AutoCAD® Civil 3D® 2010

AutoCAD® Civil 3D® 2010
Procedures and Applications

Harry O. Ward, P.E.
Nancy S. Orem

Prentice Hall

Boston   Columbus   Indianapolis   New York   San Francisco   Upper Saddle River
Amsterdam   Cape Town   Dubai   London   Madrid   Milan   Munich   Paris   Montreal   Toronto
Delhi   Mexico City   Sao Paulo   Sydney   Hong Kong   Seoul   Singapore   Taipei   Tokyo

Editor in Chief: Vernon Anthony
Acquisitions Editor: Jill Jones-Renger
Editorial Assistant: Doug Greive
Director of Marketing: David Gesell
Marketing Manager: Kara Clark
Senior Marketing Coordinator: Alicia Wozniak
Senior Managing Editor: JoEllen Gohr
Associate Managing Editor: Alexandrina Wolf
Project Manager: Louise Sette
Senior Operations Supervisor: Pat Tonneman
Operations Specialist: Deidra Schwartz

Art Coordinator: Janet Portisch
Design Coordinator: Diane Ernsberger
Cover Designer: Jason Moore
Cover Art: SuperStock
Full-Service Project Management: Lisa Garboski, bookworks publishing services
Composition: Aptara®, Inc.
Printer/Binder: Edwards Brothers
Cover Printer: Coral Graphic Services, Inc.
Text Font: Times New Roman

Certain images and materials contained in this publication were reproduced with the permission of Autodesk, Inc. © 2009. All rights reserved. Autodesk, AutoCAD, Civil 3D, DWG and the DWG logo are registered registered trademarks or trademarks of Autodesk, Inc., in the U.S.A. and certain other countries.

Disclaimer:

The publication is designed to provide tutorial information about AutoCAD® and/or other Autodesk computer programs. Every effort has been made to make this publication complete and as accurate as possible. The reader is expressly cautioned to use any and all precautions necessary, and to take appropriate steps to avoid hazards, when engaging in the activities described herein.

Neither the author nor the publisher makes any representations or warranties of any kind, with respect to the materials set forth in this publication, express or implied, including without limitation any warranties of fitness for a particular purpose or merchantability. Nor shall the author or the publisher be liable for any special, consequential or exemplary damages resulting, in whole or in part, directly or indirectly, from the reader's use of, or reliance upon, this material or subsequent revisions of this material.

Library of Congress Control Number: 2009922784

10 9 8 7 6 5 4 3 2 1

Prentice Hall
is an imprint of

www.pearsonhighered.com

ISBN-10: 0-13-507166-6
ISBN-13: 978-0-13-507166-3

This text is dedicated to my son, Joseph, and would
not have been possible without the help and support
of my wife, Kathy, and my partner, Reiko.

—Harry O. Ward

This book is dedicated to my husband, Bob,
for his never-ending love, patience, support, and
humor; and to my co-author Harry for opening
up a whole new world to me.

—Nancy S. Orem

THE NEW AUTODESK EDUCATION PRESS SERIES

Pearson/Prentice Hall has formed an alliance with Autodesk® to develop textbooks and other course materials that address the skills, methodology, and learning pedagogy for the industries that are supported by the Autodesk® Education software offerings that assist educators in teaching design.

Features of the Autodesk Education Press Series

Job Skills.   Coverage of computer-aided drafting job skills, compiled through research of industry associations, job websites, college course descriptions, and the Occupational Information Network database, has been integrated throughout the AEP books.

Professional and Industry Association Involvement.   These books are written in consultation with and reviewed by professional associations to ensure they meet the needs of industry employers

Autodesk Student Engineering and Design Community.   The Autodesk Student Engineering and Design Community provides free Autodesk design software for download and learning resources to help you get started in your academic career. Join today, go to **www.autodesk.com/ edcommunity**.

Chapter Introductions with a bulleted list of learning objectives for each chapter provide users with a roadmap of important concepts and practices that will be introduced in the chapter.

Key Terms are bold and italic within the running text and defined in the margin to help students understand and use the language of the computer-aided drafting world.

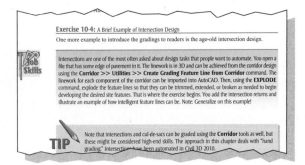

A **New to Civil 3D 2010** icon flags features that are new to the 2010 version of the Civil 3D software, creating a quick "study guide" for instructors who need to familiarize themselves with the newest features of the software to prepare for teaching the course.

Job Skills link the application of the software to the tasks that students will perform on a daily basis. They provide tips and tricks that are not discussed in other areas of the text.

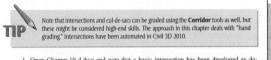

Tips relate the author's experiences to specific chapter content. These will enhance the student's success in the workplace and provide real-life tips and tricks for the problems.

Create View Frames. See Figure 12-7 for an example of the Frames created.
10. Select from the pull-down, **General >> Plan Production Tools >> Create Sheets...** The **Create Sheets - View Frame Group and Layouts** dialog box displays as shown in Figure 12-8. Hit **Next**.
11. When the **Create Sheets – View Frame Group and Layouts** dialog box appears, choose **VFG - primary road - (1)** as the new sheet set name. Hit **Next**.
12. Accept the .DST Storage location offered.
13. Accept the sheet location offered as well as the Sheet File name. Hit **Next** and the **Create Sheets - Profile Views** dialog box appears.

Note:
The software will force a Save after Step 16 so prepare yourself accordingly.

Notes provide additional, related information to the reader outside the procedure being outlined.

Example 10-1: The Section Method Done by Hand

In this example problem computed by hand, refer to Figure 10-16. Here is a simple situation in which you have a road section with two 12′ lanes and 6′ of 3:1 embankment.

Project examples throughout the text are one of the primary benefits of this book. Hundreds of examples are procedurized and set up for rapid access to the specific function being addressed. These procedures also act as problem-solving projects. They are actual contextual tasks that provide in-depth solutions for actual problems in civil engineering and surveying. Many other problems at the end of the chapter provide additional opportunity for delving further into Civil 3D's capabilities.

Exercise 10-3: "Popping Up" a Curbed Parking Lot Island

In order to provide another example of the power of the **Grading** tools in Civil 3D, you will now see how to pop a curbed island out of the asphalt paving area. The curb will be 6″ high and have a slight kilter to its face so as to avoid a vertical edge on the face of curb.

1. Open Chapter-10-c.dwg or stay in the drawing from the last exercise.
2. **Zoom** into the parking area to the west of the building. You see some plines representing the flowline of some parking islands.
3. From the **Grading** pull-down menu, select **Create Feature Lines from Objects**. Select the four parking lot islands in the parking lot. Hit **OK** to the **Create Feature Lines** dialog box.

Hands-On exercises throughout the chapters provide step-by-step walk-through activities for the student, allowing immediate practice and reinforcement of newly learned skills.

In order to provide another example of the power of the **Grading** tools in Civil 3D, you will now see how to pop a curbed island out of the asphalt paving area. The curb will be 6″ high and have a slight kilter to its face so as to avoid a vertical edge on the face of curb.

1. Open Chapter-10-c.dwg or stay in the drawing from the last exercise.
2. **Zoom** into the parking area to the west of the building. You see some plines representing the flowline of some parking islands.
3. From the **Grading** pull-down menu, select **Create Feature Lines from Objects**. Select the four parking lot islands in the parking lot. Hit **OK** to the **Create Feature Lines** dialog box.
4. From the **Grading** pull-down menu, select **Edit Feature Line Elevations** and then **Elevations From Surface**. When the **Set Elevations from Surface** dialog box displays, select **Grading Group 1** as the surface to compute to. Turn on the toggle to insert intermediate grade breaks. Hit **OK**.
5. Select object or [Multiple/Partial]: Pick all four islands one by one, and the software computes additional elevations from the asphalt pavement over and beyond the vertices in the plines. The pline islands are now "draped" onto the parking lot surface.
6. You are now ready to pop the islands up from the surface. From the **Grading** pull-down menu, select **Edit Feature Line Geometry >> Stepped Offset**. The following prompts and responses should occur:
Specify offset distance or [Through/Layer] <0.1000>: .1

To access student data files, go to www.pearsondesigncentral.com.

URLs in the margin direct students to the online student data files.

CHAPTER TEST QUESTIONS

Multiple Choice

1. Concerning Plan Production Tools, what does P&P stand for?
   a. Plan and profile
   b. Plan and production
   c. Profile and procedure
   d. None of the above
2. The expression "cutting P&P sheets" refers to which of the following?
   a. Creating sheets for preview purposes
   b. Generating plan and profile sheets for plotting purposes
   c. Separating drawings to export to another system
   d. None of the above
3. Why are plan and profile sheets created?

   c. You will see a visual concurrence happening in the plan view.
   d. None of the above
7. When creating P&P sheets, which of the following sheet settings are needed?
   a. **Plan** only
   b. **Profile** only
   c. **Plan and Profile**
   d. All of the above
8. Which of the following scale ratios might be more applicable to a plan profile sheet than the others?
   a. For the plan: 1″ = 10′ horizontal,
   For the profile: 1″ = 10′ horizontal and 1″ = 1′ vertical.

End-of-chapter material, easily located by shading on page edges, includes:

- Chapter Test Questions
- Multiple Choice
- True or False
- Student Exercises, Activities and Review Questions

to help students check their own understanding of important chapter concepts.

INSTRUCTOR RESOURCES

An Online Instructor's Manual is available to qualified instructors for downloading. To access supplementary materials online, instructors need to request an instructor access code. Go to **www.pearsonhighered.com/irc**, where you can register for an instructor access code. Within forty-eight hours after registering you will receive a confirming e-mail including an instructor access code. Once you have received your code, go to the site and log on for full instructions on downloading the materials you wish to use.

STUDENT RESOURCES

Pearson Design Central. Pearson has created an online community where students can share examples of their drawings and obtain resources for their drawing projects. Student data files needed for certain projects in this book can be obtained at **www.pearsondesigncentral.com**. URLs in the margin direct students to the online student data files.

Preface

Harry Ward, one of the authors, founded OutSource Inc. in 1991, and his company has trained and worked with thousands of engineers, planners, and surveyors during that time, both nationally and internationally. The company's success in training attracted the attention of the Carlson Software Company in 2006. As a result, the company merged with Carlson and became known as Carlson College, formally OutSource Inc., a Division of Carlson Software. In 2009 Ward founded a new company called Harken-Reidar, Inc. that is authorized as a training center by Autodesk and Carlson Software. This new company specializes in the Civil, Survey and Construction markets and sells hardware and software solutions, provides consulting nationwide, and offers world-class training by licensed engineering and surveying instructors. Harken-Reidar plays a dual role in the industry: employees are engineers, surveyors, and contractors who also have a relationship with academia. Its style of training combines civil engineering education along with the applied usage of the CADD software. The firm belief at Harken-Reidar is that a user should understand how the software works and the mathematics behind the software before using it on a project. This was Harry Ward's philosophy in developing this textbook, and it parallels some of the classes he has taught for many years at Virginia's George Mason University. Those classes consist of lectures—in which he teaches theory, formulas, and algorithms—and CADD laboratories—in which he provides lab instruction on application to CADD.

The two main purposes of this text are to provide (1) basic instruction in what someone would need to know about civil engineering in order to operate this software, and (2) procedures and examples of how to operate the software for developing civil engineering project design and drafting. The instruction covers a variety of the disciplines within the field of civil engineering, while outlining the algorithms and formulas for many design functions. It lays down procedurized groundwork for performing design and drafting. Each chapter takes the reader through step-by-step procedures for using this state-of-the-art product, while offering scores of civil engineering-related tips and tricks.

The text will help guide the reader through the paradigm shift occurring in the civil engineering and construction industries as we continue in this new millennium. That shift is directly attributable to one event—the use of three dimensions in designing and constructing projects.

Chapter 1 is an overview of the software and its interface. In Chapter 2, a complete design project is undertaken and brought from inception through completion. It rapidly acquaints the reader with the software's basic functionality. The text then traverses, chapter by chapter, through the complete and advanced usage of each of the software's capabilities. It uses a feature-training methodology in a discipline-oriented organization that mimics design tasks on actual projects.

Each chapter ends with problems, with the answers given in the Online Instructor's Manual. These could be used as test questions, additional exercises, or homework assignments.

A few years ago, one of OutSource's clients purchased an engineering software package for several thousand dollars from a relatively small software manufacturer. It cost enough to buy a small automobile. The client installed it, had some staff trained, and began using it on a project. Not long after, a frustrated user of the software at the company contacted Harry to ask whether the software would update the profiles for the company's roads if the engineers modified the horizontal alignment. He also asked whether the surface would update itself if they added breaklines or spot shots to it.

Harry informed him that the answer was no, that they would need to regenerate the various data sets and reimport them. The user said, "That is what I thought, but would you tell that to my boss?" When the principal of the company joined the conversation and Harry informed him of their discussion, the executive immediately said, "Then why did they charge me thousands of dollars if I have to do most of the work myself?"

The industry is now in the position in which the executive's question can be answered entirely differently. The answer is in the civil engineering software solution called AutoCAD® Civil 3D®. Now the response can be a resounding, "Yes, Civil 3D will update these various components of design and automatically update, regenerate, and import them." The software ripples through the data, effecting change where it is required.

Another anecdote that occurred recently involved a designer computing an earthworks quantity for a large project. He reported to his boss that the developer would require 250,000 cubic yards of fill to build the site. When the boss asked how he knew it would be 250,000 c.y., his response was, "Well, that is what the software said." This type of response always makes a boss apprehensive.

Technology has finally reached the level that many civil engineering firm owners and managers thought it was years ago. Many firms will undergo a paradigm shift in how they work as they implement Civil 3D.

SUMMARY DESCRIPTIONS OF THE TEXTBOOK CHAPTERS

Introduction: CADD—The Primary Tool of Our Trade

The text begins with an introduction to the field of civil engineering. Then there is a brief historical look back at the introduction of CADD to the field of civil engineering and a description of the introduction of Computer Aided Design and Drafting into the industry. The chapter then provides a brief description of the technologies emerging within the field and how Civil 3D begins to fill the needs of these emerging technologies.

Chapter 1: The Components and Interface of Civil 3D

This chapter describes the interface for the software and introduces the reader to some of the state-of-the-art methodologies found in the Civil 3D product.

The new philosophies found within the Civil 3D design application are introduced with discussions of the profoundly new capabilities available to CADD users, including the new interface tools; new objects for use in design; data-driven, object style libraries; and new roadway abilities.

Chapter 2: A Civil 3D JumpStart Project

The intent of this chapter is to get the reader quickly acclimated with the basic usage of the Civil 3D software. An introductory project initiates the students into the basic design process. It involves preparing an existing ground surface and then developing a parcel of property for a shopping center and parking lot. It develops an access road alignment, the road's profile, and corridor data for the access road in 3D. After this is done, the grading for the shopping center and parking lot is designed in 3D and the plans assembled for the road and the shopping center.

Chapter 3: The Simple, but Time-Honored Point

Now begins the detailed procedures of the text. The first chapter lays out expectations and discusses the interface and software components. The second chapter briefly shows how to design an entire project. From here on the text describes the detailed usage of the software on a discipline basis beginning with point usage. Chapter 3 discusses basic math related to points and provides many examples for point-based computations. Civil 3D is used to develop point aesthetics and build a library for using point descriptions and then develop point groups. Civil 3D **Point Layout** tools are used, and students learn how to compute information using points and then take on advanced points usage and tables.

Chapter 4: A Tip of the Hat to Surveyors-More Points!

This chapter provides information on additional point commands and supplements to the content provided in Chapter 3.

Chapter 5: Surveying

Surveying is usually where engineering projects commence in earnest. Base data are collected, boundaries are established, and control is set. After the designers have completed their work, very often the project returns to survey for quality checking, development of stakeout data, or conversion to 3D/GPS Machine Control data. This chapter discusses importing field-collected data, developing traverses for setting control, and balancing those traverses to eliminate (or disperse) any error that may exist.

Chapter 6: Civil 3D—The Modern Curvilinead

This chapter covers linework and geometry. It discusses mathematics and formulas for lines, triangles, arcs, and spirals and introduces different types of angles, bearings, and azimuths.

Transparent commands in Civil 3D are used in detail, and Curvilinear and Rectilinear 2D Geometry (Lines, Arcs, Spirals) is developed. This information is then used to develop Parcels using the **Parcel Layout** toolbar, develop Alignments using the **Alignment Layout** toolbar, and learn about Styles and Labels.

Chapter 7: Advanced 3D Surface Modeling

One of the most important parts of Civil 3D has to be the Surface Model because so many computations emanate from surface models. Chapter 7 first discusses the mathematics and theories for Digital Terrain Models and Surfaces and then teaches the TIN process, how ground information is used, and about contour computational methods. Students create surfaces in Civil 3D and develop contours and labels. Students use breaklines and spot shots and analyze and depict surface data.

Chapter 8: Advanced Profiles and Sections

This chapter covers using Surface Models and how to design vertical alignments. It discusses mathematics, theories, and formulas for vertical tangents and vertical curves and uses Civil 3D to create profiles and finished grade vertical alignments. Students make use of the **Profile Layout** toolbar to create vertical profiles and then develop Cross Sections and use the **Sample Line Layout** toolbar.

Chapter 9: Advanced Corridor Development

One of the strongest aspects of Civil 3D is the corridor design features. The chapter begins with a brief discussion of superelevations for roadways and corridors and the use of subassemblies. Then Civil 3D is used to develop corridor assemblies. Students compute superelevations for a corridor and discuss and develop subgrades for the road.

Chapter 10: Advanced Site Grading and Virtual Site Design™

Site grading is performed for many purposes, but the chief reason is to assure proper drainage across a site following construction. The chapter discusses the building of commercial and subdivision sites in 3D and teaches about quality control methods used in design. Students develop a commercial site in Civil 3D using feature lines and grading objects and then compute earthworks takeoffs and quantities.

Chapter 11: Piping for Storm Sewers and Drainage

This chapter begins with a brief discussion of hydrology, runoff, time of concentration, watersheds, and the rational method and then develops watersheds in Civil 3D. This is followed by a brief discussion of hydraulics and then the development of a pipe network.

Chapter 12: Plan Production Tools

As the project matures, it is plotted out as plans, plan/profiles and sections, and details. This chapter provides procedures for generating many of these plots and drawings. This covers a major function introduced in 2008.

Appendix A: Data Sharing in Civil 3D

In this appendix, several methods for sharing design data with others are discussed. These include inserting a source design file into another file using LandXML data sharing, using data shortcuts, and using projects for sharing data.

A unique aspect of this appendix is the discussion of developing data for 3D/GPS Machine Control. This growing area of engineering construction is replacing traditional stakeout activities. Engineers are under increasing pressure to deliver 3D/GPS digital data directly to the contractor for robotic machine control.

Appendix B: Labeling in Civil 3D 2010

In this appendix, labeling methods are discussed.

Appendix C: Software and Hardware Versions

The software version and system specifications section describes the software being used in the text and breaks it down by its components. Hardware specifications are discussed in an imaginative way. The perfect CADD station is specified, and the minimum requirements are identified.

Appendix D: Identify the Civil Engineering Industry

Industry components are identified and detail the major fields within the industry of civil engineering along with the tasks that are required on projects falling into these categories. The Civil 3D software is then described, and the components found within Civil 3D are introduced.

Appendix E: Civil 3D's Visualization Capabilities

Visual communications are a growing requirement in the civil engineering business today, and Civil 3D comes with a photorealistic rendering engine. This appendix contains a discussion and several examples of computer renderings and visualizations from a variety of design projects. Students then use Civil 3D to develop a surface with multiple materials and use Civil 3D for rendering the materials into a photorealistic image.

ACKNOWLEDGMENTS

To Peter J. Goldsmith, PE, whose support of Harry Ward's quest to use CADD early in his career helped make his accomplishments possible.

The authors also thank the reviewers of this text: Larry Bettes, Shasta College; Liaquat Khan, NHTI–Concord's Community College; Jeanie C. McCormack, Brevard Community College; and John J. Rose, Phoenix College.

Text Element	Example
Key Terms: Bold and italic on first mention.	***Azimuths***
Civil 3D commands: Bold and capitalized.	**ZOOM EXTENTS**
Toolbar names, menu items, and dialog box names: Bold and follows capitalization convention in Civil 3D toolbar or pull-down menu.	Unless otherwise specified to use the pull-down, the following convention indicates a menu call from the pull-down menu. **Utilities >> Task Pane.** Next go to the **Toolspace** and choose the **Prospector** tab.
Civil 3D prompts: Command window prompts use a different font.	`Specify station:`
Keyboard input: Bold with special keys in brackets. **<Enter>.**	**<300>**

Contents

Introduction: CADD—The Primary Tool of Our Trade

A BRIEF INTRODUCTION TO THE FIELD OF CIVIL ENGINEERING——

Civil 3D is software for automating solutions to design problems in the field of civil engineering. Therefore, it is important to understand a little about the field itself. Many students in the class are being introduced to civil engineering and may have only a partial understanding of the depth and breadth of the field. This introduction serves to briefly describe this; for instance, corridor design is a highly sophisticated area of the software, as is geometry development and surface modelings. The use of Civil 3D software spans the field, serving some parts very robustly.

Civil 3D: The short term used in this text for the software package officially called Autodesk Civil 3D.

Civil engineers are often referred to as "jacks of all trades" because the field is so wide and contains so many subsets and disciplines. Civil engineers typically receive training in many of these areas in their undergraduate education and then tend to specialize with a master's or doctorate degree. As one of the oldest branches in the profession of engineering, civil engineering includes the following disciplines, each one a career unto itself:

- Transportation engineering
- Geotechnical engineering
- Structural engineering
- Environmental engineering
- Surveying
- Land development
- Coastal engineering
- Process engineering
- Water resources engineering
- Construction engineering
- Geographic Information Systems (*GIS*) and Global Positioning Systems (*GPS*)

Some emerging areas within civil engineering include the following:

- Automated construction *3D/GPS Machine Control*
- Bioengineering
- Project management
- Life-cycle design
- Real-time monitoring
- Rehabilitation
- Smart systems
- Space structures

GIS: Geographic Information Systems

GPS: Global Positioning Systems

3D/GPS Machine Control: An emerging technology that allows construction equipment to obtain their earthmoving information from on-board computers with 3D data sets of the site. GPS receivers locate the vehicle, compare it to the data set, and automatically adjust the earthmoving blade to the appropriate height and angle to accomplish those goals.

HOW CADD BECAME THE PRIMARY TOOL OF THE TRADE

To understand why Civil 3D is such a breakthrough software application, you must be familiar with the software that has been used up until now. To do so, it is important to look back at how **CADD** became the predominant tool of the trade in civil engineering.

CADD: Computer Aided Design/Drafting.

PRIMITIVE AND MANUAL-BASED TOOLS OF THE TRADE

Prior to 35 years ago, the state of the art of civil design generally meant using hard-copy tables, hand-calculated formulas, and simple mechanically operated calculators. PCs did not exist, and mainframe computers were extremely rare. Engineers performed trigonometric functions by looking up values in preprinted tables and computed many engineering formulas using a slide rule.

During the 1960s, the largest organizations, such as government agencies, began acquiring mainframe computers, which consumed huge amounts of square footage. The computer memory was so small that it was common to feed a large set of data for computations into the computer several times before getting complete results. During the 1970s, computers began to appear in engineering organizations and school systems. These computers had either punch cards or paper tape rolls with holes punched in them for data storage. Some surveyors used a tabulation machine called a "Monroe." Usage of these machines tapered off after the introduction of hand calculators, which quickly became the main computational tool.

Engineers created technical drawings using ink on linen in the "old days." Mistakes in drafting were not easily tolerated as the linen was quite fragile and not highly conducive to making changes. To reproduce the drawings, blueprints were created by passing the original, opaque linens through a light machine. This affected treated paper so that the light could not be emitted through the black ink, thereby leaving a white, etched line on a blue background. Blueprints gave way to ammonia-based blueline prints when the process was reversed, whereby the light faded a treated paper to white, leaving a blue line where the light could not penetrate through the black ink.

Drafting was performed using drafting tables with drafting arms, ink pens, and pencils. The drafting arms could be set to any angle allowing technicians to lean their pens against the straightedges to draw straight lines. The arm could be rotated and locked into that position allowing for rotated lines. By placing right triangles on the arm, the draftsperson could draw orthogonal lines. Other equipment consisted of Koh-i-Noor brand pens, Pelikan brand ink, Kueffel & Esser (K&E) compasses, mechanical pencils, and so on. The tools of the drafting trade also included protractors, flexible curves, French curves, railroad curves, straightedges, triangles, and electric erasers. Engineers drew on paper, linen, and mylar.

One of the authors, Harry Ward considers himself fortunate to have had his career parallel the growth of CADD in his chosen field. After more than 20 years as a professional civil engineer specializing in the use of CADD, he personally experienced and contributed to the growth of this technology. He gained this experience when he was fairly new to the civil engineering business and performing design and drafting services using the previously mentioned tools for the City of Houston, Bridge Division in 1978. The economy was very robust with growth in all sectors, and he was soon employed in the **private sector** with Turner, Collie & Braden, a large firm doing both international and domestic work. This firm is now part of the AECom group.

private sector: The area within civil engineering that provides funding for projects that emanate from private sources. This includes land developers, homeowners, and professionals such as doctors and attorneys.

AUTOMATED TOOLS OF THE TRADE

Automation was not entirely new to Turner, Collie & Braden, as it had been using a minicomputer, with Tektronix computer terminals and homegrown COGO software. Subdivisions were computed by data entry specialists who knew the language and could assemble data files and plot files. They generated these plot files from a single set of batched commands. To make a change to a single property line required that an entire batch file be rerun. To make changes to individual objects without recomputing the entire project was a highly productive improvement. This was the idea behind interactive graphics and the advent of CADD in civil engineering.

Sometime in the mid- to late 1970s, M&S Computing began to make a presence in the civil engineering field because of its ***CAD*** product called *IGDS*. It cost about $1 million for the workstations, minicomputer, plotter, software, and maintenance. These systems tended to be regional acquisitions at that time because part of the United States was suffering from economic troubles. The price of oil and inflation combined to cripple some areas of the country as administrations changed from President Ford, with the "Whip Inflation Now" slogans, to President Carter. Therefore, certain regions, such as those including Texas and California, were doing very well under these conditions at the expense of regions such as the Northeast. Engineering and oil firms in these healthy economic areas could afford the acquisition of million-dollar CAD systems.

CAD: Computer Aided Drafting.

INTERACTIVE GRAPHICS-BASED TOOLS OF THE TRADE

Not long after Harry joined Turner, Collie & Braden, it acquired an M&S Computing CAD system at a cost of close to $1 million. Because this was such a new technology, most of the company employees were not even sure how it was supposed to be used or where it would enter and depart the workflow. The company acquired two workstations, each with a large digitizing table, a floating menu tablet, and foot pedals to control the height and angle of the table. The system came equipped with dual monitors that could interact with each other; a view from one monitor could be placed on the other monitor so it could be seen better. One monitor usually had a single large view on it, whereas the other monitor usually had four smaller views of the subject matter. To this day, most AutoCAD users still do not work in this way, even though it is highly effective and AutoCAD does support this.

Users of the system could make changes to objects and, when ready, then send them to the plotter, hence the term *interactive*. We take this for granted today, but prior methods required recomputation of the entire data set! These were called *batch computations*.

The tools available in the system at the time were basically commands that drew vector graphics such as lines, arcs, linestrings, shapes, and text. To give the system credit though, it was three-dimensional from the day the company acquired it and it was programmable. These features caused Harry, in the mid-1980s, to join a small group of progressive people in the MIS (or IT) division of the company who were writing civil engineering and surveying software that interacted with the CAD system. These were pioneering days because very few firms had discipline-oriented CAD software at that time.

When the system arrived on the company's doorstep, an employee from a company called Intergraph came in and placed an Intergraph logo on top of the M&S Computing logo that was on the machine. It turned out that M&S Computing had gone public and was now called Intergraph. The software was called *IGDS* for Interactive Graphics Design System. By the mid-1980s, the company had a half dozen workstations that ran 24 hours a day with three shifts of personnel.

PC-BASED CADD BECOMES THE PRIMARY TOOL OF THE TRADE

During the early to mid-1980s, PCs were being introduced to Harry's company and to the industry. The standard PCs had Intel 8086 and 8088 processors, often running from floppy disks. Hard disks cost over $5,000 and had to be heavily justified for purchase. Then the new Intel 286s were introduced, and the company struggled with whether to standardize on Apple or IBM-type PCs.

Around that time, PC alternatives began to develop that allowed use of Intergraph Design files on the PC at significantly less cost than a workstation. Harry recalled a couple of PC-based IGDS programs called C-CAD and Pseudo-Station. Intergraph acquired them both; C-CAD disappeared, and Pseudo-Station became MicroStation. Later, legal machinations resulted in the rights to MicroStation reverting back to the Bentley Corporation, where they remain today.

While PC-based CAD was beginning to achieve credibility, a small company called Autodesk was founded in 1982, which introduced and shipped AutoCAD. The company went public in 1985 at $11 a share. The software was originally two-dimensional and then became

3D: Three dimensions, characterized by the use of the *X, Y,* and *Z* axes in the Cartesian coordinate system resulting in real world models.

2-1/2D whereby elevational data were embedded into objects but they were not actually *3D* objects. AutoCAD popularity grew, especially among those companies and individuals that did not want to spend hundreds of thousands or millions of dollars to obtain minicomputer-based CAD. AutoCAD responded to the requests of these users and became very strong in the development of construction plans. It excelled in dimensioning and customization. Autodesk put a subset of the List Processing language into AutoCAD (called LISP), which allowed those with minimal programming knowledge to write routines to AutoCAD for redundant drafting functions. The use of the software grew between disciplines as people adapted the software to their needs using LISP.

In the late 1980s, Autodesk's AutoCAD Release 10 was introduced as a three-dimensional CAD program. The processing power on the PCs increased with each new processor announcement, and it did not take long before 3D models were being prepared on PCs and color shading was available. Autodesk launched a product in 1987 called Autoshade for this purpose as an add-on package. It then developed and introduced Autovision in 1993, which was ultimately added into AutoCAD as part of the Release 14 product. Meanwhile, a company called Discreet developed a *visualization* and modeling package called 3D Studio MAX and introduced it in 1990. Autodesk then acquired that company. The 3D Studio MAX product was split into two pieces: a professional studio production version called 3D Studio MAX and a version for engineers and architects called 3D Studio VIZ. Each solution caters to its intended market.

visualization: In the context of CADD, it is used to produce an image of something that does not exist so that the viewer can better understand the project or model being discussed.

In the mid-1980s, Dave C. Arnold, a professional engineer in New Hampshire, started a company called DCA Software, which produced civil engineering software tools that worked inside AutoCAD. The software consisted of LISP routines that helped users place points, generate *contours*, and label linework. It was fairly informal in its early days and possessed scarce documentation. DCA Software persuaded AutoCAD dealers to sell the software as an add-on when they sold AutoCAD to engineering companies. That company became Softdesk, a publicly traded company that wrote software for Autodesk products. Autodesk and Softdesk agreed to merge in late 1996 and finalized it in 1998.

contour: A linestring of a constant elevation on the site. It can be open or closed.

This merger changed how Autodesk did business because it began selling the combined products as Desktop Solutions and developed a Desktop for each discipline. For instance, Land Desktop catered to the civil engineering industry. Autodesk also produced Architectural Desktop, a Mechanical Desktop, and Building Services Desktop. Land Desktop was one of the most popular engineering programs in the business at that time. However, with the successful release of the heavily object-oriented Architectural Desktop, Autodesk was taking a similar development track for the civil engineering community.

Autodesk developed and prereleased a new-generation product called Autodesk Civil 3D in 2003. This software is not a new version of the Land Desktop; it is a new product that makes use of the object-oriented technologies that have been introduced over the years in the Land Desktop software but takes them to a much more robust level. Although Land Desktop has point objects, contour objects, and grading objects, Civil 3D increased the use of these concepts and integrated them into a project scenario.

Civil 3D has also developed a sophisticated library structure that allows design data to be embedded into it that guide the design of engineering elements. The first public release of this product, called Civil 3D 2005, occurred in late 2004. In addition to major feature enhancements for sophisticated *corridor* design, it also included a version of 3D VIZ called VIZ Render as part of the package. The second release, called Civil 3D 2006, occurred in 2005, followed by Civil 3D 2007, 2008, 2009 and now 2010.

corridor: A structure that allows passage or conveyance of people or things.

Civil 3D is rapidly becoming the state-of-the-art software for civil engineers and is the heir-apparent to Land Desktop. It has a dynamic model concept whereby the objects that customize it to work specifically for the civil industry are data-driven. The graphics and annotations are style-driven. Many objects are parametrically controlled, another first for the civil industry.

This textbook, *Autodesk Civil 3D 2010: Procedures and Applications,* details everything you need to know to use this software rapidly and expands on that knowledge using step-by-step instructions for advanced usage of the software. As you progress through the book, you will learn the theories, algorithms, and formulas behind the software. Then when the supervisor asks, "How do you know that the result is the correct answer?" you can respond with "Because I understand the data provided to the computer and how the software produces computations."

THE FUTURE OF TECHNOLOGY FOR CIVIL ENGINEERING

Now that you have learned a brief history of CADD in civil engineering, what is the future of CADD? The Autodesk Civil 3D software allows users to prepare for the future of technology in civil engineering. As the industry moves into the third dimension, engineers will be better prepared to work with the technologies that are appearing in the related fields such as surveying and construction. These businesses are moving rapidly into advanced usage of GPS even to the point of establishing GPS networks with postprocessed corrected data, 3D/GPS Machine Control whereby robots perform excavation tasks on the bulldozers and excavators that are pushing dirt, to 3D modeling and computer renderings and animations and their respective uses in civil engineering. Engineers must respond to this technology because it requires 3D surface and project data for the robotics to do their job. Harry has been consulting with engineering firms that want to start moving into 3D design because contractors are persuading developers to choose engineering firms that are more up to date. The argument is that it will help developers save money by allowing contractors to use their investments in 3D/GPS-Guided machine control equipment. Three-dimensional laser scanning is making its way into engineering and surveying firms at around $100,000 per machine. These machines can capture 3D data of subway tunnels, cityscapes, bridges, structures, and dams. They are used to help analyze movements, deflections under load, and for antiterroristic functions. The robotic-reflectorless total stations used by surveyors capture 3D data more readily than ever before. So you can see that technology is rapidly building momentum in the industry, and Civil 3D will help you meet those challenges.

The future of CADD is characterized by several trends. A few of these are the following:

1. CADD will become an interface to the geospatial database and engineering computations will occur using the data within the geospatial environment,

2. CADD will move to BIM, Building Information Modeling. More data will be attached to the CADD elements. Although this is successfully being done in the architectural field, it is only beginning in the civil field. BRiM, that is, Bridge Information Modeling, is beginning to get noticed. In the architectural arena, this means attaching information to, say, HVAC regarding manufacturer, sizes, bends, flow occurring, maintenance schedules, and so on. If this is done faithfully for all elements on the project, costs can be controlled, maintenance schedules can be derived, and conflict checking can be computed to find where trades will conflict (for example, potable water lines conflicting with sanitary piping within the building).

3. 4D and 5D will become part of many projects. This is the advent of adding time to our considerations. For example, consider a construction site, where just-in-time delivery of materials can affect costs, labor allocation, and milestone progress. This is already occurring on some mining sites throughout the world. Let's examine this for a moment.

In this text we advise that users move to Civil 3D so they can begin to design and analyze in three dimensions. This is still a foreign topic in many companies and agencies, however. Consider that surveyors have been in 3D for many years, and contractors have moved to 3D in droves with the advent of machine guidance equipment, but engineers are still trying to figure out why they should work in 3D. So, if we haven't quite embedded 3D CAD design into our normal workflow, how can we move into 4D or 5D? But even though we haven't fully accomplished entrenching 3D into our daily design routine, some parts of the industry are already moving rapidly into incorporating time and cost into the process, hence 5D. We will now explain what it means to be working in 4D and 5D, and the benefits this can provide to the construction industry.

In this discussion, 3D consists of using all three dimensions (X, Y and Z coordinates) for design and analysis. The fourth dimension (4D) is the addition of time as a functional player in the design and analysis of a plan. The fifth dimension (5D) is the addition of cost analysis. These five dimensions certainly make up our world of design and construction.

During his years as a professor at George Mason University, Harry Ward observed that a large amount of research had been conducted within the academic community on 4D and how it relates to design and construction applications. Several years ago, one of George Mason University's professors studied the effect that time has on construction by using time-lapse photography to photograph a construction site and storing the photos for study and analysis. When analyzed in a fast-motion scenario, the pictures readily demonstrated that including time considerations into the construction process improved areas of potential waste and mismanagement.

Terrance C. Ryan, Ph.D., PE, the executive director of the Engineers and Surveyors Institute in Chantilly, Virginia, performed one of these studies and wrote several papers on the topic. The research relates time-lapse photography with construction simulation modeling. For instance, Ryan described a power plant renovation where various pieces of equipment had to be moved in and out of the facility. The time-lapse methods showed how crane positioning and clearances were critical to the task, and 3D simulation identified improvements for the project. Another item found was how important just-in-time delivery of construction materials was to the project. Deliveries must be sequenced correctly and can negatively affect the contractor's payout schedule when done ineffectively.

Ryan noted that, for a project in three dimensions, the fourth dimension is the life cycle of the project, which is measured in time. It begins with research and design of the project, then moves into construction, change orders and as-builts, and finally operations and maintenance. These are all functions of time.

With regard to 4D, the mining industry has many parallels to construction. In order to mine ore that is hundreds of feet below the surface, you must uncover layers of other material or dig tunnels. The sequence of events that is required follows a timing pattern in which one task must be completed before the next begins. Mining companies have the ability to compute how fast a deadline can be accomplished and how many pieces of equipment are needed to do so. This is the essence of four-dimensional computing applied directly to real-life problems, such as resource allocation, sequencing, and timing. It is this methodology that allows a scheduler to allocate resources to the task. In fact, the methodology can be worked backward as well: If an imminent deadline is defined, computations can be performed that will predict how many different types of equipment will be needed to achieve that deadline.

But the technologies available are not limited to mining applications. They can be applied to road design and construction as well.

So then, what is 5D? Well, the fifth D stands for the dollar. With the ability of software to compute in three dimensions and to add time as a fourth factor, what the construction industry really needs is to be able to assign costs to all of this work and movement. When performing estimations and quantity takeoffs, one of the results we look for is the cost of doing the project. This is where the fifth D comes in. Civil 3D 2010 adds quantity takeoff calculations into its feature list.

Civil 3D has costs built into the 3D CAD objects that are being input or modified. Earthworks and their costs can be computed, and material quantities can now be produced as well. Subsurface materials, aggregates, and trenching can be calculated for utilities, again in 3D.

And so for our purposes today in the design, surveying, and construction field, we would all benefit from the use of 3D. And not just 3D, but 4D and 5D would be of help as well. *Some of the information on 4D and 5D technology presented here was extracted from an article Harry wrote in his column, "Virtual Stringline: Zooming from 3D to 4D and 5D," in SitePrep Magazine (March 5, 2008).*

The intent of this textbook is to introduce the reader and participant to the Autodesk Civil 3D product and show how it will perform design and drafting functions. It also discusses the algorithms and design computations that exist in the civil engineering business and how they relate to the operations of Civil 3D.

The Components and Interface of Civil 3D

1

Chapter Objectives

- Understand the field of civil engineering and its relationship with Computer Aided Design and Drafting.
- Be familiar with the applications embedded within the Civil 3D offering.
- Realize that Civil 3D is not a program; rather it is a cross-pollination of several programs integrated into a single engineering solution.
- Understand why Civil 3D is creating a paradigm shift in the civil engineering business.
- Understand the software's new philosophies, interfaces, and capabilities.

INTRODUCTION

Chapter 1 introduces Civil 3D, its philosophies, what it is composed of, and its interface. The philosophies are causing a *paradigm shift* in the civil engineering business because the software is an application with entirely new methods, interfaces, and capabilities. These will be described in concept so that the reader, upon beginning the procedurized tutorials and exercises, will at least have an impression of what to expect the software to accomplish.

paradigm shift: A fundamental change in how processes are performed.

This chapter also discusses the contents of the Civil 3D suite of software because many solutions come with its install and its adjunct installs. It describes the applications embedded within Civil 3D's capabilities.

Unlike the help system that accompanies the software, this chapter provides detailed illustrations and explanations of the interface and related icons in a single location. This will ease learning these items and undoubtedly save the reader time and reduce frustration in the use of the software. The icons have an enormous number of subtle variations that the user must be aware of in order to stay in complete control of the project data.

REVIEW OF FUNCTIONS AND FEATURES TO BE USED

The features being introduced in this chapter include what the software offers, an explanation of AutoCAD MAP 3D, what the interface tools are, and what the icons mean. This chapter explains how the software is style- and data-driven, how it uses objects for design, and the fact that it offers DOT-level highway design capabilities.

THE COMPONENTS OF AUTODESK CIVIL 3D

Civil 3D consists of the integration of several programs including AutoCAD as the foundation graphics engine. Although the full set of commands is available, only the **File**, **Edit**, **View**, and **Insert** pull-down menus are shown when the software initially launches. Augmenting AutoCAD

Figure 1-1   Civil 3D and MAP 3D pull-down menus

is the MAP 3D software, which adds GIS, important utilities, and drafting cleanup tools to the user's toolkit (see Figure 1-1). The civil engineering component of the software adds on the heavy civil engineering design software. A visualization tool completes the offering by allowing for the development of some of the industry's highest-quality visualizations.

Visualization was included in the 2006 version, but the entire AutoCAD version has been updated to include major rendering tools. This provides users with benefits in that the AutoCAD data is now directly renderable (if that is indeed a word). This textbook will describe rendering only briefly because that function is deserving of a text in itself.

Civil 3D includes a native visualization tool. It uses some of the core technology developed in Autodesk VIZ, including much of the photometric lighting and rendering technology. Civil 3D has optimized methodology to render and animate data from Civil 3D more effectively. Its user interface has been simplified. The guiding principle is that Civil 3D is the model building and organization application, whereas AutoCAD is used for visualization.

For the purposes of this text, AutoCAD knowledge is assumed to be a prerequisite, as there are many sources and textbooks available from which AutoCAD can be learned. Appendix E offers a brief discussion of visualization.

pull-down menus, icons, toolbars, pop-downs, and dialog boxes: Interface items.

Some of the conventions to be used in this text include references to ***pull-down menus, icons, toolbars, pop-downs,*** and ***dialog boxes***. An example of the pull-down menu is shown in Figure 1-2. In fact, ellipses within the pull-down menu indicate that a dialog box will display to complete the information gathering needed to fulfill the command request.

Note:
Some add-in software available for Civil 3D that is important to know about includes Trimble Link™, Carlson Connect™, and Leica Exchange. These supplements allow for data exchange with manufacturers' equipment and provide Civil 3D with the ability to send data directly to 3D/GPS Machine Control devices.

An example of a toolbar is shown in Figure 1-3; this one has three icons. Toolbars are configurable; that is, the user can reshape them by dragging one corner. Toolbars are also customizable in that commands can be added to or deleted from them.

A pop-down menu is shown in Figure 1-4, and there are usually choices to be made within them.

Dialog boxes are used frequently and might appear similar to that shown in Figure 1-5.

Figure 1-2   Menus and submenus

Figure 1-3   Example toolbar

Figure 1-4   Pop-down menu

Figure 1-5   Dialog box

INTRODUCTION TO AutoCAD MAP 3D

MAP 3D is a required and foundational aspect of Civil 3D, yet it is one of the more misunderstood and underutilized software packages. This software was an independent solution sold as an adjunct to AutoCAD for many years. It has been available for over ten years; however, it was not always sold under the name MAP. Years ago, part of it was called the Autodesk Data Extension (ADE). This software, introduced in 1993, possessed many drafting-oriented features that were missing in the main AutoCAD solution.

Together with AutoCAD, MAP 3D made for a great set of tools. Unfortunately, it was not a big seller, although those with very advanced needs probably purchased it. For those who have had a history with AutoCAD products, this was one of their business models; that is, selling "extensions" to AutoCAD. There were at least two other extensions as well: the Autodesk Modeling Extension (AME) and the Autodesk SQL Extension (ASE). SQL stands for Structured Query Language used to extend database functionality.

The Autodesk Modeling Extension was included in the base AutoCAD software in Release 14. The Data Extension and SQL Extension, combined into a new product in 1996 called AutoCAD MAP, became fairly popular, especially for civil engineering and surveying users. By combining the graphics tools with the database tools, MAP created an environment that GIS users could benefit from. The ASE toolset allowed users to attach to external databases and create links to the AutoCAD graphical entities, perform sophisticated queries, and generate robust reports and results using AutoCAD.

AutoCAD MAP 3D, introduced in 2004, added surface modeling, surface analysis, and ***point groups*** to the software. These functions are part of the Civil 3D package and as such are removed from the MAP 3D menus. Because of MAP 3D's importance as part of the software, a discussion of its capabilities follows.

point groups: A Civil 3D object representing a collection of points grouped by a relationship such as utility points, property points, and terrain points.

AutoCAD MAP 3D augments AutoCAD and enhances the creation, maintenance, and presentation of mapping information. With MAP 3D, users can do the following:

* Open and link AutoCAD drawings to associated databases.
* Develop new data or edit data to maps to make them more intelligent.
* Use many unique features to assist in cleaning up "noise" in maps.
* Use a "batch" plotting facility for easy and flexible map plotting.
* Produce basic thematic maps with legends.
* Perform geodetic transformations on graphical objects in a file. This allows for moving or rotating data from one geodetic zone to another.

- Access map data in other formats, such as Oracle, MicroStation, Mapinfo, Arcview, and ArcInfo.
- Link any external documents to objects in their maps.

MAP 3D is the foundation for Civil 3D and helps in developing and managing complex design projects. MAP 3D can increase teamwork efficiency by creating a comprehensive and cost-effective project database. It integrates multiple drawings into one seamless environment providing access, editing, and reporting of drawing, attribute, and related database information within a single AutoCAD session. You can view and edit objects from multiple source drawings in a single work session.

The basis of this product is a robust query engine designed to assist AutoCAD users working with large or complex data sets. MAP 3D lets you query AutoCAD drawings based on any combination of drawing properties, object location, or information stored in related databases. This flexibility speeds up work by allowing you to focus on just the pertinent information. The query engine enables "super cross-references" because you can access several drawings simultaneously yet limit the reference to precisely the geographic area of the drawing you want. You also have full editing access to all of these queried drawings so edits can be made concurrently.

AutoCAD MAP 3D's multiple-drawing edit capability provides a secure environment for multiple MAP users who may be sharing their data or drawings. Project teams can efficiently and safely share drawings and data. By providing simultaneous access to interrelated drawings, teams can work concurrently from the same source drawings, increasing project team flexibility and efficiency and reducing total process time.

AutoCAD MAP 3D's management tools include routines to automate linking graphic objects to database records, a system to link documents to graphic objects thereby allowing easy access to those documents from your drawings, and an object data structure for storing and accessing data within your AutoCAD drawings.

Features of MAP 3D

AutoCAD MAP 3D allows users to access and modify graphic and nongraphic data stored in multiple AutoCAD drawing (.DWG) files. Users perform these modifications from within their current "active" AutoCAD file, and the user's environment acts as a single database of information.

One of the most popular features within the package allows multiple users to access central AutoCAD drawings and perform an advanced query for objects and data within those drawings. Once queried, the user can decide where the objects should finally reside; that is, back in the source drawings, with a new drawing, or remain in the current drawing. This awesome power has now been augmented with strong SQL features, import/export capabilities, and geodetic transformations.

The ability to perform graphic data accessing is selective and can occur through multiple drawings, whereas nongraphic accessing uses the AutoCAD extended entity data (or object data). The MAP 3D module provides direct access from within AutoCAD to external database management systems (DBMS). Examples of these are Microsoft Access, dBASE, INFORMIX, ORACLE, and PARADOX. Using Extended entity data (EED), a user can also link the AutoCAD data with other applications such as word processing and spreadsheets.

The nongraphic link provides the same command set regardless of the database in use. MAP 3D has drivers for the most popular databases systems. Open DataBase Connectivity (ODBC) is supported for general databases as well.

An Application for MAP 3D

An example of a MAP 3D application is that it can be used to input and/or modify data on a large engineering project in which the data are distributed among many large AutoCAD (.dwg) files. With MAP 3D, you can establish connections between entities or symbols in the various drawings with your current drawing, without carrying the overhead associated with the unwanted data that may exist in those files.

The method of accessing the geographic limits of the data in the drawings is the use of spatial databases. Augmenting this is the ability to access the data via property selection. In other words, you can identify the boundary of the data search and bring over only the data on the Road-Centerline layer to the current working session.

For an engineering project, a key map outlining the project's boundaries may be advantageous, so that users can select data from geographic locations without becoming overwhelmed by the total volume of data. A little forethought should easily identify anticipated "subboundaries."

Main Features of MAP 3D

1. Information can be isolated and analyzed by
   - Viewing selected features and statistics
   - Exporting data to external files and accessing EED
2. Data editing. After the data are extracted, they can be
   - Changed or deleted
   - Moved to another drawing or saved back to the original drawing
   - Saved to a new drawing
3. Data Selection Enhancements exist for more effective queries, such as
   - Boolean constructs (AND, OR, XOR)
   - Transform data from one coordinate system to another
   - Match features across edges of different drawings
4. MAP 3D has unique editing features to assist in cleaning up mathematical noise in maps. This noise consists of sloppy drafting, errors where entities cross one another or are duplicated, and so on. These features help prepare maps for accurate analysis and the creation of map topologies. They comprise
   - ***Rubber sheeting*** stretches objects from one set of points to a new set of points, often used to correct scans and to compensate for map distortions
   - Boundary clipping
   - Map-edge cutting tools that create clean breaks between linear objects
   - Precisely aligned map-sheet edges
   - Neatly cut and created spaces for annotations
5. The ability exists to import/export other formats including MicroStation (DGN), Mapinfo (MIF), Arcview, Oracle, and ArcInfo file formats.
6. Basic thematic maps with legends can be produced. Create thematic maps while allowing for automatic altering of color, linetype, text, and other parameters to show correlation in database information. Thematic maps can be based on object properties such as layer and linetype, object data you define in the drawing, or SQL data linked to external databases. As well as limiting objects in the thematic display to a certain area, users can also limit objects based on specific layers or particular block names.

rubber sheeting: Stretches objects from one set of points to a new set of points, often used to correct scans and to compensate for map distortions.

AutoCAD MAP 3D also supports topologies. A Topology in GIS describes the relationship of connecting adjacent features and adds a level of "intelligence" to the data set. A user can create, modify, and delete topologies; create buffers around points, lines, and polygons; analyze maps with point, line, and polygon overlays using **INTERSECT**, **UNION**, **IDENTITY**, **ERASE**, **CLIP**, and **PASTE** operations; use "shortest path trace" to find the shortest distance between two locations, useful for emergency services; and use "flood trace" to trace out from a point a specific distance in all directions, useful, for example, for analyzing demographic data and comparing alternative retail locations based on driving or walking times. You can also use flood trace to trace out to blocks that have specific attribute, object data, or external database record value, useful, for example, for finding all valves that need to be turned off in a water network.

Security

A newly installed copy of MAP 3D contains no prebuilt securities, except one for the superuser. The superuser must set these. Login as the superuser by using SUPERUSER as the login name and SUPERUSER as the password (note all caps). To establish security, follow this procedure:

1. Use the **EDIT-USER** command to set up at least one superuser.
2. Using the **EDIT-USER** command, the superuser sets the privileges.
3. Using the **CONFIGURE** command, the superuser enables the FORCELOG variable. After this is set, users must log into MAP 3D with the **SET USER** command.

The Spatial Database

In a CAD environment, a spatial database is a set of internal and external databases for one or more related drawings. Part of the description defines a CAD drawing. The remainder itemizes nongraphic characteristics such as databases or other documents.

You can think of drawing files as part of a spatial database. MAP 3D evaluates the data that define the graphics and their associated data, and the data linked to it from external databases. A CAD drawing becomes visible only in a drawing editor, such as AutoCAD, which is really a special kind of database manager; it both writes and interprets data that represent graphic elements, called *entities*.

Thus, a spatial database describes anything that you can represent in part or completely by one or more drawings. For example, a spatial database could describe a treatment plant, a city, an oil refinery, a geographical region, and so forth. Moreover, a spatial database can represent not only shapes but also names, materials, part numbers, suppliers, dates, and the like. *The primary requirement is that all entities share a common coordinate system.*

An AutoCAD spatial database has up to three parts:

1. The Graphic database, which is a data file that contains the definitions of all the geometric entities in a drawing such as lines, circles, arcs, and so on.
2. The Extended entity data (EED) or Object data. These data define additional, nongraphic aspects of an entity. Normally unseen, they are part of the drawing file and are stored with individual entities.
3. The External database(s) contains data files that you can read with a database manager. Like the EED database, it also contains nongraphic data. However, it can be linked to entities in one or many drawings.

All of these databases are within the scope of basic AutoCAD. However, the power of MAP 3D lies in that it can take advantage of these databases in several drawings simultaneously.

The power of MAP 3D is its ability to open a working session using a *current drawing*, attaching other AutoCAD files to the working session, performing queries of external information, and importing the results of queries into the current drawing. After the data have been added, deleted, or modified, they can then be saved to a new drawing, to the current drawing, or back to the drawings from whence the data came.

Source drawings are AutoCAD drawings and any data files linked to them that contain all of a project's data (both graphic and nongraphic) on which you want to run queries. Different source files categorize a project's data in different ways. For example, they can categorize data by location—as for a set of adjacent maps—or by content—for example, by water, gas, electricity, and so on—or by any mix of these and other criteria. When you use the AutoCAD **OPEN** command, the entire drawing is loaded. All of the drawing's entities, or as many as the current view allows, appear. When MAP 3D "opens" (or attaches) one or more source drawings, no part of them appears. Instead, "attach" means that the contents of those drawings are available for querying and bringing into the current drawing. MAP 3D supports several query strategies.

Queries

Querying, as the central activity of MAP 3D, is how MAP 3D selects information from one or more drawing files. Several strategies exist for defining query criteria and for handling the entities resulting from the query. Queries range from simple to complex and can be saved for reusing, editing, and supplementing them with AutoLISP expressions. Queries access one or more source drawing files. Usually, MAP 3D queries bring entities directly into the current drawing.

A MAP 3D query has several levels of complexity that are primarily determined by query definition criteria, query mode, and method of saving queried entities.

Query Definitions.   A query definition sets the criteria for selecting entities. The definition can include graphics; Boolean operators such as AND, OR, and XOR; SQL expressions; and AutoLISP expressions. Query definitions use three types of criteria:

1. **Location.**   Selects entities based on their location in the source drawing. The location can be relative to a specific point or feature or within a window. For example, you can search for entities that lie within a given radius of a specified point or within a given distance on either side of a specified line.

2. **Properties.**   Selects entities based on properties that relate to graphic or Extended entity data (EED) in the drawing file, such as length, layer, material, part number, and so on.

3. **SQL.**   Selects entities based on data in linked SQL database tables, such as supplier, owner, cost, and so on.

Query Access Modes.   MAP 3D queries entities in source drawings in one of several query modes including Preview, Draw, and Report modes.

The modes are distinguished by how permanent the query entities in the current and source drawings will be. The Preview and Draw modes display entities in the current drawing with different degrees of completeness, with different consequences for the source drawing, and for different purposes. The Report mode exports data to a file without displaying it. While querying, MAP 3D locks the source drawing file so other users cannot access that drawing. After all the entities retrieved from the source drawings appear in the current drawing, all source drawing files are unlocked so other MAP users can have access. After data are edited, a record-locking mechanism kicks in and locks only that entity so that others cannot edit it at the same time. This prevents users from "stepping on each other's toes."

Preview Mode.   If you execute a Preview mode query, objects that match the query criteria appear on-screen but are not actually copied from the source drawings. Use the **REDRAW** command on the **View** menu to clear the screen. It displays the queried entities on the screen in the current drawing without affecting either the current or the source drawings. These queried entities typically have an entity type of ADEXXXXXXX if listed; however, this will disappear on redraw. Show mode displays queried entities in the current drawing only temporarily; however, **ZOOM** and **PAN** will work until a **REDRAW** operation occurs that causes the queried entities to disappear. Use Preview mode for a quick view of a query and to see whether you are on the right track.

Draw Mode.   If you execute a Draw mode query, objects that match the query criteria are copied into the work session, provided they have not already been copied in by a previous query. The original objects remain unchanged in the source drawings. AutoCAD MAP 3D will not place duplicate copies of an object in the work session. If a previous query copied an object into the work session, the new query will not copy it in again. If you retrieve an object that is on a locked layer, you cannot save changes back to the source drawing. To save changes back, you must open the source drawing and unlock the layer before performing the query. Draw mode copies the queried entities into the current drawing, displays the queried entities on-screen, and leaves the source drawings unchanged. Because the queried entities are copied into the current drawing, using **REDRAW** does not make the entities disappear. After data are modified, MAP 3D locks the entities in the source file. No other MAP 3D user can edit until they are saved back or released. When an object is locked, other users can view it, but they cannot edit it.

Report Mode.   If you execute a Report mode query, AutoCAD MAP 3D creates the specified text file. Use a text editor, such as Windows Notepad, to view the report file.

Additional tools that make MAP 3D a worthwhile foundation item for Civil 3D include the Drawing Cleanup commands, **TRANSFORM** and **RUBBER SHEETING**, and mass editing commands such as **BOUNDARY BREAK** and **BOUNDARY TRIM**. GIS professionals need these tools to ensure that their linework is accurate and clean, as do engineers and surveyors.

Editing and Graphical Cleanup Tools

The Drawing Cleanup commands correct linear object and node errors to create a clean topology. The commands include these abilities: **Delete Duplicates**, **Erase Short Objects**, **Break Crossing Objects**, **Extend Undershoots**, **Apparent Intersection**, **Snap Clustered Nodes**,

Dissolve Pseudo-Nodes, **Erase Dangling Objects**, **Simplify Objects**, **Zero-Length Objects**, and **Weed Polylines**. The **TRANSFORM** command scales, offsets, and rotates selected objects. The **RUBBER SHEETING** command stretches objects from one set of points to a new set of points and is often used to correct scans that were made from stretched hard copies. The **BOUNDARY BREAK** command cleans map edges by cutting lines, *2D* polylines, arcs, and circles that cross a specified edge. The **BOUNDARY TRIM** command trims objects to a selected or defined boundary.

The MAP 3D menu tools for performing data cleanup can solve problems that have vexed users for years—further evidence of why a land development professional should be using Auto-CAD MAP 3D for everyday operations. The following describe several common scenarios that can wreak havoc on engineering projects.

2D: Two dimensions, characterized by the use of the *X*- and *Y*-axes in the Cartesian coordinate system resulting in planar material.

Scenario 1.   On a site where existing surface data are defined by mass points and *breaklines*, the surveyor must process these data and build an *existing ground* surface. Engineers using Auto-CAD Land Development Desktop points and faults, on the other hand, might develop the proposed site. In either case, various situations could lead to crossing breaklines or vertical faces. Of course, surface processing does not tolerate vertical faces because the *slope* is infinity, owing to a divide by zero in the calculation.

The software, however, can locate all the invalid crossings and, depending on the type of crossing, will trim, break, or otherwise fix such incidents. Previously, users spent large amounts of time performing these tasks manually.

breaklines: 3D polylines representing breaks in the planar slopes of the terrain. A breakline causes the mathematics of the terrain modeling to avoid building triangles that would cross a breakline. The triangle thus has a side adjacent to the breakline but does not cross it.

Scenario 2.   The traditional AutoCAD user might trim and erase feverishly to clip data to specific locations or boundaries. Now, the software can break all of the objects so that their properties may be altered and can perform the trimming to boundaries. Users can easily trim data to open or close polylines.

existing ground: Natural ground

slope: A change in elevation over a horizontal distance, usually described by a ratio (3:1).

Scenario 3.   If a user inadvertently copied AutoCAD drawing data on top of itself, such an error would double not only the file size but also the plot stroking, thereby affecting the quality of the plot. MAP 3D can help users avoid such a nightmare by deleting duplicate objects while preserving the integrity of the original file data.

Each of these scenarios demonstrates how the software can perform sophisticated drawing cleanup operations in a simple, common-sense fashion.

Among other features of the cleanup tools are the following:

- MAP 3D can automatically eliminate the speckling inherent in scanned images and can automatically extend or trim property lines that do not close, according to user-specified tolerances. It can weed out densely populated vertices in polyline data.

- The conversion utilities will redefine lines, arcs, 3D polylines, and circles into polylines.

- After editing, the **Mapping** commands provide the ability to modify the original entities, create new entities but retain the original ones, or create new entities and delete the original ones.

- Users can perform object selection for editing by using automatic algorithms or by simply selecting objects using traditional AutoCAD methods.

- Rubber sheeting of data is supported in a user-friendly way. Paper stretch can cause inherent errors in data that have been scanned and converted to vector data. The software tools allow users to correct this situation.

Geodetic Transformations

One of the most powerful commands in MAP 3D's repertoire for a surveyor is the ability to assign a geodetic coordinate system (Global Coordinate System) and transform data from one geodetic coordinate system to another.

Note:
You will need to configure the database to use with MAP 3D and that is out of the scope of this text. The addition of GIS into CADD software has become increasingly powerful. The reader is advised to seek additional resources to learn MAP 3D because this text is dedicated to Civil 3D.

CIVIL 3D—A CIVIL ENGINEERING DESIGN APPLICATION WITH NEW PHILOSOPHIES

Civil 3D continues to provide a unique software solution that offers a revolutionary approach to civil engineering design and drafting. It consists of the fusion of several Autodesk solutions including AutoCAD, MAP 3D, and the Civil 3D toolset along with Trimble Link™, Carlson Connect™, and Leica Exchange. Trimble, Carlson, and Leica are independent companies that provide links into Civil 3D so their users can use this product within their respective software solutions. They typically supply these add-ons after Civil 3D is released and they will probably do so again for the 2010 version. All of the traditional AutoCAD commands exist and can be accessed through the usual toolbars, pull-down menus, Custom User Interface, or type-in commands.

The new philosophies included within this software are data-driven design, reactive object technology, "ripple-through effectiveness," state-of-the-art interface enhancements, and an interactive and dynamic library of settings. The data-driven design refers to how objects will design themselves based on how the settings data are established. For instance, the horizontal curves for a road can be established such that they always meet a minimum standard allowable curve for the state or county in which they are being designed. Reactive object technology refers to items such as annotation automatically updating itself and reorienting itself when objects change or when the view is altered or rotated. The ***ripple-through effect*** refers to the impact that modifying an alignment has on the corridor's profiles, sections, and assemblies, whereas they automatically recompute their new values attributable to the modification. The interactive and dynamic library of settings refers to how the objects developed will take on aesthetic and visual characteristics based on how their display settings have been configured. The objects will change their appearance based on any changes to these settings automatically as well.

ripple-through effect: A term coined to describe the dynamic modeling characteristics of Civil 3D in performing automatic updates to data.

What Civil 3D Introduces

In addition to Civil 3D's fundamentally sound and traditional routines, it introduces profoundly new capabilities to civil engineering users of CADD. These include the following:

- New interface tools, support for ribbons

- New objects specifically developed for civil design

- Dynamic, model-based design, data-driven methods, and the ripple-through effect

- Data-driven, object style libraries that control graphics appearances and text

- DOT-level highway design capabilities

- Rehabilitation and reconstruction design tools

Note:

Ribbons, which were introduced in Office 2007 by Microsoft as an interface enhancement. They consist of a bar across the top of your program window that shows the functions that can be performed from a single location. Ribbons try to consolidate the program's functions into a familiar place so that the user does not need to pick through multiple levels of menus, toolbars, or task panes.

Interface Tools.   The Civil 3D interface tools are evident in the **Tool Palettes** and **Toolspace**, as the software is launched, as shown in Figure 1-6. The interface for 2010 fully supports the ribbons found in Vista and Microsoft Office products. In the figure ribbons are shown for the menu command Modify. Note that the Modify tab is selected. Civil 3D commands can be selected likewise. (We will leave it to the readers to investigate the ribbons on their own. This text will continue to refer to the commands from the pull-down menus.) Autodesk has gone to great lengths to place more functionality at the user's fingertips, and the invention of the hide-away **Toolspace** and **Tool Palettes** provides excellent examples. For this book it is much easier for us to refer to commands by pull-down menu rather than to try to describe which icon picture to select when choosing commands. Therefore, it is recommended that you set up your workspace for production as it is in Figure 1-10. Notice that the Civil 3D program is not maximized. In order to set your system up so that it is conducive with the textbook references and descriptions perform the following exercise.

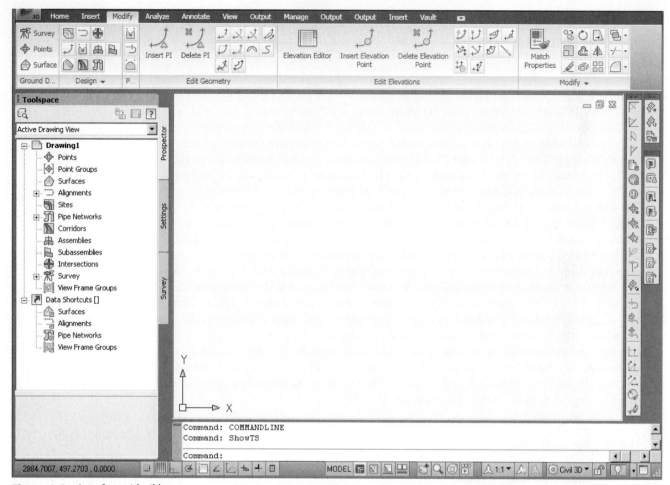

Figure 1-6 Interface with ribbons

Exercise 1-1: Ribbons and Menus

1. In the small toolbar at the upper left corner of the screen, click on the down arrow. Select the command to **Show Menu Bar** as shown in Figure 1-7. This will bring up the normal menu commands that we will use to choose our routines from.
2. Then right click to the right of the ribbons and the menu shown in Figure 1-8 will display. Select **Close** to terminate the ribbon display.
3. In the bottom right corner of the system, click on the **Workspace Switching** button shown in Figure 1-9 and select the Civil 3D workspace. This should place Civil 3D menus at the top of the screen. If not, select it again and you should see the display shown in Figure 1-10.

Figure 1-7 Show menu bar

Figure 1-8 Terminate the ribbon display

Figure 1-9 Workspace switching

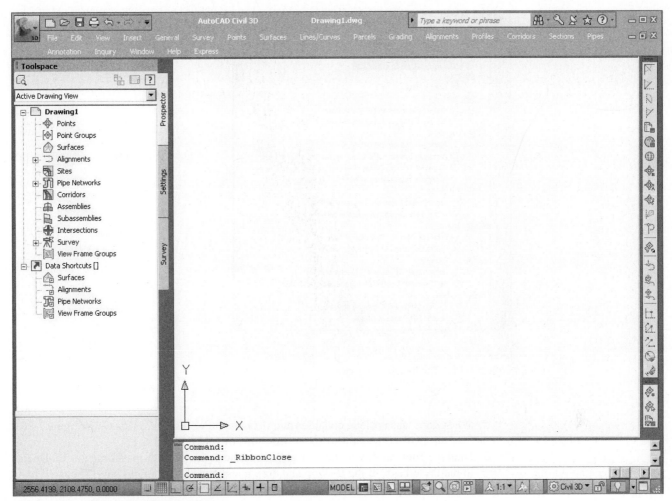

Figure 1-10   Proposed workspace setup

An entire set of Survey-related tools exists in the software as evidenced by the **Survey** pull-down menu.

The following procedure shows you how to accomplish this user workspace. Note that it is not required for the use of the software; it simply places the maximum amount of power at your fingertips without sacrificing design space. The advantage is that you have maximized the working area for design but have left the **Tool Palettes** and **Toolspace** available. Simply passing the mouse over these palettes opens them. When you finish making a selection from one of them, the palettes automatically close up.

Exercise 1-2: Set Up Production Workspace

1. Launch the Civil 3D software by double-clicking the icon on the desktop.
2. The system may appear similar to that shown in Figure 1-10.

An Inquiry Toolspace, with instantaneous readouts of many types of data, is included as part of the interface and can be found under the **General** menu. See Figure 1-11.

3. If the **Palettes** and **Toolspaces** are not displayed, select **Toolspace...** and **Tool Palettes Window** from the **General** pull-down menu.
4. Right-click on the spine of each palette and select **Auto-hide** (Figure 1-12).

You can hold the **<Ctrl>** key down when moving palettes to prevent them from docking or uncheck the **Allow Docking** option in the shortcut menu.

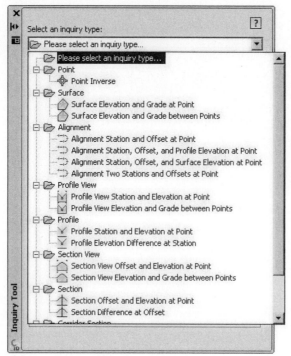

Figure 1-11   The Inquiry Toolspace

Figure 1-12   Right-click menu on palettes

5. When done, each palette collapses and floats in the workspace, as shown in Figure 1-13.
6. Size the Civil 3D window to about two-thirds of your desktop size.
7. Drag the **Tool Palettes** to the far right side of the desktop and drop it. Drag the **Toolspace** to the far left side of the desktop and drop it and click on the minus sign. They will both contract.

Figure 1-13   Collapsed palettes

8. Resize the Civil 3D window from the upper left and lower right corners to fit completely between the contracted palettes. You have now maximized your functionality without sacrificing drawing space.
9. Trying to set this up without using a procedure similar to this will cause the palettes to "dock," thereby reducing your overall drawing area. See Figure 1-14.

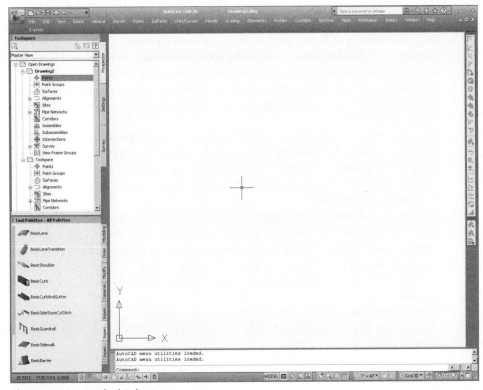

Figure 1-14   Docked Palettes

Panorama Palette.   The **Panorama** window is a multipurpose palette with the primary purpose of displaying data such as points, alignment entities, and description keys. The **Panorama** is also a **Tool Palette** that provides users with an **Event Viewer** to view messages that are logged during an Autodesk Civil 3D session. For example, if a surface is being created, you will read about the breaklines that may have been imported into the AutoCAD file.

If there are crossing breaklines (where one breakline physically crosses over or under another), that breakline is not added into the data set for surface modeling. The **Event Viewer** informs you of this occurrence. See Figure 1-15.

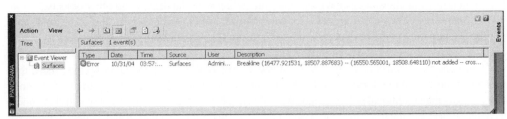

Figure 1-15   Panorama

Toolspace Palette.   The Civil 3D environment includes the **Toolspace**, shown in Figure 1-16. The **Toolspace** has two panels: one called a **Prospector** for data and the other for **Settings**. The **Toolspace** allows the user to view project data and status at any time and updates itself dynamically to show the status of all design data within the drawing.

Figure 1-12 shows that when Points exist, they are displayed when the cursor is on the **Points** item. Observe also that the **Surfaces** item is expanded and shows one surface in existence.

Figure 1-16   Toolspace Prospector

Exercise 1-3: Investigate Toolspace

This exercise investigates the **Toolspace** more closely.

1. Make sure that you are in Civil 3D and that your **Toolspace** is displayed. If it is not, select **General >> Toolspace....**

A **Survey Item** and a **Survey** tab can be seen as well. These allow surveyors to work with graphical and dynamic objects in the same way as designers can in their part of the **Toolspace**.

2. Save your drawing to Toolspace.dwg in your project location.
3. There are two essential parts to the **Toolspace: Prospector** and **Settings**. The **Prospector** is the command central for many operations and reviewing tasks.
4. After starting a Civil 3D session, click in the **Toolspace** on the **Prospector** tab.
5. There is a pop-down window in the top left of the palette. Select **Master View** if it is not already selected.
6. Three collections of information can be viewed using the **Master View: Open Drawings**, **Projects**, and **Drawing Templates**. Expand the **Open Drawings** item, and you see your AutoCAD filename of Toolspace. That file can be expanded to see the potential data types stored within it, such as Points, Point Groups, Surfaces, Sites, Corridors, Assemblies, and Subassemblies.
7. Right-click on **Points**. The **Prospector** displays a shortcut menu pertaining to points. Because this is a new file, the only options are **Create...**, **Transfer...**, and **Refresh**. Hit **Create...**, and a **Create Points** toolbar appears, allowing for the creation of points.
8. Take a moment to explore some of the icons in the toolbar. They include **Miscellaneous Manual**, **Intersection**, **Alignment**, **Surface**, **Interpolation**, **Slope**, and **Import Points** functions.
9. Choose **Miscellaneous Manual**. Following the prompts, set a point inside your AutoCAD file. Give the point an elevation **112.33** and a description of **FG**. The point should display where you placed it.
10. Select the point you placed with a left-click; then right-click, and a shortcut menu appears. Choose **Edit Points...**, and a **Panorama** palette appears. Notice that you can change the elevation value from 112.33 to 113.22, and when you close the **Panorama**, the point is updated.
11. Close the **Create Points Creation** toolbar.

These were just some very basic examples of using some of the new interface tools. As the text progresses, you will use these tools in detail.

New Objects for Design and Drafting.   A wide variety of objects is available to use in designing. Many of these objects were introduced in Land Desktop; however, they are now more fully implemented. But what are objects? Specifically, we are referring to Intelligent Objects, which are Autodesk data types that provide a programming structure for a variety of design items that contain data, functions, and allowable behaviors while interacting with the design and other objects.

A **Networks** Item and a **Figures** Item can be observed as Object types. These are found under the **Survey** item in the **Prospector**. These items will populate as the surveyor imports or creates traverse networks or linework defined as a figure.

The concept of object relationships is not new to Autodesk users. Land Desktop introduced this in a much more primitive form. Land Desktop contours were objects because they tried to act more like contours than traditional polylines did. What this meant is that the contour label would slide along a contour object when it was moved. It brought the break under the text with it and healed up the location from which it came. Civil 3D takes this to the next logical level. Contours are no longer objects because they are a part of the bigger picture, but they are now treated as a display option for the Surface Object. The Surface Object contains all the surface data within it, and the user uses style libraries to display the surface in a variety of analytical ways; for example, as contours, as slope shaded analyses, as a rendered object, and so forth. The Surface Object itself is affected by changes to its source data; that is, the points, the breaklines, or other surface data that were used to develop the surface.

The novel and revolutionary aspect of Civil 3D objects is that, because they are style-based and dynamic, they react and interact with other Civil 3D objects. Introducing links between design objects that react dynamically minimized the need for many manual tasks, such as ensuring that modifications are enacted between linework and labels, alignments and profiles, and the like. This process creates a ripple-through effect of actions and reactions and updates the data within the design automatically. Changes in one object can be passed automatically to objects associated to it at the user's option. For instance, if a curve within an alignment is altered, any grading using that alignment as a baseline can be consequently updated. Furthermore, all related alignment stationing, linework labels, and other alignment-related data are likewise updated.

These relationships are quite extensive, and you should have a feel for which objects update other objects. Some rules of thumb are listed here.

- When Points are modified, they can directly influence Surfaces.
- When Surfaces are modified, they can directly influence Grading Objects and Profiles.
- When Parcels are modified, they can directly influence Grading Objects and Corridors.
- When Alignments are modified, they can directly influence Grading, Corridors, Profiles, and Sections.
- When Grading Objects are modified, they can directly influence Surfaces and Corridors.
- When Subassemblies are modified, they can directly influence Assemblies and Corridors.
- When Assemblies are modified, they can directly influence Corridors.

A relationship exists among design objects, the styles that control their display, and the labels that control their annotation. These styles and labels are also managed as objects within Autodesk Civil 3D.

Objects are the basic working mechanism of the engineering design workflow. The underlying methodology for Civil 3D uses an object-oriented architecture. Therefore, design components such as points, surfaces, and alignments are intelligent and maintain relationships with other objects. The classic example is a horizontal alignment that has associated profiles and cross sections. If the alignment is manipulated, the profiles and sections linked to that alignment are automatically updated accordingly.

The major object types in Civil 3D are represented as follows.

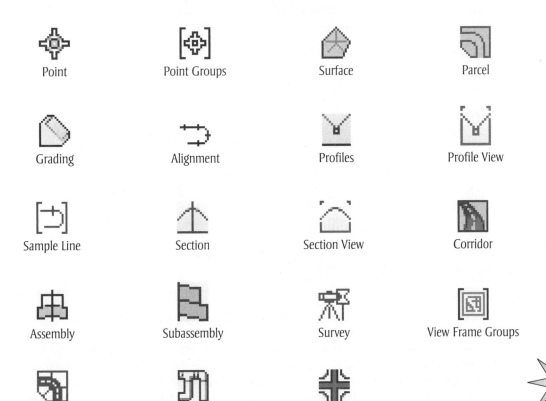

Point	Point Groups	Surface	Parcel
Grading	Alignment	Profiles	Profile View
Sample Line	Section	Section View	Corridor
Assembly	Subassembly	Survey	View Frame Groups
Sites	Pipe Networks	Intersections	

Civil 3D software is the first version of AutoCAD for civil engineering users in which lines, arcs, and polylines will *not* be the predominant data types for design and drafting. Rather, surface, roadway, parcel, and point objects will be the predominant design objects that are created and modified. Although other civil-oriented software solutions are on the market, none have taken this reactive technology as far as Civil 3D has. The ability to perform storm sewer drafting and compute watershed locations is also available in Civil 3D.

Dynamic, Model-Based Design, Data-Driven Methods, and the Ripple-Through Effect.   The concept of a live, dynamic model is new to the civil engineering field and consists of the ability to make changes to integral design components and have those changes update any related project components. The classic example is a horizontal alignment that has associated profiles and cross sections. If the alignment is modified, the alignment annotation, the profiles, and the sections linked to that alignment are updated automatically. Another example could be parcels with associated distance, bearing, and area labels that are updated automatically when the parcel geometry is altered.

Survey networks and figures are dynamic parts of the software. This means that changes to setups or backsights can be automatically recalculated in the network object.

Data-Driven, Object Style Libraries.   Object style libraries are very important to the use of the software in that they control the appearance and design characteristics of the object. When a new object is created, a predefined style can be applied to control how it displays. Styles can be modified on the fly and are retroactive. For example, if contours appear red and the user would like them to appear blue, a style modification can occur and be applied to the contours. They will then inherit the property of displaying blue. If the style definition is modified, the changes are immediately applied to all objects using that style, similar to Text Styles or Dimension Styles.

The styles are managed on the **Toolspace Settings** tab shown in Figure 1-17. All Civil 3D objects have a Standard style that can be used as is, or new ones can be created as needed. The best approach would be to have someone in the organization predevelop all of the styles needed as part of the implementation of the software. Styles can be organized and stored in a drawing template (.dwt) file.

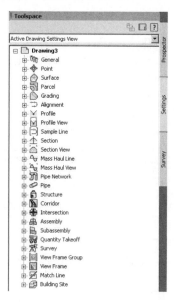

Figure 1-17   Toolspace Settings

A set of Survey settings exists in the **Settings** tab. This tab allows the user to create Figure Prefix Libraries for defining linework or figures and Equipment Databases where settings for ambient conditions and other equipment parameters are contained. The management of the Survey databases occurs here as well.

When developing a style for an object, the object will be physically placed on a main layer. However, component objects can reside on supplemental layers in order to control the display of those components. So an alignment object can reside on the CL layer, but the lines can reside on the CL-Lines layer while the arcs reside on the CL-Arc layer. The user can issue this instruction by using an * to denote using the object's layer as a prefix or suffix. It becomes an interesting visual when the user would like to inspect the arcs within an alignment separate from the linear components.

DOT-Level Highway Design Capabilities.   Civil 3D offers Autodesk users high-end highway design tools that allow for multiple baseline designs and multiple regions with each baseline. Baselines are centerlines for adjacent roadway occurrences. Regions are areas within those baselines where different things might be happening, such as ***superelevations*** or different assemblies.

Rehabilitation and Reconstruction Design Tools.   Civil 3D provides a highly customized and very specific toolset for designers who are working in the area of roadway rehabilitation and maintenance design. These tools include subassemblies and routines for sidewalk replacement, curb replacement, and several variations on milling and overlaying pavements. The initial installation of Civil 3D may not import these into the **Tool Palettes**, but they can be accessed through the Catalogs and dragged and dropped into a **Tool** palette of your making.

User control functions exist in the very useful user-defined boundaries as well as the ability to add station-based assembly insertions.

Channel and Retaining Wall Sub-assemblies add to the rehabilitation tools.

Figures 1-18 and 1-19 indicate the rehabilitation capabilities of Civil 3D.

> **superelevations:** Refers to the cross slope introduced into a cross section of a roadway in order to compensate for the centrifugal forces created by horizontal curves. According to the laws of mechanics, when a vehicle travels on a curve it is forced outward by centrifugal force. On a superelevated roadway, this force is resisted by the vehicle weight component parallel to the superelevated surface and the side friction between the tires and pavement. The pavement is essentially tilted to counter the forces described above.

Page (1 of 2) 1 2   Next

OverlayBrokenBackBetweenEdges
Overlays a four lane crowned corridor between gutter flange points.

OverlayBrokenBackOverGutters
Overlays a four lane crowned corridor over gutter.

OverlayCrownBetweenEdges
Overlays a simple crowned roadway between two known edge-of-pavement points.

OverlayMedianAsymmetrical
Widens an existing divided highway inward over a depressed median, with an asymmetrical barrier.

OverlayMedianSymmetrical
Widens an existing divided highway inward over a depressed median, with a symmetrical barrier.

OverlayMillAndLevel1
Overlay with milling or leveling on an uncrowned roadway.

OverlayMillAndLevel2
Overlay with milling or leveling on a crowned roadway.

OverlayParabolic
Inserts parabolic travel lanes between know flange points.

OverlayWidenMatchSlope1
Overlay and widening, matching existing slope on a

OverlayWidenMatchSlope2
Overlay and widening, matching

Overlay and widening, matching existing slope on a crowned roadway.

Figure 1-18   Rehabilitation tools, page 1

OverlayWidenWithSuper1
Overlay and widening of a roadway using Outside Lane superelevation.

UrbanReplaceCurbGutter1
Replaces an existing curb and gutter, with known back of curb profile.

UrbanReplaceCurbGutter2
Replaces an existing curb and gutter, tying to existing inside edge of sidewalk.

UrbanReplaceSidewalk
Replaces an existing sidewalk, from outside edge towards the curb.

Figure 1-19   Rehabilitation tools, page 2

TIP In addition to these fine tools, Autodesk has also developed the ability for designers to create designs where the old roadway will be repaired. This is in contrast to prior solutions in which the assumption was that all roads were new roads. An enormous amount of roadway repair occurs throughout the world, and these abilities allow for milling, overlaying, sidewalk, or curb and gutter replacements on existing roadways.

Engineers, drafters, and roadway repair workers will benefit not only from the ability to design DOT-level roadways but from the roadway rehabilitation tools as well. Many regions in the country or in the world do not have a lot of new growth; however, they do perform a large amount of roadway maintenance. These skills will provide new productivity for that staff.

Understanding Civil 3D Icons

The following information offers the user a description of the icons in Civil 3D. Although Civil 3D Help provides this information, it is scattered around and sometimes difficult to locate. This text places all of these items in this single location for easy reference.

The icons at the top of the **Prospector** palette control the display of icons within the **Prospector** panel, display the **Panorama** window, and provide access to **Help.** The icons and their respective meanings are outlined next, as found in Civil 3D Help.

 Toggles the display of **Project Item State** icons in the **Prospector.** The **Project Item State** icon indicates its status with respect to the project, such as whether it is checked in or out. Details for these icons are shown.

If no icon is displayed, then the drawing has been added to the project, but you do not have a local copy.

 The drawing is available to be checked out, the **Vault** copy matches your local copy.

 The drawing is available to be checked out, but your local copy is newer than the **Vault** copy.

 The drawing is available to be checked out, the **Vault** copy is newer than your local copy.

 The drawing is checked out to you, but you do not have a local copy.

 The drawing is checked out to you, the **Vault** copy matches the local copy.

 The drawing is checked out to you, your local copy is newer than the **Vault** copy.

 The drawing is checked out to you, the **Vault** copy is newer than your local copy.

 The drawing is checked out to someone else, and you do not have a local copy.

 The drawing is checked out to someone else, and your local copy matches the **Vault copy**.

 The drawing is checked out to someone else, and your local copy is newer than the **Vault copy**.

The drawing is checked out to someone else, and your local copy is older than the **Vault copy**.

 This icon is displayed next to the drawing name in the **Prospector** when the local copy becomes out-of-date.

 Toggles the display of **Drawing Item State** icons in the **Prospector.** The **Drawing Item State** icon indicates the state of an object within a drawing, including whether or not it is locked.

The following icons describe the possible states of information.

 The object is locked.

 The object is referenced by another object.

 The object is a reference to an object in another drawing.

 Toggles the display of **Drawing Item Modifier** icons at the top of the **Prospector**. The **Drawing Item Modifier** icon indicates the status of the item relative to the project or the drawing. A description of the **Drawing Item Modifier** icons is provided here.

No icon means the object is **Not** out of date and **Does Not** violate constraints, the Local copy of the object **Is** more recent than the Project copy, and the Local copy of the object has **Not** been edited relative to the Project object.

 The object **Is** out of date or **Does** violate constraints, the Project copy of the object **Is** more recent than the Local copy, and the Local copy of the object **Has** been edited relative to the Project object.

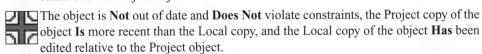 The object is **Not** out of date and **Does Not** violate constraints, the Project copy of the object **Is** more recent than the Local copy, and the Local copy of the object **Has** been edited relative to the Project object.

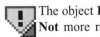 The object **Is** out of date or **Does** violate constraints, the Project copy of the object is **Not** more recent than the Local copy, and the Local copy of the object **Has** been edited relative to the Project object.

 The object is **Not** out of date and **Does Not** violate constraints, the Project copy of the object is **Not** more recent than the Local copy, and the Local copy of the object **Has** been edited relative to the Project object.

 The object **Is** out of date or **Does** violate constraints, the Project copy of the object **Is** more recent than the Local copy, and the Local copy of the object **Has Not** been edited relative to the Project object.

 The object is **Not** out of date and **Does Not** violate constraints, the Project copy of the object **Is** more recent than the Local copy, and the Local copy of the object **Has Not** been edited relative to the Project object.

 The object **Is** out of date or **Does** violate constraints, the Project copy of the object is **Not** more recent than the Local copy, and the Local copy of the object **Has Not** been edited relative to the Project object.

 Toggles the display of the **Panorama** window, if the **Panorama** window contains active vistas.

 Indicates that data do exist in this area.

The view in the **Prospector** might appear similar to Figure 1-20. The name of the drawing is EG Drawing. Points do exist, and Point Groups exist. When the tree for a drawing is expanded, AutoCAD icons are displayed in front of each drawing name. If the icon is blue, it means that the drawing is in the project. If the icon is red, then the drawing is currently open.

Figure 1-20   Data and Project icons

The **Toolspace** has Windows Explorer style expansion and contraction facilities that are called Trees. They display items in a hierarchical structure. Any item containing other items below it is called a Collection. In Figure 1-20, Open Drawings, EG Drawing, Point Groups, and Surfaces, are Collections. A symbol may be shown to the far left of each Collection name; this is called a Tree Node. Its intent is to provide information about the display of the items in the Collection. The following list describes these Tree Node symbols:

This icon means that the collection contains items that are not displayed; expand the tree and display the items.

This icon means that the items contained in the collection are displayed and you can collapse the tree and hide the items, if desired.

This icon means that the collection contains items that cannot be displayed in the tree. You can click on the Collection name to list the items in a **Toolspace** item view, which is another pane displayed beside or below the tree.

This icon means that the Collection's data need to be refreshed. You can right-click on the collection and choose **Refresh**.

This icon means that the item is a reference to an item located elsewhere in the tree. You can double-click the reference to navigate to the actual item.

This icon means that the Collection contains no items.

Other icons exist for Survey items that include Control Points, Non-Control Points, Directions, Setups, and Traverses, and can be seen in the **Toolspace** under Survey.

Pipe Utilities Grips

Several grips that allow for modifying pipe and components are described here.

The Endpoint Free Grip.   Clicking the endpoint free grip in the **Plan** view moves that endpoint of the pipe to a new point. The midpoint and opposite endpoint of the pipe are maintained during this edit so the length does not change. Curved pipes behave identically to an AutoCAD arc.

The Midpoint Free Grip. Clicking the midpoint free grip moves the whole pipe to a new, specified point. Curved pipes behave identically to an AutoCAD arc.

The Length Constraint Grip. Pipe length can be increased or decreased by gripping the end of the pipe, and only that end shortens or lengthens. The direction of the pipe does not change in this mode of operation.

The Midpoint Resize Constraint Grip. This grip allows you to reset the pipe's width based on the pipe sizes available in the parts list and part catalog. When the midpoint resize grip is used on a pipe, a series of parallel lines display next to the pipe, whereby each set of parallel lines represents an available pipe width. A tooltip displays the pipe width, and you can snap to any of the parallel lines to select a new pipe width on the fly.

Sheet Set Manager Palette

Another interface item in Civil 3D is the **Sheet Set Manager**, an AutoCAD 2005 enhancement that is included in the Civil 3D product. Sheet sets organize, create, and publish multiple drawing layouts into a single set of plans. Before the **Sheet Manager** existed, a set of drawings was organized using manual procedures. The individual drawings in the set may have emanated from several different AutoCAD files, and the process of ensuring that they were properly maintained, ordered, and correctly numbered was very time consuming. Open the **Sheet Set Manager** by typing **Sheetset**. The **CREATE SHEET SET** command in the **File** menu opens a Wizard that guides you through the process of creating a sheet set. You can also right-click in the **Sheet Set Manager** window and obtain the menu shown in Figure 1-21.

Once in the Wizard, there are two ways to create a sheet set. You can use a sample sheet set provided by Autodesk or use an existing drawing set of your own. The sample sheet set option works like a template and provides the organization and default settings for the new sheet set. After the setup is complete, you can compose individual sheets within the set by importing layouts and placing saved views as needed. The individual sheets created using this method are saved as separate drawing files, in which the original drawing files are linked as referenced drawings. The sheet set is saved as a separate file with the extension of .DST.

If you have already created layouts for the desired drawings and now need to assemble them together into a plan set, you would use the second option. You can specify one or more folders that contain drawing files, and the layouts can be imported into the sheet set. In this case, no new drawing files are created. Keep in mind, though, that this option will not fully utilize the capabilities of the sheet set feature to manage and organize such items as sheet numbers, callouts, and such because the title blocks and views have already been defined.

The **Sheet Set Manager** palette performs the management of the sheets. The user can create new sheet sets, open existing ones, list the sheets, and observe the views within a particular sheet. The sheets can also be arranged into individual groups to assist in navigation and organization. Figure 1-22 shows that a variety of details are available as well as a thumbnail preview if so desired.

The sheet file can be opened by double-clicking on it. If the sheet set was created using the **Sample Sheet Set** option, you must specify the folder location of the AutoCAD files whose views are to be used. These become support drawings and are displayed in the **Sheet Set Manager** dialog box along with their saved views, which can be chosen and placed on a sheet. The sheets and their views are routinely numbered and update dynamically when changes are made to a name or a number. After the sheet set has been developed, the complete set or just certain selected sheets can be published (or plotted). Publishing is a term now used for outputting the data to an external source. Not all plots are printed to hard copy anymore; some outputs go to the .DWF format for viewing in the Express Viewer or on the Internet. Of course, outputting to a plotter is still a normal function for creating hard copies. The **Sheet Set Manager** has made plotting drawings individually an obsolete endeavor. Other enhancements include the **eTransmit** option, which allows for the creation of a transmittal package formatted in the Zip format, and the **Archive** option, which creates a compressed archive of the entire sheet set.

Figure 1-21   Sheet Set Manager menu

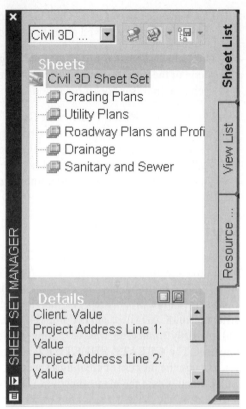

Figure 1-22   Sheet Set Manager palette

Chapter Summary

This chapter introduced Civil 3D and its capabilities for model building and organization. It also gave an explanation of MAP 3D, a foundational aspect of Civil 3D that adds GIS, important utilities, and drafting cleanup tools to the user's toolkit. Now that we've covered the basics, we move into a design project in Chapter 2.

Chapter Test Questions

Multiple Choice

1. The Civil 3D user must know which of the following in order to use Civil 3D for typical subdivision design?

   a. AutoCAD
   b. Geometry concepts
   c. Surface or DTM concepts
   d. All of the above

2. A user must understand which Civil 3D interface items in order to negotiate through the data effectively?

   a. **Tear-off** palettes
   b. **Toolspace**
   c. Slide Sorter
   d. **Kiosk** tools

3. Which of the components allows users to access all of the Properties of project data?

   a. **Settings** tab
   b. **Preview** window
   c. Right-clicking on the **Surfaces** item
   d. All of the above

4. Some of the add-in software available for Civil 3D includes which of the following?

   a. Trimble Link
   b. Carlson Connect
   c. Leica X-Change
   d. All of the above

5. MAP 3D can connect and provide read/write access to which of the following?

   a. Microstation files
   b. Photoshop files
   c. Microsoft Access
   d. None of the above

6. One user can use MAP 3D to access many AutoCAD drawings simultaneously. How many users can attach to the same AutoCAD drawing simultaneously?

   a. One
   b. None
   c. An unlimited number
   d. Two

7. Which components consist of the AutoCAD spatial database for MAP 3D?

   a. Graphic database
   b. Extended entity data (EED) or Object data
   c. External database(s)
   d. All of the above

8. Drafting technicians should know how to use MAP 3D in conjunction with Civil 3D in which of the following ways?

   a. Attaching multiple drawings to a working session
   b. Performing drawing cleanup operations
   c. Importing/exporting data to other manufacturers' programs
   d. All of the above

9. Drawing Cleanup tools allow for which of the following?

   a. Deleting Duplicate Objects, Erasing Short Objects, and Breaking Crossing Objects
   b. Raster and pixel-based photo editing
   c. OLE cleanup and editing
   d. Altering audio sounds from MP3 and WAV files

10. The **Panorama** performs which of the following functions?

   a. Road design
   b. Site grading
   c. Utility piping layout
   d. None of the above

True or False

1. True or False: GIS capabilities are not part of the Civil 3D solution.

2. True or False: All Civil 3D data can be reformatted into 3D/GPS Machine Control data.

3. True or False: 3D surfaces can be formatted to 3D/GPS Machine Control data.

4. True or False: MAP 3D can link AutoCAD graphics to external databases such as Microsoft Access and Oracle.

5. True or False: Rubber sheeting can allow the user to correct the inherent errors in data that has been scanned in and converted to vector data.

6. True or False: Civil 3D cannot use the AutoCAD **Sheet Set Manager** because it can open only one drawing at a time.

7. True or False: Every icon in the Civil 3D **Toolspace** will invoke an engineering command.

8. True or False: Some icons appear in the **Prospector** when project objects are out of date.

9. True or False: The **Prospector** shows when project items are populated with data.

10. True or False: Users can access project data in various ways through the **Prospector**.

CHAPTER EXERCISES

1. What are the major object types Civil 3D uses? Why would we use them?

2. What would be some examples of uses for object technology? How does this compare to parametric technology?

3. What is GIS? Explain what it is used for and how it differs from CAD.

4. What is GPS? Explain what it is used for and how the future of engineering and surveying will be changed by the advances in this area.

5. What is a spatial database as related to GIS?

6. Civil 3D is comprised of what software components?

7. Do you think the cost of designing engineering projects is more than, less than, or the same as it was 30 years ago? Explain your answer.

8. Explain the uses for alignments; provide examples of their use and the benefits they provide to designers.

9. Explain the uses for Corridor Profiles; provide examples of their use and the benefits to designers.

10. If you were provided a series of stations, offsets, and elevations relative to an alignment, explain what this means and what usefulness it might present. What can be accomplished with this information?

11. Write a few paragraphs on how visualizations (or renderings) can be used in the civil engineering industry.

12. If engineers work in two dimensions, what limitations do they have compared with someone working in three dimensions? Explain your response.

13. How can laser-guided machine control be used in conjunction with GPS-guided machine control to automate earth-moving tasks?

A Civil 3D JumpStart Project

2

Chapter
Objectives

- Perform basic functions of Civil 3D on all facets of a project because the chapter goes through an entire project from start to finish.
- Prepare an existing ground surface from actual 3D project data, create contours, and label them.
- Develop a property parcel for a shopping center and prepare the labeling required for its drafting.
- Develop an alignment for an access road to the shopping center.
- Develop a finished ground profile and a corridor to put the road into 3D.
- Design the grading for the shopping center and the parking facility.

INTRODUCTION

This chapter commences immediately with a design project. The details and advanced usage of the commands are reserved until subsequent chapters; however, this chapter takes you through an entire project from start to finish, with only a minimal amount of settings manipulations. You prepare an existing ground surface from actual 3D project data, create contours, and label them. You develop a property parcel for a shopping center and prepare the labeling required for its drafting. Then you develop an alignment for an access road to the shopping center, and a *finished ground* profile and a corridor to put the road into 3D. The next step is to design the grading for the shopping center and the parking facility.

REVIEW OF FUNCTIONS AND FEATURES TO BE USED

This chapter uses engineering functions to create a terrain or surface model and shows you how to use this "Object," display it in different ways, and label it. The project creates a Parcel object from primitive geometry entities and displays it to show directional and distance labels as well as parcel areas. It also develops an alignment from primitive geometry and defines it as an object. Styles will be used to control its appearance as well as that of the other objects. You will create a *profile view* with an *existing ground profile* and then develop a finished ground profile for the access road again. Assemblies are created from subassemblies, and a corridor object is designed using assemblies. Grading objects are also developed for the site of the shopping center.

finished ground: The improved conditions for the site.

profile view: A Civil 3D term for the location in Civil 3D where profiles are displayed. Each profile view displays new or existing profiles and offsets for one horizontal alignment. Although you can create profiles without displaying them on a profile view, when a profile view is created, the complete list of profiles for the alignment is displayed so that a profile can be selected for display in the profile view.

existing ground profile: The vertical alignment for the roadway as defined by the location of the horizontal alignment draped onto the existing ground terrain model.

You will benefit from the ability to see rapidly what Civil 3D can do from a broad-brush approach. This chapter and its accompanying procedures start with existing ground data and end with a completed (albeit, simple) design project.

Job Skills

PROJECT DESIGN APPLICATION——

Part One: Project Design Application

To begin, you create an Existing Ground surface. You also select some basic settings to make the surface react and display the way you wish. Your first task is to open a drawing with raw data in it and inspect the contents of the data.

Note:
These data were prepared without the benefit of a Civil 3D template and, as a result, have few to no settings predeveloped within them. Here some of the important ones will be set. For actual projects, you are strongly advised to configure the product to adhere to your organization's CADD standards.

Exercise 2-1: Open Drawing and Inspect Data

To access student data files, go to www.pearsondesigncentral.com.

1. Launch Civil 3D and close the Drawing.dwg that initially opens.
2. Select **File** from the pull-down menu, then **Open**, and choose the Chapter-2a.dwg in your student data files.
3. Notice that there are breaklines and mass points in the file, which together represent the existing ground conditions.
4. On inspection of the data, notice that there is a road running east to west. Zoom in and you will see a cul-de-sac heading toward the south from the road.
5. Click on a breakline somewhere in the file and notice the grips. Place your cursor in one of the grips, but do not click it. Simply look at the lower left corner of the screen and observe that the X, Y, Z coordinates are shown for the grip. Notice that the Z coordinate or elevation has a value representing the elevation of the surface at that location.

Note:
The mass points are actually Auto-CAD blocks floating at the correct elevation. An aerial photogrammetist developed the breaklines using stereodigitizing techniques. The three-dimensional breaklines have elevations at each vertex. The mass points are placed in the data set to densify the surface data.

After having observed the data set, you can prepare a Civil 3D surface for Existing Ground. Before doing that, inspect some important surface-related settings. The first one to change is the Precision of the Contour label. Because we are labeling even contours that are multiples of 2, there is no need to have thousandths-place precision on the annotation when whole numbers will suffice. The precision is unneeded, and the extra decimal places tend to clutter up the drawing. Additionally you need to create a layer on which the annotation will reside.

Exercise 2-2: Develop Settings

1. Go to the **Toolspace**. Go to the **General** pull-down menu and choose **Toolspace...** or type **Showts** to display the **Toolspace** palette if it is not already there. Click on the **Settings** tab.
2. In the **Master View**, expand **Drawings**. Then expand **Surface**. Then expand **Label Styles**.
3. Choose the **Contour** label style, and note that one exists called **Standard**.
4. Click on the **Standard** label style, right-click the mouse, and choose **Edit....**
5. The **Label Style Composer** dialog box displays. Click on the **Information** tab and observe the contents of the panel. Click on the **General** tab and observe the contents of the panel.
6. Click the **Layout** tab. Several properties exist in the **Property** column.
7. Click on **Text**; expand text. Choose **Contents** and then refer to the **Value** column. Click on the value for **Contents**. Choose the button with the three dots called ellipses **(...)**.
8. This brings up the **Text Component Editor—Contents** dialog box.
9. Click into the **Preview** window on the right side of the dialog box, highlight the data there, and erase them so that the window is blank.
10. Click on **Precision** in the **Modifier** column.
11. The value for the Precision is 0.001, which is not appropriate for your contour label because you do not wish to have decimal points on even contours. Click on 0.001 and select **1** from the pop-down window in the **Value** column.

12. Then click the **gray arrow** at the top of the dialog box to populate the **Preview** window with the new data settings.
13. Look on the **Preview** window, and you will see some code indicating that new settings exist. Hit **OK**.
14. In the **General** tab, for the **Layer** property, click on the **Value** where it shows Layer 0 and notice that a button with ellipses (...) exists. Choose the button, and a **Layer Selection** dialog box appears. Choose **New**. In the **Create Layer** dialog box, click on the value for **Layer** property where it says **Layer1**, and type in a new layer name of **C-Topo-Labl**.
15. Hit **OK** until you've terminated the command.

Note:

A unique feature of this text is that examples for practical use are provided for and shown as Tips that describe when these commands might be used on actual projects.

Exercise 2-3: Set Up a Surface

1. Choose **Surfaces** from the pull-down menu.
2. Select **Create surface....**
3. The **Create Surface** dialog box appears.
4. Several types of surfaces can be created: a TIN surface, a Grid surface, and two types of Volume surfaces.

TIP   The Volume surfaces are created during earthwork take-off computations. The Grid surface is used when a surface of evenly spaced rectangular data whose elevations are interpolated from the data is desired.

5. We want a *TIN* surface. In the window below is the informational item that includes the name of the surface. Click on the **Value** column for the Surface name.
6. The Surface name is incremental, so the first surface is **Surface1**, the second surface is **Surface2**, and so on. Click in this field and type **Existing Ground** as your name. Hit **OK**.
7. To the right of the **Type** is the **Layer** field. Pick on the button on the right side of the dialog box for **Surface** layer. An **Object Layer** dialog box appears. Where it says **Base Layer Name**, choose the button on the right for **Layer**, and the **Layer Selection** dialog box opens.
8. Hit the button for **New** layer and enter **C-Topo** in the field for **Layer1**. Hit **OK** twice. Then where it says **Modifier Value**, select **Suffix** from the pop-down window.
9. When the **Modifier Value** field to the right becomes available, type in a dash and an asterisk **(-*)**. This will create a layer with the name of the surface as a suffix to the layer name. You should get a layer called **C-Topo-Existing Ground**, as can be seen in the **Preview** window.
10. Type **Existing Ground** for the **Description** also.
11. Leave all else as default and click **OK**.
12. Next go to the **Toolspace** and choose the **Prospector** tab.
13. Look under **Open Drawings** for your drawing. Expand **Surfaces** to show the new surface you just created for Existing Ground.

TIN: Triangulated Irregular Network representing the surface.

The next step is to identify the 3D surface data and build the surface.

Exercise 2-4: Build Surface

1. Expand the **Existing Ground Surface** item. You see an item for **Definition**.
2. Expand **Definition**, and you see all the data types that can go into the preparation of the surface. These include **Breaklines**, **Contours**, **DEM files**, **Drawing Objects**, and other data types.
3. Our data set contains breaklines and blocks, as discussed earlier. Therefore, use the commands for adding **Breaklines** and use **Drawing Objects** to add the blocks.
4. Begin by clicking on **Breaklines**, then right-click on **Breaklines** and select **Add....**
5. A dialog box for **Add Breaklines** displays. Add a **Description** of **EG**.

TIP The choices allow for **Proximity breaklines**, **Wall breaklines**, and **Breaklines from a file**. Proximity breaklines are 2D polylines that have points with elevations at each vertex in the polyline. The point elevations will be used by the software in creating 3D breaklines from the 2D polylines. The Wall breakline option is used to represent vertical components of surfaces. In actuality, they are not truly vertical because this would cause issues in the software relating to a divide by zero in the denominator for various slope computations. Therefore, the software allows for Wall breaklines that contain wall height data, but the top of the wall is slightly offset from the bottom of the wall so as to avoid the vertical computational issue. The last choice is to bring in breaklines from an external text file.

6. Use **Standard** breaklines as the type of breakline but notice that other choices exist in the pop-down list.
7. Use **Standard** breaklines, which are the 3D polylines in the file. The last setting is a **Mid-ordinate distance** field, which is available for creating 3D breaklines from 2D polylines that have curves in them. In this case if you use the default of 1′, a 3D polyline would be created such that small chords simulate the curve but do not deviate from the arc by more than 1′.
8. Hit **OK**. When you are prompted to Select objects:, place a window around the data. Do not worry if there are points mixed in with the selection set of breaklines because the software filters anything that is not a breakline.
9. A **Panorama** dialog box may appear that indicates that there are two crossing breaklines. Coordinates are displayed so you can check the severity of the issue. In this case, it has been determined that this will not harm your surface integrity, and so continue on. Click the green check mark in the top right of the **Panorama** dialog box to continue. Upon completion of this function, the software creates the surface, as shown by a yellow boundary.
   Crossing breaklines can be found using the **Zoom to** option in the **Panorama**.
10. Now in the **Prospector**, choose **Drawing Objects** under the **Definitions** area of the **Exiting Ground Surface**. Right-click and choose **Add....**
11. For the **Object type**, choose **blocks**.
12. Type **EG** as the **Description** field in the dialog box and hit **OK**.
13. When you are prompted to Select objects:, place a window around the data. Do not worry if breaklines are mixed in with the selection set of points because the software filters out the data it does not need.
14. On completion, the yellow surface boundary is updated to include the blocks.

Now that the surface is created, you typically want to view contours representing the surface.

Exercise 2-5: Develop Contours for Surface

1. In the **Toolspace**, choose the **Settings** tab. Choose **Surface >> Surface Styles >> Standard**. Right-click on **Standard** and choose **Edit....**
2. In the **Surface Style** dialog box, choose the **Display** tab.
3. With the view direction in the pop-down window set to **Plan**, click on the lightbulb to turn on the **Major** and **Minor** contours and turn off the lightbulb for **Border**. Note the colors are preset and can be changed here, if so desired.
4. On leaving the dialog box, the contours in Civil 3D are automatically updated to show the contours as defined in the Style.
5. The next step is to create **Contour** labels on the **Contours**. Choose **Surfaces >>Add Surface Labels >> Add Surface Labels . . . Contour-Multiple at Interval** from the pull-down menu.
6. When prompted to Select a surface:, select the surface. Then you are prompted to Pick first point: in order to identify a start point for the labeling to begin. Place a point at the top of the site and place a second point to the bottom and outside the site. When you are prompted Interval along contour <100.000>: type **500′**.

7. Hit **<Enter>**. On completion of the command, zoom in and inspect the data and the contour labels every 500' across the site.

8. Save your file to a name with your initials as the suffix of the name, Chapter-2-a-hw.dwg.

Part Two: Project Design Application

Part Two of this exercise is to develop a property parcel. It consists of a fairly simple four-sided shape that is 500' wide by 500' long. Please note that the software is certainly not limited to this simplicity; rather, this introductory exercise is planned to keep it simple in order to make several conceptual points clear.

You will open the drawing Chapter 2-b.dwg from the student data files, a file that contains the completed surface data from the previous set of exercises. The next objective is to develop a parcel boundary in which you design a commercial shopping center. The first step is to create the primitive geometry for the boundary lines. Following that using the Civil 3D functionality will create Parcel objects from the primitive linework.

Exercise 2-6: Develop Geometry for Parcel Boundary

1. Open the drawing called Chapter 2-b.dwg.

2. Begin by creating a layer called **C-Prop-Bndy**; set the color to **yellow**, and set it to be the current layer. Draw a polyline as described next. Select the icon for **Polyline** in AutoCAD or type **PL <Enter>**. The system responds as shown:

```
Command: PLINE
Specify start point: <Polar off> 15600,18540
Current line-width is 0.0000
Specify next point or [Arc/Halfwidth/Length/Undo/Width] : <Coords
off> <Coords on> @500<0
Specify next point or [Arc/Close/Halfwidth/Length/Undo/Width] : @500<90
Specify next point or [Arc/Close/Halfwidth/Length/Undo/Width] : @500<180
Specify next point or [Arc/Close/Halfwidth/Length/Undo/Width] : CL
```

3. Next you will address the settings for the boundary to place the Civil 3D parcel on the **C-Prop-Bndy** layer.

4. From the **Parcels** pull-down menu, choose the **CREATE PARCEL FROM OBJECTS** command. When you are prompted with Select lines, arcs, or polylines to convert into parcels or [Xref] :, select the polyline you just drew, hit **<Enter>**.

5. The **Create Parcels—From objects** dialog box opens (Figure 2-1). Accept the default Site name and Parcel style.

6. Now select an existing layer for the Parcel layer. In the area for **Layers**, click on the button to the right of **Parcel layer:** This opens the **Object Layer** dialog box. For the parameter called **Base Layer Name:**, click on the button to the right for **Layers**. Click on the layer **C-Prop-Bndy**. Hit **OK**.

7. In this example, you create a layer to use for the Parcel segment layer. Click on the **Layer** button to the right of the **Parcel segment layer:** This opens the **Object Layer** dialog box. For the parameter called **Base Layer Name**, click on the button to the right for **Layers**. Click on the button for **New…**. In the **Value** column for **Layer Name**, type in **C-Prop-Bndy-Line** and then hit the value for Color and select **red**. Hit **OK** until you return to the **Create Parcels—From objects** dialog box.

8. Turn on the **Automatically add segment labels** option at the bottom of the dialog box. Use **Standard** for all of the settings. Ensure that the check mark is **On** for **Erase existing entities**. Hit **OK** to exit and execute.

9. The Parcel object should be created in AutoCAD. Check in the **Toolspace** and click on the **Prospector**. Under **Open Drawings**, expand your current drawing named Chapter-2b.dwg. Expand the **Sites**, and you see **Site 1**, which was created when you created the parcel. Expand **Site 1** and you see **Parcels**; expand **Parcels** to see your parcel, called **Standard_100**. If you click on this item, you see the parcel in the right-hand preview window panel. Figures 2-2 and 2-3 show the **Prospector** panel and the AutoCAD data.

10. Save and close your drawing.

To access student data files, go to www.pearsondesigncentral.com.

Figure 2-1   Create Parcels—From objects

Figure 2-2   Parcel Preview

Figure 2-3   Parcel in AutoCAD

Now that there is a parcel boundary for the property, continue on with the design. The next step is to develop an entrance road to the shopping mall. You will reconfigure the road that runs east to west just south of our parcel boundary. First, draw the primitive geometry for the roadway centerline alignment.

Exercise 2-7: Develop a Horizontal Alignment for Access to the Parking Lot

1. Open the drawing called Chapter-2c.dwg. It contains the surface you developed and the parcel boundary.

2. Create a layer called **C-Road-Cntr**, set the color to **green**, and set the layer current.

3. Type **L** for **Line** in AutoCAD. When prompted for the start point, type **15925,18543 <Enter>**.

4. Then type **@330<S <Enter>**.

5. Then type **@500<N55dE <Enter>**.

6. Then type **@600<E <Enter>**.

7. Next you place curves into the linework using the **FILLET** command by typing **F** for **Fillet**. Type **R** for **Radius** and set the first radius to **100**. Then pick the first two *tangents* that you drew, and a 100′ radius curve will be drawn. Type **F** for **Fillet** again. Type **R** for **Radius** and set the radius to **500**. Then pick the second and third tangents that you drew, and a 500′ radius curve will be drawn.

8. Type **PE** for **PolyEdit**. Select the first polyline drawn. When you are prompted with: Do you want to turn it into one? **<Y>**, hit **<Enter>**. The software responds with Enter an option [Close/ Join/Width/Edit vertex/Fit/Spline/Decurve/ Ltypegen/Undo] :. Type **J <Enter>**. You will be asked to Select objects. Select the first tangent, the first curve, the second tangent, the second curve, and finally the third tangent. Hit **<Enter>** when done. The geometry for the center of the road is now a polyline.

9. From the *Alignments* pull-down menu, choose **Create Alignment from Polyline....** When you are prompted with Select the first line/arc/polyline or [Xref] :, select the polyline for your roadway. On selecting the polyline, the **Create Alignment—From Polyline** dialog box appears. Select, Alignment (<[Next Counter (CP)]>). Type: Centerline, Site 1 for the site, and the Alignment style of Standard. Now click on the **Layer** button to the right of **Alignment Layer**. This opens the **Object Layer** dialog box. For the parameter called **Base Layer Name:**, click on the button to the right for **Layers**. Click on the button for **New....** In the **Value** column for **Layer name**, type in **C-Road-Cntr**, hit the value for Color, and select **green**. Hit **OK** until you return to the **Create Alignment from Objects** dialog box.

10. Use the default for **Alignment label set** of **Standard**. Click the **down arrow** next to the button to the right of **Alignment label set**. Click on **Edit Current Selection** (a check mark may already be set here, which is fine). The **Alignment Label Set—Standard** dialog box appears.

11. At the top of the dialog box in the **Labels** tab, shown in Figure 2-4, are pop-down windows for the **Type:** of label and the **Major Station Label Style:**. Make sure that the **Type:** is **Major *Stations*** and the **Major Station Label Style:** is **Standard**. Then, click on the **down arrow** next to the button to the right of the **Major Station Label Style:** pop-down menu. Select **Edit Current Selection**. The **Label Style Composer—Standard** dialog box displays. Choose the **General** tab.

    Under the **Property** column is a **Label** item. A subitem for the **Label** is **Layer**. Select i the **Value** column for the **Layer Property**, and see the **Layer** button with ellipses (...). Select that button to change the layer for labels. Choose the **C-Road-Cntr** layer for the labels. Hit **OK**. Hit **Apply** and **OK** for the **Label Style Composer—Standard** dialog box.

12. Next, change the **Type:** to **Minor Stations** and ensure that the **Minor Station Label Style:** is **Standard**. Click on the **down arrow** next to the button to the right of the **Minor Station Label Style:** pop-down menu. Select **Edit Current Selection**. The **Label Style Composer—Standard** dialog box displays. Choose the **General** tab. Under the **Property** column is a **Label** item. A subitem for the **Label** is **Layer**. Select in the **Value** column for the **Layer Property**, and see a button with ellipses (...). Select that button to change the layer for labels. Choose the **C-Road-Cntr** layer for the labels. Hit **OK**. Hit **Apply** and **OK** for the **Label Style Composer—Standard** dialog box.

To access student data files, go to www.pearsondesigncentral.com.

tangent: Intersects a circle once. A tangent line is perpendicular to the radius drawn to the point of tangency (or point of contact with the arc or circle). If a line is perpendicular to a radius at its outer endpoint, then it is tangent to the circle.

alignment: A series of two-dimensional curvilinear geometry elements, used to represent features such as road centerlines where it is beneficial to understand the relationship that these elements have to each other.

stations: A distance along a horizontal alignment that is usually divided by 100′. Therefore 12 stations is 1200′. In metric, this might represent kilomenters such that station 10 is 10 kilometers.

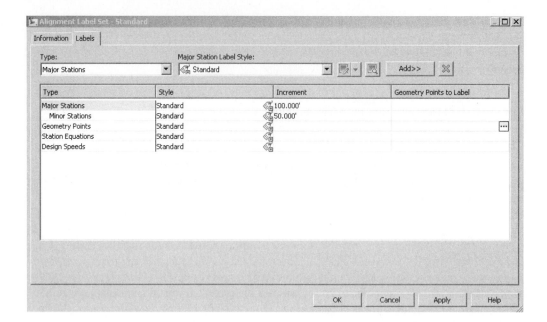

Figure 2-4 Alignment Label Set—Standard

13. Next, change the **Type:** to **Geometry Points** and ensure that the **Geometry Points Label Style:** is **Standard**. Click on the **down arrow** next to the button to the right of the **Geometry Points Label Style:** pop-down menu. Select **Edit Current Selection**. The **Label Style Composer—Standard** dialog box displays. Choose the **General** tab. Under the **Property** column is a **Label** item. A subitem for the **Label** is **Layer**. Select in the **Value** column for the **Layer Property**, and see a button with ellipses (…). Select that button to change the layer for labels. Choose the **C-Road-Cntr** layer for the labels. Hit **OK**. Hit **Apply** and **OK** for the **Label Style Composer—Standard** dialog box.

14. Hit **Apply** and **OK** to exit the **Alignment Label Set— Standard** dialog box.

15. In the area for **Conversion Options**, turn off the toggle for **Add curves between tangents,** because you have already added them using the **FILLET** command. Hit **OK**.

16. You should see a roadway alignment, fully labeled on the **C-Road-Cntr** layer. Observe in the **Prospector** that Alignment-(1) exists under the **Sites, Site 1, Alignments, Centerline Alignments** item. If you click on **Alignment-(1)**, a preview of the alignment shows up in the panel to the right. If it does not, ensure that the button at the top left of the dialog box is toggled on. Right-click on **Alignments** and check the **Show Preview** option. Then right-click on **Alignment-(1)**.

17. Save and close your drawing.

> **Note:**
> Chapters 6 and 7 on road design go into detail about road design works, whereas the intent of this exercise is to prototype a site rapidly.

Now there is a horizontal alignment for the access road into the shopping area. The next task is to develop a vertical profile for the roadway you just created. To accomplish this, develop a Profile along the alignment and computed from the **Existing Ground** surface. It will be placed inside a Profile View, which is the Civil 3D object that displays profiles. Chapter 8 on Profiles discusses this in more detail, but in summary, the Profile View is a Civil 3D concept that contains the grid that profiles are drawn in. The Horizontal Axis of the grid reflects the *stationing*, or linear distance along the horizontal alignment, and the Vertical Axis represents elevational data. The Profile View will include the existing ground profile with annotation. The settings in the **Toolspace** that control the Profile View are in the Profile View Style, which sets the display and spacing of gridlines, profile titling, and the annotation of stations and elevations within the grid. The **Profile View Label Styles** control the display of text and annotation. Once you develop the Profile View and the Existing Ground profile, then you develop a finished *grade* profile for your road.

stationing: Distance along a baseline. It is measured in units of 100 feet in Imperial units and, typically, 1000 meters in metric. Therefore, 1 station = 100′ and is illustrated as 1 + 00.

grade: A change in elevation over a horizontal distance, usually described in percent (%).

To access student data
files, go to
www.pearsondesigncentral.com.

Exercise 2-8: Develop a Profile View

1. Open the drawing called Chapter-2d.dwg. It contains the surface you developed, the parcel boundary, and the roadway centerline.
2. From the *Profiles* pull-down menu, click **Create Profile from Surface...**, and the **Create Profile from Surface** dialog box appears. In the **Alignment** pop-down, **Alignment-(1)(1)** should already be there from the alignment creation performed earlier.
3. Click on the **Existing Ground** surface in the window on the right. Click the **Add>>** button to send it to the bottom window for calculation. The station range should be correct from the alignment computations.
4. Now click on the **Draw in Profile View** button.

profiles: An object containing elevation data that is related to a horizontal alignment. It can apply to existing conditions or proposed conditions. The information within the profile is typically referred to by stations and elevations.

TIP — If you hit **OK**, the computation is active but has no place to display the results because the Profile View has not been established.

5. The **Create Profile View** dialog box appears (see Figure 2-5). In the **Profile view name:** field, type **Access Road**, and from the **Select Alignment:** pop-down window, select **Alignment-(1)(1)**. It should already be in the window. Accept the default layer name of **C-Road-Prof**. In the center of the dialog box is a pop-down window called **Profile view style:**. Choose the style called **Major Grids**. You can edit this style if changes to the display of the Profile View are needed. Accept the defaults.

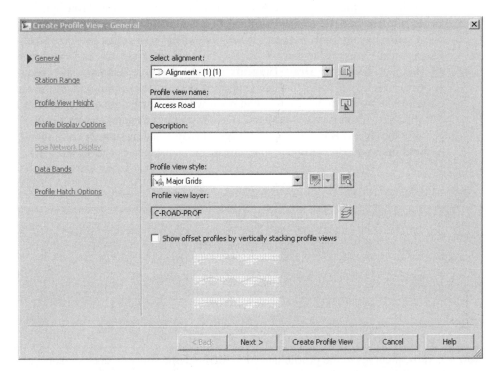

Figure 2-5   Create a Profile View

6. For the **Station Range** and the **Profile View Height**, accept the defaults. Click **Create Profile View**.
7. When you are prompted to `Select profile view origin:`, type **18000,21000** as the coordinate for the location of the Profile View. This is up and to the right of the Plan View. Zoom into the grid representing the Profile View. The evenly spaced horizontal and vertical lines are the grid lines with spacing inherited from the **Major Grids** settings. Vertical blue lines are drawn wherever keypoints for the alignment's horizontal geometry exist, such as *PCs* and *PTs*.
8. Save and close your drawing.

PC: Point of Curvature.

PT: Point of Tangency.

vertical tangents: Linear objects in the profile representing a grade between PVIs. These are linear three-dimensional components of the vertical alignment denoted with a grade usually in percentage (%).

PVI: The Point of Vertical Intersection of the incoming and outgoing vertical tangents.

vertical curves: Parabolic curves located around a PVI to smooth the road as it transitions from one tangent grade to another. These curvilinear three-dimensional components of the vertical alignment denoted by a PVI and a length of curve are typically parabolic with an ever-changing radius.

To access student data files, go to www.pearsondesigncentral.com.

Draw the Existing Ground Profile in the Profile View

The Profile View displays surface profiles and also provides the grid on which you can develop a layout profile or finished grade profile. Each Profile View displays new and/or existing profiles and offset profiles for a single horizontal alignment. Profiles can be created without choosing to display them in the Profile View. When a Profile View is developed, a complete list of profiles for the alignment in question is available so that it can be selected for inclusion in the view.

We have succeeded in developing a Profile View and the Existing Ground profile for the Access Road [or Alignment-(1)(1)]. The next task is to create a finished ground profile in the Profile View. Begin with the *vertical tangents*, which are primitive geometry elements for the profile. At the Points of Vertical Intersection (or *PVIs*), you add vertical curves. These curves differ from the horizontal alignments in that they are not simple arcs; rather, they are parabolic curves. The curve on a hill is known as a *crest curve*, whereas the curve in a depression is known as a *sag curve*. The mathematics behind *vertical curves* will be discussed in Chapter 8 on profiles.

Exercise 2-9: Add Vertical Tangents

1. Open the drawing called Chapter-2e.dwg.
2. From the **Profiles** pull-down menu, choose the command **CREATE PROFILE BY LAYOUT....** When you are prompted to Select profile view to create profile:, pick the text box above the profile. The **Create Profile-Draw New** dialog box appears.
3. Notice that it knows you are dealing with Alignment-(1)(1). In the **Name** field, type **Access Road FG**. Type **Access Road FG** in the **Description** field as well.
4. At the bottom of the dialog box in the pop-down window for **Profile label set**, choose the style called **Complete Label Set**. Accept the default for the **Profile layer** option. Accept the default **Design Style** for the **Profile style** option. Hit **OK**.
5. The **Profile Layout Tools—Access Road FG** toolbar opens up at the top of the screen. When you are prompted to Select a command from the Layout tools:, choose the first icon button for **Draw Tangents without Curves**. When you are prompted to Specify start point:, pick an **Endpoint** snap on the leftmost end of the **Existing Ground** linework. Choose your second point when prompted at about station 3+50 and elevation 320. Choose your third point at about station 7+00 and elevation 345. The last point for the **Access Road** will be an **Endpoint** snap to the rightmost part of the **Existing Ground** linework. Hit **<Enter>** to terminate the sequence.

TIP When estimating the location of the stations and elevations at which to place these points, use the tooltips that pop up when the cursor is paused. Do not allow the cursor to be snapping, or it tells the snap being computed. Rather, just place the cursor near a line but not on it, and the tooltip will pop up to tell you what the station and elevation is. Use this to estimate the station and elevation requested in the procedure.

Exercise 2-10: Add Vertical Curves

Now add vertical curves to the profile tangents. Although the software does support both symmetrical as well as asymmetrical vertical curves, you use symmetrical at this point.

The software has the concept of Fixed, Free and Floating Vertical curves. This concept is similar to the earlier philosophy for horizontal curves and lines and is discussed in Chapter 6 on geometry. Basically, the concept involves constraint-based commands and the creation of Fixed, Floating, and Free vertical tangents and vertical curves. These objects can be edited dynamically and retain their tangencies.

A Fixed entity is fixed in its position and is defined by criteria such as a radius or located points. It is not dependent on other entities for geometry development or tangency. A Floating entity is always tangent to one entity and is defined by the parameters provided or is dependent on one entity to define its geometry. A Free entity is always tangent to an entity before and after it and must have at least two other entities to attach to which define its geometry.

1. From the **Profile** pull-down menu, choose the command **EDIT PROFILE GEOMETRY....**
2. When prompted to Select the profile; click on the finished ground profile tangents just drawn, and the **Profile Layout Tools** toolbar appears. Click on the sixth button from the left; the tooltip should say **Draw fixed parabola by three points**.

     This prompt will change as do others in the software, depending on the choice last selected by the user. From the pop-down menu, choose the option for **Free Vertical Curve (Parameter)**. When you are prompted to Select first entity:, click near the first incoming tangent to the PVI. When you are prompted to Select next entity:, click near the outgoing tangent.
3. When you are prompted to Specify curve length or [Radius/K] :, type **300 <Enter>**.
4. The software then assumes you will continue with additional PVIs and prompts you to Specify first entity: again. Click near the second PVI and you are prompted again to Select next entity;, Click near the outgoing tangent. When you are prompted to Specify curve length or [Radius/K], type **300 <Enter>**. **<Enter>** terminates the routine.
5. You see two vertical curves now added where the PVIs are.
6. Save and close the file.

Exercise 2-11: Create a Corridor for the Access Road

Now develop the remaining part of the road, that is, the finished ground *cross section* conditions for the pavement. Civil 3D introduces a corridor design capability that completes the road design cycle. It builds on the horizontal and vertical alignments that you have worked on so far. A *corridor* is a Civil 3D object and as such is linked to the horizontal and vertical alignments, surfaces, and assemblies that were used to create it. If one of these components is altered, the corridor is correspondingly modified. The next step is to modify subassembly properties for your design criteria, create an *assembly* from the *subassemblies*, and create the corridor model.

     For our Access Road, we have the following design requirements: The road will be a crowned section with a pavement width of **12′**. The cross slope of the lane is **–2.08%** from the crown to allow for drainage off the roadway when it rains. A shoulder for this road will be **4′** wide with a cross slope of **–4%** from the edge of pavement. The side sloping from the shoulder will be **3:1** until it hits existing ground.

Note: Subassemblies are the primitive components of assemblies, and they instruct the software in how to handle lanes, curbs, guardrails, or shoulders and related side sloping. Autodesk provides many subassemblies to begin with, and you can access them from **Tool Palettes**. The assemblies, on the other hand, are stored in the drawing and can be accessed from the **Project Toolspace** under **Assemblies**. They contain the definition of the typical section being designed and are developed by piecing together subassemblies.

Note: A 3:1 side slope is a condition describing an elevation rise of 1′ for every 3′ horizontally and is usually denoted by this ratio.

cross section: A tranverse view of the surface.

corridor: A structure that allows passage or conveyance of people or things.

assembly: Objects that manage collections of subassemblies; used for the basic structure of a corridor object.

subassemblies: The fundamental building blocks used to create assemblies. It defines the geometry of a component used in a corridor section and includes predeveloped components for such things as travel lanes, curbs, side slopes, and ditches. It has intelligent behavior built into it and can automatically adapt to design conditions comprising superelevations and cut or fill requirements.

TIP These subassemblies are some of the first examples of parametric technology being introduced to the civil engineering community. Once these objects are created, the parameters within them can be changed on the fly. The dynamic modeling abilities of the software then can cause a ripple-through effect as the changes are applied to all related objects in the corridor.

To access student data
files, go to
www.pearsondesigncentral.com.

Exercise 2-12: Create the Assembly

1. Open the drawing called Chapter-2f.dwg.
2. Type **Z** for **Zoom** at the command prompt, then type **C** for **Center** and type **17000,20000**. When asked for a height, type **50**.
3. This places you in a location where the assembly can be created. There is nothing special about this location; it is simply out of the way and zoomed to a height of **50′**.
4. From the **Corridors** pull-down menu, select **Create Assembly...**. The **Create Assembly** dialog box opens.
5. Enter the name as **Access Road**. Leave the remaining settings as default and hit **OK**.
6. When you are prompted to `Specify assembly baseline location:`, pick a point in the middle of the screen. A small symbol with a red line will show up. This indicates the assembly location to which you will attach subassemblies.

If you look in the **Prospector** and expand the tree for **Assemblies**, you see the assembly name. Now you will attach the subassemblies to both the left and the right sides of the assembly location.

Exercise 2-13: Attach Subassemblies to the Assembly Marker

1. From the **Civil 3D Imperial-Basic** palette, click the **BasicLane** subassembly and the **Properties** dialog box appears.
2. Look under the **Advanced** menu parameters at the bottom of the **Properties** palette.
3. Set the **Side** to **Right** and notice the lane width is **12′**. Change the parameter **%Slope** to **-2.08**. Set the depth to **1.0**.
4. In the drawing, pick the assembly baseline location, which is the circular symbol in the middle of the assembly that you created. Hit **Enter** twice. The lane should show up on the right side of the assembly marker.
5. From the **Civil 3D Imperial-Basic** palette, click the **BasicShoulder** subassembly. Look in the **Properties** palette and set the parameter for **Side** to **Right**. Set the depth to **0.67**. Ensure that the width is set to **4.0** and the **% Slope** is **-4.00**. When you are prompted to `Select marker point within assembly or [RETURN for Detached]`: pick the perimeter edge of the circle symbol located at the top right corner of the **BasicLane** subassembly. Hit **Esc**. The shoulder should extend to the right of the lane.
6. From the **Civil 3D Imperial-Basic** palette, click the **BasicGuardrail** subassembly. Look in the **Properties** window and select **Right** side from the pop-down parameter for **Side**. When you are prompted to `Select marker point within assembly or [RETURN for Detached]`: pick the perimeter edge of the circle symbol located at the top right of the shoulder. Hit **Esc**.
7. At this point you can mirror the subassemblies to create the left side of the road. Select the three subassemblies that you created. Right-click, then click mirror.
8. From the **Imperial-Generic** palette, click the **LinkOffsetAndSlope** subassembly. Again, the **Properties** dialog box opens each time a subassembly is picked. In this case, ensure that the **%Slope** is set to **–2**. Also set the **Offset from Baseline** to **22.0** (which produces a **6′** area past the guardrail before sidesloping kicks in). A positive number for the offset indicates that it heads off to the right, whereas a negative offset indicates to the left.
9. Then pick inside the drawing and then pick the perimeter edge of the circle symbol located at the right, center **BasicGuardrail** subassembly. The **Link** should extend to the right of the guardrail.
10. Look back into the **Properties** palette and set the **Offset from Baseline** parameter to **–22.0**, so it will be applied to the left.
11. Then pick the perimeter edge of the circle symbol located at the left, center **BasicGuardrail** subassembly. The **Link** should extend to the left of the guardrail.
12. From the **Imperial-Basic** palette, click the **BasicSideSlopeCutDitch** subassembly. Review the settings for the parameters in the **Properties** palette and accept the defaults. Set the **Side** to **Right**.
13. Then pick the perimeter edge of the circle symbol located at the right, center **LinkOffsetAndSlope** subassembly. The **Link** should extend to the right.
14. Go back to the **Properties** palette and set the **Side** to **Left**.

Figure 2-6   Access Road
Assembly

15. Then pick the perimeter edge of the circle symbol located at the left, center
    LinkOffsetAndSlope subassembly. The **Link** should extend to the left.
16. Press **<Enter>** twice or hit **Esc** to finish the command. Save the file.

You have now created the assembly. Figure 2-6 shows how it should appear. Keep in mind
that the designer can build the right side independently of the left if desired. The assembly does
not have to be symmetrical, and on actual projects, it often may not be symmetrical. If a developer is developing a project on the east side of the road, it may proffer to improve that side of the
road while allowing a future developer to improve the west side of the road.

Now move forward to creating the roadway. In this task, the pieces to the Corridor puzzle
come together. You have all the components for the Corridor. To summarize, you developed
the primitive geometry for the alignment and developed a completed alignment. You then computed and drew an Existing Ground profile inside a Profile View. From there you designed a finished ground profile for the Access Road. You then set the settings for some subassemblies and
created an assembly. Now create the Corridor and the finished design surface.

Exercise 2-14: Create a Corridor

1. Open the drawing called Chapter-2g.dwg.
2. We will restore a pre-saved view to place our view around the centerline.
3. Type **V<Enter>** for **View** at the command prompt to obtain the **View Manager** dialog
   box. Choose the **Access Road Plan View**, hit **Set Current**, then hit **OK**. You are at the centerline of the Access Road. There is also a view setup for the profile should you need it.
4. From the **Corridors** pull-down menu, select **Create Simple Corridor....**
5. The **Create Simple Corridor** dialog box appears. Enter **Access Road** for the name and
   hit **OK**.
6. When you are prompted to `Select a baseline alignment <or press enter`
   `key to select from list>:`, pick the green centerline in the view then hit
   <Enter>. This brings up the **Select an alignment** dialog box. Hit **OK**.
7. You are prompted to `Select a profile <or press enter key to select from`
   `list>:`.
8. Hit **<Enter>**, and the **Select a Profile** dialog box appears. Choose the **Access Road FG**
   and hit **OK** (Figure 2-7).
9. You are prompted to `Select an assembly <or press enter key to select from`
   `list>:` hit **<Enter>** and the **Select an Assembly** dialog box appears. Select **Assembly-1**
   from the list and hit **OK** (Figure 2-8).
10. A large window of data will display for **Target Mapping**, as in Figure 2-9. Do not close
    this box yet.

To access student data
files, go to
www.pearsondesigncentral.com.

Figure 2-7   Select a Profile

Figure 2-8   Select an Assembly

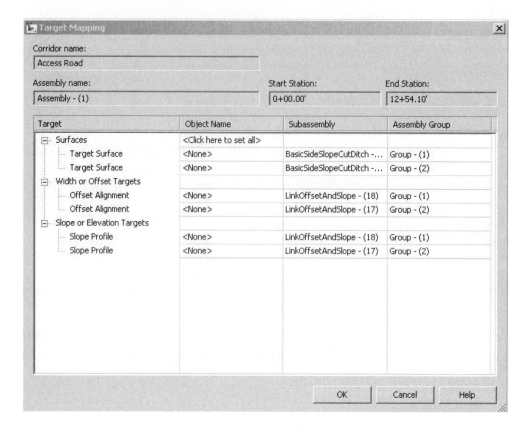

Figure 2-9   Target
Mapping

Exercise 2-15: Target Mapping

Target Mapping is a technical way of assigning the particular alignments, profiles, and surfaces required by the subassemblies to create the complete assembly. For instance, the **BasicSideSlopeCutDitch** subassembly needs to know which surface it will be computing to, and so the **Target Map** for this would be the Existing Ground surface.

1. In the second column and in the row for **Surfaces** is a cell that says <Click here to set all>.
2. When you click on the cell, a dialog box called **Pick a Surface** displays. Choose the **Existing Ground** and click **OK**. You will see the Target Surface is now Existing Ground. Click **OK**, and the corridor will generate, as shown in Figure 2-10.
3. Close the **Panorama** if it appears and inspect the results of the processing. A Corridor model will be evident in the drawing.
4. Restore a pre-saved view to place your model in a bird's-eye perspective with shading to help see the road better. Type **V<Enter>** for **View** at the command prompt to obtain the **View Manager** dialog box. Click the **ISO View**, hit **Set Current**, then hit **OK**.
5. You see the road is 3D, complete with representation of the guardrails, as shown in Figure 2-11.

Figure 2-10   Corridor
Created

Figure 2-11   Corridor ISO

6. Type **ZP <Enter>** to return to the previous view when you are finished viewing.
7. Save and close the file.

Exercise 2-16: Viewing Additional Results of the Corridor Design

The Corridor model is now built, but it is necessary to discuss a few methods that exist to review the model. One is to investigate what the finished sections look like. Follow this procedure to observe the section conditions.

1. Open the drawing called Chapter-2h.dwg. The previously created corridor is shown.
2. Under the **Corridors** pull-down menu, choose **View/Edit Corridor Section**. When you are prompted to `Select a Corridor <or press enter to select from list>:`, pick any part of the corridor that you can.
3. Once the corridor is selected, the first station of the section displays along with a **Section Editor** toolbar that allows you to move up and down the alignment, viewing any section desired. This is displayed in Figure 2-12.
4. Take a few moments to zoom in and out and review the section that appeared. Notice where the lanes, the ditch, and the tie-out slopes are.
5. Then move forward to the next station and observe the display.
6. Continue observing and when you are ready, close the toolbar; the normal view will return as it was before you entered this facility.

To access student data files, go to www.pearsondesigncentral.com.

Many aspects of the Corridor model can be manipulated and many of them will be in Chapter 9 on corridors. However, here is a brief example of the powers. You follow a procedure that identifies some basic *feature lines* of the corridor, such as the centerline, the edge of the pavement (or EP), the bottom of the ditch, and the daylight cut and fill lines. These will be inspected for quality control purposes, but they serve a purpose later in establishing construction information because they can also be exported as alignments or grading feature lines. Grading feature lines are discussed in Chapter 10 on site grading.

feature line: An object that the grading commands can work with. It represents breaks in the surface features. For example, the edges of pavement, ditches, or daylighting could be feature lines. Their appearance is controlled by feature line styles.

Exercise 2-17: Corridor Feature Lines

1. Select the Corridor model by picking it, and it will highlight. Right-click and select **Corridor Properties...** from the shortcut menu.
2. The **Corridor Properties** dialog box displays. Select the tab for **Feature Lines** (Figure 2-13).
3. By default, all of the feature lines are assigned to the **Standard** feature line style. In order to see some of the objects within the corridor better, assign **Feature Line Styles** to the **Daylight_Cut**, the **Daylight_Fill**, and the **Edge of Travel Way** (ETW) feature lines. When you return to Civil 3D, they will appear differently as a result of this style modification.
4. In the **Code** column, pick the **Daylight_Cut** code and look in the **Feature Line Style** column. Pick the **blue** icon in this column, and a dialog box called **Pick Feature Line Style** will display. In the pop-down window, select the style called **Daylight Line—Cut**, and hit **OK**.
5. In the **Code** column, pick the **Daylight_Fill** code and look in the **Feature Line Style** column. Pick the **blue** icon in this column, and a dialog box called **Pick Feature Line**

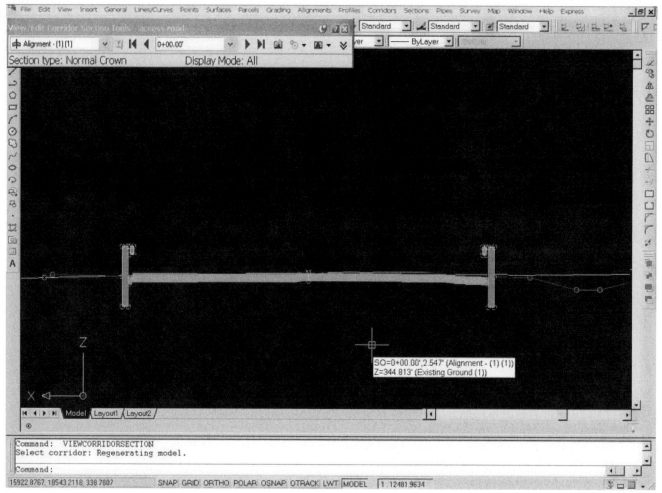

Figure 2-12   Corridor Section Editor

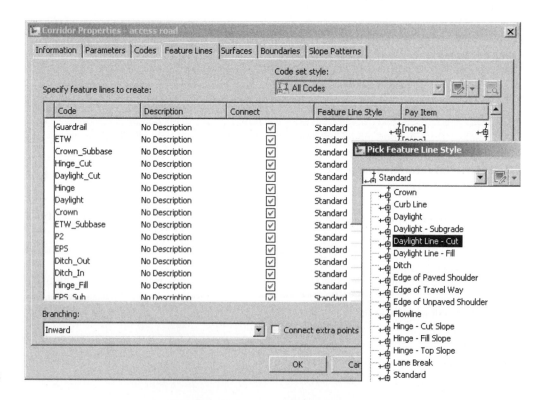

Figure 2-13   Feature Lines

Style will display. In the pop-down window, select the style called **Daylight Line—Fill**, and hit **OK**.

6. In the **Code** column, pick the ETW code and look in the **Feature Line Style** column. Pick the **blue** icon in this column, and a dialog box called **Pick Feature Line Style** will display. In the pop-down window, select the style called **Edge of Travel Way**.

7. Then click the **down arrow** button on the right side of the pop-down window. Choose **Edit Current Selection** from the options (Figure 2-14).

Figure 2-14   Edit Current Selection

8. The **Feature Line Style** dialog box will display. Choose the **Display** tab. Change the **Feature Line Color** to **Yellow** and change the **Lineweight** to **0.80 mm**. Hit **OK**.

9. Hit **OK**. Hit **OK** one more time to exit the main **Corridor Properties** dialog box. The system will regenerate the Corridor. If you do not see the alterations, click the **LWT** button, the ninth from the left, at the bottom of the screen to **On**.

10. The corridor should appear as shown in the graphic. The cut is red and fill is green per the alterations just made to the display of the corridor. The edge of pavement is yellow and a heavy lineweight. If the **Panorama** displays, close it.

11. Save the file and close the drawing.

At this point in the project, you have created the terrain model, a parcel for the design of our site, an alignment, a profile, an assembly, and a corridor that provides access to the commercial shopping center being designed. Refer to Figure 2-15. Some basic adjustments to the display of our data have been made along the way.

Figure 2-15   Cut and Fill Colored

Site Design

The next task is to create some building pads for the stores and a parking lot for the commercial site being designed. The design criteria for the site are as follows:

- A Building Restriction Line *(BRL)* of 25′ prevents any structures from being within 25′ of the property line.
- The finished floor of the stores will be at 350′.
- The parking lot slope is indicated with callouts in the drawing or with points placed at various critical locations in the file. You will draw 3D Polylines to help guide the drainage over the parking lot.
- The parking lot ties into the access road edges of pavement at 344.58′. The crown of the Access Road is at 344.78′.

BRL: Building Restriction Lines indicate the limits for construction of structures inside a property. They ensure that structures are not built too close to other structures.

- A 6′ wide sidewalk with a –2% grade exists around the stores except on the north and west sides.

- The majority of the drainage flow will be directed toward the Access Road, where it will be conveyed until station 3 + 56, at which a drain inlet will be placed to divert it offsite.

- The site ties out to natural ground at a 3:1 side slope.

- A layer in the drawing called **Site Geometry** contains the buildings for the shopping center.

- A layer called **Site Drainage Criteria** indicates where the Feature Lines will go that will guide the drainage and become Feature Lines.

Exercise 2-18: Design the Shopping Center Building Finished Floor Slabs and the Parking Lot

To access student data files, go to www.pearsondesigncentral.com.

1. Open the drawing called Chapter-2i.dwg. The previously created corridor is shown with the visual adjustments that were made to it. There are buildings in the file with their elevation set to **0.0** and an accompanying **6′** wide sidewalk.

2. Change the properties of the buildings to place them on the **3D-Data** layer. To do this, type **Properties** to invoke the **Properties** dialog box. Select the polyline and change the elevation parameter to **350.0**. Hit **Enter** and **Esc** to end the task.

3. Repeat this for the sidewalk, but make the elevation **349.88**, which represents a –2% drop over 6′.

4. Then offset the edge of sidewalk away from the buildings using the **OFFSET** command and a distance of **0.4′**. This represents the Top of Curb of the sidewalk.

5. Then offset the Top of Curb again, away from the building, a distance of **0.1′**. This now represents the Flowline of the Curb.

6. With the **Properties** dialog box open, select the Flowline of Curb, and change the elevation to **349.38**, which is a 0.5′ drop from the Top of Curb.

7. You will see that this coincides with two points (Points 1 and 2) placed in the file at the same elevations, that is, 349.38. These two points represent the start of our flow divide, and now you can see how they were determined.

8. Ensure that your current layer is set to **3D-Data**.

9. Type in **3P** at the command prompt to invoke the **3DPOLY** command. Use a **Node** snap and snap to Point 1 for the first point. Use a **Node** snap and pick Point 8. Continue by picking another **Node** snap and selecting Point 9. Hit **<Enter>** to terminate. You might notice that the 3D Polyline is now set to 3D due to snapping to the nodes that had elevations.

10. Type in **3P** or hit **<Enter>** at the command prompt to invoke the **3DPOLY** command again. Use a **Node** snap and snap to Point 2 for the first point. Use a **Node** snap and pick Point 8. Hit **<Enter>** to terminate.

11. Type in **3P** or hit **<Enter>** at the command prompt to invoke the **3DPOLY** command again. Use a **Node** snap each time to snap to Points 4, 5, 6, and 7. Hit **<Enter>** to terminate.

At the north end of the site, notice that Point 3 has been placed at an elevation of 349.6. This represents a –2% cross-slope over that pavement distance. This pavement area is for the loading and unloading of trucks and supply vehicles. The asphalt pavement flows away from the buildings at –2% and then at –1% to the east and west of Point 3. Now you will create grading for the perimeter of the site and parking lot.

12. In the **Grading** pull-down menu, select the **CREATE FEATURE LINES FROM OBJECTS** command. Choose the two cyan-colored lines touching Point 3, representing the perimeter of the parking lot.

    When the dialog displays click the **Style** field **On** and select **Edge of Travelway** for the feature lines. Hit **OK**.

13. Each of these are grading feature lines. Click on the **West** feature line and right-click. Select the **Elevation Editor....**

14. Refer to Figure 2-16 and set the first elevation to **349.6** if it is not already set. Then establish all the grades for the segments at **–0.5%**, except for the last segment. Set the last segment to **–1%**, which should set the last elevation to **344.56**.

Station	Elevation	Length	Grade Ahead	Grade Back
0+00.00	349.600'	5.364'	-0.500%	0.500%
0+05.36	349.573'	275.634'	-0.500%	0.500%
2+81.00	348.195'	292.753'	-0.500%	0.500%
5+73.75	346.731'	41.623'	-0.500%	0.500%
6+15.37	346.523'	56.628'	-0.500%	0.500%
6+72.00	346.240'	171.349'	-0.500%	0.500%
8+43.35	345.383'	82.208'	-1.000%	1.000%
9+25.56	344.561'			

Figure 2-16   Elevation Editor

15. Click on the **Eastern** feature line and right-click. Select the **Elevation Editor....**
16. Refer to Figure 2-17 and set the first elevation to **349.6** if it is not already set.
17. Then in the **Grade** column, set the first segment's grade to **−1.0%**.
18. Set the next segment to **−0.5%**.
19. Set the next segment to **−1.0%**.
20. Set the last segment to **−2.185%**, which should set the last elevation to **344.58**.

The 3D linework should now all reside on the **3D-Data** and the **C-Topo-Grad-Flin** layers for easy selection later. Next set the grading for the perimeter of the site as it ties out to natural ground.

Station	Elevation	Length	Grade Ahead	Grade Back
0+00.00	349.600'	96.337'	-1.000%	1.000%
0+96.34	348.637'	121.125'	-0.500%	0.500%
2+17.46	348.031'	267.823'	-0.500%	0.500%
4+85.28	346.692'	31.987'	-1.000%	1.000%
5+17.27	346.372'	50.911'	-2.185%	2.185%
5+68.18	345.260'	31.095'	-2.185%	2.185%
5+99.28	344.580'			

Figure 2-17   Elevation Editor Data

Exercise 2-19: Establish a 3D Grading Perimeter

1. From the **Grading** pull-down menu, select **Create Grading....** These are called **Grading Creation Tools**. A toolbar called **Grading Creation Tools** will display, shown in Figure 2-18.

Figure 2-18   Grading Creation Tools

Use of this tool is detailed in Chapter 10 on site grading; however, it is necessary to set some of the parameters now in order to move forward with this exercise. The first button from the left sets the **Grading Group**. The second button sets the **Target Surface**. The third button sets the **Grading Layers**.

2. Select the first icon button from the left of the toolbar. This invokes the **Select Grading Group** dialog box (Figure 2-19) to allow you to name the Grading Group. Under **Group name:**, type **Parking Lot Grading Group**. Then hit **OK**. You may note that this creates a **Parking Lot Grading Group** in the **Prospector** under **Sites**, **Site 1**, **Grading Groups**.

Figure 2-19   Select Grading Group

3. Select the second icon button from the left of the toolbar. This invokes the **Select surface** dialog box to allow you to select the surface to which you are going to tie out. Choose **Existing Ground** when the dialog box displays, hit **OK**.

4. Select the third icon button from the left of the toolbar. This invokes the **Set Grading Layers** dialog box to allow you to develop layers for the grading feature lines. The default should be **C-TOPO-GRAD** for the Grading. Hit **OK**.

5. Now select the fourth button item ⟨ Standard ⟩ from the left to **Select a Criteria Set**. This opens a dialog box that might default to **Standard**. Open the pop-down window and choose the **Basic Set**. Hit **OK**. The pop-down window now has several options available. Choose the option called **Surface @ 3-1 Slope** (Figure 2-20).

6. Now hit the second button just to the right of the pop-down window in the **Grading Creation Tools** toolbar. It should have a tooltip called **Create Grading** if you pause your cursor over the button. If not, click the **down arrow** and select **Create Grading** (Figure 2-21).

Figure 2-20   Pop-down options

Figure 2-21   Create Grading

7. When this command is invoked, the command prompt will ask you to select the feature. Click on the Western perimeter feature line.

8. When prompted to `Select the grading side:` choose a point to the West of the site. When prompted to `Select the start point:` hit **<Enter>** for Yes.

9. Without leaving the command, when prompted to `Select another Feature Line:`, select the Eastern perimeter line and pick a point to the East of the site for the direction.

10. When complete, hit **<Enter>** and close the toolbar. You should see the perimeter graded out to the Existing Ground. The red indicates Cut activity and the green indicates Fill. The perimeter is the Daylight where the proposed ties into the existing.

11. Save and close the file.

The next step is to create a finished ground surface representing the Access Road and the grading for the parking lot and the commercial shopping center.

Exercise 2-20: Create a Finished Ground Surface

1. Open the drawing called Chapter-2j.dwg. The previously created corridor and parking lot grading are shown in Figure 2-22.
2. Go to the **Prospector** and expand the **Open Drawings** collection. Then expand Chapter-2j.dwg.

To access student data files, go to www.pearsondesigncentral.com.

Figure 2-22   Corridor and parking lot grading

3. Then expand **Surfaces**, right-click on **Existing Ground**, and choose **Surface Properties....** Set the **Surface Style** to **Contours (Background)** and choose the button to the right to get the pop-down menu. Choose **Edit Current Selection**, choose the **Contours** tab, and set the **Contour Interval** to **2′** and **10′** (see Figure 2-23). Hit **OK** twice.
4. Then expand **Sites**, **Site 1**, and **Grading Groups**. You see the **Parking Lot Grading Group**. Left-click on the **Parking Lot Grading Group**, and you will see a preview of the group in the right pane if the **Show Preview** is checked under **Grading Groups**. Right-click on the **Parking Lot Grading Group** and choose **Properties....** The **Grading Group Properties** dialog box will open.
5. In the **Information** tab, turn **On** the toggle for **Automatic Surface Creation**. This will invoke the **Create Surface** dialog box.
6. The **Type** will be a **TIN surface**, which is the default. The layer will default to **C-TOPO**.
7. Ensure that the name **Parking Lot Grading Group** is in the **Name** field under **Information**.
8. Provide the **Description** of **Parking Lot Grading Group**.
9. Under the **Properties**, **Style**, click on the name **Standard** to invoke the ellipses (...), choose **Border and Contours**. Hit **OK**. Hit **OK** twice to execute.

Notice that contours now exist for the finished ground around the parking lot. Figure 2-22 shows some leaders pointing to the finished ground contours. The next step is to add in the feature lines for the drainage vectors, the sidewalks, and the buildings.

Exercise 2-21: Creating Feature Lines

1. In the **Prospector**, expand the **Surfaces** collection and then expand the **Parking Lot Grading Group** item. Expand the **Definition** item, and you see **Breaklines**. Right-click on **Breaklines** and hit **Add...** to invoke the **Add Breaklines** dialog box.

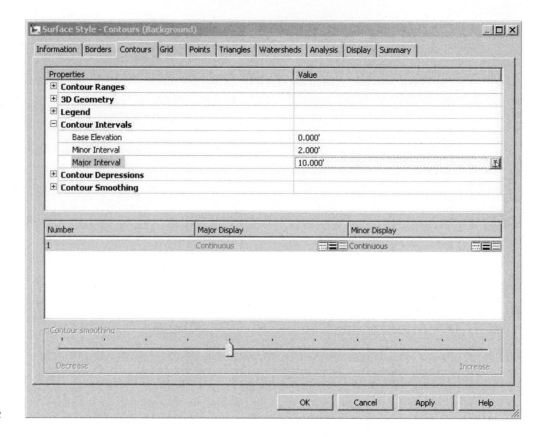

Figure 2-23   Surface Style

2. Type **Parking Lot Breaklines** into the **Description** field. **Type:** will be **Standard**, and the **Mid-ordinate distance:** will be **1′**, as shown in Figure 2-24. Hit **OK**.
3. When you are prompted to `Select objects:`, select the two building pads, the sidewalk breaklines, the two drainage vectors in the middle of the parking lot, and the last vector on Points 4 through 7. Hit **<Enter>** when finished picking the breaklines.
4. Turn off the **3D-Data** and **C-Topo-Existing Ground** layers, and you will see the Parking Lot contours.

Figure 2-25 shows that if you place your cursor inside the parking lot, a tooltip pops up and automatically provides elevational information for the Existing Ground as well as the Parking Lot surfaces. The next step is to develop contours for a corridor from the Corridor model.

Figure 2-24   Add Breaklines

FF=350.00

FF=350.00

−1.67% Grade

STANDARD_ 100
250000 SQ FT
5.74 ACRES

into EOP of Access Road

SO=4+78.62',-311.469' (Alignment - (1) (1))
Z=352.407' (Existing Ground (1))
Z=346.244' (Parking Lot Grading Group)

Figure 2-25   Site Contours

Exercise 2-22: Create Contours

1. Zoom into the corridor, or type **V** for **View** and select the **Access Road Plan View**, set it current, and hit **OK**.
2. Go to **Prospector**, expand **Corridors**, right-click **access road,** and choose **Properties....**
3. Choose the **Surfaces** tab, shown in Figure 2-26.
4. Click the first button on the top left that has a tooltip of **Create a corridor surface**. It uses the **Data type:** of **Links** and the **Specify code:** of **Top**.

Figure 2-26   Corridor Properties-access road

5. The name **Access Road Surface** appears in the window below.
6. Click the button with the plus sign to the right of the **Specify code:** pop-down menu with a tooltip of **Add surface item**. It should be set to **Top**. The name **Access Road** can be expanded now, and you should see **Top**. This is the surface data from which the surface will be created.
7. Now select the **Boundaries** tab, as shown in Figure 2-27. This option trims the contours for the roadway right at the daylight cut and fill lines to ensure clean tie-out of the contours.

Figure 2-27   Corridor Properties Boundaries

8. Right-click on the **Access Road Surface** name.
9. Choose the **Add Automatically** option and then choose **Daylight** from the submenu. Hit **Apply**, then hit **OK**.
10. The contours for the Corridor should be displayed in AutoCAD now.

Congratulations! You have developed a corridor and a shopping center, all in 3D. Now place some property corner points on the parcel.

11. Zoom back to the **Plan View** of the parking lot.
12. From the **Points** pull-down menu, select **Create Points Miscellaneous**, then **Manual**. Using the **Endpoint** snap, set a point on each corner of the parcel. When prompted for the name, enter **1**, then name the rest by an increment of **1**. Hit **<Enter>** Specify a point elevation <.>: Hit **<Enter>**.
13. Save your file and close the drawing.

Now the last step shows preparation of the Plan & Profile sheets for plotting the project.

Exercise 2-23: Setting Up a P&P Sheet

To access student data files, go to www.pearsondesigncentral.com.

1. Open the drawing called Chapter-2k.dwg. The previously created Corridor and Parking Lot are shown with their respective contours, as shown in Figure 2-28 and Figure 2-29.
2. Type **V** for **View**, choose the **Access Road Profile** view, set it current, and hit **OK**. The profile is now displayed.
3. Click on a grid in the **Profile** and then right-click. Choose **Edit Profile View Style....**
4. Select the **Graph** tab. On the right side of the dialog box is a parameter to set the **Vertical Exaggeration**. Set it to **10.00**. Hit **OK**.

Figure 2-28   Corridor and Parking Lot are shown with Contours

Figure 2-29   Close-up of Corridor and Parking Lot are shown with Contours

5. Right-click the button next to the **Model** button at the bottom of the screen to display the **Layout** tabs.
6. Right-click on the **Layout 1** tab and choose **Page Setup Manager...**. When the dialog box appears, select the **Modify** button to get to the **Page Setup** dialog box shown in Figure 2-30.

Figure 2-30   Page Setup

7. Set the **Plotter name:** to **DWF6 ePlot.pc3**.
8. Set the **Paper size** to **ARCH D, 36 × 24**. Hit **OK** and **Close**.

TIP
Selecting an exaggeration of **10.0** means that the vertical scale for the profile will be 1/10th that of the horizontal scale. This often-used factor can be switched to **5.0** for a flatter profile or even sometimes to **1.0** for a profile that is not exaggerated.

9. From the **View** pull-down menu, select **Viewports**. Select **New Viewports...**. A dialog box appears.
10. Choose **Two: Horizontal**. Hit **OK**. Pick a point in the upper left of the screen, then the lower right. Two viewports appear. Click on the viewport, then right-click, and choose **Properties**. Set the **Annotation scale** to **1″ = 50′**. Repeat for the second viewport.

11. At the bottom of the screen, toggle the **PAPER** button to **MODEL**. Pan the **Plan View** so you can see the corridor.
12. Pan the Profile into the Profile View so you can see it. Toggle back to **PAPER**.
13. Choose the **View** pull-down menu and select **Regen All**.
14. Right-click on **Layout 1**, and choose the **Rename** option. Rename it to **Plan & Profile**.
15. Now click on the **Layout 2** tab. After it is finished regenerating, right-click on **Layout 2**. Repeat the setup commands to create a 24″×36″ viewport. This time choose **Single** from the viewport options.
16. Stretch the viewport to take advantage of the whole sheet. Then click on the viewport; then right-click and choose the **Properties** command. Set the **Standard scale** for this viewport to **1:20**. If this will not fit on the paper, use a **1:30** scale.
17. Right-click on the **Layout 2** tab, and choose the **Rename** option. Rename it to **Plan Parking Lot**.
18. Choose the **View** pull-down menu and select **Regen All**.
19. These sheets or layouts are now ready for plotting. Refer to Figure 2-31.

Figure 2-31   Plan & Profile

Note that you can make changes to the various styles involved so that finished ground contours appear differently than the Existing Ground contours. Refer to Figure 2-32. More detailed concepts like this will be covered in the later chapters.

Congratulations! You have completed the chapter's goal.

Job Skills will benefit from this chapter because it covered an entire project from start to finish using Civil 3D. Although it was fairly simple in scope, it touched on developing multiple surfaces, parcels, property corner points, centerlines, profiles, assemblies, and corridors. The project was completed by creating construction plans in paper space. These functions could be called *Minimum Proficiency Requirements*.

Minimum Proficiency Requirements are those tasks that everyone in design should be capable of performing. A manager in the company should be able to approach any designer or technician and ask that a surface be assembled, a centerline be created, a profile be computed, or a plot be output. Of course, the real value in being able to do these tasks is to understand the mathematics behind them. This chapter assumes that you understand at least the rudimentary math behind the automated computations; however, the remaining chapters in the book do not. The advanced chapters that follow begin by going over the math behind Civil 3D, provide instruction in many of the formulas, and teach the algorithms that you need to know to use the software properly.

Figure 2-32 Completed site

CHAPTER SUMMARY

This chapter took you through a design project from start to finish. You prepared the ground surface from actual 3D project data, developed a property parcel for a shopping center, and prepared the labeling required for its drafting. Finally, you developed a finished ground profile and a corridor to put the road into 3D. Now we move on to points and point settings.

CHAPTER TEST QUESTIONS

Multiple Choice

1. One of the things that this chapter prepares you to do is
   a. Develop an alignment for an access road to the shopping center
   b. Design a hydraulic grade line for a storm sewer
   c. Design the shopping center buildings, walls, and roof trusses
   d. None of the above

2. Which of the following are Civil 3D objects?
   a. Corridors
   b. Surfaces
   c. Earthworks
   d. a and b

3. Mass points are
   a. Often from Photogrammetric sources
   b. In 3D with elevations
   c. Fairly evenly spaced across the site and are intended to densify the surface data
   d. All of the above

4. The following are types of surfaces:
   a. TIN and GRID
   b. Superelevation

   c. Building Restriction Lines
   d. Earthworks

5. Proximity breaklines
   a. Are 2D polylines
   b. Have elevations at each vertex in the polyline
   c. Are converted to 3D polylines for surface creation
   d. All of the above

6. A Wall breakline is
   a. Vertical
   b. Nearly vertical
   c. Flat
   d. None of the above

7. In a Profile View, which of the following are correct?
   a. The Horizontal Axis of the grid reflects the stationing
   b. Vertical Axis represents elevational data
   c. The grids represent specified spacing criteria
   d. All of the above

8. A vertical alignment may have the following components:
   a. A PI, PC, and PT
   b. A PRC and a PCC
   c. A broken back curve
   d. A PVI, PVC, and PVT

9. Vertical curves can be which of the following?

   a. Sag curves
   b. Crest curves
   c. Parabolic
   d. All of the above

10. A crest curve is

    a. Usually at the bottom of a valley
    b. At the top of a hill
    c. A flat segment of roadway
    d. None of the above

True or False

1. True or False: Working with Civil 3D is easier and more effective when a template is selected with no styles preset within it.

2. True or False: The precision for contour labeling should always be set for two decimal places.

3. True or False: The Contour Label Control Line should be set to fall on the **Zero** layer.

4. True or False: The user does not have to set Surface Names in Civil 3D.

5. True or False: A template for Surface Naming can be established, and it can be automatically incremented such that Surface 2 is created after Surface 1.

6. True or False: A Grid surface is for a surface of evenly spaced rectangular data whose elevations are interpolated from the data is desired.

7. True or False: Breaklines can be Proximity breaklines, Wall breaklines, and Breaklines from a file.

8. True or False: The Wall breakline option is used to represent perfectly vertical components of surfaces.

9. True or False: Parcels can have only four sides in Civil 3D.

10. True or False: The Profile View displays surface profiles but will not display a grid.

11. True or False: The Profile View displays new and/or existing profiles but not offset profiles for a single horizontal alignment.

12. True or False: Vertical tangents are segments that go only straight up in the air.

13. True or False: Vertical curves are often parabolic.

14. True or False: Vertical curves usually have a constant radius.

15. True or False: Subassemblies are made from assemblies.

16. True or False: Subassemblies allow for user definable parameters that can change the design of the corridor.

17. True or False: Assemblies govern the proposed corridor development.

18. True or False: A 3:1 side slope is a condition describing an elevation rise of 3′ for every 1′ horizontally.

19. True or False: Corridor feature lines have fixed properties and always look the same.

20. True or False: A Building Restriction Line (BRL) outlines the location of wetlands.

CHAPTER EXERCISES

1. How are the Existing Ground and finished ground interrelated?
2. How much horizontal distance is needed to tie out a sideslope of 3:1 when the elevation difference between the tie-out point and the ground is 10′?
3. How much horizontal distance is needed to tie out a sideslope of 4:1 when the elevation difference between the tie-out point and the ground is 10′?
4. What is a breakline as a concept when looking at a roadway of a ditch compared with the purpose of a breakline as used by the software in preparing a TIN model?
5. Can a contour have different elevations on its vertices?
6. What is the difference between subassemblies and assemblies?
7. How does the software differentiate between a slope and a grade?
8. Provide some examples of where styles come into play when designing and drafting a project in Civil 3D.
9. What types of data components can be added to a surface?
10. Are Parcels automatically annotated on creation, and if so, what controls this?
11. Why are vertical curves added to proposed roadway profiles?
12. Can a corridor be viewed in 3D?

The Simple, but Time-Honored Point

3

Chapter Objectives

- Create, edit, report, and label Civil 3D Point objects.
- Set Point settings involved in the aesthetics of point display.
- Use Geodetics with a combination of MAP 3D commands and POINT commands.
- Use and create Point Styles, Point Groups, and Description Key Sets.

INTRODUCTION

It is often proclaimed that the civil engineering business, with its adjunct partner of surveying, is a highly skilled and educated career and that individuals make a lot of money drawing invisible lines on the ground. Examples of these invisible lines are centerlines of roads and utilities and property, easement, and *right of way (ROW)* lines. They can be drawn in a CADD file, but engineers use points to identify them on the ground in the field, the idea being that these invisible lines begin and end at these points. The setting of these points has been referred to as *COGO*, or coordinate geometry.

Points are locations in space defined by *X*, *Y*, and *Z* values in the *Cartesian* coordinate system. These points have been used to identify objects for much of the history of civil engineering and surveying; hence, they are simple and time-honored.

Earlier in this text, you learned some of the background involving CADD related to civil engineering and the interface elements of the Civil 3D software. In Chapter 2, you explored the basic usage of the software, created a surface from Existing Ground data, and developed a shopping center on a piece of property with an access road and corridor providing ingress/egress to the shopping center. This provides an excellent background on which the remainder of the textbook will build. The detailed functionality of Civil 3D will be presented from this chapter forward.

right of way (ROW): The property typically owned by a government agency and usually dedicated for roadway usage. The roads must be built inside the state R.O.W. so that they are not running across private property.

COGO: Software geared toward solving coordinate geometry problems.

Cartesian: A word variation relating to the French mathematician René Descartes.

REVIEW OF FUNCTIONS AND FEATURES TO BE USED

This chapter uses engineering functions to create point data. There are 50 different ways to compute point data, almost all of which are crucial to developing project data in 2D as well as 3D. What sets this chapter apart from training manuals or software **Help** tools is that all of the exercises are paired with an AutoCAD file that has data set up to perform the commands instantly. No setup work is required to try out these functions. If you know some of these routines, you can easily try new routines by simply opening the file and running through that specific procedure.

Designers use several concepts in creating points that comprise a *bearing/bearing intersect*, a *distance/distance intersect*, and a variety of combinations of these operations. This chapter discusses the theory of what these mean before you commence performing computations. A review of some of the distance and angular concepts is necessary before performing computations based on them.

bearing/bearing intersect: Set points at the intersection of two bearings.

distance/distance intersect: Set points at the intersection of two distances.

Job skills will benefit from knowledge of point management because all phases of civil engineering use point data. Engineers use them when surveying the base information, whether collected via total station or GPS. Engineers also set points for proposed objects and finished grade spot shots. Contractors use them in construction by way of stakeout points, stringlines, and GPS data.

POINT BASICS

Points are very simple in concept. They occupy a specific location in 3D space and are defined by a numerical value for *X*, *Y*, and *Z* in the Cartesian coordinate system. These work well because AutoCAD's default system is also a Cartesian coordinate system. A simple method for keeping track of the *X*, *Y*, and *Z* axes is to use the *three-finger* rule. Make a fist with your left hand. Then extend your pointer finger straight out in front of you. Lift your thumb straight up. Extend your middle finger to the right so it is at a 90° angle to the pointer finger. Hold that position. The *X*-axis is equivalent to the pointer, the *Y*-axis is your thumb, and the *Z*-axis is represented by your middle finger. Now if you maintain that relationship, you can rotate your hand around, and the axes are all related to each other. There can be many *X* axes depending on what angle in which your pointer finger is pointing; however, the other fingers always maintain that orthogonal relationship, just like in a CAD system.

The two-dimensional Cartesian coordinate system is a subset of the three-dimensional coordinate system and is used by those performing 2D drafting functions. Civil 3D is a three-dimensional system, but it is flexible enough to operate in either two or three dimensions. Both options will be investigated in the following discussions.

real numbers: Expressed by allowing decimals that have an infinite sequence of digits to the right of the decimal point.

The coordinate system is such that the location of a point, which we can call *P*, is established by three **real numbers** indicating the positions of the perpendicular projections from the point to three fixed, perpendicular, measured lines, called *axes*. The horizontal coordinate is denoted as *X*, the vertical coordinate is denoted as *Y*, and the height coordinate is called *Z*.

Correspondingly, the axes are called the *X*-axis, the *Y*-axis, and the *Z*-axis, and the point that fills that space is defined as $P = (X, Y, Z)$. The *Y*-axis is located 90° from the *X*-axis. Together the *X*- and *Y*-axes produce a plane. The *Z*-axis projects orthogonally from the *X*-*Y* plane and is positive in one direction and negative in the other.

A point that has a coordinate of (0, 0, 0) is located at the origin of the coordinate system. Points can also occupy locations along the negative portions of the axes. Therefore, points defined as follows can all be legitimate:

$P = (10, 30, 55)$
$P = (12.3345, 111.3333, 0.0000)$
$P = (-45.33, -33.22, -10.00)$
$P = (10.55, 22.66, -66.67)$
$P = (2.02030405 \times 10^6, 3.01223344 \times 10^6, 1.43276566 \times 10^6)$
$P = (2.02030405 \times 10^{-6}, 3.01223344 \times 10^{-6}, 1.43276566 \times 10^{-6})$

Civil engineers usually express these values in terms of the *Y*-axis being a Northing, the *X*-axis being an Easting, and the *Z*-axis as an Elevation and refer to them in that order. Note that the *X*- and *Y*-axes are reversed from the standard Cartesian order in civil engineering. Therefore, a civil engineering/surveying point is denoted as $P = $ (N: 5000.0, E: 7500.00, Elev: 120.0), whereas in the Cartesian system, the same point would be represented as $P = $ (*X*: 7500.0, *Y*: 5000.0, *Z*: 120.0).

What can be accomplished with points and why are they used? Some uses for points in civil engineering and surveying are as follows:

- Property corners for parcels of ownership
- Roadway alignment curves and tangent locations
- Building corners and Column locations
- Stakeout locations for the construction of features such as Edges of Pavement

In fact, virtually everything drawn in a CAD system such as AutoCAD uses point-based information somewhere because AutoCAD is a vector-based drawing system. This means that each graphic element must have a starting point and some formulaic method for constructing the location of where that element exists. For instance, objects are defined in several ways, and CAD systems do not always agree on the definitions, which can complicate translations between software applications. For instance, a horizontal arc can be located and defined using the radius point, a start angle, and an ending angle for the arc.

Example 3-1: In Figure 3-1, we have an arc defined by the center point of $X = 17.5219$ $Y = 7.3619$ $Z = 0.0000$, the radius length of 10.0000, a start angle of 22.5000, and an ending angle of 45.0000.

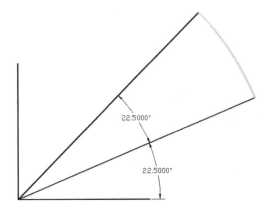

Figure 3-1   Angles

Another CAD program might use an entirely different algorithm to locate the same arc. For instance, the same arc could be described as having a center point of $X = 17.5219$ $Y = 7.3619$ $Z = 0.0000$, and a start angle dictated by a matrix containing the sine of the angle from the horizontal axis (sine $22.5° = 0.3826834$) and congruent with the sine of the angle from the vertical axis (sine $-67.5 = -0.92387953$). The start angle is positive from the horizontal axis because it increases in the counterclockwise direction and negative from the vertical axis because it increases in a clockwise direction. This matrix places the arc in the correct quadrant. It then has a sweep angle of $22.5°$ from the angle computed from the matrix.

Before using Civil 3D to help solve point-based problems, it is important to know the algorithms and formulas behind these computations. Let us discuss some of the mathematical formulas involving point data by reviewing how to calculate a vector between two points.

A line (or vector) is defined as the connection between the beginning point and its corresponding ending point. Therefore, a line would exist if it connected from a point called $P1$ to a point called $P2$. A line would also exist if it began at a point $P1$, had a known angle from the X- or Y-axis, and had a distance component. The basic formula for a line is $AX + BY + C = 0$. In solving for Y,

$$Y = -AX/B - C/B$$

Substituting $m = -A/B$ and $b = -C/B$, the equation reduces to $Y = mX + b$, where the Y value is the location along the Y-axis, m is the slope of the line, X is the coordinate value along the X-axis, and b is the Y intercept (or the position the line crosses the Y-axis).

Example 3-2: If, for a line, the slope (m) $= .5$ and the Y-intercept (b) $= 3$, any value of Y along the line is a function of where X is. So if you know X, you can compute where the Y coordinate falls on the line. Therefore, for a line where $X = 10$, you get:

$$Y = (.5)(10) + 3 = 8$$

The length of the line is computed using the principals of a triangle that has sides A and B with a hypotenuse of C. Sides A and B are the horizontal and vertical components of the right triangle, and C is the hypotenuse.

The Pythagorean theorem of $A^2 + B^2 = C^2$ reduces to $C = \sqrt{A^2 + B^2}$

Following the same thought process, the length of a line bounded by two coordinates would be solved as shown here. These coordinates are in the X, Y, Z format.

$P1 = (10, 20, 0)$
$P2 = (5, 15, 0)$

Solve for ΔX or the change in X values $= (10 - 5) = 5$. This is the horizontal component.
Solve for ΔY or the change in Y values $= (20 - 15) = 5$. This is the vertical component.
Solve for ΔZ or the change in Z values $= (0 - 0) = 0$.

$$\therefore C = \sqrt{25 + 25} = \sqrt{50} = 7.0710678$$

If the line has a Z (or elevational) coordinate, then expand the formula as follows:

$P_1 = (10, 20, 5)$
$P_2 = (5, 15, 10)$

Solve for ΔX or the change in X values $= (10 - 5) = 5$. This is the horizontal component.
Solve for ΔY or the change in Y values $= (20 - 15) = 5$. This is the vertical component.
Solve for ΔZ or the change in Z values $= (5 - 10) = -5$. This is the elevational component. Note that the negative change in Z values is made into an absolute value by squaring it in the equation. Therefore, -5 squared $= 25$.

$$\therefore C = \sqrt{25 + 25 + 25} = \sqrt{75} = 8.66025$$

Point Aesthetics

Now that the chapter has covered various concepts of how to compute with points, discussion continues on issues regarding how points appear. A point conveys nothing else in its purest sense besides its position; however, civil engineers and surveyors do expect more from a point. For instance, in addition to the location of a point, points represent the locations of a variety of objects in the field, such as property corners, building corners, trees, manholes, or even locations of linear objects such as edges of pavement or sidewalks. Therefore, knowing what the point represents as well as its X, Y, and Z location are critical pieces of information.

In order to visualize what a point represents, you may want the ability to view the point differently depending on what the point's representation is. Sometimes there is text associated with the point that simply states what it is, such as "Ground Shot" or "Waterline." Another option is to vary the shape or symbol of the point. For example, the point shape might change depending on whether it is a property corner, perhaps displayed as a small circle $\bigcirc$, or if it represents a ground shot it might appear as an **X**-shaped tick mark.

Civil 3D has a myriad of ways to depict points and what they represent. The following short exercises begin an introduction to this. They create a New Point Style, which affects how the point appears; a New Label Style, which affects how the labeling for the point appears; a New Point File Format, which allows points to be imported or exported with your choice of formats; and a Description Key Set, which controls the point codes indicating what the point actually represents. In the procedures that follow, you also create a customized table for reporting point data.

To access student data files, go to www.pearsondesigncentral.com.

point styles: A definition of how the point should appear.

Exercise 3-1: Creating Point Styles

1. Create a new drawing in Civil 3D, use the template **_AutoCAD Civil 3D (Imperial) NCS Base.dwt**.
2. Choose the **Settings** tab on the **Toolspace** palette.
3. Expand **Point >> *Point Styles*** and notice a preset style called **Standard**, as shown in Figure 3-2. You could edit that or create a new one by right-clicking on **Standard**. This yields **Edit, Copy, Delete**, and **Refresh**, which are style management functions. Instead, create a new style.
4. Right-click on **Point Styles** and choose **New....**
5. Figure 3-3 shows the tabs for establishing a Point Style: **Information, Marker, 3D Geometry, Display**, and **Summary**.
6. The **Information** tab is used to change the style name from **New Point Styles** to the name you prefer; in this case, call it **Prop-Corner**. Then select the **Marker** tab to identify the

Figure 3-2   Point Styles

Figure 3-3   Point Style
dialog box

aesthetic appearance of a point symbol in AutoCAD. The marker can be an AutoCAD Point symbol or, more likely, a Civil 3D marker, which is selected from the panel of buttons. The buttons on the left indicate what the point should look like when placed. The two additional buttons on the right are superimposition buttons that can be laid over the style chosen on the left. Experiment with the options. Choose the "×" and note the **Preview** display on the right. Choose the cross "+" and observe the **Preview**. Now choose the superimposed circle and note the **Preview**. The **Custom marker style** options are shown in Figure 3-4.

Custom marker style:

Figure 3-4   Custom marker styles

7. Now select the second button from the left (that has no symbol on it) but leave the superimposed circle turned on. This option might be used by a surveyor in denoting a property corner. The size and inches option in the top right of the box indicates that the symbology will plot a 0.1″ at the scale of the drawing. If you desire it to be larger or smaller, this value can be adjusted accordingly. You can also choose an option of **Use Fixed Scale**, **Use size in absolute units**, or **Use size relative to screen**, whereby the size of the marker is a percentage of the drawing screen size, in addition to **Use drawing scale**.

8. Continuing this exploration, note the lower left quadrant of the dialog box. You see an option called **Marker rotation angle**. This value can rotate the selected marker so that it always comes in, in a rotated position. One last option is choosing an AutoCAD block instead of a Civil 3D marker.

TIP   If blocks have been preset, they can simply be selected from the window. If your window is empty or if your organization wants you to use in-house-developed symbols, then right-click inside the window and choose **Browse....** Then locate the drive, folder, and block you would prefer to use.

9. In this case, use **AutoCAD BLOCK symbol for marker** and select the **AeccTickCircle**. Check the **Preview** and notice a circle symbol shows up. So any symbol you desire can be established for the marker.

10. Select the **3D Geometry** tab. Expand the **3D Geometry** item. Poke into the pop-down window for **Point Display Mode** under the **Value** column. Notice that a point can actually reside in three dimensions at the elevation of the point, it can be "flattened" to an elevation, or the elevation can be exaggerated by a scale factor. Selecting any of these options makes the **Point Elevation** or the **Scale Factor** option available as needed. Leave the option as it was at **Use Point Elevation**.

11. Now select the **Display** tab. This is where the layer, color, and so on are set for the Point Style in both 2D and 3D views. You can also preset if the marker and its associated label are to be turned on by default. To create a layer for the point, pick a point in the **Layer** column for the **Marker** row. A **Layer Selection** dialog box appears. Hit the **New...** button, and a **Create Layer** dialog box displays. Click under the **Values** column for **Layer Name**. Enter a layer name of **VF-Node-Ctrl-Ipf**. For the **Color** option, choose the button to select a color and choose **red**. Everything else will remain the default. Hit **OK.** You are back in the **Layer Selection** dialog box. Select the new layer **VF-Node-Ctrl-Ipf**. Hit **OK**. You are now back in the **Point Style—Prop Corner** dialog box, and the layer for the marker is set.

12. Now select the **Layer** cell for the **Label** row. Hit the **New...** button, and a **Create Layer** dialog box displays. Click under the **Values** column for **Layer Name**. Enter a layer name of **VF-Ctrl-Text**. For the **Color** option, choose the button to select a color and choose **green**. Everything else will remain the default. Hit **OK**. You are back in the **Layer Selection** dialog box. Select the new layer **VF-Ctrl-Text**. Hit **OK**. You are now back in the **Point Style—Prop Corner** dialog box, and the layer for the label is set. Under the **Color** column change the Layer colors to **ByLayer**. Hit **OK**.

13. On the **Toolspace** palette, right-click on **Point Styles** and choose **New...** again.

14. The **Information** tab is used to change the style name from **New Point Style** to the name you prefer; in this case call it **Planimetrics**. From the **Marker** tab, choose the "." and note the **Preview** display on the right. Leave the other settings in this tab as the default.

15. Now select the **Display** tab. This is where the layer, color, and so on are set for the Point Style in both 2D and 3D views. To create a layer for the point, pick a point in the **Layer** column for the **Marker** row. A **Layer** dialog box appears. Hit the **New...** button, and a **Create Layer** dialog box displays. Click under the **Values** column for **Layer Name**. Enter a layer name of **VF-Node-Topo**. For the **Color** option, choose the button to select a color and choose **blue**. Everything else will remain the default. Hit **OK**. You are back in the **Layer Selection** dialog box. Select the new layer **VF-Node-Topo**. Hit **OK**. You are now back in the **Point Style—Planimetrics** dialog box, and the layer for the marker is set.

16. Now select the **Layer** cell for the **Label** row. Hit the **New...** button, and a **Create Layer** dialog box displays. Click under the **Values** column for **Layer Name**. Enter a layer name of **VF-Topo-Text**. For the **Color** option, choose the button to select a color and choose **green**. Everything else will remain the default. Hit **OK**. You are back in the **Layer Selection** dialog box. Select the new layer **VF-Topo-Text**. Hit **OK**. You are now back in the **Point Style—Planimetrics** dialog box, and the layer for the label is set.

17. Hit the **Summary** tab to inspect your settings. When ready, hit **Apply** and **OK**. Notice that there is a new Point Style name called **Planimetrics** in the **Settings** palette.

18. Save this drawing as **My Point Style-Initials.dwg**, substituting your initials where it says "initials" in the filename.

Exercise 3-2: Creating Label Styles

In this exercise, a new Label Style is created.

1. Open My Point Style.dwg.
2. Choose the **Settings** tab on the **Toolspace** palette.
3. Expand **Point >> Label Styles** and notice a preset style called **Standard**. You can edit that or create a new one by right-clicking on **Standard**. This yields **Edit, New, Copy, Delete**, and **Refresh**, which are style management functions. Instead, create a new style.
4. Right-click on **Label Styles** and choose **New....**
5. In the **Label Style Composer** dialog box, the tabs for establishing the Label Style are **Information, General, Layout, Dragged State**, and **Summary**. In the **Information** tab, change the name to **My Point Label Style**.
6. Select the **General** tab in Figure 3-5, and change the **Text Style** to **Romans** (which has been preset in the drawing). Notice that the text style changes in the **Preview** to the right.

To access student data files, go to www.pearsondesigncentral.com.

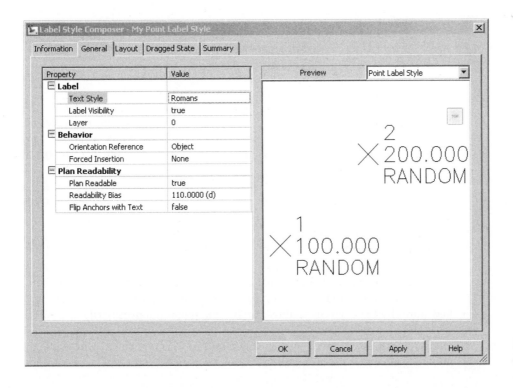

Figure 3-5 Label Style Composer dialog box

7. Leave the remaining defaults as they are. Hit **Apply** and **OK**.
8. From the **Points** pull-down menu, choose **Create Points...** to invoke the toolbar for point creation. Click on the first button and choose **Manual**.
9. Set a point at a coordinate of **1000,1000**. Give it a point description of **FG** and an elevation of **101.330**, and terminate the command.
10. In the **Toolspace**, go to the **Prospector** tab.
11. In the **Master View**, expand the item for your open drawing and expand the **Point Groups** item.
12. Right-click on **All Points**, and select **Properties....** The **Point Group Properties** dialog box opens as shown in Figure 3-6.

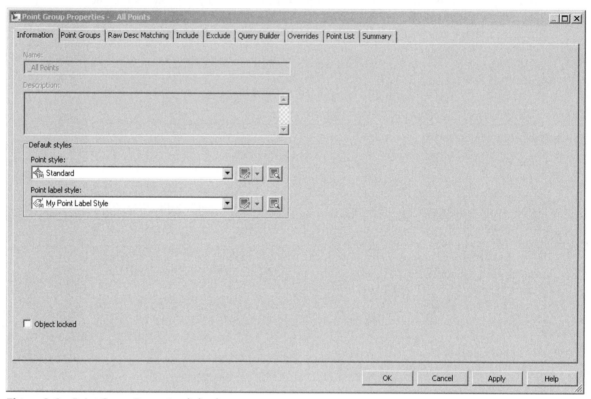

Figure 3-6   Point Group Properties dialog box

13. In the **Information** tab, go to the **Point label style:** option, pick in the pop-down window, and select **My Point Label Style** which you just created. Hit **Apply** and **OK**.
14. In AutoCAD, type **Z** for **Zoom** and **C** for **Center**. Type in a coordinate of **1000,1000** and a magnification or height of **25**.
15. You see a point placed with the Romans text style you requested (Figure 3-7). To see how your other changes to the settings affect the display, twist the drawing. Type in **Dview** and select the point you just placed when asked by the prompt. Hit **<Enter>**.
16. Choose **TW** for **Twist** and provide an angle of **215** (which would turn the point upside down). Hit **<Enter>** to complete the routine. Notice that the UCS icon and the point marker have rotated 215°, but the text orientation remained readable. The setting changed for **Orientation Reference to View** allows the point always to remain readable even when you Twist the view, usually for plotting purposes. This exercise shows how powerful the Civil 3D settings can be, and this is not necessarily a recommended setting for all points. Type **U** to **Undo** the creation of the point. Depending on how many commands you ran since you set the point, keep typing in **U** for Undo until the point is gone.

Figure 3-7   A Point

17. You can right-click on the **All Points** item and select **Properties**. When the **Properties** dialog box opens, in the **Information** tab, go to the **Point Label Style** option, pick in the pop-down window, and select **Standard**. Hit **Apply** and **OK**, and your points no longer use the style you created.

POINT GROUPS

Points are not actually Civil 3D objects in the same sense that surfaces and alignments are objects, although they share many characteristics with Civil 3D objects. For instance, points can be displayed in a drawing and modified graphically, and their manifestation is controlled using Styles and Label Styles. Yet they are technically not Civil 3D objects.

An excellent feature in Civil 3D is that points can be defined such that they fall into Point Groups; this helps immensely with organization. A Point Group is an object, and the point is a subset of the Point Group object. Whether a point is or is not an object does not make any real difference to you in practice, although knowing this may help you to understand better how points work.

There are two examples of how points will react differently than if they were objects. First, when a point is right-clicked and the **Properties** option is selected, this invokes the AutoCAD **Properties** dialog box, which describes the Point Group to which the point belongs but not the point itself. Second, when a point is selected, the **Layer** toolbar lists the **Point Group** layer information but not the actual **Point** layer information.

Point Groups are named collections of points that are used to organize and control points and their appearances in drawings. Point Groups have the following characteristics:

- They have enduring properties that can be easily reviewed or modified, either beforehand or retroactively.

- Displaying a points list shows the points included in a Point Group, and it can be updated automatically. This can occur when new points are input or modified that match the Point Group's properties or when the properties of a Point Group are modified.

- A Point Group can be locked to avoid unintentional modifications. Some aspects of Point Groups can be observed, accessed, and managed at the project level through the **Toolspace**.

A strong feature of Point Groups is that they allow you to manage many points at one time by using their group name. Point Groups give the computer the ability to sort through only the points needed for accessing or review. They also allow you to exclude unwanted points from a task such as exporting a point dump. Point Groups organize points that have similar descriptions such as "EP" for edge of pavement shots or points that are related by function such as DTM spot shots. There are many methods for developing Point Groups including defining them from a selection set or providing a range of point numbers. Further, these methods can be compounded on one another. In other words, the points in a Point Group called Road Points can also be included in a Point Group called Proposed DTM Points. Once they are established, they can be saved into the template for automatic use on future projects, thereby becoming part of the organization's CADD standards.

Job skills would benefit from the imaginative use of point groups beyond the obvious of grouping points according to their description or function. In other words, a point group called Monday's Points can be established for a surveyor importing point data for a job shot and collected on, say, Monday. This can be repeated for those obtained on Tuesday with a point group called Tuesday's Points. Then the surveyor can refer back to those groups to identify which points were collected on Monday versus those collected on Tuesday. Another possible use of point groups is to separate 3D points that are satisfactory for inclusion into a surface's development versus those that are two dimensional and not appropriate for use.

DESCRIPTION KEY SETS

The key to success in defining point groups is to have a strong description library for the point codes and their intended functions. If this is accomplished, you can assign point styles based on point descriptions, assign point symbology based on descriptions, and automatically populate point groups based on the descriptions. Obviously, this would benefit anyone setting points because a standardized mechanism would be used every time someone sets a storm manhole point. If all users used the preset description of, say, DMH for storm drain manholes, they would achieve a consistent look to their storm manhole symbologies and annotations in AutoCAD. In other words, the same symbol would always appear for the storm manhole along with a standardized description next to the point.

Description Key Sets: A library of codes that control how points are created, where they are created, and what they respresent.

The CADD file layers would always be correct, and the point would always reside in the correct point group. The tool to accomplish this is called *Description Key Sets*. Table 3-1 shows an example of many of the point description codes that you may find on a survey project. The first column shows the description key code, the second column the description of the code, the third column the suggested layer for the point, the fourth column the symbol for the point, and the last column the related point symbol layer.

In the following two exercises, a Description Key Set (formerly called a Description Key Library for Land Desktop users) and then a Point Group are created.

Exercise 3-3: Creating Description Key Sets

The Description Keys built here can be used in developing Point Groups in Exercise 3-4.

To access student data files, go to www.pearsondesigncentral.com.

1. Launch Civil 3D and open My Point Style.dwg. Make sure that the **Toolspace** is displayed.
2. Click the **Settings** tab of the **Prospector** to view the **Settings** panel. Pick **Master View** in the pop-down window at the top. Expand the **My Point Style.dwg** drawing name. Expand the **Point** item.
3. Right-click on the **Description Key Sets** and select **New....**
4. In the **Description Key Sets Name** field, change the name from **New DescKey Set** to **MY-DESCRIPTIONS**. Hit **OK** to create the new Description Key Set and observe that it now exists under the **Description Key Sets** item.
5. Now that the Description Key Set called **MY-DESCRIPTIONS** is created, the keys can be defined for point and label styles. Click on **MY-DESCRIPTIONS** and right-click. Select **Edit Keys....** This displays a **Panorama** dialog box listing all currently defined keys, shown in Figure 3-8. The new Description Key appears in capital letters.

Figure 3-8   Description Key settings

Table 3-1   A Sample Listing of Description Keys

Code	Desc	Layer	Symbol	Symbol Layer
AC	AC UNIT	VF-NODE-TOPO	CG78	VF-TOPO-MISC
BB	BB/TOE	VF-NODE-BRKL-TOE	CG32	VF-BRKL
BD	BUILDING	VF-NODE-BLDG	CG32	VF-BLDG
BM	BENCH MK	VF-NODE-CTRL-BMRK	CG85	VF-CTRL
BP	BOLLARD	VF-NODE-TOPO-BOLL	CG33	VF-TOPO-MISC
BR	SOIL BORING	VF-NODE-TOPO-BORE	CG85	VF-TOPO-MISC
BSL	BRUSH LINE	VF-NODE-BLIN	CG32	VF-SITE-VEGE-BRSH
CD	CL DITCH	VF-NODE-DTCH-CNTR	CG32	VF-DTCH-CNTR
CF	CG FACE	VF-NODE-CURB-ROAD	CG32	VF-ROAD-CURB-FACE
CM	CONC MON	VF-NODE-CTRL-CMON	CG74	VF-CTRL
CO	CLEANOUT	VF-NODE-MHOL-SSWR	CG01	VF-SSWR-MHOL
CP	CLR	VF-NODE-ROAD-CNTR	CG32	VF-ROAD-CNTR
CV	ELECT UGND VLT	VF-NODE-POWR-EVLT	GV	VF-POWR-UNDR
DF	DRAINFIELD	VF-NODE-SSWR	CG32	VF-SSWR-DF
DK	BLDG DECK	VF-NODE-BLDG-DECK	CG32	VF-BLDG
EC	DRWY CONC	VF-NODE-DRIV-CONC	CG32	VF-DRIV-CONC
EG	EDG SHLDER	VF-NODE-PVMT-GRVL	CG32	VF-PVMT-GRVL-SLDR
ELM	ELEC MTR	VF-NODE-INST-EMTR	CG88	VF-POWR-INST-EMTR
EM	EVERGRN MED	VF-NODE-TREE-EVMD	EM	VF-SITE-VEGE-TREE
EP	EOP	VF-NODE-PVMT	CG32	VF-PVMT-EDGE
ES	EVERGRN SMLL	VF-NODE-TREE-EVSM	ES	VF-SITE-VEGE-TREE
EW	EDGE WATER	VF-NODE-TOPO-EWAT	CG32	VF-TOPO-EWAT
FC	FILLER CAP	VF-NODE-POWR-FCAP	CG33	VF-POWR-UNDR
FF	FIN FLR	VF-NODE-BLDG-FFLR	CG04	VF-BLDG
FH	FIRE HYD	VF-NODE-WATR-STRC	FH	VF-WATR-FIRE-HYDT
FLM	FENCE METAL	VF-NODE-SITE-FENC-METL	CG32	VF-SITE-FENC
FLV	FENCE VINYL	VF-NODE-SITE-FENC-VINL	CG32	VF-SITE-FENC
FLW	FENCE WOOD	VF-NODE-SITE-FENC-WOOD	CG32	VF-SITE-FENC
FLY	FLY	VF-NODE-CTRL-FLY	FLY	VF-CTRL
FO	FIBER OPT	VF-NODE-COMM-FOPT	CG32	VF-COMM-FOPT
GD	GROUND SHOT	VF-NODE-TOPO-SPOT	CG36	VF-TOPO-SPOT
GR	GRD RAIL	VF-NODE-SITE-GDRS	CG32	VF-SITE-GRDS
GW	GUY WIRE	VF-NODE-POLE-GUYW	GW	VF-POWR-POLE
HC	HANDICAP MARKINGS	VF-NODE-MRKG-PRKG	HANDI	VF-PRKG-STRP
HR	HEDGEROW	VF-NODE-HEDG	CG32	VF-SITE-VEGE-HEDG
HS	HEAD STONE	VF-NODE-TOPO	CG78	VF-TOPO-MISC
IN	INLET	VF-NODE-STRM-INLT	CG04	VF-STRM-STRC
IPF	I PIPE FOUND	VF-NODE-CTRL-IPF	CG41	VF-CTRL
IPS	I PIPE SET	VF-NODE-CTRL-IPS	CG41	VF-CTRL
IRF	I ROD FOUND	VF-NODE-CTRL-IRF	CG41	VF-CTRL
IRS	I ROD SET	VF-NODE-CTRL-IRS	CG41	VF-CTRL
IV	IRRI VALV	VF-NODE-WATR-IRVA	CG94	VF-WATR-VALV
JW	WALL	VF-NODE-SITE-JWLL	CG32	VF-SITE-WALL
LA	LANDSCAPE	VF-NODE-VEGE-MISC		VF-SITE-VEGE-MISC
LE	EVERGRN LG	VF-NODE-TREE-EVLG	EL	VF-SITE-VEGE-TREE
LP	LIGHT POL	VF-NODE-POLE-LITE	CG92	VF-POWR-POLE

Table 3-1 (*Continued*)

MB	MAIL BOX	VF-NODE-TOPO	MAILBOX	VF-TOPO-MISC
MS	SDMH	VF-NODE-MHOL-STRM	CG01	VF-STRM-MHOL
MW	WATER MH	VF-NODE-MHOL-WATR	CG49	VF-WATR-MHOL
NV	INVERT	VF-NODE-STRM-STRC	CG04	VF-STRM-STRC
OH	OH WIRES	VF-NODE-POLE-OHWR	CG32	VF-POWR-POLE
OV	OVERHANG	VF-NODE-BLDG-OHAN		VF-BLDG
PD	TELE PED	VF-NODE-COMM-PED	CG34	VF-COMM
PH	PHOTO CTRL	VF-NODE-CTRL-PHOT	PH	VF-CTRL
PM	LANE STRIPES	VF-NODE-MRKG-ROAD	CG32	VF-ROAD-MRKG
POR	PORCH	VF-NODE-BLDG-PORC	CG32	VF-BLDG
PP	POWER POLE	VF-NODE-POLE-POWR	UPOLE	VF-POWR-POLE
RI	RIP RAP	VF-NODE-RRAP	CG32	VF-RRAP
RW	RET WALL	VF-NODE-SITE-RTWL	CG32	VF-SITE-WALL
SATV	SAT TV	VF-NODE-COMM-SATV	CG03	VF-COMM-SATV
SB	SHRUB	VF-NODE-SHRUB	CG134	VF-SITE-VEGE-BRSH
SM	SMH	VF-NODE-MHOL-SSWR	CG01	VF-SSWR-MHOL
SN	SIGN	VF-NODE-SIGN	SN	VF-SITE-SIGN
SP	TREE	VF-NODE-TREE-SPEC	CG133	VF-SITE-VEGE-TREE
STL	SEPTIC LID	VF-NODE-SSWR		VF-SSWR-MHOL
STON	PLANTED STONE	VF-NODE-CTRL-STON	CG43	VF-CTRL
STP	STEPS	VF-NODE-SITE-STPS	CG32	VF-SITE-STPS
STW	STONE WALL	VF-NODE-SITE-STWL	CG32	VF-SITE-WALL
TB	TOP OF BANK	VF-NODE-BRKL	CG32	VF-BRKL
TC	CG TOP	VF-NODE-CURB-ROAD	CG32	VF-ROAD-CURB-TOP
TF	TRANSF	VF-NODE-POWR-TRAN	TF	VF-POWR-TOWR
TL	TREE LARGE	VF-NODE-TREE-LARG	TL	VF-SITE-VEGE-TREE
TLN	TREE LINE	VF-NODE-TRLN	CG32	VF-SITE-VEGE-TROW
TM	TREE MED	VF-NODE-TREE-MED	TM	VF-SITE-VEGE-TREE
TR	TRAVERSE	VF-NODE-CTRL-TRAV	CG48	VF-CTRL
TS	TREE SMALL	VF-NODE-TREE-SM	TS	VF-SITE-VEGE-TREE
TX	TRAF SIG BOX	VF-NODE-POWR-STRC	TRAFCNTL	VF-POWR-STRC
UE	ELEC UGND	VF-NODE-POWR-UNDR	CG32	VF-POWR-UNDR
UG	GAS UGND	VF-NODE-POWR-UGAS	CG32	VF-POWR-UNDR
UM	UNKNOWN MH	VF-NODE-TOPO	MH_UTIL	VF-TOPO-MISC
UT	TELEPHONE	VF-NODE-COMM-UTEL	CG32	VF-COMM
UTV	UG CABLE TV	VF-NODE-CATV-UNDR	CG32	VF-CATV-UNDR
UW	IWATER UNGD	VF-NODE-WATR-UNGD	CG32	VF-WATR-VALV
VDH	VDOT MON	VF-NODE-CTRL-VDOT	CG73	VF-CTRL
WA	WALL ALIGN	VF-NODE-SITE-WAAL	CG32	VF-SITE-WALL
WE	WELL	VF-NODE-WATR-STRC	CG01	VF-WATR-WELL
WK	WALK	VF-NODE-TOPO-WALK	CG32	VF-TOPO-WALK
WM	WATER METER	VF-NODE-WATR-METR	WM	VF-WATR-MAIN
WT	WETLANDS	VF-NODE-WLND	CG01	VF-SITE-VEGE-WLND
WV	WATER VALV	VF-NODE-WATR-VALV	WV	VF-WATR-VALV
YH	YARD HYDRANT	VF-NODE-WATR-YAHY		VF-WATR-VALV

6. In the first cell of the **Code** column, enter **AC***.
7. In the next column, click the **Point Style** toggle **On**.
8. Click on the word **<default>** in the **Style** column, and the **Point Style** dialog box displays.
9. Use the list arrow to observe the list of available styles; select **Planimetrics** from the list, and hit **OK**.
10. In the next column, click the **Point Label Style** toggle **On**.
11. Click on the **<default>** in the **Point Label Style** column, and the **Point Label Style** dialog box displays. Choose **Standard**.
12. In the **Format** column, type **AC UNIT**. When these points are placed in Civil 3D, they will always be annotated as AC Units.
13. Then in the next column for **Layer**, click the **Layer** toggle **On**.
14. Click in the cell to the right of that toggle, and from the **Layer** list, select the **VF-Node-Topo** layer and hit **OK**.
15. Now create another Description Key. Right-click on the **AC** key and choose **Copy** from the shortcut menu. A **Copy of AC*** is created.
16. Click on the **Copy of AC*** and change the name to **IPF***.
17. Click in the **Style** column, and the **Point Style** dialog box displays.
18. Use the list arrow to observe the list of available styles; select **Prop-Corner** from the list, and hit **OK**.
19. In the next column, click the **Point Label Style** toggle **On**.
20. Click in the **Point Label Style** column, and the **Point Label Style** dialog box displays. Choose **Standard**.
21. In the **Format** column, type **I Pipe Found**. When these points are placed in Civil 3D, they will always be annotated as I Pipe Found.
22. Then in the next column for **Layer**, click the **Layer** toggle **On**.
23. Click in the cell to the right of that toggle, and from the **Layer** list, select the **VF-Node-Ctrl-Ipf** layer and hit **OK**.
24. Next create yet another Description Key. Right-click on the **AC** key and choose **Copy** from the shortcut menu. A **Copy of AC*** is created.
25. Click on the **Copy of AC*** and change the name to **MB***.
26. Click in the **Style** column, and the **Point Style** dialog box displays.
27. Use the list arrow to observe the list of available styles; select **Planimetrics** from the list, and hit **OK**.
28. In the next column, click the **Point Label Style** toggle **On**.
29. Click on the **<default>** in the **Point Label Style** column, and the **Point Label Style** dialog box displays. Choose **Standard**.
30. In the **Format** column, type **Mailbox**. When these points are placed in Civil 3D, they will always be annotated as Mailbox.
31. Then in the next column for **Layer**, click the **Layer** toggle **On**.
32. Click in the cell to the right of that toggle, and from the **Layer** list, select the **VF-Node-Topo** layer and hit **OK**.
33. The **Settings** should appear as shown in Figure 3-9. Now there are Description Keys for three items to use in preparing Point Groups in the following exercise.
34. Click the check mark in the upper right of the **Panorama** dialog box to save and close the Desckey Editor. Close the **Panorama** dialog box.

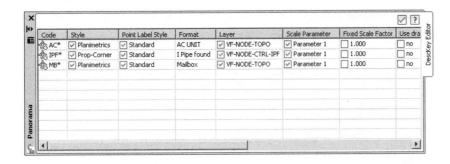

Code	Style	Point Label Style	Format	Layer	Scale Parameter	Fixed Scale Factor	Use dra
AC*	☑ Planimetrics	☑ Standard	AC UNIT	☑ VF-NODE-TOPO	☑ Parameter 1	☐ 1.000	☐ no
IPF*	☑ Prop-Corner	☑ Standard	I Pipe found	☑ VF-NODE-CTRL-IPF	☑ Parameter 1	☐ 1.000	☐ no
MB*	☑ Planimetrics	☑ Standard	Mailbox	☑ VF-NODE-TOPO	☑ Parameter 1	☐ 1.000	☐ no

Figure 3-9 Desckey Editor

Exercise 3-4: Creating Point Groups

This task defines a Point Group to help organize your points. It helps in accessing points, reporting on them, or exporting them. The Point Group is made up of our Property corner control points. By default, Civil 3D creates a point group called ALL.

1. While remaining in the same drawing, click the **Prospector** tab in the **Toolspace**.
2. Expand the drawing name item to view the Civil 3D object list.
3. Expand **Point Groups** to show the Point Group list.
4. Click on the **Point Group** item, right-click, and select **New...** from the shortcut menu.
5. In the **Information** tab, its name is Point Group-(1). Change the **Point Group** name to **Planimetrics**. Give it a description of **2D Planimetrics**. Refer to Figure 3-10.
6. Click the **Raw Description Matching** tab and toggle on **AC*** and **MB***.

Figure 3-10   Point Group Editor

TIP   This instructs Civil 3D to include only those points that match the raw descriptions of AC* and MB*. As other Planimetric keys are defined, they can be added here as well by revisiting this procedure.

7. Click the **Include** tab and notice that the same two Description Keys are selected here. Hit **OK**.
8. The **Point Group**, **Planimetrics**, is now evident on the **Point Group** list. See Figure 3-10.
9. Now create a Point Group for the Control points. Click on the **Point Group** item, right-click, and select **New...** from the shortcut menu.
10. In the **Information** tab, its name is Point Group-(2). Change the **Point Group** name to **Control**. Give it a description of **Control Points**.
11. Click the **Raw Description** tab and toggle on **IPF***.
12. This instructs Civil 3D to include only those points that match the raw descriptions of IPF*. As other Control keys are defined, they can be added here as well by revisiting this procedure. Hit **OK**.
13. Under **Point Groups**, you will now see **All Points**, **Planimetrics**, and **Control**.

Now that the data organization is created within Civil 3D, the next step is to create some points to sample how this should work.

Exercise 3-5: Create Points

1. Type **Z** for **Zoom** and **<Enter>**. Then type **C** for **Center** and **<Enter>**. When asked for the center point, type **1000,1000**. When asked for the Magnification or Height, type **500**.
2. From the pull-down menus, choose **Points >> Create Points....**
3. The **Create Points** toolbar displays. Select the first button, with the tooltip called **Miscellaneous: Manual**.

4. When you are prompted with `Please specify a location for the new point:` Type **1000,1000**. The software then responds as follows.
5. `Enter a point description <.>:` **AC**
6. `Specify a point elevation <.>:` **112.33**
7. `Please specify a location for the new point:` **1100,1000**
8. `Enter a point description <AC>:` **IPF**
9. `Specify a point elevation <112.330'>:` **114.32**
10. `Please specify a location for the new point:` **1100,1100**
11. `Enter a point description <IPF>:` **MB**
12. `Specify a point elevation <114.320'>:` **<Enter>**
13. `Please specify a location for the new point:` **<Enter>** to terminate the command.
14. If, after the points are in place, there is an icon indicating that the object data are Out of Date, then right-click on the item **(Point Groups**, **Planimetrics)** and select **Update**. That should eliminate the icon indicating Out of Date and place the points into the Point Group object. Repeat for any other Point Groups that are Out of Date.

The data shown in the **Master View** of the **Prospector** are updated automatically to show the current status of data in the drawing. The **Prospector** dynamically updates its contents as you add and remove data and civil objects. Icons adjacent to the data entry tell you the status of the data, for example, if a surface is out of date or if a point group has changed. The **Prospector** should appear similar to Figure 3-11 after the Point Groups are created and the points are entered.

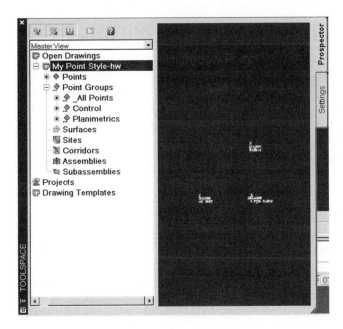

Figure 3-11   Prospector and Preview

Exercise 3-6: Creating Point File Formats

In this task, a **Point File Format** is defined to help when importing or exporting point data to external locations. Formats indicate the relative positions of the point data in the string being read. For instance, what is the first item in the string: a point number or a Northing? What is the second item in the string: an elevation or an Easting? By default, Civil 3D has a lot of predeveloped formats, but if you require one not already developed, it helps to know how to create a format.

point file format: Preformatted definitions for importing or exporting points.

1. While remaining in the same drawing, click the **Settings** tab in the **Toolspace**.
2. Expand the drawing name item to view the Civil 3D object list.
3. Click on the expand tree icon next to **Point File Formats** to show the list.
4. Click on the **Point File Formats** item, right-click, and select **New...** from the shortcut menu.
5. When the **Select Format Type** dialog box opens, choose **User Point file** and hit **OK**.
6. The **Point File Format** dialog box opens. Type in a format name of **LatLong**, as shown in Figure 3-12.

Figure 3-12   Point File
Format

7. Choose the option for **Delimited by**: and type a comma **(,)** in the open field.
8. Near the bottom is a wide window with column headers labeled **unused**. Click on the first header on the left. A **Selection** dialog box opens. Click in the pop-down window and choose **Point Number**. Hit **OK**.
9. Click on the second header. Click in the pop-down window and choose **Latitude**. Hit **OK**.
10. Click on the third header. Click in the pop-down window and choose **Longitude**. Hit **OK**.
11. Click on the fourth header. Click in the pop-down window and choose **Point Elevation**. Hit **OK**. Hit **OK** to close out.

You have created a format that allows for importing or exporting data using **LatLong** data.

EXTERNAL DATA REFERENCES

External Data References: Additional data files that can augment how point data are stored.

Civil 3D can create and maintain point database files that contain all of the point information in the project. *External Data References* are adjunct databases that can amend the information in this database. The data stored include the point number, optional point name, Northing, Easting, elevation, and point description. External Data References can allow you to either substitute point elevations when points are accessed through a point group or substitute point raw description data.

TIP   External Data References can be useful if your project is in Imperial units, but periodically you must report your elevations in Metric units.

External Data References allow you to link your custom point databases to Civil 3D. They are also called XDRefs. The XDRef is a pointer to a column of data in a custom Microsoft Access database. The key field is typically the point number. Then, when an XDRef is used to access a value for a point, the point number is looked up in the custom database, and the value from the specified column is used instead of the point's original value. These files are nondestructive in that they do not overwrite or alter the points in the drawing. Although this is not a highly used function, it can be very handy when the occasion arises.

Now that you have gained some experience in establishing Point Groups and related Description Key Sets, you will learn how to set points using some of the many **Point Creation** tools provided within the software. These are obtained using the **Points** pull-down menu, and these commands are described next.

The **Points** pull-down menu (Figure 3-13), is very clear and succinct, characteristic of all the pull-down menus. Some software manufacturers load up the menus with many commands, and users are often lost in finding the right command at the right time. Civil 3D menus are compact and easy to understand. The **POINTS** commands are as follows:

- **Create Points...** invokes the **Create Points** toolbar for setting points. There are 48 commands in this toolbar for sophisticated point geometry creation.

- **Create Point Group...** allows for the creation of Point Groups.

- **Edit Points** allows for modification of points.

- **Add Tables...** allows for importing point information in tabular format.

- **Utilities** allows for exporting points, identifying where points are located, transfer facilities, a Geodetic calculator, and the ability to create blocks from points.

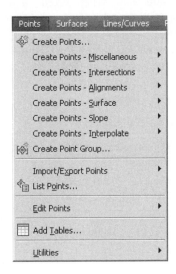

Figure 3-13   Points pull-down menu

Point Computations

The text mentioned earlier that there are 48 different methods for computing point data. The **Create Points** toolbar (Figure 3-14) contains these commands.

Figure 3-14   Create Points toolbar

Each button has an accompanying pop-down arrow for making selection choices. The buttons in the toolbar include the following functions:

- **Miscellaneous** sets 2D points using basic techniques.

- **Intersection** sets 2D points using intersectional criteria.

- **Alignment** sets 2D points using alignment-based information.

- **Surface** sets 3D points using Surface information and 3D criteria.

- **Interpolation** sets 3D points typically densifying the data.

- **Slope** sets 3D points using Grade and Slope criteria.

- **Import Points** allows for bringing points into the drawing from other sources, drawings, projects, or programs.

Each of these commands will be discussed independently, so you can use them on projects easily.

Exercise 3-7: CREATE POINTS Commands

To access student data
files, go to
www.pearsondesigncentral.com.

1. Open the drawing called Chapter-3-Points.dwg.
2. Type **Z** for **Zoom** and **<Enter>**. Then type **C** for **Center** and **<Enter>**. When asked for the center point, type **1000,1000**. When asked for the Magnification or Height, type **200**. You can also type in **V** for **View** and choose a saved view called **Points-A**. Hit **Set Current** and hit **OK**.
3. Select the **Points** pull-down menu and choose the **CREATE POINTS...** command. The toolbar displays. Investigate the first tools in the leftmost icon first.

Miscellaneous Point Creation Commands

Exercise 3-8: Miscellaneous—MANUAL Command

 Figure 3-15 shows the **MANUAL** command, which allows you to pick the origin of the point using a mouse or key-in value.

Figure 3-15   Create Points—Manual

 The **MANUAL** command can be used to set points manually wherever they are needed.

 Job skills benefit because engineers always set points on objects representing property lines, easements, road centerlines, pipelines, and so on.

1. Select the first pop-down arrow and ensure that **Manual** is checked by clicking on it. This will also invoke the command.
2. Civil 3D responds in the command prompt with the following. Enter the responses as indicated.
3. `Please specify a location for the new point:` type **1000,1000 <Enter>**.
4. `Enter a point description <.>:` **IPF**
5. `Specify a point elevation <.>:` **122.45**
6. `The software responds with: N: 1000.0000' E: 1000.0000'`
7. `Please specify a location for the new point:`
8. This time use your mouse and pick a point about 3″ (on the screen) to the right and 3″ (on the screen) downward from the first point. At the prompt: `Enter a point description <.>:` Type **IPF**, `Specify a point elevation <.>:` **112.44**.
9. The software responds with: `N: 941.60139 E: 1077.4403'` (of course, your coordinates may differ because you are picking the point with your mouse). Hit **OK** to terminate.
10. Draw a line on the screen from the **Node** snap of Point 1 to the **Node** snap of Point 2.
11. Now select **Manual** again. This time when prompted to: `Please specify a location for the new point:` Select the Midpoint snap and snap to the midpoint of the line you just drew.
12. When prompted to Enter a point description <.>:, Type **IPF**. When prompted to `Specify a point elevation <.>:`, type **116.77**. Hit **OK** to terminate.

The result should appear similar to Figure 3-16.

Figure 3-16   Result of Manual creation

Exercise 3-9: Miscellaneous—GEODETIC DIRECTION AND DISTANCE Command

 The next command, ***GEODETIC DIRECTION AND DISTANCE***, allows for computing points based on the geodetic datum set in the drawing.

 TIP   The **GEODETIC DIRECTION AND DISTANCE** command is typically used when setting points over long distances where the face of the Earth becomes a consideration.

Job skills benefit here because some software manufacturers charge extra to obtain software that can perform this function.

geodetic direction and distance: Computing a point using a geodetic datum, a geodetic azimuth, and a distance along the mathematical face of the Earth for that part of the country. For instance, 1000′ along the face of the Earth is less than 1000′ horizontally, since the Earth is curved.

1. Type **Z** for **Zoom** and **<Enter>**. Then type **C** for **Center** and **<Enter>**. When asked for the center point, type **11626006, 6865528**. When asked for the Magnification or Height, type **300**. You can also type in **V** for View and choose a saved view called **Points-B**. Hit **Set Current** and hit **OK**.

2. From the **Create Points** toolbar, choose the pop-down arrow on the first button and select **Geodetic Direction and Distance**. Respond to the prompts as follows.

3. Please specify a location for the start point:, type **11626006,6865528<Enter>**. The system responds with `Northing: 6865528.0000' Easting: 11626006.0000', Grid Northing: 6865528.0000' Grid Easting: 11626006.0000', Convergence: 0° 18' 43.40" Scale Factor: 1.000, Latitude: N38° 30' 00.00" Longitude: W78° 00' 00.01"`

4. `Geodetic azimuth <0° 00' 00.00">`: Hit **<Enter>**

5. `Geodesic distance <1.000>`: Type **100<Enter>**.

6. `Northing: 6865627.9936' Easting: 11626005.4554', Grid Northing: 6865627.9936', Grid Easting: 11626005.4554', Convergence: 0° 18' 43.40" Scale Factor: 1.000, Latitude: N38° 30' 00.99", Longitude: W78° 00' 00.01"`

7. `Enter a point description <.>`: **IPF**

8. `Specify a point elevation <.>`: **112.45**

9. `Please specify a location for the start point`: **<Enter>** to terminate.

azimuth: The North azimuth measures angles from the North axis, in a clockwise direction to 360°.

A Point 4 is created at a geodetic distance of 100′ along the curvature of the Earth in NAD 83 in northern Virginia at a geodetic *azimuth* of zero degrees. In order to test how this handled the computation, draw a line from the initial coordinate to the point placed and list the line for its length and direction.

10. Type **L** for line, and specify the first point at **11626006,6865528**.
11. Specify the next point using a **Node** snap to the point created from the last command.
12. Then type **LI** for **List** and select the line.
13. Civil 3D responds as follows:

```
LINE Layer: "0"
Space: Model space
Handle = 629
from point, X = 11626006.0000 Y = 6865528.0000 Z = 0.0000
to point, X = 11626005.4554 Y = 6865627.9936 Z = 112.4500
In Current UCS, Length = 99.9951, Angle in XY Plane = 90.3121
3D Length = 150.4793, Angle from XY Plane = 48.3552
Delta X = -0.5446, Delta Y = 99.9936, Delta Z = 112.4500
```

Notice the length of 99.9951, when you clearly entered 100′. The 100′ was the length along the face of the Earth; hence, the horizontal length of the line is something shorter. Save your drawing and remain in the drawing with your initials for the next exercise.

Exercise 3-10: Miscellaneous—RESECTION Command

 The next command is **RESECTION**. A resection creates a point at a location calculated from the measured angles between three known points.

 This function is often used to locate a coordinate when you can see three other known positions and can measure their angles.

 Job skills benefit in that sailors use this same technique to locate their positions on the sea. If you plan to sail during your vacations or retirement, this routine will be helpful.

In this exercise, you are located to the upper right of Points 1, 2, and 3. Measure their angles as shown, where the angle from Point 2 to 3 is **28.7538°** and the angle from Point 2 to 1 is **56.7010°**.

1. Type **V** for **View** and choose a saved view called **Points-A**. Hit **Set Current** and hit **OK**.

2. From the **Create Points** toolbar, choose the pop-down arrow on the first button and select **Resection**. Respond to the prompts as follows.
3. `Specify first (backsight or reference) point:` Snap to Point 2 using a **Node** snap.
4. `Specify second point:` Snap to Point 3 using a **Node** snap.
5. `Specify third point:` Snap to Point 1 using a **Node** snap.
6. `Specify the angle between the first and second point <0.0000(d)>:` Type **28.7538**
7. `Specify the angle between the first and third point <0.0000(d)>:` Type **56.7010**
8. `Enter a point description <.>:` **IPF**
9. `Specify a point elevation <.>:` **0**

Notice in Figure 3-17 that Point 5 shows up at the convergence of the linework indicating the angles shot by the surveyor. Now you have a coordinate for your location. Save your drawing and remain in the drawing with your initials for the next exercise.

Figure 3-17   Result of Resection

Exercise 3-11: Miscellaneous—STATION/OFFSET OBJECT Command

 The next command, **STATION/OFFSET OBJECT,** creates a point based on the station and offset of a line or other object chosen for the computations. The offset is to the right if a positive value is indicated and to the left for a negative value.

 The **STATION/OFFSET OBJECT** command can be used to set a point such as a manhole at a specific location relative to a known linear or curved object nearby.

1. From the **Create Points** toolbar, choose the pop-down arrow on the first button and select **Station/Offset Object**. Respond to the prompts as follows.
2. `Select an arc, line, polyline, lot line, or feature line:` Pick the line connecting Points 2 to 1 near Point 2 but not on Point 2.
3. `Starting station <0.000>:` Hit **<Enter>**.
4. `Specify a desired station <0.000>:` Type **55<Enter>**
5. `Specify an offset <0.000>:` Type **–45<Enter>**
6. `Enter a point description <.>:` **IPF**
7. `Specify a point elevation <.>:` **0**
8. `Specify another desired station:` Hit **<Esc>** or **<*Cancel*>** several times to terminate the routine.
9. Notice Point 6 shows up 55′ from Point 2 in a direction toward Point 1 and 45′ to the left of the line. This works on several types of objects, however, only on independent objects.

If you wish to set points using stations/offsets based on alignments, then use a command upcoming in the third button from the left called **Alignment: Station/Offset**.

Save your drawing and remain in the drawing with your initials for the next exercise.

Exercise 3-12: Miscellaneous—AUTOMATIC Command

 The next command, **AUTOMATIC**, creates points based on the curvilinear objects selected by the operator.

 TIP This method allows very rapid point placement on many objects at once and can be used to establish property corner points for a parcel.

To access student data files, go to www.pearsondesigncentral.com.

1. In the same drawing, Chapter-3-Points.dwg or Chapter-3-Points (with your initials).dwg, turn on the layer called **V-Misc-Objs**. Some lines and arcs will display. Type **Regen** if the arcs are not obvious.
2. From the **Create Points** toolbar, choose the pop-down arrow on the first button and select **Automatic**. Respond to the prompts as follows.
3. `Select arcs, lines, lot lines, or feature lines:` Select all of the linework that was on the layer that you just turned on.
4. `Enter a point description <.>:` **IPF**
5. `Specify a point elevation <.>:` **<Enter>**
6. `Enter a point description <IPF>:` **<Enter>**
7. `Specify a point elevation <.>:` **<Enter>**
8. Repeat this for all other requests for point description and Elevation.
9. Hit **<Enter>** to terminate when complete.
10. Notice that points are automatically placed on all of the key geometric locations of the arcs and lines, including radius points of the arcs.

Save your drawing and remain in the drawing with your initials for the next exercise.

Exercise 3-13: Miscellaneous—ALONG LINE/CURVE Command

curvilinear objects: These include arcs and spirals. Arcs or circular curves have a constant radius from beginning to end. Spirals have constantly changing radii from start to end.

 The next command, **ALONG LINE/CURVE**, creates points based on *curvilinear objects* at a distance along the object.

1. In the same drawing, and from the **Create Points** toolbar, choose the pop-down arrow on the first button and select **Along Line/Curve**. Respond to the prompts as follows.
2. **Select an arc, line, polyline, lot line, or feature line:** Pick the yellow arc on the Layer **V-Misc-Objs**.
3. `Specify a distance:` Type **25**
4. `Enter a point description <.>:` **IPF**
5. `Specify a point elevation <.>:` **<Enter>**
6. `Specify a distance:` **50**
7. `Enter a point description <IPF>:` **<Enter>**
8. `Specify a point elevation <.>:` **<Enter>**
9. `Specify a distance:` **<Enter>** to terminate.
10. You now have points (18 and 19) along the yellow arc at distances of 25′ and 50′ from the beginning of the arc. Refer to Figure 3-18.

Exercise 3-14: Miscellaneous—ON LINE/CURVE Command

 The next command, **ON LINE/CURVE**, creates points based on curvilinear objects at their key points. This command is similar to **AUTOMATIC** in its results.

Figure 3-18   Result of Miscellaneous Along Line/Curve

Exercise 3-15: Miscellaneous—DIVIDE OBJECT Command

The next command, **DIVIDE OBJECT**, creates points by the number of segments you request on an object. This command could be used to set stakeout points for landscape planting off to the side of a property line.

In this case, the landscape architect may have outlined that four equally spaced trees are to be planted in order to meet *greenspace* requirements for the subdivision. You usually do not want to set stakeout points at the actual location of the prospective trees because as soon as the contractor begins digging, the stakes will be knocked out of the ground. So it usually is a good idea to set them safely off to the side of the construction area.

greenspace: An area dedicated to the preservation or replacement of vegetation that may be reduced as a result of construction. Planning professionals often ensure that requirements for greenspace are met for a project.

1. To begin this routine, **Draw** a line from **850,1050** to **930,1075**.
2. Then from the **Create Points** toolbar, choose the pop-down arrow on the first button and select **Divide Object**. Respond to the prompts as follows.
3. `Select an arc, line, polyline, lot line, or feature line:` Select the line you just drew at the right end.
4. `Enter the number of segments <1>:` **3**
5. `Specify an offset <0.000>:` **25**
6. `Enter a point description <.>:` **IPF**
7. `Specify a point elevation <.>:` **<Enter>**
8. `Enter a point description <IPF>:` **<Enter>**
9. `Specify a point elevation <.>:` **<Enter>**
10. `Enter a point description <IPF>:` **<Enter>**
11. `Specify a point elevation <.>:` **<Enter>**
12. `Enter a point description <IPF>:` **<Enter>**
13. `Specify a point elevation <.>:` **<Enter>**
14. Hit **<Enter>** to terminate.
15. Save the drawing. You can close and open it as needed as you progress through these exercises.

The system places Points 20 through 23, in this case, where the line would have three segments including the endpoints, and at an offset of 25′. Of course you could set an offset of 0 and achieve the points right on the object. Save your drawing and remain in the drawing with your initials for the next exercise.

Exercise 3-16: Miscellaneous—MEASURE OBJECT Command

 This exercise sets points using the **CREATE POINTS—MEASURE OBJECT** command. Notice that the **DIVIDE OBJECT** and **MEASURE OBJECT** commands seem like companion commands to the **DIVIDE** and **MEASURE** AutoCAD commands. They work essentially as they do in AutoCAD, except that they set point objects as shown in Figure 3-19.

Figure 3-19 Result of Measure Object

 The **MEASURE OBJECT** command could be used to set stakeout points to the side of a culvert. You usually do not want to set stakeout points right on the centerline of a culvert because as soon as the contractor begins digging, the stakes will be knocked out of the ground, rendering them useless. So it usually is a good idea to set them safely off to the side of the construction area.

Miscellaneous—POLYLINE VERTICES—MANUAL Command

 The next computations set points on polylines. The first example, using the **POLYLINE VERTICES—MANUAL** command, sets points on a polyline using a manual approach. You might use this when you want to create points on a building pad that has a specific, flat elevation. Type in the desired elevation before setting the points, and the software will use it when creating the points.

Exercise 3-17: Miscellaneous—POLYLINE VERTICES—AUTOMATIC Command

 The next computation, using the **POLYLINE VERTICES—AUTOMATIC** command, sets points on polylines automatically. The previous command was pretty automatic, so how is this different? This one sets the elevations for the building pad automatically, assuming that the pad is set at the correct elevation to start with. You might use this when you want to create points on a building pad that has a preset, flat elevation.

1. Continuing on in the same drawing, erase the points from the previous command using the **ERASE** command in AutoCAD.
2. Now use the **MOVE** command in AutoCAD to move the building object up to an elevation of **100**. Type **M<Enter>**, select the pad and hit **<Enter>**. When prompted to `Specify base point or displacement:` Type **0,0,100<Enter><Enter>**.
3. This has caused the building to move up to an elevation of 100′.
4. From the **Create Points** toolbar and using the pop-down arrow next to the first icon, choose **Polyline Vertices—Automatic**. Respond to the prompts as follows.
5. `Select a polyline object:` Select the polyline you just moved to elevation 100.
6. `Enter a point description <.>:` **IPF**

7. `Enter a point description <IPF>:` **\<Enter\>**
8. `Enter a point description <IPF>:` **\<Enter\>**
9. `Enter a point description <IPF>:` **\<Enter\>**
10. You will be prompted to `Select a polyline object` when it has set points on your object. Hit **\<Enter\>** to terminate. Notice all of the points are automatically set with an elevation of 100 because the software read it directly from the polyline.

Save your drawing and remain in the drawing with your initials for the next exercise.

Miscellaneous—CONVERT AUTOCAD POINTS Command

 The next tool uses the **CONVERT AUTOCAD POINTS** command to create Civil 3D points from AutoCAD points. You might use this when you have a drawing that already has points; however, they are simple AutoCAD points, without any point numbers, elevation, or descriptions.

 You may use **CONVERT AUTOCAD POINTS** when points have been created from a GIS system and you wish to use them in Civil 3D with intelligence.

Miscellaneous—CONVERT SOFTDESK POINT BLOCKS Command

 The last command in this area, **CONVERT SOFTDESK POINT BLOCKS**, creates Civil 3D points from Softdesk points. This is a legacy item for users of Softdesk software. Refer back to the discussion in the introduction to this text for information on the role Softdesk played in the development of Civil 3D software.

 You might use the **CONVERT SOFTDESK POINT BLOCKS** command when you have a drawing that already has points in it that were generated by Softdesk software and you want them to be used in Civil 3D.

Intersection-Related Point Creation Commands

The commands that are investigated next are those related to intersections of a variety of objects. These types of commands have been used in surveying for a long time, but they were possibly referred to by other terms. For instance, the first command shown in Figure 3-20, called

Figure 3-20   Direction/Direction

DIRECTION/DIRECTION, begins by asking for a point from a known position and angle toward a specific direction pointing toward infinity. It then asks for a second point and an angle also pointing toward infinity. Unless these angles are equal, producing a parallel set of vectors, they must intersect at some location. This is where a point will be created. Very often in surveying tasks, the angle would be established by using a *bearing*. This routine function then would typically be called a Bearing, Bearing intersect. Although the software does allow for the angle entry to be in bearings, it also allows for azimuths and other methods for establishing the angle; hence the name of the command is **DIRECTION/DIRECTION**, because it is not limited only to bearing entry. This next section of the text explores how these commands operate and identifies the reasons for using them.

bearings: Measure a heading and are broken into four 90° quadrants: North, South, East, and West.

Exercise 3-18: Intersection—DIRECTION/DIRECTION Command

The **DIRECTION/DIRECTION** command is used to create a point that is the result of the intersection of two vectors.

TIP   This is also called a Bearing/Bearing intersect by many surveyors.

Job Skills   There are many reasons to use this routine, but one might be that a tangent is established for the centerline of a roadway, let us call it Main Street. Another vector was established for First Avenue. While the surveyor was collecting the data, he or she determined that shooting a point at the intersection of First and Main was too dangerous due to traffic volume. However, the surveyor made a note that the vectors would continue as established, with no curves or additional bends until they met at the intersection. This would be a good example of using the **DIRECTION/DIRECTION** command to set the point at the intersection of First and Main.

To access student data files, go to www.pearsondesigncentral.com.

1. Open the drawing called My Point Style-Intersections.dwg.
2. Using the **V** for **View** command, highlight the view called **Points-A**, hit **Set Current**, and then hit **OK**.
3. Select the **Points** pull-down menu and choose the **Create Points...** command. The toolbar displays. First investigate the tools in the second button from the left. Notice the drop-down arrow to the right of the second icon from the left. It shows the information in Figure 3-20 starting with **Direction/Direction**. Select **Direction/Direction**.
4. When you are prompted to Specify a start point: Type in an *X, Y* coordinate of **850, 950**.

A tick mark displays with a rubber-banding red vector emanating from the tick, indicating an angular data entry is required. The prompt allows for **B** for bearings entry, **Z** for Azimuth entry.

5. Respond to the prompts as follows. `Specify direction at start point or [Bearing/aZimuth]`: Type **B** (for Bearing).
6. `Quadrants - NE = 1, SE = 2, SW = 3, NW = 4`, as shown in Figure 3-21.
7. `Specify quadrant (1-4) or [aZimuth/Angle]`: Type **1**
8. `Specify bearing or [aZimuth/Angle]`: Enter **64.5631**
9. `Specify an offset <0.000>`: **<Enter>**

The software not only allows for a Bearing/Bearing intersect to be computed but also allows for a Bearing, offset at a specified distance to be computed to the intersection of another Bearing, offset at a specified distance. Hit **<Enter>** for the defaulted 0.000 for these offsets. This information sets the first vector and a tick mark with a vector arrow displays. It now needs the second vector information to continue.

10. `Specify start point`: Enter **1000,950**

Figure 3-21   Quadrant angles

11. `Specify direction at start point or [Bearing/aZimuth]`: Type **B** (for Bearing).
12. `Quadrants - NE = 1, SE = 2, SW = 3, NW = 4`
13. `Specify quadrant (1-4) or [aZimuth/Angle]`: **4**
14. `Specify bearing or [aZimuth/Angle]`: **48.1752** (Figure 3-22).

Figure 3-22   Entering Bearings

15. `Specify an offset : <0.000>:` **<Enter>**
16. `Enter a point description <.>:` **IPF**
17. `Specify a point elevation <.>:` **<Enter>**
18. A point is now placed at the desired location (Figure 3-23).
19. Hit **<Esc>** to terminate.

Figure 3-23   Two angles established for Direction/Direction

Exercise 3-19: Intersection—DISTANCE/DISTANCE Command

The next routine creates a point from the intersection of two circles. You establish a center point and a radius for the first circle; a center point and a radius for the second circle; and the system computes whether one or more solutions is found, tells you about it, and then asks you to select the one point that solves your problem or allows you to accept multiple points if they are found. This is called the **DISTANCE/DISTANCE** command.

TIP   The **DISTANCE/DISTANCE** command may be used to compute an arc on a piece of property for which the radius and the starting and ending points of the arc are known, say from a curve table on a plat. Or perhaps little else is known and it needs to be drawn.

In this on-the-job example, a parcel exists on a cul-de-sac. The side lot lines are known by distance and bearings on the plat, but the only information available to draw it is the arc radius. So the trick here is to locate the center of the arc because then AutoCAD can be used to draw the arc using the **Start**, **Center and End** option. This is a great use for the **DISTANCE/DISTANCE** command because the arc begins and ends at the ends of the property lines.

To access student data files, go to www.pearsondesigncentral.com.

1. Continue in the same drawing, or open the drawing called My Point Style-Intersections.dwg.
2. Using the **V** for **View** command, highlight the view called **Points-B**, hit **Set Current**, and then hit **OK**. You see the property lines. An arc with a 50′ radius will close the property.
3. Select the **Points** pull-down menu and choose the **Create Points...** command. The toolbar displays. First investigate the tools in the second button from the left. Notice the drop-down arrow to the right of the second icon from the left. Select **Distance/Distance**. Respond to the prompts as follows.
4. Please specify a location for the radial point: Pick an **Endpoint** snap at the end of the open side of the left property line. Enter radius <0.000>: Type **50**
5. Please specify a location for the radial point: Pick an **Endpoint** snap at the end of the open side of the right property line. Enter radius <0.000>: Type **50**
6. The software computes two possible solutions and asks, Point or [All] <All>: Use the mouse to pick a point near the bottom green tick mark in Figure 3-24, because that is where the arc radius is intended to be.

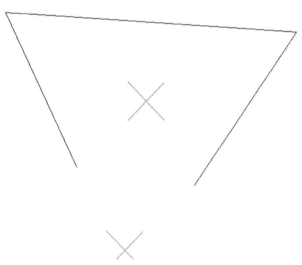

Figure 3-24   Distance/Distance command

7. Enter a point description <.>: **IPF**
8. Specify a point elevation <.>: **<Enter>**
9. Hit **<Esc>** to terminate the command when asked, Please specify a location for theradial point:, because the software thinks you will continue with more problems.
10. Now type **A** for **Arc** in AutoCAD; using the **Endpoint** osnap, select the open end of the right parcel line. Then type **C** for **Center** of arc and use the **Node** osnap to select the point you just located. Finish by using the **Endpoint** osnap and select the open end of the left parcel line. An arc now exists representing the cul-de-sac.
11. Save the file.

Exercise 3-20: Intersection—DIRECTION/DISTANCE Command

Civil 3D performs many more related functions but varies the parameters in each solution. Continue with these functions so that you try each one at least once.

TIP Perhaps you are trying to identify a conflict with a 200-year-old elm tree. The proposed roadway may be the direction vector and the tree needs to have a 55′ clearance in order to remain healthy. Does the proposed roadway conflict with this clear zone?

1. Continue in the same drawing, or open the drawing called My Point Style-Intersections.dwg.
2. Using the **Layer** command, turn on the layer called **V-Misc-Objs**.
3. Using the **V** for **View** command, highlight the view called **Points-A**, hit **Set Current**, and then hit **OK**. You see a vector arrow and a circle for which you need to compute points. Compute one or more points for where the vector crosses the circle. It has a radius of 55′.
4. Select the **Points** pull-down menu if the **Create Points** toolbar is not displayed, and choose the **Create Points...** command. The **Create Points** toolbar displays.

To access student data files, go to www.pearsondesigncentral.com.

You are still investigating the tools in the second button from the left. Using the drop-down arrow to the right of the second icon from the left, choose **Direction/Distance**. Respond to the prompts as follows.

5. `Please specify a location for the radial point:` Pick a point at the center of the circle in the view using the **Center** osnap.
6. `Enter radius <0.000>:` Type **55** for the radius.
7. `Specify start point:` Pick the left end of the vector arrow using the **Endpoint** osnap.
8. `Specify direction at start point or [Bearing/aZimuth]:` Pick the end of the vector arrow at the arrowhead using the **Endpoint** osnap.
9. `Specify an offset <0.000>:` **<Enter>** Accept 0.000 because you will not be off-setting the vector as it intersects with the circle.
10. The software solves the problem and offers two potential solutions, as shown in Figure 3-25. You can pick a point near the green tick mark to indicate your choice of solution or hit **<Enter>** for **All**. `Point or [All] <All>:` **<Enter>**
11. `Enter a point description <.>:` **IPF**
12. `Specify a point elevation <.>:` **<Enter>**
13. `Enter a point description <.>:` **IPF**
14. `Specify a point elevation <.>:` **<Enter>**
15. When asked to continue the routine with the prompt: `Please specify a location for the radial point:` Hit **<Esc>** to cancel out and terminate.

Two points exist on the perimeter of the circle where the vector would cross it, if it did. So in this example, there is a conflict between the proposed road and the tree's clear zone. The road must be moved a little farther away from the tree. Refer to Figure 3-26.

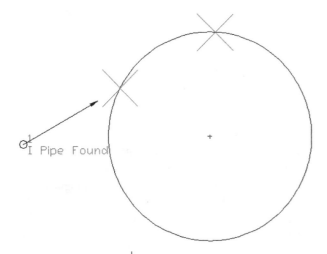

Figure 3-25   Two possible solutions

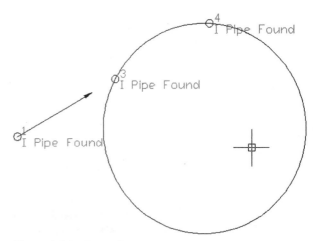

Figure 3-26   Two points are set

Exercise 3-21: Intersection—DIRECTION/PERPENDICULAR Command

 The next command, **DIRECTION/PERPENDICULAR**, can be used to compute the location of a point on a property line from the corner of a building.

 TIP   We often must locate points on a property line from the corner of a building to ensure that we have met minimum clearances to the building restriction lines or property lines as dictated by the local ordinances.

To access student data
files, go to
www.pearsondesigncentral.com.

1. Continue in the same drawing, or open the drawing called My Point Style-Intersections.dwg.
2. Using the **Layer** command, turn on the layer called **V-Misc-Objs**.
3. Using the **V** for **View** command, highlight the view called **Points-C**, hit **Set Current**, and then hit **OK**. You see a property parcel surrounding a house. Compute a point where the house corner is perpendicular to the right property line.
4. Select the **Points** pull-down menu and choose the **Create Points**... command. The **Create Points** toolbar displays.
5. Using the drop-down arrow to the right of the second icon from the left, choose **Direction/Perpendicular**. Respond to the prompts as follows.
6. `Specify start point:` Pick a point using the **Endpoint** osnap on the property corner at the top of the parcel.
7. `Specify direction at start point or [Bearing/aZimuth]:` Pick a point using the **Endpoint** osnap on the property corner at the bottom right of the parcel. A yellow vector appears on the right parcel line. Refer to Figure 3-27.

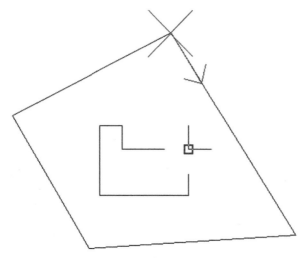

Figure 3-27   Direction/Perpendicular command

8. `Specify an offset <0.000>:` Type **10** indicating a 10′ building restriction line.
9. `Please specify a location for the perpendicular point:` Using the **Endpoint** osnap, pick a point on the right corner of the structure as shown in Figure 3-27.
10. `Enter a point description <.>:` Hit **<Enter>**
11. `Specify a point elevation <.>:` Hit **<Enter>**
12. When asked to continue the routine with the prompt: `Specify start point:` Hit **<Esc>** to cancel out and terminate.
13. A point is placed at the desired location.

Exercise 3-22: Intersection—DISTANCE/PERPENDICULAR Command

 The next command, **DISTANCE/PERPENDICULAR**, can be used to compute the location of a point on a property line from the corner of a building to a circular set of parameters.

 TIP The **DISTANCE/PERPENDICULAR** command can be used to set a point on the arc of a cul-de-sac radially from the corner of a building.

1. Continue in the same drawing, or open the drawing called My Point Style-Intersections.dwg.
2. Using the **Layer** command, turn on the layer called **V-Misc-Objs**.
3. Using the **V** for **View** command, highlight the view called **Points-B**, hit **Set Current**, and then hit **OK**. You see a property parcel surrounding a house. Compute a point where the house corner is perpendicular (or radial) to the property line.
4. Select the **Points** pull-down menu and choose the **Create Points**... command. The **Create Points** toolbar displays.
5. Using the drop-down arrow to the right of the second icon from the left, choose **Distance/Perpendicular**. Respond to the prompts as follows.
6. `Please specify a location for the radial point:` Using the **Center** osnap, pick a point on the arc to locate the radius point of the arc.
7. `Enter radius <0.000>:` Using the **Endpoint** osnap, pick a point at the end of the arc so it can compute the radius from the two points.
8. `Please specify a location for the perpendicular point:` Using the **Endpoint** osnap, pick a point at the corner of the building nearest the arc.
9. `Enter a point description <.>:` **<Enter>**
10. `Specify a point elevation <.>:` **<Enter>**
11. When asked to continue the routine with the prompt: `Please specify a location for the radial point:` Hit **<Esc>** to cancel out and terminate.

You see a point placed on the arc, radially from the corner of the house in Figure 3-28.

To access student data files, go to www.pearsondesigncentral.com.

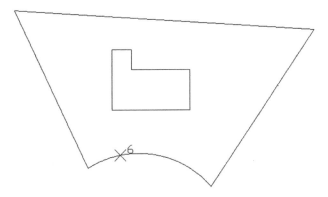

Figure 3-28   Distance/Perpendicular command

Exercise 3-23: Intersection—DIRECTION/OBJECT Command

 The next command, **DIRECTION/OBJECT**, can be used to compute a point along a direction toward an object.

 TIP An example of use for the **DIRECTION/OBJECT** command is to set the location of a point on a property line from the corner of a building to a circular set of parameters. You want to compute a point where the culvert crosses the back property line.

Job skills benefit from being able to perform geometry commands such as these because they are required skills for every designer and surveyor.

To access student data
files, go to
www.pearsondesigncentral.com.

1. Continue in the same drawing, or open the drawing called My Point Style-Intersections.dwg.
2. Using the **V** for **View** command, highlight the view called **Points-D**, hit **Set Current**, and then hit **OK**. You see a property parcel surrounding a house. Compute a point where the culvert crosses the back property line.
3. Select the **Points** pull-down menu and choose the **Create Points**... command. The **Create Points** toolbar displays.
4. Using the drop-down arrow to the right of the second icon from the left, choose **Direction/Object**. Respond to the prompts as follows.
5. `Select an arc, line, polyline, lot line, or feature line:` Pick the back property line.
6. `Specify an offset <0.000>:` **<Enter>**
7. `Specify start point:` Using the **Endpoint** osnap, pick a point at the top end of the culvert line.
8. `Specify direction at start point or [Bearing/aZimuth]:` Using the **Endpoint** osnap, pick a point at the bottom end of the culvert line.
9. `Specify an offset <0.000>:` **<Enter>**
10. `Enter a point description <.>:` **<Enter>**
11. `Specify a point elevation <.>:` **<Enter>**
12. `Select an arc, line, polyline, lot line, or feature line:` Hit **<Esc>** to cancel out and terminate.

A point is placed on the property line where the culvert crosses it. Refer to Figure 3-29.

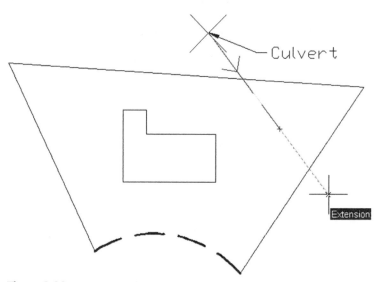

Figure 3-29   Direction/Object command

Exercise 3-24: Intersection—DISTANCE/OBJECT Command

The next command, **DISTANCE/OBJECT**, can be used to compute the location of a point(s) at a distance from an object to another object.

The **DISTANCE/OBJECT** command would allow placement of a point(s) on a property line from, say, the corner of a building to a minimum distance from the building corner.

A job skill evident in a command such as this might include being able to compute a point(s) for trees to be placed on the property line so that they are not closer to the house than 35′.

1. Continue in the same drawing, or open the drawing called My Point Style-Intersections.dwg.
2. Using the **V** for **View** command, highlight the view called **Points-D**, hit **Set Current**, and then hit **OK**. You see a property parcel surrounding a house. Compute point(s) on the right property line to plant trees no closer than 35′ from the house.
3. Select the **Points** pull-down menu and choose the **Create Points**... command. The **Create Points** toolbar displays.
4. Using the drop-down arrow to the right of the second icon from the left, choose **Distance/Object**. Respond to the prompts as follows.
5. `Select an arc, line, polyline, lot line, or feature line:` Select the right property line.
6. `Specify an offset <0.000>:` **<Enter>**
7. `Please specify a location for the radial point:` Using the **Endpoint** osnap, pick a point at the bottom right corner of the house.
8. `Enter radius <0.000>:` **35**
9. `Point or [All] <All>:` **<Enter>**
10. `Enter a point description <.>:` **<Enter>**
11. `Specify a point elevation <.>:` **<Enter>**
12. `Enter a point description <.>:` **<Enter>**
13. `Specify a point elevation <.>:` **<Enter>**
14. `Select an arc, line, lot line, or feature line:` Hit **<Esc>** to cancel out and terminate.

Two points (Figure 3-30) are placed on the property line, each at a minimum distance of 35′ from the house corner.

To access student data files, go to www.pearsondesigncentral.com.

Figure 3-30   Distance/Object command

Exercise 3-25: Intersection—OBJECT/OBJECT Command

The next command, **OBJECT/OBJECT**, can be used to compute the location of a point that results from the intersection of two objects.

You may want to compute a point where the culvert would intersect the right (or east) property line if it were to be extended.

To access student data
files, go to
www.pearsondesigncentral.com.

1. Continue in the same drawing, or open the drawing called My Point Style-Intersections.dwg.
2. Using the **V** for **View** command, highlight the view called **Points-D**, hit **Set Current**, and then hit **OK**. You see a property parcel surrounding a house. Compute a point where the culvert crosses the right property line if it were to be extended.
3. Select the **Points** pull-down menu and choose the **Create Points...** command. The **Create Points** toolbar displays.
4. Using the drop-down arrow to the right of the second icon from the left, choose **Object/Object**. Respond to the prompts as follows.
5. `Select an arc, line, polyline, lot line, or feature line:` Select the right property line.
6. `Specify an offset <0.000>:` **<Enter>**
7. `Select an arc, line, lot line, or feature line:` Select the culvert line.
8. `Specify an offset <0.000>:` **<Enter>**
9. `Enter a point description <.>:` **<Enter>**
10. `Specify a point elevation <.>:` **<Enter>**
11. `Select an arc, line, polyline, lot line, or feature line:` Hit **<Esc>** to cancel out and terminate.

Notice a new point was placed on the right property line where the culvert would cross it if it did (Figure 3-31).

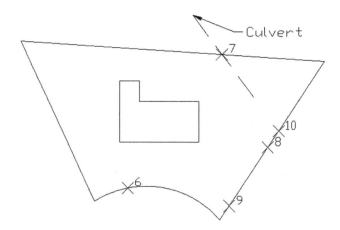

Figure 3-31   Object/Object
command

Exercise 3-26: Intersection—PERPENDICULAR Command

 The next command, **PERPENDICULAR**, can be used to compute the location of a point that results from the intersection of two objects. This command allows you to compute the perpendicular easily.

Many objects in civil engineering are perpendicular to items, and this routine simplifies these computations. For instance, side lot lines are usually perpendicular to front or back property lines, or side roads are typically perpendicular to main roads. Because computing a perpendicular is relatively easy, doing so can cut down on construction and surveying stakeout errors.

To access student data
files, go to
www.pearsondesigncentral.com.

1. Continue in the same drawing, or open the drawing called My Point Style-Intersections.dwg.
2. Using the **V** for **View** command, highlight the view called **Points-D**, hit **Set Current**, and then hit **OK**. You see a property parcel surrounding a house. Compute a point perpendicular to the back property line from a point outside the parcel.
3. Select the **Points** pull-down menu and choose the **Create Points...** command. The **Create Points** toolbar displays.
4. Using the drop-down arrow to the right of the second icon from the left, choose **Perpendicular**. Respond to the prompts as follows.

5. `Select an arc, line, polyline, lot line, or feature line:` Select the back property line.
6. `Please specify a location for the perpendicular point:` **890,1570**
7. `Enter a point description <.>:` **<Enter>**
8. `Specify a point elevation <.>:` **<Enter>**
9. `Select an arc, line, polyline, lot line, or feature line:` Hit **<Esc>** to cancel out and terminate.

A new point has been placed along the back property line as shown in Figure 3-32, indicating the perpendicular intersection to the property line from the point beginning at 890,1570.

The next several commands all have to do with computing points from criteria that intersect with alignments.

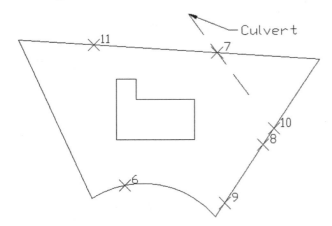

Figure 3-32 Perpendicular command

Exercise 3-27: Intersection—DIRECTION/ALIGNMENT Command

 The next command, **DIRECTION/ALIGNMENT**, can be used to compute the location of a point that results from the intersection of an angle with an alignment.

 You might use the **DIRECTION/ALIGNMENT** command to compute a point using the incoming bearing of a side road and where it intersects the main roadway, which has been defined as an alignment. The example might be similar to that used in the **DIRECTION/DIRECTION** command; however, this uses a predefined alignment.

1. Continue in the same drawing, or open the drawing called My Point Style-Intersections.dwg.
2. Using the **V** for **View** command, highlight the view called **Points-E**, hit **Set Current**, and then hit **OK**. You see an alignment. Compute a point where a bearing crosses the alignment.
3. Select the **Points** pull-down menu and choose the **Create Points**... command. The **Create Points** toolbar displays.
4. Using the drop-down arrow to the right of the second icon from the left, choose **Direction/Alignment**. Respond to the prompts as follows.
5. `Select an alignment object:` Select someplace on the alignment.
6. `Specify an offset <0.000>:` **<Enter>**
7. `Specify start point:` **50,1500**
8. `Specify direction at start point or [Bearing/aZimuth]:` **B**
9. The system reminds us of the quadrant numbers. `Quadrants - NE = 1, SE = 2, SW = 3, NW = 4`
10. `Specify quadrant (1-4) or [aZimuth/Angle]:` **3**
11. `Specify bearing or [aZimuth/Angle]:` **60.4931**
12. `Specify an offset <0.000>:` **<Enter>**
13. `Enter a point description <.>:` **<Enter>**
14. `Specify a point elevation <.>:` **<Enter>**
15. `Select an alignment object:` Hit **<Esc>** to cancel out and terminate.

Notice that a new point has been placed on the alignment between stations 3+50 and 4+00.

To access student data files, go to www.pearsondesigncentral.com.

Exercise 3-28: Intersection—DISTANCE/ALIGNMENT Command

The next command, **DISTANCE/ALIGNMENT**, can be used to compute the location of a point that results from the intersection of a circular distance from a point with an alignment.

The **DISTANCE/ALIGNMENT** command could be used to compute a point 100′ from the end of an alignment.

To access student data files, go to www.pearsondesigncentral.com.

1. Continue in the same drawing, or open the drawing called My Point Style-Intersections.dwg.
2. Using the **V** for **View** command, highlight the view called **Points-E**, hit **Set Current**, and then hit **OK**. You see an alignment. Compute a point 100′ from the end of the alignment.
3. Select the **Points** pull-down menu and choose the **Create Points**... command. The **Create Points** toolbar displays.
4. Using the drop-down arrow to the right of the second icon from the left, choose **Distance/Alignment**. Respond to the prompts as follows.
5. `Select an alignment object:` Select someplace on the alignment.
6. `Specify an offset <0.000>:` **<Enter>**
7. `Please specify a location for the radial point:` Using the **Endpoint** os-nap, pick a point at the northern end of the alignment.
8. `Enter radius <0.000>:` **100**
9. `Enter a point description <.>:` **<Enter>**
10. `Specify a point elevation <.>:` **<Enter>**
11. `Select an alignment object:` Hit **<Esc>** to cancel out and terminate.

Notice that a point was placed at around station 6+00 on the alignment.

Exercise 3-29: Intersection—OBJECT/ALIGNMENT Command

The next command, **OBJECT/ALIGNMENT**, can be used to compute the location of a point that results from the intersection of a circular distance from a point with an alignment.

You might use the **OBJECT/ALIGNMENT** command to compute a point on the alignment where a culvert crosses the alignment.

The job skill apparent in this routine is that designers and surveyors need these types of computations on a daily basis because utilities intersect with alignments routinely.

To access student data files, go to www.pearsondesigncentral.com.

1. Continue in the same drawing, or open the drawing called My Point Style-Intersections.dwg.
2. Using the **V** for **View** command, highlight the view called **Points-E**, hit **Set Current**, and then hit **OK**. You see an alignment. Compute a point on the alignment where a culvert crosses the alignment.
3. Select the **Points** pull-down menu and choose the **Create Points**... command. The **Create Points** toolbar displays.
4. Using the drop-down arrow to the right of the second icon from the left, choose **Object/Alignment**. Respond to the prompts as follows.
5. `Select an alignment object:` Select someplace on the alignment.
6. `Specify an offset <0.000>:` **<Enter>**
7. `Select an arc, line, polyline, lot line, or feature line:` Select someplace on the culvert that is around station 1+25.

8. `Specify an offset <0.000>:` **\<Enter>**
9. `Enter a point description <.>:` **\<Enter>**
10. `Specify a point elevation <.>:` **\<Enter>**
11. `Select an alignment object:` Hit **\<Esc>** to cancel out and terminate.

Notice that a point was placed at around station 1+25 on the alignment exactly where the culvert crossed the alignment.

Exercise 3-30: Intersection—ALIGNMENT/ALIGNMENT Command

 The next command, **ALIGNMENT/ALIGNMENT**, can be used to compute the location of a point that results from the intersection of one alignment to another alignment.

 You might use the **ALIGNMENT/ALIGNMENT** command to compute a point where a 12′ edge of pavement on the main road meets the 12′ edge of pavement for the side street.

1. Continue in the same drawing, or open the drawing called My Point Style-Intersections.dwg.
2. Using the **V** for **View** command, highlight the view called **Points-F**, hit **Set Current**, and then hit **OK**. You see an alignment. Compute a point where a 12′ edge of pavement on the main road meets the 12′ edge of pavement for the side street.
3. Select the **Points** pull-down menu and choose the **Create Points**... command. The **Create Points** toolbar displays.
4. Using the drop-down arrow to the right of the second icon from the left, choose **Alignment/Alignment**. Respond to the prompts as follows.
5. `Select an alignment object:` Select someplace on the longer alignment (it has a curve in it).
6. `Specify an offset <0.000>:` **12**
7. `Select an alignment object:` Select someplace on the shorter alignment (it has no curve in it).
8. `Specify an offset <12.000>:` **\<Enter>**
9. `Enter a point description <.>:` **\<Enter>**
10. `Specify a point elevation <.>:` **\<Enter>**
11. `Select an alignment object:` Hit **\<Esc>** to cancel out and terminate.

To access student data files, go to www.pearsondesigncentral.com.

Notice that a point was placed at around station 3+00 on the main road alignment at a 12′ offset. If an offset of **-12** were provided, the point would be on the left side of the roadway.

These commands and exercises conclude the Intersection-based commands in Civil 3D.

Alignment-Related Point Commands

The next set of **POINT CREATION** commands have to do with Alignments. An alignment must exist for these to do their job.

Exercise 3-31: Alignment—STATION/OFFSET Command

 The next command, **STATION/OFFSET**, can be used to compute the location of a point(s) that have station and offset values relative to an alignment.

 The **STATION/OFFSET** command might be used to locate Planimetric features such as fire hydrants or mailboxes at a variety of stations when they are a standard distance off the face of a curb.

Surveyors usually develop stakeout points at the end of every project to identify for the construction contractor where structures need to be built. This routine accomplishes that.

To access student data files, go to www.pearsondesigncentral.com.

1. Continue in the same drawing, or open the drawing called My Point Style-Intersections.dwg.
2. Using the **V** for **View** command, highlight the view called **Points-G**, hit **Set Current**, and then hit **OK**. You see an alignment. Compute points representing mailboxes at the stations provided at offsets that are 16′ to the right and left of the roadway centerline.
3. Select the **Points** pull-down menu and choose the **Create Points**... command. The **Create Points** toolbar displays.
4. Using the drop-down arrow to the right of the third icon from the left, choose **Station/Offset**. Respond to the prompts as follows.
5. `Select alignment:` Select someplace on the alignment.
6. `Specify station along alignment:` **75**
7. `Specify an offset <0.000>:` **16** (which indicates 16′ to the right of the alignment).
8. `Enter a point description <.>:` **MB**
9. `Specify a point elevation <.>:` **<Enter>**
10. `Specify station along alignment:` **75**
11. `Specify an offset <16.000>:` **-16**
12. `Enter a point description <.>:` **MB**
13. `Specify a point elevation <.>:` **<Enter>**
14. `Specify station along alignment:` **150**
15. `Specify an offset <-16.000>:` **<Enter>**
16. `Enter a point description <.>:` **MB**
17. `Specify a point elevation <.>:` **<Enter>**
18. `Specify station along alignment:` **150**
19. `Specify an offset <-16.000>:` **16**
20. `Enter a point description <.>:` **MB**
21. `Specify a point elevation <.>:` **<Enter>**
22. `Specify station along alignment:` **225**
23. `Specify an offset <16.000>:` **<Enter>**
24. `Enter a point description <.>:` **MB**
25. `Specify a point elevation <.>:` **<Enter>**
26. `Specify station along alignment:` **225**
27. `Specify an offset <16.000>:` **-16**
28. `Enter a point description <.>:` **MB**
29. `Specify a point elevation <.>:` **<Enter>**
30. `Specify station along alignment:` **300**
31. `Specify an offset <-16.000>:` **<Enter>**
32. `Enter a point description <.>:` **MB**
33. `Specify a point elevation <.>:` **<Enter>**
34. `Specify station along alignment:` **300**
35. `Specify an offset <-16.000>:` **16**
36. `Enter a point description <.>:` **MB**
37. `Specify a point elevation <.>:` **<Enter>**
38. `Specify station along alignment:` **<Enter>** to terminate.

Figure 3-33 shows eight points representing mailboxes that will be placed along the alignment at the specified stations and 16′ to the right and left of the roadway up to station 3+00.

Exercise 3-32: Alignment—DIVIDE ALIGNMENT Command

The next command, **DIVIDE ALIGNMENT**, can be used to compute the location of a point(s) that have station and offset values relative to an alignment.

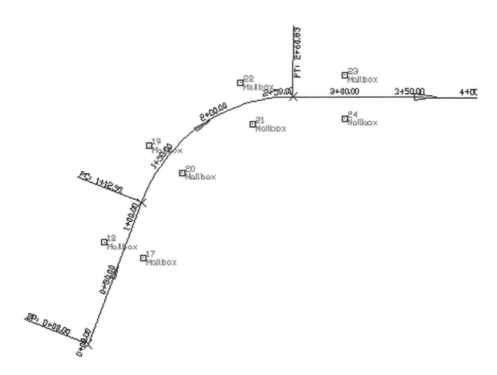

Figure 3-33 Station/ Offset command

> The **DIVIDE ALIGNMENT** command might be used to compute points for the excavation for tree bulbs such that there are 22 trees planted at an offset of 50′ to the right side of the roadway following construction.

1. Continue in the same drawing, or open the drawing called My Point Style-Intersections.dwg.
2. Using the **V** for **View** command, highlight the view called **Points-G**, hit **Set Current**, and then hit **OK**. You see an alignment. Compute points for the excavation for tree bulbs such that there are 22 trees planted on the right side of the roadway following construction.
3. Select the **Points** pull-down menu and choose the **Create Points**... command. The **Create Points** toolbar displays.
4. Using the drop-down arrow to the right of the third icon from the left, choose **Divide Alignment**. Respond to the prompts as follows.
5. `Select alignment:` Select someplace on the alignment.
6. `Enter the number of segments <1>:` **21**
7. `Specify an offset <0.000>:` **50**, which indicates that they will be placed to the right side.
8. `Enter a point description <.>:` **<Enter>**
9. `Specify a point elevation <.>:` **<Enter>**

Continue hitting **<Enter>** as the software prompts for point descriptions and point elevations until it is finished putting 22 points on the right side of the road. When prompted to Select alignment: hit **<Enter>** to terminate. You see the points on the right side of the road.

To access student data files, go to www.pearsondesigncentral.com.

Exercise 3-33: Alignment—MEASURE ALIGNMENT Command

 The next command, **MEASURE ALIGNMENT**, can be used to compute the location of a point(s) that has station and offset values relative to an alignment.

> The **MEASURE ALIGNMENT** command might be used to compute points for the stake-out of the road. You may want points placed at 25′ intervals at an offset of 50′ to the left side of the roadway.

A large part of a surveyor's job is to produce construction stakeout points for roadways, and this is exactly how they would be developed.

To access student data files, go to www.pearsondesigncentral.com.

1. Continue in the same drawing, or open the drawing called My Point Style-Intersections.dwg.
2. Using the **V** for **View** command, highlight the view called **Points-G**, hit **Set Current**, and then hit **OK**. You see an alignment. Place points at 25′ intervals at an offset of 50′ to the left side of the roadway.
3. Select the **Points** pull-down menu and choose the **Create Points**... command. The **Create Points** toolbar displays.
4. Using the drop-down arrow to the right of the third icon from the left, choose **Measure Alignment**. Respond to the prompts as follows.
5. `Select alignment:` Select someplace on the alignment.
6. `Starting station <0+00.00>:` **<Enter>**
7. `Ending station <6+58.53>:` **<Enter>**
8. `Specify an offset <0.000>:` **-50**, which indicates that the points will be on the left side of the road.
9. `Enter an interval <10.000>:` **25**
10. `Enter a point description <.>:` **<Enter>**
11. `Specify a point elevation <.>:` **<Enter>**

Continue hitting **<Enter>** as the software prompts for point descriptions and point elevations until it is finished putting points on the left side of the road. When prompted to `Select alignment:` hit **<Enter>** again to terminate. You see the points on the left side of the road in Figure 3-34.

Figure 3-34 Measure Alignment command

Exercise 3-34: Alignment—AT GEOMETRY POINTS Command

The next command, **AT GEOMETRY POINTS**, can be used to compute the location of a point(s) that has station and offset values relative to an alignment.

TIP You want points placed at the geometrically important locations of the alignment; namely, the Points of Curvature (PCs), Points of Tangency (PTs), Spiral to Curve, Radius Points, and Points of Intersections (or PIs). If spirals are included, their corresponding points will be placed as well. These are defined and detailed in Chapter 6 on alignments. With these points identified, a surveyor has the criteria needed to lay out the centerline of the road on the construction site.

1. Continue in the same drawing, or open the drawing called My Point Style-Intersections.dwg.
2. Using the **V** for **View** command, highlight the view called **Points-G**, hit **Set Current**, and then hit **OK**. You see an alignment. Place points at the geometrically important locations of the alignment.
3. Select the **Points** pull-down menu and choose the **Create Points**... command. The **Create Points** toolbar displays.
4. Using the drop-down arrow to the right of the third icon from the left, choose **At Geometry Points**. Respond to the prompts as follows.
5. `Select alignment:` Select someplace on the alignment.
6. `Starting station <0+00.00>:` **<Enter>**
7. `Ending station <6+58.53>:` **<Enter>**
8. `Specify a point elevation <.>:` **<Enter>**
9. `Specify a point elevation <.>:` **<Enter>**

Continue hitting **<Enter>** as the software prompts for point elevations until it is finished putting points on the alignment. When prompted to `Select alignment:` hit **<Enter>** again to terminate. You see the points located at all of the critical geometric points of the road. The point descriptions are automatic because they relate to the point being located such as the BOA (Beginning of Alignment), EOA (End of Alignment), PC, PT, PI, or RP.

Exercise 3-35: Alignment—RADIAL OR PERPENDICULAR Command

 The next command, **RADIAL OR PERPENDICULAR**, can be used to compute the location of a point(s) that has station and offset values relative to an alignment.

 TIP You often need to compute points at radial or perpendicular locations from an alignment.

This command can be used to locate where a side street may intersect the roadway.

1. Continue in the same drawing, or open the drawing called My Point Style-Intersections.dwg.
2. Using the **V** for **View** command, highlight the view called **Points-G**, hit **Set Current**, and then hit **OK**. You see an alignment. Place points at radial or perpendicular locations on the alignment.
3. Select the **Points** pull-down menu and choose the **Create Points**... command. The **Create Points** toolbar displays.
4. Using the drop-down arrow to the right of the third icon from the left, choose **Radial or Perpendicular**. Respond to the prompts as follows.
5. `Select alignment:` Select someplace on the alignment.
6. `Specify a point that is radial or perpendicular to the current alignment:` Pick a point using the **Endpoint** osnap at the end of the arc at station 5+77.23. The software will confirm this as Station: 5+77.23 with Offset: 74.096′ (Figure 3-35).
7. `Enter a point description <.>:` **<Enter>**
8. `Specify a point elevation <.>:` **<Enter>**
9. `Select alignment:` **<Enter>** to terminate.

Exercise 3-36: Alignment—IMPORT FROM FILE Command

 The next command, **IMPORT FROM FILE**, can be used to import points that were generated based on an alignment and use station, offset values relative to that alignment. The software uses the next available point numbers and prompts for the information needed as it goes.

To access student data files, go to www.pearsondesigncentral.com.

To access student data files, go to www.pearsondesigncentral.com.

Figure 3-35   Radial or Perpendicular command

To access student data
files, go to
www.pearsondesigncentral.com.

1. Continue in the same drawing, or open the drawing called My Point Style-Intersections.dwg.
2. Using the **V** for **View** command, highlight the view called **Points-G**, hit **Set Current**, and then hit **OK**. You see an alignment. Import alignment based points.
3. Select the **Points** pull-down menu and choose the **Create Points...** command. The **Create Points** toolbar displays.
4. Using the drop-down arrow to the right of the third icon from the left, choose **Import from File**.

To access student data
files, go to
www.pearsondesigncentral.com.

5. A dialog box opens called **Import Alignment Station and Offset File**. Select the file called **Points-import file-sta-off.txt** in the Support files folder for this textbook and hit the **Open** button.
6. The software then prompts you to choose the format for this file. The options are as follows: `1. Station, Offset, 2. Station, Offset, Elevation, 3. Station, Offset, Rod Reading, HI, 4. Station, Offset, Description, 5. Station, Offset, Elevation, Description, 6. Station, Offset, Rod Reading, HI Description`.
7. `Enter file format (1/2/3/4/5/6):<0>:` **1** (This file uses format 1, station, offset.)
8. It then needs to know what the delimiter is between data items. Our file uses commas.
9. `1. Space, 2. Comma`
10. `Enter a delimiter (1/2): <0>:` **2**
11. `Enter an invalid indicator for Station Offset <-99999>:` **<Enter>**
12. `Select alignment:` pick alignment.

Notice that several points enter the file to the left and right of the alignment as shown in Figure 3-36.

This concludes the segment on placing Alignment-based points into your project. The file My Point Style-Intersections-Complete.dwg shows the results of these examples.

Surface-Related Point Commands

This next segment delves into procedures for placing Surface-related points into a project drawing.

The next command in this toolbar item is for creating new points based on an alignment's profile information. This can be used for creating 3D stakeout data of the roadway's crown, for example. The command is called **PROFILE GEOMETRY POINTS**. You are requested to select the alignment and the profile in question. The software then sets the points on the alignment with 3D elevations.

The ability to adjust point elevations based on a surface also exists. This is a very beneficial routine if points have been set to a surface using the **RANDOM POINTS** command. If the surface is modified and updated, the points that were dependent on that surface can be updated automatically. Change the elevation for a point or a group of points by selecting a location on a surface. This command can be found under the **Points** pulldown >> **Edit Points** >> **Elevations from Surface...**

Figure 3-36   Import from File command

Exercise 3-37: Surface—RANDOM POINTS Command

 The next command, **RANDOM POINTS** (Figure 3-37), can be used to set points based on surface data.

Figure 3-37   Random Points command

 The elevation values for these points are extracted directly from the surface information. This avoids having to hand-calculate the elevations and place them in manually. Hand calculations are prone to typographical errors and miscalculation.

The software uses the next available point numbers and prompts for other information as it goes.

1. Open the drawing called Chapter 3-a.dwg.
2. Using the **V** for **View** command, highlight the view called **Points-H**, hit **Set Current**, and then hit **OK**. You see a surface. Set some points based on this surface.
3. Select the **Points** pull-down menu and choose the **Create Points**... command. The **Create Points** toolbar displays.
4. In the **Create Points** toolbar, and using the drop-down arrow to the right of the fourth icon from the left, choose **Random Points**.

To access student data files, go to www.pearsondesigncentral.com.

Figure 3-38   Closed contours

You see some closed contours in the view (Figure 3-38), and you will be placing a couple of points within the closed contours to give others an idea of the elevations in this area. Respond to the prompts as follows.

5. `Select a surface object:` Pick any contour for the surface.
6. `Please specify a location for the new point:` Select a point within one of the closed contours, as shown in Figure 3-38, for Point 1.
7. `Enter a point description <.>:` **FG**
8. `Please specify a location for the new point:` Select a point within one of the closed contours, as shown in Figure 3-38, for Point 2.
9. `Enter a point description <FG>:` **<Enter>**
10. `Please specify a location for the new point:` Select a point within one of the closed contours, as shown in Figure 3-38, for Point 3.
11. `Enter a point description <FG>:` **<Enter>**
12. `Please specify a location for the new point:` **<Enter>**
13. `Select a surface object:` **<Enter>** to terminate.

Exercise 3-38: Surface—ON GRID Command

 The next command, **ON GRID**, can be used to set points in a grid based on surface data. The elevation values are extracted directly from the surface information. This avoids having to hand-calculate the elevations and place them in manually. The software uses the next available point numbers and prompts for other information as it goes.

 You often need to place points on the corners of a grid overlaid onto a surface. It provides a representative sampling of the elevations occurring on that surface.

 If the **ON GRID** command is used on a Grid Volume type of surface, you can achieve cut and fill values of the proposed work as compared with those of the existing surface.

To access student data
files, go to
www.pearsondesigncentral.com.

1. Continue in the same drawing, or open the drawing called Chapter 3-a.dwg.
2. Using the **V** for **View** command, highlight the view called **Points-H**, hit **Set Current**, and then hit **OK**. You see a surface. Set some points based on this surface.
3. Select the **Points** pull-down menu and choose the **Create Points**... command. The **Create Points** toolbar displays.
4. Using the drop-down arrow to the right of the fourth icon from the left, choose **On Grid**. Respond to the prompts as follows.
5. `Select a surface object:` Pick any contour for the surface.
6. `Specify a grid basepoint:` **14900,18275**
7. `Grid rotation <0.0000 (d)>:` **<Enter>**
8. `Grid X spacing <5.0000>:` **50**
9. `Grid Y spacing <50.0000>:` **<Enter>**
10. `Specify the upper right location for the grid:` **15150,18475**
11. `Change the size or rotation of the grid/grid squares [Yes/No] <No>:` **N**
12. `Enter a point description <.>:` **FG**
13. Continue hitting **<Enter>** as the software prompts for point descriptions until it is finished putting points on the grid. When prompted to `Select a surface:` again, hit **<Enter>** to terminate. See Figure 3-39.

Figure 3-39 Points set on a Grid

Exercise 3-39: Surface—ALONG POLYLINE/CONTOUR Command

The next command, **ALONG POLYLINE/CONTOUR**, can be used to set points on a polyline or contour at a user-defined interval. The elevation values are extracted directly from the surface information. This can be used to set points on an alignment directly from the surface in 3D. The software uses the next available point numbers and prompts for other information as it goes.

TIP   The **ALONG POLYLINE/CONTOUR** command can be used to set the rim elevations of manholes with a distance of 300′ between manholes on the proposed road surface.

1. Continue in the same drawing, or open the drawing called Chapter 3-a.dwg.
2. Using the **V** for **View** command, highlight the view called **Points-H**, hit **Set Current**, and then hit **OK**. You see a surface and a polyline along the road running east to west. Set some points based on this surface right on the polyline.
3. Select the **Points** pull-down menu and choose the **Create Points**... command. The **Create Points** toolbar displays.

To access student data
files, go to
www.pearsondesigncentral.com.

4. Using the drop-down arrow to the right of the fourth icon from the left, choose **Along Polyline/Contour**. Respond to the prompts as follows.
5. `Select a surface object:` Pick any contour for the surface.
6. `Distance between points <10.0000>:` **50**
7. `Select a polyline or contour:` Select the Polyline with the heavy lineweight.
8. `Enter a point description <.>:` **FG**
9. Continue hitting **<Enter>** as the software continues to place a point every 50′ along the alignment. Hit **<Enter>** to terminate.

Notice in Figure 3-40 that the polyline now has points every 50′ along it.

Figure 3-40 Along Polyline/Contour command

Exercise 3-40: Surface—POLYLINE/CONTOUR VERTICES Command

 The next command, **POLYLINE/CONTOUR VERTICES**, can be used to set points on a polyline or contour at the vertices of the polyline, and elevation values are extracted directly from the surface information. This can be used to set points on a building pad when the surface already has the pad elevations built into it. The software uses the next available point numbers and prompts for other information as it goes.

TIP This routine can be used for many tasks such as establishing a daylight buffer for grading a site out. A polyline can be drawn at an offset from the property boundary, and points can be established on this polyline from the existing ground surface. When those points are included in the Proposed ground surface, they ensure a tie-out to the existing ground. This example sets points on the centerline based on the existing ground surface.

To access student data files, go to www.pearsondesigncentral.com.

1. Continue in the same drawing, or open the drawing called Chapter 3-a.dwg.
2. Using the **V** for **View** command, highlight the view called **Points-H**, hit **Set Current**, and then hit **OK**. You see a surface and a polyline along the road running east to west.
3. Select the **Points** pull-down menu and choose the **Create Points...** command. The **Create Points** toolbar displays.
4. Using the drop-down arrow to the right of the fourth icon from the left, choose **Polyline/Contour Vertices**. Respond to the prompts as follows.
5. `Select a surface object:` Pick any contour for the surface.
6. `Select a polyline or contour:` Select the rectangular polyline.
7. `Enter a point description <.>:` **FG**, continue hitting **<Enter>** until points are placed at all the corners, hit **<Enter>** to terminate.

Notice that points now exist on the building corners.
This concludes our segment on placing Surface-based points into your project.

Exercise 3-41: IMPORT POINTS Command

To access student data files, go to www.pearsondesigncentral.com.

To access student data files, go to www.pearsondesigncentral.com.

 Our next command is **IMPORT POINTS** and can be used to import point data from an external file. A good option within this routine is the ability to create a point group as it executes.

1. Continue in the same drawing, or open the drawing called Chapter 3-a.dwg.
2. Using the **V** for View command, highlight the view called **Points-L,** hit **Set Current** and then hit **OK**. You will see existing ground contours. We will import point data from a file provided with your data set for this text.

3. Select the **Points** pull-down menu and choose the **Create Points**... command. The **Create Points** toolbar displays.

4. Use the seventh icon from the left to choose **Import Points**. A dialog will display. Use the **PNEZD (comma delimited)** format option. A display of other formats is shown in Figure 3-41. PNEZD stands for Point, Northing, Easting, Elevation, Description.

Autodesk Uploadable File
ENZ (comma delimited)
ENZ (space delimited)
External Project Point Database
NEZ (comma delimited)
NEZ (space delimited)
PENZ (comma delimited)
PENZ (space delimited)
PENZD (comma delimited)
PENZD (space delimited)
PNE (comma delimited)
PNE (space delimited)
PNEZ (comma delimited)
PNEZ (space delimited)
PNEZD (comma delimited)
PNEZD (space delimited)

Figure 3-41   Formats

5. Select the source file in the student data files called **POINTS-IMPORT FILE-PNEZD.TXT**.

6. Toggle **On** the **Add Points** to **Point Group** option as shown in Figure 3-42.

7. Hit the button to the right of the pop-down window and provide a name for the new Point Group called **Import-EG Points**.

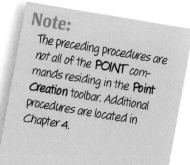

Figure 3-42   Import Points, Add Points to Point Group

8. Turn **Off** the toggles for the **Advanced Options** and hit **OK**.

9. The points in this file are imported into the project shown in Figure 3-43 and are in the preset view called **Points-L**.

10. Save this drawing as we will use it again later.

Note:
The preceding procedures are not all of the **POINT** commands residing in the **Point Creation** toolbar. Additional procedures are located in Chapter 4.

You will also notice that the **Prospector** tab in the **Toolspace** (Figure 3-44) shows the new Point Group called **Import-EG Points**. When selected, it displays all of the points within the group.

Figure 3-43 Imported Points

Figure 3-44 Prospector tab shows the new Point Group

TIP

There is one additional icon on the far right of the toolbar. This allows for the toolbar to be expanded or contracted. If it is expanded, some fields show up that allow for the creation of Point Styles, Point Label Styles, and Point Layers in the event you would like to create or switch these on the fly. Also, notice that a pushpin is included in the banner of the toolbar. This pins the toolbar, placing it in a fixed location, and also shrinks the toolbar down to a small placeholder when the cursor moves outside the toolbar. To display the expanded toolbar, move the cursor over the placeholder.

Continue with the Points Pull-Down Menu

Next is a discussion of some other capabilities within the **Points** pull-down menu in Civil 3D (Figure 3-45).

The **CREATE POINT GROUP...** command allows the creation of point groups such as the one created in Exercise 3-41 on **Import Points**.

Figure 3-45   The Points pull-down menu

The **EDIT POINTS, POINTS...** commands modify points. The choices follow.

- **Points...** allowing for the tabular editing of point data where the **Panorama** displays with cells of all pertinent point data as shown in Figure 3-46. By clicking in a cell, you can edit the information on the fly. By checking the green check mark on the upper right of the box, you can effect the change immediately.

Point Number	Easting	Northing	Point Elevation	Name	Raw Description	Full Description	Description
3	14561.9281'	18563.3096'	325.528'		FG	FG	
4	14611.6411'	18557.9596'	324.513'		FG	FG	
5	14661.3540'	18552.6095'	325.148'		FG	FG	
6	14711.0670'	18547.2595'	325.913'		FG	FG	
7	14760.7799'	18541.9094'	326.654'		FG	FG	
8	14810.4929'	18536.5594'	327.387'		FG	FG	
9	14860.2058'	18531.2094'	328.070'		FG	FG	
10	14909.9188'	18525.8598'	328.965'		FG	FG	
11	14959.6603'	18520.7844'	329.820'		FG	FG	
12	15009.4510'	18516.2160'	330.445'		FG	FG	

Figure 3-46   Point Editor Panorama box

- **Point Groups...** (Figure 3-47) allows you to change the display order for point groups in a drawing and allows for updating out-of-date point groups. This dialog box can also be used to select a point group when you need it for an application such as adding a point group to a surface data set. The **Show Point Group Differences** button in the top left of the dialog box allows for reviewing and updating out-of-date point groups. The **Update Point Group** button, the second button in the top left of the dialog box, allows updating all out-of-date point groups. A point group is out of date when an exclamation mark within a yellow shield is displayed next to a point group name.

- **Datum...** updates points that were set, perhaps to an assumed elevation, to a corrected benchmark elevation. Points with no elevation values are not adjusted. Points that need to be changed individually can be altered via the **Edit/List Points** command. This command does not really warrant further procedure because it asks only one question, `Change in elevation or .[Reference]:` to which you type in the amount of elevation change you want to accomplish.

Figure 3-47   Point Groups

- **Elevations from Surface...** assigns surface elevations to a feature line, survey figure, parcel line, or 3D polyline.
- **Renumber...** allows points to be renumbered by using an additive factor. In other words, say that you have points already set from Point 1 through Point 115. Now a field crew is bringing in a new set of points that happen to overlap your point numbers. You cannot have multiple points with the same point number, so something has to give and someone must renumber his or her points. In Civil 3D, use the **Renumber** command to add a factor of, say, 1000 to the points already set and you then have points ranging from 1001 to 1115, thereby clearing the way for new points in the 1 to 115 range. This command does not really warrant further procedure because it asks only one question, `Enter an additive factor for point numbers:` to which you type in the amount of change you want to add to the existing numbering.

Exercise 3-42: Creating Automated Tables—ADD TABLES Command

The next command in the **Points** pull-down menu is the **ADD TABLES...** command. Refer to Figure 3-48. This builds point tables based on the points or point groups in the drawing.

Figure 3-48   Creating Automated Tables

1. Continue in the same drawing, or open the drawing called Chapter 3-a.dwg. Type **Z** **<Enter> for Zoom and E <Enter> for Extents**..

2. Under the **Points** pull-down menu, choose the **Add Tables...** command. A **Point Table Creation** dialog box displays.

3. If you want a customized table for the points, select a predeveloped one under the **Table style** pop-down or use the arrow in the drop-down arrow next to the icon just to the right of the **Table style** window. Select **Create New** or **Edit Current Selection** to customize a table. In this example, click the **Edit Current Selection** and the **Table Style—Standard** dialog box opens, shown in Figure 3-49. Under the **Information** tab, you can change the name, which would make sense if you selected **New**. Otherwise, choose the **Data Properties** tab, where you can elect to wrap text or to have the table maintain view orientation (in the event that your view is twisted to accommodate a plotting orientation). Also you can affect how your titling and column headers display when the table splits, if it is set up to split. **Title style**, **Header style**, and **Data style** are selected here as well. In the **Structure** window, the table can be customized to show any related columns that you wish.

To access student data files, go to www.pearsondesigncentral.com.

Figure 3-49 Table Style dialog box

4. You can customize this table to show latitude and longitudinal values along with the co-ordinates, point numbers, and elevations for the points in your drawing. The buttons to the right of the window allow you to **add** columns or **delete** them. Hit the **Plus** button to add a column. A new column becomes available next to the **Easting** column, albeit with no header yet.

5. Double-click on the blank header and a **Text Component Editor—Column Contents** dialog box appears. In the black window, type **Latitude** and hit **OK**.

6. Now double-click in the cell in the **Latitude** column and in the **Column Value** row. A **Text Component Editor—Column Contents** dialog box opens. Make sure you are in the **Properties** tab. In the **Properties** pop-down, select **Latitude** from the alternatives.

7. Then click the **arrow** button just to the right of the window, to send the option into the black window on the right.

8. Notice that you can choose the **Format** tab and change text properties if you wish. Hit **OK**. You are in the **Table Style—Standard** dialog box again.

9. Repeat this sequence to add in the longitudinal information.
10. Hit the **Plus** button to add a column. A new column becomes available next to the **Latitude** column, again with no header yet.
11. Double-click on the blank header and a **Text Component Editor—Column Contents** dialog box appears. As shown in Figure 3-50, in the black window, type **Longitude** and hit **OK**.

Figure 3-50 Text Component Editor

12. Now double-click in the cell in the **Longitude** column and in the **Column Value** row. A **Text Component Editor—Column Contents** dialog box opens, shown in Figure 3-51. Make sure you are in the **Properties** tab. In the **Properties** pop-down, select **Longitude** from the alternatives.

Figure 3-51 Text Component Editor—Column Contents

13. Then click the **arrow** button just to the right of the window, to send the option into the black window on the right.
14. Notice that you can choose the **Format** tab and change text properties if you wish. Hit **OK**. You are in the **Table Style—Standard** dialog box again.
15. Click on the **Display** tab (Figure 3-52). Here you can set colors, component layers, and such for appearance's sake. Hit **OK**.
16. You are in the **Point Table Creation** dialog box.
17. In the center of the dialog box, hit the button where it says **No Point Groups** selected.
18. Choose the Point Group created in the **Import Points** exercise called **Import EG-Points**, and hit **OK**. The dialog box should now appear as in Figure 3-48.
19. Leave the **Split table** option checked **On** and retain the default values.
20. Hit **OK**. When prompted for `Select upper left corner:` pick a point well outside the site and off to the right.

Figure 3-52   Table Style Display

21. The table appears with the data it had initially as well as with the latitude and longitude because the file has a geodetic datum established for northern Virginia, NAD 83, U.S. foot.

The next command in the **Points** pull-down menu are the **UTILITIES** commands, which include the following:

- **Quick View Project** displays a tick mark where points exist in the external project point information, assuming one exists.

- **Draw Project Extents** draws a rectangle around the extents of the project's points from external project point information, assuming one exists.

- **Zoom to Project Extents** places your view as if it did a **ZOOM EXTENTS** of the project's points from external project point information, assuming one exists.

- **Replace Softdesk Point Blocks** converts Softdesk point blocks to AutoCAD Civil 3D points.

- **Convert Land Desktop Points...** converts AutoCAD Land Desktop points to AutoCAD Civil 3D points.

- **Convert from AutoCAD Points** converts AutoCAD point objects to AutoCAD Civil 3D points.

- **Create Blocks from COGO Points...** creates blocks at the location of specified COGO point locations.

- **Geodetic Calculator** allows for computing a coordinate from a lat/long, or a lat/long from a coordinate, once a geodetic zone is set in the file.

CHAPTER SUMMARY

Understanding and using points is essential to civil engineering. Points are locations in space defined by X, Y, and Z values; they are used to identify objects such as property corners. This chapter discussed computation methods and concepts necessary for performing computations; coordinate systems; Point Groups; and Description Key Sets. It then moved into point computations using commands found on the **Create Points** toolbar.

CHAPTER TEST QUESTIONS

Multiple Choice

1. Some uses for points in civil engineering and surveying are:

   a. Property corners for parcels of ownership
   b. Roadway earthworks computations
   c. Developing renderings and animations
   d. None of the above

2. Point groups have the following characteristics:

   a. They have enduring properties that can be easily reviewed or modified, either beforehand or retroactively.
   b. Displaying a points list shows the points included in a point group and it can be updated automatically.
   c. A point group can be locked to avoid unintentional modifications.
   d. All of the above

3. Which of the following codes can be used in the Description Key Set?

   a. AC
   b. YARDINLET
   c. 1033
   d. All of the above

4. The **Point Creation** toolbar allows for the following operation:

   a. Automatically checking that all points on a project are correct
   b. Setting points by snapping to objects
   c. Setting all points to the correct elevational value required by the project
   d. None of the above

5. Points can be created for which of the following circumstances?

   a. Locating points related to alignments
   b. Locating points related to surfaces
   c. Importing points from external files
   d. All of the above

6. Points can be established when the user has which of the following criteria?

   a. Elevations
   b. A starting point, a distance, and a grade
   c. A starting point and a slope
   d. All of the above

7. Points can be:

   a. Defined or set
   b. Edited or modified
   c. Reported on
   d. All of the above

8. Editing of points can be accomplished using which of the following?

   a. **Panorama**
   b. AutoCAD **MOVE** command
   c. **Prospector**
   d. All of the above

9. A point can be located if the user has which of the following criteria?

   a. An Easting, an X coordinate, and a Z coordinate
   b. Two Northings and a Time value
   c. A line depicted by a beginning and an ending location
   d. None of the above

10. Some typical needs for a designer to set points would be for:

   a. Stakeout purposes
   b. Identifying the locations of existing condition planimetrics
   c. Spot shots
   d. All of the above

True or False

1. True or False: COGO is an acronym for Consolidated, Orthogonal Geometry Organization.

2. True or False: Points are defined using the Cartesian coordinate system and consist of X, Y, and Z values.

3. True or False: The Y-axis is located 180° from the X-axis.

4. True or False: A line (or vector) is defined as the connection between the beginning point and its corresponding ending point.

5. True or False: A line exists if it begins at a Point $P1$, has a known slope distance, and has a distance component.

6. True or False: The Civil 3D user must first perform several setup options in order to use the **Points** commands.

7. True or False: Contractors will never use the points that engineers set.

8. True or False: Civil 3D has a myriad of ways to depict points and what they represent, and Point Styles is the vehicle used to accomplish this.

9. True or False: Point Styles is limited to Civil 3D symbols, and user-defined blocks may not be used.

10. True or False: Point Groups are named collections of points and are used to associate points that have relationships, such DTM points, Property Corner points, and so on.

11. True or False: Points in Point Groups cannot be overlapped with other Point Groups.

12. True or False: Description Key Sets are used to authorize the use of the Civil 3D software.

13. True or False: Point File Formats can be customized to include formats not delivered with the Civil 3D software.

14. True or False: External Data References (XDRefs) are AutoCAD files that can be cross-referenced into the AutoCAD drawing.

15. True or False: The **Points** pull-down menu is a very sophisticated menu with over 50 **Point Creation** commands.

CHAPTER EXERCISES

1. What is the difference between coordinate values of X, Y and N, E?
2. What is the value of Y for a line represented by a formula of $Y = (.25)(10) + 5$?
3. Find the length of the vector between Points $P1 = 10,10,0$ and $P2 = 15, 12,0$.
4. Plot that same point in AutoCAD. What angle exists between this vector and the X-axis?
5. What is the slope of this vector?
6. If a line starts at $P3 = 5,5,0$ and has a slope of .333 and a length of $10'$, what is the ending coordinate?
7. Create a **Point Group**.
8. Using the **Points >> Create Points** toolbar, select **Miscellaneous Convert AutoCAD Points** to convert AutoCAD points to Civil 3D points.

    Type **Point** at the command prompt to create an AutoCAD point (which is not a Civil 3D point). The software responds with Specify a point: Type a coordinate of **1850,1975,230.54**. Notice a dot shows up inside the parcel polyline you were working with in the last couple of exercises. It actually resides at an elevation of 230.54. Use **Miscellaneous Convert AutoCAD Points** to create a Civil 3D point at this precise location in 3D.

9. The next example is to set points using the **Create Points—Measure Object** command.

    To begin this exercise, **Draw** a line from **850,1025** to **930,1050**.

    Then from the **Create Points** toolbar, choose the pop-down arrow on the first button and select **Measure Object**.

    Use a Starting station of **0.0000** and an Ending station of **83.815**, set points using a $20'$ offset right, from the line, with an interval of **10.00**, a point description of IPF, and just hit **<Enter>** for the point elevation. Set 7 points each at a $20'$ offset to the right of the line every $10'$.

10. This question has you set points on polylines using the **Polyline Vertices—Manual** command.

    Using the **Zoom Center** command, choose a zoom center point of **2000,2000** with a magnification or height of **500**.

    Draw a polyline starting at an X, Y coordinate of **1750,1900** to **1850,2100** to **2100,2000** to **2100,1875**, and close it by typing **C**.

    From the **Create Points** toolbar and using the pop-down arrow next to the first icon, choose **Polyline vertices— Manual** and set a point on each vertex using a default elevation of **100.0** for the proposed building pad, and use the IPF description for each point as it is set.

A Tip of the Hat to Surveyors—More Points!

4

Chapter Objectives

The objectives of this chapter are similar to those of Chapter 3 in that many point setting routines are described. These additional examples are probably more geared toward surveyors because of their heavy reliance on point information during their daily workflow. However, designers could also use some of these functions to save time in performing a variety of computations.

INTRODUCTION

This material was in the appendix in previous versions of the text. Due to the increasing interest of surveyors in the product, however, we moved it to this chapter to make it follow Chapter 3. This information is included to provide surveyors, instructors, and the reader with additional routines and procedures for using the extensive set of Point-related commands in the **Create Points** toolbar. The commands in this chapter are no less powerful nor less useful than those in Chapter 3 and should be given equal respect in learning and use in production.

REVIEW OF FUNCTIONS AND FEATURES TO BE USED

The features in this chapter are the same as those for Chapter 3, but with more examples to help surveyors make greater use of Civil 3D during their daily workflow.

When using the files for this chapter, please note that the files are still referenced to Chapter 3 because they are all point-related examples.

CREATING "THINKING POINTS"

The next segment delves into procedures for placing Interpolation-related points into a project drawing. Refer to Figure 4-1. These commands allow the ability to generate "thinking points."

Figure 4-1   "Thinking points"

Thinking points are points that may or may not be used in design, but they will assuredly be used to develop other data.

Consider that you know the elevation of a flow line of a curb and are wondering what the elevation would be if you went in a specified direction for a specified distance at a specific grade or slope. And then, depending on where it landed, you would make a decision on what would happen next. Decide whether the point is too high or too low or erase it and provide different criteria. These are thinking points because they allow you to see the results of design criteria rapidly and then either proceed forward or step back and try again with little or no cost.

Exercise 4-1: Interpolation—INTERPOLATE Command

 The next command, **INTERPOLATE**, can be used to set intermediate points in 3D. The software uses the next available point numbers and prompts for other information as it goes.

The **INTERPOLATE** command might be used to densify a data set for DTM triangulation.

To access student data files, go to www.pearsondesigncentral.com.

1. Continue in the same drawing, or open the drawing called Chapter 3-a.dwg.
2. Using the **V** for **View** command, highlight the view called **Points-I**, hit **Set Current**, and then hit **OK**. You see two points already set, Points 1001 and 1002. You will densify these by adding three points in between them at prorated elevations based on the two points' elevations.
3. Select the **Points** pull-down menu and choose the **Create Points** command. The **Create Points** toolbar displays.
4. Using the drop-down arrow to the right of the fifth icon from the left, choose **Interpolate**.
5. `Pick a first point object`: Select Point 1001 with your mouse; no Osnap is needed.
6. `Pick a second point object`: Select Point 1002 with your mouse; no Osnap is needed.
7. `Enter number of points <0>`: **3**
8. `Specify an offset <0.000>`: **0**, this will create the new points on line with the 1001 and 1002.
9. `Enter a point description <.>`: **Spot**
10. `Enter a point description <Spot>`: **<Enter>**
11. `Enter a point description <Spot>`: **<Enter>**
12. Hit **<Esc>** to terminate.

Notice that three new points were created in between Points 1001 and 1002.

Exercise 4-2: Interpolation—BY RELATIVE LOCATION Command

 The next command, **BY RELATIVE LOCATION**, can be used to set points in 3D by using Grade, Slope, Elevational, or Difference based criteria.

The **BY RELATIVE LOCATION** command can be used to create proposed ground points based on the engineer's desired slope, grade, or elevation. These thinking points can be used to test what elevations, slopes, and grades might result based on the data you are providing in your design.

To access student data files, go to www.pearsondesigncentral.com.

1. Continue in the same drawing, or open the drawing called Chapter 3-a.dwg.
2. Using the **V** for **View** command, highlight the view called **Points-I**, hit **Set Current**, then hit **OK**. You see two points already set, Points 1001 and 1002. You will set a point from one of the contour endpoints toward Point 1001 at a grade of 2%.

3. Using the drop-down arrow to the right of the fifth icon from the left, choose **By Relative Location**.
4. `Specify first point or [Entity]` : Pick a point at an endpoint of a contour with the **Endpoint** Osnap.
5. `Specify an elevation for the first control point <356.000'>`: **<Enter>**
6. `Specify second point`: Pick a point on Point 1001 using the **Node** Osnap.
7. `Specify an elevation for the second control point or [Difference/Slope/Grade] <356.911'>`: **g**

TIP

Note that a comment is warranted here to explain the other options available. **Difference** allows you to enter a change in height from the first elevation and can be either plus or minus. So if the first elevation is 360.00, a difference can be applied of, say, 5' so that the second elevation becomes 365.00. **Slope** is similar to **Grade** except that it refers to a ratio instead of a percentage. Slopes are in values such as 2:1, 3:1, and so forth, where the 2:1 means 2' horizontally for every 1' vertically. Of course, you are using the **Grade** option in the example where 2% is 2' vertically for every 100' horizontally.

8. `Grade (percent) or [Slope] <0.00>`: **2**
9. `First Elev: 356.000', Second Elev: 358.617', Elevation Difference: 2.617 Horiz Dist: 130.850, Grade: (percent): 2.00, Slope: (run:rise): 50.00:1`
10. `Distance`: **100**
11. `Specify an offset <0.000>`: **<Enter>**
12. `Enter a point description <.>`: **Spot**
13. Hit **<Esc>** to terminate.

Notice that a new point showed up 100' from the contour endpoint you selected. The elevation is established at a 2% grade from the contour elevation in a direction toward the Point 1001.

Exercise 4-3: Interpolation—BY RELATIVE ELEVATION Command

 The next command, **BY RELATIVE ELEVATION**, can be used to set points in 3D by using Grade, Slope, Difference, or Elevational criteria. This is different from the previous command in that it establishes the grade to be met but then requests the final elevation to be set. It then sets a point at the desired elevation using the grade computed at whatever horizontal distance it takes to meet the elevation prescribed.

TIP

Again, these can establish thinking points that allow you to consider the results of moving ahead with your actions. They can be used to find out where a point falls running at, say, −2% until it hits a critical hydraulic grade elevation of, say, 101.33. If the point falls into the next county, then it likely is not feasible. If it falls near the ditch flowline, then maybe it makes sense.

1. Continue in the same drawing, or open the drawing called Chapter 3-a.dwg.
2. Using the **V** for **View** command, highlight the view called **Points-I**, hit **Set Current**, and then hit **OK**. You see two points already set, Points 1001 and 1002. You will set a point starting at 1002, heading toward 1001, and hold the grade between them such that it keeps traveling until it meets the elevation specified.
3. Using the drop-down arrow to the right of the fifth icon from the left, choose **By Relative Elevation**.
4. `Specify first point or [Entity]` : Pick a point on Point 1002 with the **Node** Osnap.

To access student data files, go to www.pearsondesigncentral.com.

5. `Specify an elevation for the first control point <360.000'>:` **\<Enter\>**
6. `Specify second point:` Pick a point on Point 1001 using the **Node** Osnap.
7. `Specify an elevation for the second control point or [Difference/Slope/Grade] <356.911'>:` **\<Enter\>**
8. `First Elev: 360.000', Second Elev: 356.911', Elevation Difference: −3.089, Horiz Dist: 187.628, Grade: (percent): −1.65, Slope: (run: rise): −60.74:1, Elevation <0.000'>:` Type in **356** to see where a point of elevation 356 would land if it held the slope between Point 1002 and Point 1001.
9. `Specify an offset <0.000>:` **\<Enter\>**
10. `Enter a point description <.>:` **\<Enter\>**
11. It then allows you to continue setting new points at new specified elevations, so hit **\<Esc\>** to terminate. Notice that a point was set to the right of Point 1001 at exactly the elevation of 356.00.

Exercise 4-4: Interpolation—NUMBER BY DISTANCE Command

 The next command, **NUMBER BY DISTANCE**, can be used to set interpolated points in 3D by using the Grade between two other 3D objects.

 The **NUMBER BY DISTANCE** command can be used to densify your data set. This can be important when you have too little data where the TIN activity can cause ambiguous results.

To access student data files, go to www.pearsondesigncentral.com.

1. Continue in the same drawing, or open the drawing called Chapter 3-a.dwg.
2. Using the **V** for **View** command, highlight the view called **Points-I**, hit **Set Current**, and then hit **OK**. You see two points already set, Points 1001 and 1002.
3. Using the drop-down arrow to the right of the fifth icon from the left, choose **Number By Distance**.
4. `Specify first point or [Entity] :` Pick a point on a contour vertex using the **Endpoint** Osnap.
5. `Specify an elevation for the first control point <356.000'>:` **\<Enter\>**
6. `Specify second point:` Pick a point on Point 1002 with the **Node** Osnap.
7. `Specify an elevation for the second control point or [Difference/Slope/Grade] <360.000'>:` **\<Enter\>**
8. `First Elev: 356.0009, Second Elev: 360.000', Elevation Difference: 4.000, Horiz Dist: 97.374, Grade: (percent): 4.11 Slope: (run:rise): 24.34:1`
9. `Enter number of points <0>:` **3** so you set three intermediate points between these two objects.
10. `Specify an offset <0.000>:` **\<Enter\>**
11. `Enter a point description <.>:` **\<Enter\>**
12. `Enter a point description <.>:` **\<Enter\>**
13. `Enter a point description <.>:` **\<Enter\>**
14. `Enter number of points <0>:` **\<Esc\>** to terminate.

Exercise 4-5: Interpolation—PERPENDICULAR Command

 The next command, **PERPENDICULAR**, can be used to set points in 3D at a perpendicular location from a point to a vector.

 On a project, you often need to identify the elevation of a centerline for a driveway as it hits the flowline of a curb. The **PERPENDICULAR** command can be used to accomplish that or similar 3D perpendicular tasks.

To access student data
files, go to
www.pearsondesigncentral.com.

1. Continue in the same drawing, or open the drawing called Chapter 3-a.dwg.
2. Using the **V** for **View** command, highlight the view called **Points-I**, hit **Set Current**, and then hit **OK**. You see two points already set, Points 1001 and 1002.
3. Using the drop-down arrow to the right of the fifth icon from the left, choose **Perpendicular**.
4. `Specify first point or [Entity] :` Pick a point on Point 1002 with the **Node** Osnap.
5. `Specify an elevation for the first control point <360.000'>:` **<Enter>**
6. `Specify second point:` Pick a point on Point 1001 with the **Node** Osnap.
7. `Specify an elevation for the second control point or [Difference/Slope/Grade] <356.911'>:` **<Enter>**
8. `First Elev: 360.000', Second Elev: 356.911', Elevation Difference: −3.089, Horiz Dist: 187.628, Grade: (percent): −1.65, Slope: (run: rise): −60.74:1`
9. `Please specify a location that is perpendicular to the interpolated line:` Pick a point on the circle in the view with the **Center** Osnap.
10. `Specify an offset <0.000>:` **<Enter>**
11. `Enter a point description <.>:` **<Enter>**
12. Hit **<Esc>** to terminate.

Exercise 4-6: Interpolation—INCREMENTAL DISTANCE Command

 The next command, **INCREMENTAL DISTANCE,** can be used to set points in 3D by using Grade, Slope, Elevational, or Difference based criteria. The variation of this command is that it sets points at specified intervals, say, every 25′.

 TIP This routine might be used to create a centerline of driveway elevations at the flowline of a curb section every 75′ based on the grade of the curb section.

To access student data
files, go to
www.pearsondesigncentral.com.

1. Continue in the same drawing, or open the drawing called Chapter 3-a.dwg.
2. Using the **V** for **View** command, highlight the view called **Points-I**, hit **Set Current**, and then hit **OK**. You see two points already set, Points 1001 and 1002.
3. Using the drop-down arrow to the right of the fifth icon from the left, choose **Incremental Distance**.
4. `Specify first point or [Entity] :` Pick a point on a contour vertex using the **Endpoint** Osnap.
5. `Specify an elevation for the first control point <356.000'>:` **<Enter>**
6. **Specify second point:** Pick a point on Point 1001 with the **Node** Osnap.
7. `Specify an elevation for the second control point or [Difference/Slope/Grade] <356.911'>:` **<Enter>**
8. `First Elev: 356.000', Second Elev: 356.911', Elevation Difference: 0.911, Horiz Dist: 44.815, Grade: (percent): 2.03, Slope: (run:rise): 49.19:1`
9. `Distance between points <10.0000>:` **<Enter>**
10. `Specify an offset <0.000>:` **<Enter>**
11. `Enter a point description <.>:` **<Enter>**
12. `Enter a point description <.>:` **<Enter>**
13. `Enter a point description <.>:` **<Enter>**
14. `Enter a point description <.>:` **<Enter>**
15. `Distance between points <10.0000>:` Hit **<Esc>** to terminate.

Exercise 4-7: Interpolation—INCREMENTAL ELEVATION Command

 The next command, **INCREMENTAL ELEVATION**, can be used to set points in 3D by using Grade, Slope, Elevational, or Difference based criteria. The variation of this command is that it will set points at specified Elevational intervals, say, every 1′.

> This routine might be used to create points that have only even elevations, such as 360.0, 361.0, 362.0, 363.0. This could be helpful in a planning exercise in which the planner is trying to obtain a rough feel for the design possibilities.

To access student data files, go to www.pearsondesigncentral.com.

1. Continue in the same drawing, or open the drawing called Chapter 3-a.dwg.
2. Using the **V** for **View** command, highlight the view called **Points-J**, hit **Set Current**, then hit **OK**. You see two contours that you will work with that have white circles identifying them.
3. Using the drop-down arrow to the right of the fifth icon from the left, choose **Incremental Elevation**.
4. `Specify first point or [Entity] :` Pick a point on a contour vertex inside the circle on the green contour using the **Endpoint** Osnap.
5. `Specify an elevation for the first control point <360.000'>:` **<Enter>**
6. `Specify second point:` Pick a point on a contour vertex inside the circle on the brown contour using the **Endpoint** Osnap.
7. `Specify an elevation for the second control point or [Difference/ Slope/Grade] <366.000'>:` **<Enter>**
8. `First Elev: 360.000', Second Elev: 366.000', Elevation Difference: 6.000, Horiz Dist: 250.535, Grade: (percent): 2.39, Slope: (run:rise): 41.76:1`
9. `Elevation Difference <0.000'>:` **1**
10. `Specify an offset <0.000>:` **<Enter>**
11. `Enter a point description <.>:` **<Enter>**
12. `Enter a point description <.>:` **<Enter>**
13. `Enter a point description <.>:` **<Enter>**
14. `Enter a point description <.>:` **<Enter>**
15. `Enter a point description <.>:` **<Enter>**
16. `Elevation Difference <1.000'>:` Hit **<Esc>** to terminate.

Exercise 4-8: Interpolation—INTERSECTION Command

 The next command, **INTERSECTION**, can be used to set points in 3D by using the slope of a vector defined via two points or a 3D object with another object that crosses the first object's path.

> The **INTERSECTION** command could be helpful in determining the elevation at the edge of pavement where an underground utility crosses the edge of pavement, or where a roadway crown might intersect another roadway centerline. This occurs in 3D.

To access student data files, go to www.pearsondesigncentral.com.

1. Continue in the same drawing, or open the drawing called Chapter 3-a.dwg.
2. Using the **V** for **View** command, highlight the view called **Points-J**, hit **Set Current**, then hit **OK**. You see two contours that you will work with that have white circles identifying them. You also see a white line that crosses the path if the two circles were connected.
3. Using the drop-down arrow to the right of the fifth icon from the left, choose **Intersection**.
4. `Specify first point or [Entity] :` Pick a point on a contour vertex inside the circle on the green contour using the **Endpoint** Osnap.
5. `Specify an elevation for the first control point <360.000'>:` **<Enter>**
6. `Specify second point:` Pick a point on a contour vertex inside the circle on the brown contour using the **Endpoint** Osnap.

7. `Specify an elevation for the second control point or [Difference/`
   `Slope/Grade] <366.000'>:` **<Enter>**
8. `First Elev: 360.000', Second Elev: 366.000', Elevation Difference:`
   `6.000, Horiz Dist: 250.535, Grade: (percent): 2.39, Slope: (run:rise):`
   `41.76:1`
9. `Specify an offset <0.000>:` **<Enter>**
10. `Specify first point or [Entity]:` **e**
11. `Select an arc, line, lot line, feature line, or polyline or [Points]:`
    Select the line crossing the path between the two circles.
12. `Specify offset from entity <0.000>:` **<Enter>**
13. `Enter a point description:` **<Enter>**
14. Hit **<Esc>** to terminate.

This concludes this segment on placing Interpolation-based points into your project.

PERFORMING SLOPE-BASED COMPUTATIONS

This next segment delves into procedures for placing Slope-based points in the file. See Figure 4-2. These additional 3D commands can be used as thinking points or directly within the design as 3D data points. These commands are interesting because they solve real-life problems that engineers encounter. For instance, the **SLOPE—HIGH/LOW POINT** command can take a known slope in one direction, intersect it with a known slope in another direction, and set the intersection point in 3D.

Figure 4-2   Placing Slope-based points

Exercise 4-9: SLOPE—HIGH/LOW POINT Command

 The next command, **HIGH/LOW POINT**, can be used to set points in 3D by using the slope of one vector and intersecting it with the slope of another vector. This could be helpful in the following situation.

 TIP   This can be solved for many design conditions, but one example in particular might be in a subdivision, while grading between two houses. There is a drainage envelope around each house, assuring that drainage occurs away from the house. If one house is higher than the other and has a differing drainage slope, you may want to locate a center of swale point where the two envelopes intersect so you can guide the drainage toward either the front or the back of the houses.

1. Continue in the same drawing, or open the drawing called Chapter 3-a.dwg.
2. Using the **V** for **View** command, highlight the view called **Points-K**, hit **Set Current**, then hit **OK**. You see two house templates with drainage envelopes around them. You will set a high/low point between the two houses, which are at different finish floor elevations and have 10′ drainage envelopes.
3. Using the drop-down arrow to the right of the sixth icon from the left, choose **High/Low Point**.
4. `Specify start point:` Select a point on the lower right drainage envelope corner of the left house using the **Endpoint** Osnap.

To access student data files, go to www.pearsondesigncentral.com.

5. `Specify second point:` Select a point on the lower left drainage envelope corner of the right house using the **Endpoint** Osnap.
6. `First Slope (run:rise) or [Grade] <Horizontal>:` **g** to indicate that you will give it a grade (in %).
7. `Grade (percent) or [Slope] <0.00>:` **–5,** this is a 5% downward grade. (Remember that grades are in % whereas slopes are in ratios.)
8. `Grade: (percent): −5.00, Slope: (run:rise): −20.00:1`
9. `Second Grade (percent) or [Slope] <−5.00>:` **–.05,** to indicate that the second grade will be 1/2 % downward. Therefore, the first grade is coming down faster because the house is at a 2′ higher elevation while the second grade is coming down slower because that house is lower. This allows an intersection point to be computed between the two drainage envelopes that can be used as a center of swale point. The swale can guide drainage between the houses to either the front or the back of the property.
10. `Grade: (percent): −0.05, Slope: (run:rise): −2000.00:1, New point: X: 15876.168, Y: 19170.945, Z: 348.997.` Note that a tick mark displays where the new computed point will be placed if you proceed with the command. If the point will fall in an unsatisfactory location, type **n** for **No** at the next prompt and redo the command with different, more satisfactory data.
11. `Add point [Yes/No] <Yes>:` **y**
12. `Enter a point description <.>:` **<Enter>**
13. `Specify start point:` Hit **<Esc>** to terminate.
14. Save this drawing as you will use your results to perform the next two exercises.

Exercise 4-10: Slope—SLOPE/GRADE—DISTANCE Command

 The next command, **SLOPE/GRADE—DISTANCE,** can be used to set points in 3D by using the elevation of an object and providing it with Slope, Grade, and Distance criteria to set another point in 3D.

> The **SLOPE/GRADE—DISTANCE** command could be helpful in designing a swale between two houses after a low point has been constructed as was accomplished in the previous exercise. A designer can extend the swale between the houses for, say, 50′ at a grade of −2%, thereby ensuring drainage away from the houses toward the front or back of the property.

To access student data files, go to www.pearsondesigncentral.com.

1. Continue in the same drawing.
2. Using the **V** for **View** command, highlight the view called **Points-K**, hit **Set Current**, and then hit **OK**. You see two house templates with drainage envelopes around them. You will use the high/low point set in the last exercise to design a swale to convey drainage between the two houses.
3. Using the drop-down arrow to the right of the sixth icon from the left, choose **Slope/Grade—Distance**.
4. `Specify start point:` Select the point placed using the **High/Low Point** command in the last example using the **Node** Osnap.
5. `Elevation <348.997′>`
6. `Specify a point to define the direction of the intermediate points:` Pick a point in the front yard of the houses (in other words, to the north and between the two houses).
7. `Slope (run:rise) or [Grade] <Horizontal>:` **g**
8. `Grade (percent) or [Slope] <0.00>:` **–1**
9. `Grade: (percent): −1.00, Slope: (run:rise):−100.00: 1`
10. `Distance:` **100,** you will set points 100′ from the first point you picked.
11. `Enter the number of intermediate points <0>:` **4,** you will set four intermediate points along the way with one last point at 100′.
12. `Specify an offset <0.000>:` **<Enter>,** this allows for offset points if desired; you will say none.

13. `Add ending point [Yes/No] <Yes>:` **\<Enter\>**
14. `Enter a point description <.>:` **\<Enter\>**
15. `Enter a point description <.>:` **\<Enter\>**
16. `Enter a point description <.>:` **\<Enter\>**
17. `Enter a point description <.>:` **\<Enter\>**
18. `Enter a point description <.>:` **\<Enter\>**
19. `Elevation <348.997'>:` **\<Enter\>**
20. Specify a point to define the direction of the intermediate points: Hit **\<Esc\>** to terminate.

You should see several points developed between the two houses in Figure 4-3.

Figure 4-3   Points set between two houses

Exercise 4-11: Slope—SLOPE/GRADE—ELEVATION Command

 The next command, **SLOPE/GRADE—ELEVATION**, can be used to set points in 3D by using the elevation of an object and providing it with Slope, Grade, and Elevation criteria to set another point in 3D.

> This **SLOPE/GRADE—ELEVATION** command differs from the previous command in that it asks for the ending elevation instead of a distance. You can use it to lay some points out for the front yard of the left house in the example.

1. Continue in the same drawing.
2. Using the **V** for **View** command, highlight the view called **Points-K**, hit **Set Current**, and then hit **OK**. You see two house templates with drainage envelopes around them. The points you placed between the two houses should be there from the previous exercise. Use the last point placed in the front yard to set some new points. Select the last point in the front yard, provide a direction to the west (or left), and travel at a grade of positive 4% until you hit an elevation of 351.5.
3. Using the drop-down arrow to the right of the sixth icon from the left, choose **Slope/Grade—Elevation**.
4. `Specify start point:` Select the last point placed in the front yard from the last exercise using the **Node** Osnap.
5. `Elevation <347.997'>:` **\<Enter\>**
6. `Specify a point to define the direction of the intermediate points:` Pick a point in the front yard of the left house (in other words, to the left, but somewhere in the front yard of the left house).

7. Slope (run:rise) or [Grade] <Horizontal>: **g**
8. Grade (percent) or [Slope] <0.00>: **4**
9. Grade: (percent): 4.00, Slope: (run:rise): 25.00:1 Ending Elevation: **351.5**
10. Enter the number of intermediate points <0>: **3**
11. Specify an offset <0.000>: **<Enter>**
12. Add ending point [Yes/No] <Yes>: **<Enter>**
13. Enter a point description <.>: **<Enter>**
14. Enter a point description <.>: **<Enter>**
15. Enter a point description <.>: **<Enter>**
16. Enter a point description <.>: **<Enter>**
17. Elevation <347.997'> **<Enter>**
18. Specify a point to define the direction of the intermediate points: Hit **<Esc>** to terminate.

Notice that the last point placed has an elevation of 351.500, as shown in Figure 4-4, which is what was requested. The points are placed such that their grade is 4% from the first point chosen.

Figure 4-4   The last point placed is at elevation 351.500

CHAPTER SUMMARY

Because this chapter simply expands on the previous chapter, the summary is the same as it was for Chapter 3. In essence, understanding point-based features is important for anyone working on a civil project. Some team members place different emphasis on points depending on their contribution to the project. Make no mistake about it, however, someone is establishing points for everything on the site at some time during the project cycle.

CHAPTER TEST QUESTIONS

Multiple Choice

1. What are "thinking points"?
   a. Points used to help construct additional data
   b. Points that might create temporary locational information that can be used to carry on with a thought process
   c. Points that allow the user to see the results of design criteria so that moving forward on that track can be analyzed
   d. All of the above

2. Which type of design information can be developed with "thinking points"?
   a. Deciding how much flow exists in a channel
   b. Deciding whether a point is satisfactory with regard to elevations, slopes, and grades based on the data the user is providing
   c. Deciding if a surveyor should stake out the point or allow GPS machine guidance to do it
   d. All of the above

3. How is the term *slope* different from *grade*?

   a. Slope refers to anything with a percentage, such as 2%.
   b. Slope refers to a rise:run relationship.
   c. Grade refers to something underground.
   d. Grade refers to run:rise relationships.

4. A data set of points can be used to:

   a. Densify a data set based on information from raw data
   b. Densify a data set with additional points constructed from criteria from other points
   c. Densify a data set to reduce the number of points within it
   d. None of the above

5. Points can be set in 3D at specified intervals of, say, 50′ by using:

   a. **Grade** or **Slope**
   b. Elevational criteria
   c. Difference based criteria
   d. All of the above

6. If the user wanted to create points that have only even elevations such as 100.0, 101.0, 102.0 they would use which routine?

   a. **INCREMENTAL DISTANCE**
   b. **INCREMENTAL ELEVATION**
   c. **BY RELATIVE LOCATION**
   d. **INTERPOLATE**

7. A point can be set in 3D by intersecting the slope of one vector and intersecting it with the slope of another vector using which command?

   a. **INTERSECT POINT**
   b. **SLOPE/GRADE—DISTANCE**
   c. **HIGH/LOW POINT**
   d. None of the above

8. Which of the following commands might be used to densify a DTM?

   a. **DENSIFY DTM VERTICES**
   b. **THINKING POINTS**
   c. **INTERPOLATE**
   d. All of the above

9. Which of the following routines would best solve a traverse balancing issue for a non-closed traverse?

   a. **BY RELATIVE LOCATION**
   b. **INTERPOLATE**
   c. **BY RELATIVE ELEVATION**
   d. None of the above

10. Which of the following routines can be used to set points based on a percent and distance from another object?

   a. **SLOPE DISTANCE STORY STAKE**
   b. **FIXED SLOPE FROM OBJECT**
   c. **SLOPE/GRADE—DISTANCE**
   d. All of the above

True or False

1. True or False: A line exists if it begins at a point P1, has a known slope distance, and has a distance component.

2. True or False: Point file formats can be customized to include formats not delivered with the Civil 3D software.

3. True or False: The **Points** pull-down menu is a very sophisticated menu with over 50 point creation commands.

4. True or False: The **NUMBER BY DISTANCE** command can be used to densify your data set.

5. True or False: The **INTERSECTION** command cannot determine the elevation at the edge of a pavement where an underground utility crosses the edge of the pavement.

6. True or False: "Thinking points" are never used in design.

7. True or False: "Thinking points" should never be plotted.

8. True or False: The **INCREMENTAL ELEVATION** command is used to set points at specified distance intervals.

9. True or False: The **HIGH/LOW POINT** command allows you to set a point in a swale.

10. True or False: The **INCREMENTAL ELEVATION** command cannot be used to set points by slope.

CHAPTER EXERCISES

1. Using the **SLOPE/GRADE—DISTANCE** routine, how many points can be set between two other points if a distance of 100 is used with the number of points being set to 10 with an ending point?

2. Using the **HIGH/LOW POINT** command, what is the value of a new point being created from two objects of equal elevation, 10 feet apart, if they both extend at a 2% grade?

3. Using the **HIGH/LOW POINT** command, what is the value of a new point being created from two objects of equal elevation, 10 feet apart, if they both extend at a 2:1 slope?

4. Using the **SLOPE/GRADE—ELEVATION** command, what is the elevation of a new point if you started at a

location of elevation 100′ at 5% with an ending elevation of 120′, with 10 intermediate points and an ending point?

5. In the example above, how many points are created?

6. Using the **SLOPE/GRADE—ELEVATION** command, what is the elevation of a new point if you started at a location of elevation 100′ at 5% with an ending elevation of 120′, with 10 intermediate points and no ending point?

7. In the example above, how many points are created?

8. Using the **INCREMENTAL DISTANCE** routine, how many points are generated using an entity of 20′ in length, equal elevations of 0.0, and a distance between points of 10′?

9. Using the **BY RELATIVE LOCATION** routine, how many points are generated using an entity of 20′ in length, equal elevations of 0.0, and a distance of 5′?

10. Using the **NUMBER BY DISTANCE** command, how many points are generated if you are asked to `Enter number of points` and respond with 5?

Surveying

5

Chapter Objectives

- Understand how the Surveying interface operates within Civil 3D.
- Understand the application of Surveying Objects.
- Perform traverse balancing tasks.
- Understand how to reduce field data collection files.

INTRODUCTION

This chapter introduces you to surveying with Civil 3D. This technology was added to the 2007 release and largely completes the offering for use throughout the enterprise. With this technology, the surveying department can now develop the entire base data required for a project; the planning department can perform initial, preliminary designs; and the engineering department will take the project to final design. On completion, the project's data are likely to return to the surveying department for quality assurance/control and stakeout, or Machine Control data preparation.

The Civil 3D surveying functionality includes the following functions and abilities:

- The Prospector's Survey interface. Surveyors can view the numeric data along with previews; locate data visually, such as traverse or figures, in AutoCAD; and even change properties and values of the data using simple, succinct pull-down menus.

- Import, manage, and edit data collector field data.

- Enter, edit, balance, and report on open or closed traverses.

- Manage and edit survey equipment libraries.

- Manage and edit figure prefix libraries for automatic linework generation. This concept is similar to what has been offered in Autodesk's Land Desktop software, in which linework is collected in the field and given a prefix. For example, tops of curbs can be given prefixes such as TC1, TC2, and so on. The figure prefix library contains an entry called TC, so the software treats anything beginning with TC as a TC item, thereby correctly establishing the layering for the linework. This allows multiple edges of pavement to be open in the data collector simultaneously. The user should build this carefully so that other linework items do not mistakenly fall into the prefix. Consider something like a Tree and a Traverse station. If a Tree is prefixed with TR*, TRV descriptions would also be captured.

- The **Prospector's** inclusion of an interface collection for traverse networks, figures, and survey points, and the ability to manage and oversee these collections visually.

- Create survey figures directly from AutoCAD linework. This is even new to Land Desktop users.

- Develop terrain model breaklines from figures that have a specific prefix. In other words, perhaps linework coded with a BRKL prefix is intended to be breaklines for the Digital Terrain Model (DTM), and so many include tops and toes of channels, ridge lines, and so on. Users can now send those figures that have a BRKL prefix, for example, directly into the surface.

- The use of the Vault to protect the data for which surveyors are ultimately responsible.
- Output design data and surfaces in formats compatible with Topcon (via Carlson Connect), Trimble (via Trimble Link), and Leica (via Leica X-change) GPS Machine Control equipment.

The purpose of this chapter is to introduce you to some fundamental surveying concepts and provide basic procedures for developing survey data on projects.

REVIEW OF FUNCTIONS AND FEATURES TO BE USED

The text provides instruction in the functions for traverse entry, balancing traverse angles, how to compute the errors that are inherent in traverse computations, and the mathematics behind balancing the error of a traverse. Once the theories and algorithms are covered in the chapter, the discussion moves into automating these calculations in Civil 3D.

SURVEYING FUNCTIONS

Surveyors perform many functions in the process of developing engineering projects. They are responsible for collecting the base information consisting of existing conditions prior to design. This often includes identifying the property's boundary; the environmental conditions affecting the site such as wetlands and water bodies; the planimetric features, which are the buildings and other infrastructure on the site; and the topography, which consists of the three-dimensional conditions.

The method for collecting these data begins at the courthouse to identify the legal bounds of the property. These bounds are drawn up by the surveyor in a Civil 3D file using the Parcels and Rights of Way discussed in Chapter 6. These might be augmented by existing centerlines, easements, and so on.

Surveying of Parcels

There are two main methods for specifying parcel geometries: metes and bounds, and the U.S. Public Lands Survey System.

Metes and bounds are used primarily in the original colonial states in the United States. They were found to be too ambiguous, and the country converted to the U.S. Public Lands Survey System to improve confidence in the system. Metes and bounds describe property as beginning at a certain point, often a physical feature such as a tree or fence post. The property is then described by distances and bearings to another physical feature. Because a property's physical features deteriorate over time, they become ambiguous. Consider a parcel defined by a river's edge. During flooding the edge may move significantly, so the owner might actually lose land as the river erodes the banks or when a tree falls down.

The U.S. Public Lands Survey System (PLSS) was created to eliminate these ambiguities because rectangular-shaped boundaries use a methodical formula. The system is regulated by the U.S. Department of the Interior, Bureau of Land Management (BLM). The PLSS generally divides land into 6-mile-square townships. Townships are divided into 36 one-mile-square sections. Sections can be further divided into quarter sections, quarter-quarter sections, or irregular government lots as shown in the figure on page 129. The government sets a permanent survey monument at each section corner and at quarter-section corners.

The north-south line in the figure that runs through the initial point is called the Principal Meridian. The east-west line that runs through the initial point is called a Base line and is perpendicular to the Principal Meridian. Once the parcel is less than 10 acres, metes and bounds are used to further quantify the boundary.

Township Grid

Example 5-1: A PLSS Description

Each section may be subdivided into smaller parcels (aliquot parts). For example, a ten-acre parcel could be described as:

- NE 1/4 SE 1/4 SE 1/4 sec. 15, T2N, R2W Minsk, Ne.

- Translation: the Northeast quarter of the southeast quarter of the southeast quarter of section 15, Township 2 North, Range 2 West of the Minsk Meridian.

Descriptions are read from left to right, but locating the property is easier if one reads from right to left or from a larger division to a smaller one.

Example 5-2: Metes and Bounds

The metes and bounds description below defines the property shown in the following figure.

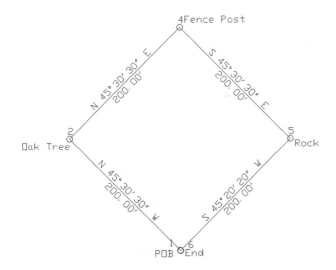

Beginning at a POB;
Thence n 45°30'30" w a distance of 200.00' to an oak tree;
Thence n 45°30'30" e a distance of 200.00' to a fence post;
Thence s 45°30'30" e a distance of 200.00' to a rock;
Thence s 45°20'20" w a distance of 200.00' to end;
Which is the point of beginning.

Following the collection of data or simultaneously, field collection techniques are employed to find physical evidence for the information on the site. GPS or total station equipment may be used to locate these data accurately. Precise 2D and 3D Control must be established for the project before any significant work is performed. In other words, monuments are established on the properties that are tied into state-certified control. These monuments can be occupied time and time again, and allow specific relations to be performed, as surveying and construction occur so that all aspects of the site are perfectly related.

The developed control has errors in its initial calculations due to either equipment or human error. The error is then eliminated from the control, creating a perfectly closed polygon, the vertices of which become the control monuments.

Other surveying techniques include aerial photogrammetry, GIS research, and GPS surveying. An example of an aerial photogrammetry project in Chapter 7 consists of about 200 acres of natural ground. Photogrammetry is the surveying task of flying above a project and photographing it using a zigzag pattern in which similar images at slightly different angles are photographed. Photographs are placed in the stereodigitizer and calibrated using Visually Identifiable Objects (VIOs) that are set using GPS or total station equipment. These now have accurate 3D coordinates that are set to the VIOs in the photos, thus calibrating everything in the photos to a coordinate. Digitizing then captures features and breaklines. This excellent method for collecting large amounts of data quickly has accuracies of about 0.01' for every thousand feet the aircraft is flying above the site. These data are typically verified by localized equipment such as total stations to ensure that the accuracies are met. The data produced from the stereodigitizing consist of CAD data usable by software such as Civil 3D.

A rapidly increasing methodology for collecting data is through the use of GPS equipment. Base stations are set on the project, again tied into state monumentation. The surveyor uses a rover with a GPS antenna that communicates with the base station to compute relative coordinates of the distance the rover is from the base station. Because the base station is tied down, the rover can be tied down relative to it, thus producing very accurate results. A new technology under development all over the world is the use of Imaginary Reference Stations. Using this technology, organizations collect a variety of certified base stations, tie them into a central server, amass errors, and correct for those errors. When a rover ties into the network, its location is computed, and an imaginary base station is created virtually at the location of the rover. Interpolated error corrections occur on the server and send postcorrected data (that is, coordinates) directly to the rover for immediate, and direct use in surveying or construction. See Figures 5-1 and 5-2 for graphics on how this works.

These systems are operational in many parts of the world. In the United States, they tend to be accessible in certain regions where this technology is in development. Many state DOTs are behind this development, as are private interests.

Developing Traverse Data

When a surveyor creates the traverse, he or she occupies a known location and typically backsights another known location. The angle between the two locations is now established. Then foresights are shot to new locations that may be accessible to the project. The idea is to locate positions that will be needed as the site is surveyed and built. These positions should be in as open an area as possible so they can be seen from as many points of view as possible in order to establish control for that portion of the project. A position would be useless if the surveyor could not see it. This then determines how many traverse points are required.

Once the setup station is identified and a backsight is created, turned angles and distances are captured to establish the next location (turned angles are discussed in Chapter 6).

Figure 5-1 The process for Imaginary Reference Stations—initializing the rover

Figure 5-2 The process for Imaginary Reference Stations—error corrections obtained

---

Example 5-3: Creating a Traverse

You now create a traverse using the following data. The procedure here is simple in order to convey the ideas involved, but the same techniques can be used on larger, more sophisticated traverses.

The traverse setup is on Point *A* located at 1000,1000. Backsight *B* is located 500′ at a bearing of South 45-00-00 West of Point *A*. A turned angle of 90-00-00 degrees and a distance of 500′ produces Point *C*. Then *C* is occupied with Point *A* being the backsight. A turned angle of 269-50-00 and a distance of 499.90′ produces Point *D*. Point *D* is then occupied with *C* being the backsight to locate Point *E*. A turned angle of 270-00-00 and a distance of 500′ are used to locate Point *E*. Then *E* is occupied with a backsight to *D* to locate Point *A* again at a turned angle of 270-00-00 and a distance of 500′. Refer to Figure 5-3. There is not a closed traverse because error has been placed into the computations. Clearly, surveyors do not intentionally

Figure 5-3 Traverse data

add error, yet the equipment might, or perhaps a prism is not held perfectly plumb to the shot. Maybe ambient conditions such as heat or fog have affected the line of sight. To replicate this error, the bust of 0.1′ and 1 degree has been entered, and a method known as the Compass rule will be used to correct this error. This method has been used for many years and still holds some favor because it is easily hand-calculated for verification purposes. Computer automation has improved traverse balancing by allowing surveyors to use a much more sophisticated method called least squares, but this exercise concentrates on the Compass rule.

Using the Compass rule, first correct for the bad angles and then for the bad distances. To correct for the angles, this figure should be closed. The intention was to start at Point A and return to Point A, but with the error it was impossible to close back precisely. You need to determine how much angular error and distance error there is. It is necessary to know how many degrees should be in the figure, and certain simple methods can obtain that information. Closed figures with n sides are n-gons and the angles sum up to

$$(n-2) \times 180$$

TIP

So a figure with

3 sides is a triangle and has 180°.

4 sides is a rectangle and has 360°.

5 sides is a pentagon and has 540°.

6 sides is a hexagon and has 720°.

7 sides is a heptagon and has 900°.

8 sides is an octagon and has 1080°.

9 sides is a nonagon and has 1260°.

10 sides is a decagon and has 1440°.

12 sides is a dodecagon and has 1800°.

15 sides is a 15-gon and has 2340°.

So, based on this information there should be 360° in Figure 5-3. Let us find out what we have and correct it in the following manner (see Table 5-1).

Table 5-1 Adjustment of Angles			
Point	Measured Interior Angle	Average Correction (Degrees)	Adjusted Angle (Degrees)
A	89.5139	−0.1285	89.3854
C	90.5	−0.1285	90.3715
D	90.0	−0.1285	89.8715
E	90.5	−0.1285	90.3715
Result	360.5139	.514	359.9999

Note that the sum of the interior angles is 360.5139 (it should be 360-00-00); therefore, the average correction is .5139/4 vertices = 0.1285. This is applied to the angles, and because it is an average, it is subtracted. By the time the error is applied to Point E, the entire error of .5139 degrees has been distributed.

Computation of Azimuths for the Traverse

Now compute the relative azimuths of each traverse segment. The azimuth of $AB = 225.0$ degrees and with the turned angle of $BAC = 90.0$ degrees, the azimuth of $AC = 315.0$ degrees. Next you occupy each setup, then backsight the previous setup, and turn an interior angle to obtain the next setup. Then apply the corrected turned angle from Table 5-1 to each vertex.

$315.0 = AC$
-180 to flip the line of sight looking from C to A
$135.0 = CA$
$-90.3715 = C$, subtract adjusted interior angle of C from azimuth
$\overline{44.6285 = CD}$
$+180$ to flip the line of sight looking from D to C
$\overline{224.6285 = DC}$
$-89.8715 = D$
$\overline{134.757 = DE}$
$+180$
$\overline{314.757 = ED}$
$-90.3715 = E$
$\overline{224.3855 = EA}$
$+180$
$\overline{404.3855 = AE}$
$-89.3854 = A$
$\overline{315.0 = AC}$

This check proves it is now balanced because this result is the same angle where you began.

Example 5-4: Computing a Traverse Misclosure and Relative Precisions

Here you compute the nonclosure or linear misclosure based on the incorrect distance(s). You compute how far off the error is in the x direction and the y direction. These values are the departure and latitude (refer to Figure 5-4).

Departures are eastings/westings, whereas latitudes are northings/southings.

Departures = L sin (alpha)
Latitudes = L cos (alpha)

where the angle alpha is from north (straight up) to line L.

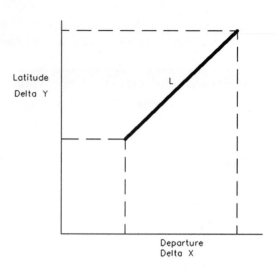

Figure 5-4   Departure and latitude diagram

Linear misclosure is the square root of the departure of misclosure squared plus the latitude of misclosure squared or

$$\sqrt{(\text{dep. misclosure})^2 + (\text{lat. misclosure})^2}$$

See Table 5-2.

Station	Preliminary Azimuths	Length	Departures	Latitudes
Table 5-2 Table Computation of Departures and Latitudes				
A	315.0	500	−353.533	353.553
C	44.6285	499.9	351.183	355.767
D	134.757	500	355.049	−352.051
E	224.3855	500.0	−349.741	−357.324
A				
		Sum = 1999.9	2.958	−.065

Linear misclosure $= \sqrt{(-2.958)^2 + (.065)^2}$

$\qquad\qquad\qquad = \sqrt{(8.749 + .004)} = 2.958'$

Relative precision $=$ Linear misclosure/Traverse length

$\qquad\qquad\qquad = 2.958/1999.9 = 0.0015 = 1/648$

The Compass rule adjusts the departures and latitudes of traverse courses in proportion to their lengths. See Table 5-3.

Correction in departure for $AC =$

$$-\frac{(\text{Total departure misclosure})}{\text{Traverse perimeter}} \times \text{Len } AC$$

Correction in latitude for $AC =$

$$-\frac{(\text{Total latitude misclosure})}{\text{Traverse perimeter}} \times \text{Len } AC$$

$-2.958/1999.9 \times 500.0 = -.771'$

$0.065/1999.98 \times 500.0 = .016'$

Table 5-3   Table of Compass Rule

| Station | Preliminary Azimuths | Unadjusted | | | Balanced | | Coordinates | |
		Length	Dep.	Lat.	Dep.	Lat.	X East	Y North
A			(−.771)	(.016)			1000	1000
	315.0	500	−353.553	353.553	−354.32	353.55		
C			(−.771)	(.016)			645.608	1353.55
	44.6285	499.9	351.183	355.767	350.412	355.783		
D			(−.771)	(.016)			996.02	1709.333
	134.757	500	355.049	−352.051	354.278	−352.035		
E			(−.771)	(.016)			1350.298	1357.29
	224.3855	500	−349.741	−357.324	−350.512	−357.308		
A							999.786	999.99
Summary =		1999.9	2.958	−.065	−.142	−.01		

For C to D:

$0 - 2.958/1999.9 \times 499.9 = -.739'$

$-.065/1999.9 \times 499.9 = .016'$

ELECTRONIC FIELD RECORDERS OR DATA COLLECTORS

Using field records, surveyors also collect data. When the rod person places the prism on the shot to be located, a shot code and a possible linecode will be determined if the shot also represents linework such as a crown or edge of pavement. Point codes were discussed in Chapter 3 (see Table 3-1). These codes describe the points, and the libraries place the shot on the correct layers, with the correct symbology and annotation. In the case of linework, there are also linecode libraries.

SURVEY LANGUAGE

This is also known as the field book format.

Point Creation Commands

AD = ANGLE DISTANCE, locates points/linework by a turned angle, distance

AD (point) [angle] [distance] (descript)

AD [VA] (point) [angle] [distance] [vert angle] (descript)

AD [VD] (point) [angle] [distance] [vert distance] (descript)

AUTO PT NUMBERING, for automatic point numbering

AP ON (point)

AP OFF

BEARING DISTANCE, locates points/linework by bearing, distance

BD (point) [bearing] [quadrant] [distance] (descript)

BD [VA] (point) [bearing] [quadrant] [distance] [vert angle] (descript)

BD [VA] (point) [bearing] [quadrant] [distance] [vert distance] (descript)

DEFLECTION DISTANCE, locates points/linework by deflection angle, distance

DD (point) [angle] [distance] (descript)

DD [VA] (point) [angle] [distance] [vert angle] (descript)

DD [VD] (point) [angle] [distance] [vert distance] (descript)

FACE 1, locates point from a traverse station. Using horizontal angle measured on face 1, distance

FACE 2, locates point from a traverse station. Using horizontal angle measured on face 2, distance

F1 (DIRECT), F2 (INVERTED)

F1/F2 (point) [angle] [distance] (descript)

F1/F2 [VA] (point) [angle] [distance] [vert angle] (descript)

F1/F2 [VD] (point) [angle] [distance] [vert distance] (descript)

LAT LONG (point) [latitude] [longitude] (descript)

NE, sets a 2D point.

Is a Control Point and is not moved in traverse balancing

NEZ, sets a 3D point.

Is a Control Point and is not moved in traverse balancing

NE SS, 3D pt side shot (not fixed in observation database, can be overwritten)

NE (point) [North] [East] (descript)

NEZ (point) [North] [East] (elev) (descript)

NE SS (point) [North] [East] (elev) (descript)

PRISM [height]

PT OFFSET (point) [offset] (ahead)

SKIP

STADIA, reduces a distance measured using stadia rod intercept

STADIA (point) [angle] [distance] [rod] (vert angle) (descript)

AZ = AZIMUTH DISTANCE, locates points/linework by azimuth, distance

ZD (point) [azimuth] [distance] (descript)

ZD [VA] (point) [azimuth] [distance] [vert angle] (descript)

ZD [VD] (point) [azimuth] [distance] [vert distance] (descript)

Point Location Commands

AZ [point 1] [point 2] [azimuth]

B [point1] [point 2] [bearing] [quadrant]

BS [point] (orientation), **backsight a known point**

STN [point] (inst. height) (descript), **occupy a station**

Point Information Commands

A [point 1] [point 2] [point 3]

AZ [point 1] [point 2]

B [point 1] [point 2]

D [point 1] [point 2]

DISP PTS (point 1) (point 2)

GRADE [point 1] [point 2]

INV PTS [point 1] [point 2]

INVERSE RADIAL [backsight] [station]

SLOPE [point 1] [point 2]

SD [point 1] [point 2]

VD [point 1] [point 2]

Point Editing Commands

DEL PTS [point 1] (point 2)

MOD DESC [point 1] [descript]   MOD EL [point 1] [elev] MOD ELS [point 1] [point 2] [elev]

MOD ELS BY [point 1] [point 2] [amount]

Figure Commands

AREA [figure]

BEG [figure], **begins a figure called {FIGURE}**

C3, next three shots are on a curve. The first shot should be on the beginning of the curve, the next shot about midway around the arc, and the last shot should be on the end of the curve.

CLOSE

CLOSE BLD, closes to connect the last point to the first point by creating two right-angled segments to close a building

CLOSE RECT [offset], closes objects such as sheds, storm structures

CONT [figure], continues a figure called {FIGURE}. This command assumes that the last point in the existing figure is the point to continue from. It continues a figure from the back end.

CRV = TANGENT CURVE

CRV [DELTA, LENGTH, DEFL, MID, TAN, CHORD] [radius] [value]

END, ends the current figure

These Figure commands draw figures using a data collector or manual input; they do not set points.

FIG AD [angle] [distance] FIG DD [deflection] [distance] FIG ZD [azimuth] [distance]

FIG BD [bearing] [quadrant] [distance]   FIG NE [Northing] [Easting]

ID FIG

INVERSE FIG [figure]

MAPCHECK [figure]

OFFSET [figure] [distance]

PC, next shot is on PC. The shot after that must be a PT.

POINT [point]

RT [distance], is a great command for drawing a building that has 90-degree corners and measured wall lengths

SET (point)

START [figure], restarts a figure called {FIGURE} from the beginning of the figure

These XC commands are for drawing nontangential curves.

XC = EXTEND CURVE

XC ZD (BULB) [radius] [chord-az] [chord-dis]

XC BD (BULB) [radius] [chord-brg] [quad] [chord-dis]

XC AD (BULB) [radius] [chord-angle] [chord-dis]

XC DD (BULB) [radius] [chord-defl] [chord-dis]

XC C3 [pt on curve] [endpt]

XC PTS [radius] [radpt] [endpt]

Intersection Commands

AZAZ [pnt 1] [az 1] [off 1] [pt 2] [az 2] [off 2]

BB [pnt 1] [brg 1] [quad 1] [off 1] [pnt 2] [brg 2] [quad 2] [off 2]

LNLN [pnt 1] [pnt 2] [off 1] [pnt 3] [pnt 4] [off 2]

RKAZ [point] [radius] [pnt 1] [azimuth] [offset]

RKBRG [point] [radius] [pnt 1] [brg] [quad] [offset]

RKLN [point] [radius] [pnt 1] [pnt 2] [offset]

RKRK [pnt 1] [radius 1] [pnt 2] [radius 2]

SAVE [NORTH, SOUTH, EAST, WEST, 1, 2, ALL] (point) (descript)

SAVE [NEAR, FAR] (point) [ref pt#] (descript)

SAVE PICK (point) (descript)

SQ [ref 1] [ref 2] [ref]

Figure Correction and Manipulation Commands

DEL FIG [fig]   DISP FIGS

Equipment Correction Commands

ANGLES [RIGHT, LEFT] [ZENITH, NADIR, HORIZ]

ATMOS [ON, OFF] COLL [ON, OFF] CR [ON, OFF]

EDM OFFSET [offset]

HORIZ ANGLE [RIGHT, LEFT]

PRESS [pressure] [INCH, MBAR, MM]

SF [factor]

PRISM CONSTANT [constant]   PRISM OFFSET [offset]

TEMP [temperature] [F, C, K]

UNITS [METER, FOOT] [DMS, DECDEG, GRAD, MILS, RADIANS]

VERT ANGLE [ZENITH, NADIR, HORIZ]

Baseline Commands

BL IS [point 1] [point 2] [station]   BL PT (point 1) [station] (offset)(descript)

BL INV [point 1] (point 2)

Centerline Commands

CL IS [figure] (station) (point)

CL INV [point 1] (point 2)

CL PT (point) [station] (offset) (skew angle) (descript)

CL PT BY [point] [station 1] [offset] [distance] (station 2) (descript)

CL ELEV (point) [station] [offset] [elev] (descript)

CL ROD (point) [station] [offset] [rod] (descript)

CL VD (point) [station] [offset] [vert distance] (descript)

HI [elev]

XS [station]

XS ELEV (point) [offset] [elev] (descript)

XS ROD (point) [offset] [rod] (descript)

XS VD (point) [offset] [vert distance] (descript)

AutoCAD Related Commands

PAN   SHELL   REDRAW   ZOOM PT [point]

ZOOM [WINDOW, EXTENTS, PREVIOUS, W, P, E, A]

Miscellaneous Commands

CALC [formula]   DITTO   [ON, OFF]   HELP (command)   HISTORY
OUTPUT [ON, OFF] TRAV [ON, OFF]

Unit Conversions for Distance

Unit	Symbol	Equation
Inches	"	
Feet	'	1 ft = 12 inches
Yards	Y	1 yd = 3 ft
Rods	R	1 rod = 16.5 ft
Chains	C	1 chain = 66 ft
Links	L	1 link = 1/100 chain = 0.66 ft
Meters	M	1 ft = 0.3048 m
Millimeters	MM	1 mm = 1/1000 m
Centimeters	CM	1 cm = 1/100 m
Kilometers	KM	1 km = 1000 m

Mathematical Operations

Sometimes a surveyor needs to compute distances, angles, bearings, or azimuths, and these commands also perform mathematical calculations. Occasionally, an angle, bearing, or distance is needed, but the surveyor may be unsure of what the value is. However, it might be possible to define this information from existing points.

The following commands—**ANGLE, AZIMUTH, BEARING, SLOPE, GRADE, VERTICAL DISTANCE, SLOPE DISTANCE, and DISTANCE** commands—display angle, azimuth, or distance values. However, when they are placed inside parentheses, they can be used to compute these values and send them into other commands. For instance:

ZD 5000 (AZ 500 501) (D 503 504) uses the azimuth from point 500 to point 501, and the distance from point 503 to point 504 to set point 5000.

The built-in functions can also be used in conjunction with the [Calc] command. For example:

CALC (A 10 20 30)/2 returns half the angle from point 10 to point 20 to point 30.

The **ANGLE** and **AZIMUTH** commands always return an angle. This value can be used in any command that requires an angle or an azimuth. For example:

ZD 5000 (SLOPE 10 20) 1000 uses the slope angle between point 10 and point 20 to set point 1000.

AD VA 5000 250.3000 600.00 (SLOPE 10 20).

Files Produced When Balancing

When an analysis is run and the network is adjusted, the following files are created and stored:

- **an<traversename>.trv:** Displays the horizontal closure and angular error
- **fv<traversename>.trv:** Displays a report of raw and adjusted elevations from the vertical adjustment methods
- **ba<traversename>.trv:** Displays the adjusted station coordinates derived from balancing the angular error and horizontal closure with no angular error
- **<traversename>.lso:** Displays the adjusted station coordinates based on Horizontal Adjustment Type setting (Compass rule)

Secrets of Survey Functions

A file exists in the folder C:\Documents and Settings\All Users\Application Data\Autodesk\C3D 2010\enu\Survey\ called **translat.ref** File. This file can be customized to control the order in which the user would prefer to enter the data parameters.

```
# Translator File for SURVEY
# Line
# —
# 1   Description
# 2   Command Number, # of Command Phrases, # of data elements,
#          Auto Point Data #, Check for last literal,
#          Variable command element, Variable data element,
#          Batchable command
# 3   Command Phrase1 #, Command Phrase2 #, ...
# 4   Data Mnemonic1, Data Mnemonic2, ...
# 5   Data Order1, Data Order2, ...
# 6   NULL
# 7   Blank Line
```

Example
```
BD
32,1,4,1,1,0,0,1
12
P,B,Q,D
1,2,3,4
NULL
```

Another file that exists in the same folder is called **language.ref file**. It contains the potential synonyms for each of the commands in the field book language. For instance, if the user would prefer to call the AD command "LOC" for *locate,* then LOC can be added to command #1.

A listing of the default synonyms is shown here; however, this file can be customized for use in Civil 3D.

```
# SYNONYM FILE FOR SURVEY
# Phrase Number, SYNONYM1, SYNONYM2, SYNONYM3, ....
1,AD,ANG-DIST
2,ADJ,ADJUST
3,A,ANG,ANGLE,ANGLES,ANGS
```

4,AUTO,AP

5,ATMOSPHERE,ATMOS

6,AZ,AZM,AZIMUTH

7,AZAZ

8,AZ-DIST,ZD

9,AZSP,AZSPI,AZ-SPI,AZ-SPIRAL

10,B,BEARING,BRG,BRGS,BEARINGS

11,BB,BRG-BRG

This allows for your preference in using these commands. If your common terminology is not shown, it can be added to this file. For instance, instead of storing a point using NE, we like to say STO and add this to number 74.

12,BD,BRG-DIST

13,BEG,BEGIN,BEGINS

14,BL,BASELINE

15,BOWDITCH,COMPASS

16,BRK,BRG-ARC,BARC,BRG-RK

17,BS,BACKSIGHT,BACKSITE

18,BSP,BRG-SPI,BSPI

19,BY,INC,INCRE,INCREMENT

20,CHORD,CHRD

21,CL,CENTERLINE,CLINE

22,COLL,COLLIMATION

23,CONSTANT

24,CONT,CONTINUE

25,CR,CURVATURE

26,CRANDALL,CRAND

27,CV3,C3

28,CURVE,CRV,CV

29,DD,DEFL-DIST

30,DESC,DESCR,DESCRIPT,DESCRIPTION

31,DEL,DELETE

32,DEPTH

33,DISPLAY,DISP,DSP,LIST

34,D,DIST,DISTANCE,DIS,HD,HDIST,LENGTH

35,DELTA

36,EDM

37,EL,ELEV,ELEVATION

38,ELEVATIONS,ELS,ELEVS

39,END,ENDS,E

40,ENTITY,ENT

41,EXIT,QUIT,STOP

42,FC1,F1,FACE1

43,FC2,F2,FACE2

44,FACTOR,FACT

45,DEFL,DEFLECTION

47,FILE

49,FOR

50,FROM

51,FS,FORESIGHT,FORESITE

53,HI

56,INDEX

57,INV,INVERSE

58,IS

59,JOB

61,LEVEL,LV

62,LINE,LN

63,LINE-LINE,LNLN

64,LINE-SPI,LNSP

65,LOC,LOCATE,LOCATION

66,LOW,LO

72,MOD,MODIFY

74,NE,NORTH-EAST

75,NEW

76,NEZ

77,NULL

78,OBJ,OBJECT

79,OFF

80,OFFSETS,OFFSET

81,ON

82,PT,POINT,PNT

83,PNTS,PTS,POINTS

84,PAN

85,PC

86,PD,PAR-DIST,PAR-DIS

87,PRC

88,PRESS,PRESSURE

89,PRISM

90,RAD,RADIAL,RADIUS

91,RECALL

92,REDRAW,R

94,RK,ARC

95,RKB,ARCB,ARC-BRG,RKBRG

96,RKAZ,ARCAZ,ARC-AZ,RKZ

97,RKLN,ARCLN,ARC-LINE

98,RKRK,ARCARC,ARC-ARC

99,RKSP,ARCSP,ARCSPI,ARC-SPIRAL,ARC-SPI

100,ROD

101,ROTATE,ROT

102,SAVE,KEEP

103,SCALE
104,SCS
105,SIDESHOTS,SIDESHOT,SS
106,SF,SCALEFACTOR
107,SL,SEA-LEVEL
108,SYMBOLS,SYM,SYMBOL
109,SPIRAL,SPI,SP
110,SPSP,SPISPI,SPI-SPI,SPIRAL-SPIRAL
111,SQ,SQ-OFF,SQOFF,SQUARE-OFF,SQUARE
112,STADIA
113,START
114,STN,STATION,STA
115,TAN-OFF,TANOFF
116,TAN,TANGENT
117,TEMP,TEMPERATURE
118,TIME,DATE
119,TO
120,TRANSIT
121,TRANSLATE,TRANS
122,TRAVERSE,TRAV,TRV
123,UNIT,UNITS
125,VA
126,VD,VDIST
127,VERTICAL,VERT
128,VIEW
129,W,WINDOW
130,XSECT,XS,XSECTION
131,SD,SDIST
132,ZOOM,Z
137,COMMAND,CMD
138,INFO,INFORMATION
139,EXTENTS,E
140,PREV,P,PREVIOUS
141,DITTO
142,SQRT
144,WAIT
145,WHILE
146,SIGNATURE
147,OUTPUT,OUT
148,MID,MIDORD,MID-ORDINATE
149,PICK
150,NEAR
151,FAR
152,ALL
153,XC,NC
154,BULB

155,RUN

156,BATCH

157,FBK

200,RIGHT,RT,RT-TURN

201,ZENITH

202,HORIZ,HORIZONTAL,HOR

203,NADIR

204,LEFT,LT

205,USFOOT,USFEET

206,METER,METERS,METRIC

207,FOOT,FEET

208,DMS

209,GRAD,GRADS

210,DECDEG

211,MIL,MILS

212,FAHREN,F,FAHRENHEIT

213,K,KELVIN

214,CELSIUS,CENTIGRADE,C

215,MM

216,INCH,INCHES

217,MBAR

218,GRADE,G

219,SLOPE

220,NORTH

221,SOUTH

222,EAST

223,WEST

224,MAPCHECK,MAPCHK,CHECK,CHK

225,AREA

226,RECT,RECTANGLE,RECTANG

227,CIRC,CIRCLE

228,CLOSE

229,RENAME

230,NAME

231,SSS

232,SAS

233,SAA

234,SSA

235,ASS

236,ASA

237,AAS

238,TRIANGLE,TRI,TRIANG

239,SOLVE

241,BLDG,BUILDING,BLD,BUILD

242,FIGURE,FIG

243,FIGURES,FIGS

244,SKEW

245,SET

246,LAT,LATITUDE

247,LONG,LON,LONGITUDE

248,ID,IDENT,IDENTIFY

249,SKIP

250,BACKUP

251,HISTORY,HIST,H

252,CALCULATE,CALC,CA

253,HELP,?

254,EDIT

255,MCS

256,MCE

257,RADIANS,RADS

Example 5-5: Computing a Traverse Adjustment in Civil 3D

The following procedure takes the reader through an entire survey project, beginning with a closed traverse taken from field notes to entering the field shot locations and then checking the traverse with a cross loop. This is usually done for quality assurance/control and accuracy purposes.

Field Notes

BS	STA @	FS	Angle RT.	DISTANCE
4	1	2	278-05-06	513.43
		(6)Mon 101	61-14-49	214.84
		(7)IPF A	311-23-25	23.85
1	2	3	291-45-07	440.52
		(8)Mon 102	163-14-58	221.69
2	3	4	260-24-37	308.20
		(9)IPF B	49-04-04	54.45
3	4	1	249-45-10	347.68
		(10)IPF C	54-31-01	49.62

Cross Loop Field Notes

BS	STA @	FS	Angle RT.	DISTANCE
2	1	1A	53-28-13	204.12
1	1A	1B	150-14-00	198.54
1A	1B	3	230-27-34	171.85
1B	3	4	297-59-58	308.20

Coordinates for Mon 101: $N = 10177.65460149$ $E = 10446.77951350$

Mon 102: $N = 10094.69083254$ $E = 9532.42708331$

The survey task is as follows:

1. Enter and adjust traverse loop 1–4.
2. Rotate to control monuments.
3. Enter and rotate boundary to pipe found and complete ties.
4. Enter and adjust cross loop.

The following procedure should allow the user to complete this task.

5. Set up drawing, set up points settings, description keys.
6. Set point for Traverse #1 by N/E (occupied station).
7. Set point for Traverse #4 by N/E (BS).
8. Traverse settings are no vertical, angles right.
9. Traverse entry (occupy #1, BS 4, Locate 2,3,4,1).
10. Traverse loops, define loops, should be OK.
11. Traverse loops, check adjust loop.
12. Traverse loops, adjust loop.
13. Command line, traverse/sideshots, sideshot settings
14. Command line, traverse/sideshots, sideshot entry

Now enter the monuments.

15. Set point for Mon 101, 102 by N/E (using real coordinates).
16. Set layer for boundary.
17. Draw boundary using COGO, Lines, By direction.
18. Set label preferences.
19. Label property lines.
20. Check closure of property lines.
21. Fillet, R = 0, to close.
22. Align to fit into place.
23. Checkpoints, modify project.
24. Update labels if needed.
25. Enter cross loop.
26. Edit Points, Erase 101-102.
27. Edit field book file (ensure that N/E exists for points 1–4).
28. Define traverse loop.
29. Traverse analysis.

Civil 3D File for Adjusting a Closed Traverse

The following FBK file can be built to automate the traverse development in Example 5-5. This can be conducted in Windows Notepad and run by using the **Import Field Book** option, which is available when right-clicking on the traverse created in the **Survey Toolspace**.

NE 1 2000 2000 "TRV 1"
NE 4 2347.68 2000 "TRV 4"
STN 1
BS 4
AD 2 278.050600 513.43 "TRV 2"
STN 2
BS 1
AD 3 291.450700 440.52 "TRV 3"
STN 3
BS 2
AD 4 260.243700 308.20 "TRV 4"
STN 4
BS 3
AD 1 249.451000 347.68 "TRV 1"

Civil 3D File for Adjusting a Traverse Cross Loop

This FBK file for Example 5-5 can be edited in Notepad as well and run by right-clicking on a new traverse created in the **Survey Toolspace**.

NE 1 10070.5376 10260.5491 "TRV 1"

NE 2 10132.4980 9750.8695 "TRV 2"

NE 3 10518.9622 9962.3056 "TRV 3"

NE 4 10418.1471 10253.5486 "TRV 4"

STN 1

AUTO OFF

BS 2

AD 101 53.281300 204.12 "TRV 1A"

STN 101

BS 1

AD 102 150.140000 198.54 "TRV 1B"

STN 102

BS 101

AD 3 230.273400 171.85 "TRV 3"

STN 3

BS 102

AD 4 297.595800 0.00 "TRV 4"

Refer to Figure 5-5 for an image of the completed traverse following import.

Figure 5-5   Completed imported traverse

Exercise 5-1: Computing a Traverse Reduction in Civil 3D—1

1. Open the drawing Chapter 5-a.dwg.
2. In the **Toolspace**, click on the **Survey** tab.
3. Right-click on the **Survey Databases** item; select **New local survey database….**
4. Name it **Chapter 5** when the dialog box appears to name the database.
5. In the **Toolspace**, right-click on **Networks** and choose **New…**; when the dialog box for naming appears, type in **Chapter 5**.
6. Expand **Networks**, right-click on **Chapter 5**, and select **Edit field book…**; select **Survey-TRAV.fbk** from where your files are stored for the textbook. It contains the following data, all in the field book language:

   UNIT FOOT DMS

   HORIZ ANGLE RIGHT

To access student data files, go to www.pearsondesigncentral.com.

```
PRISM CONSTANT 0
PRISM OFFSET 0
EDM OFFSET 0
CR OFF
ATMOS OFF
COLLIMATION OFF
JOB CHAP-5
!NOTE TRAVERSE DEMO
TRAVERSE DEMO
SCALE FACTOR 1.000000
VERT ANGLE ZENITH
END
NE 1 1000 1000 "STA1"
NE 2 646.44660941 646.44660941 "STA2"
END
STN 1
!AZ 1 2 225.000000
!PRISM 0.000000
BS 2
AD 3 90.0 500.000 "STA3"
STN 3
BS 1
AD 4 269.5 499.9 "STA4"
STA 4
BS3
AD 5 270 500 "STA5"
STA 5
BS 4
AD 1 269.5 500
STA 1
BS 5
```

7. This data set stores Points 1 and 2 using a **Control Point** command (NE). It then occupies Point 1, backsights 2, and locates 3. It then occupies 3, backsights 1, and locates 4. Then it occupies 4, backsights 3, and locates 5. Then it occupies 5, backsights 4, and locates 1 again.
8. Close the file.
9. Expand **Networks**, right-click on **Chapter 5**, and select **Import> Import field book...**; the **Field book filename (.FBK)** dialog box appear. Select **Survey-TRAV.fbk** from where your files are stored for the textbook. The **Import Field Book** dialog box displays, as shown in Figure 5-6. Accept the data as shown and hit **OK**.
10. When the import is complete, the traverse shown in Figure 5-7 is computed.
11. Note in the **Survey** tab under **Chapter 5** that two control points, 1 and 2, have been created. These will not be moved during traverse balancing. Expand **Setups** and notice that Stations 1, 3, 4, 5, and 1 are described.
12. Right-click on **Traverses**, select **New...**, and type in **Chapter 5** in the naming dialog box.
13. Then click on **Traverses**, Fill in the Initial Station (1), Initial Backsight (2), Stations (3-5,1), and Final Foresight (1) fields, as shown in Figure 5-8.
14. Then a dialog box, shown in Figure 5-9, may appear that indicates you have made changes and not applied them. Hit **Yes** to apply the changes now.

Figure 5-6 Import Field Book dialog box

Figure 5-7 Imported traverse

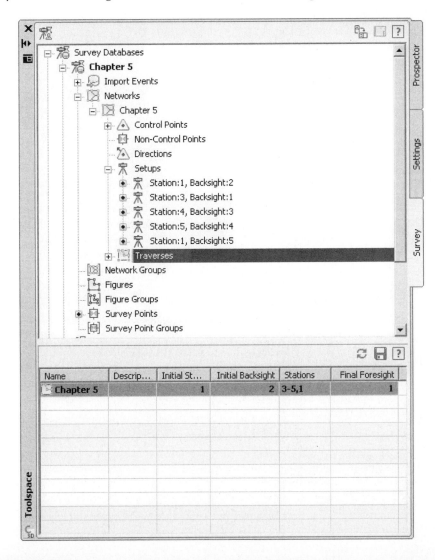

Figure 5-8 Defining the traverse stations

Figure 5-9

15. Click **Chapter 5** under Traverses and right-click. From the choices, select **Traverse analysis...** .
16. The dialog box shown in Figure 5-10 is displayed.
17. Accept the settings and hit **OK**.
18. You may get a dialog box that reads, **WARNING: User-specified traverse limits not met**. Hit **OK**. A notepad opens with traverse information.
19. Then a dialog box, shown in Figure 5-9, may appear that indicates you have made changes and not applied them. Hit **Yes** to apply the changes now.
20. Then click **Chapter 5** and right-click again. From the choices, select **Traverse analysis....**
21. The Notepad files are shown in Figures 5-11, 5-12, and 5-13 display. They are the Compass rule, a balanced angle analysis, and the traverse analysis.

Property	Value
Do traverse analysis	☑ Yes
Do angle balance	☑ Yes
Horizontal adjustment method	Compass rule
Vertical adjustment method	Length weighted distribution
Horizontal closure limit 1:X	15000.00000000
Vertical closure limit 1:X	15000.00000000
Angle error per set	0.00050000
Update survey database	☑ Yes

OK   Cancel   Help

Figure 5-10   Traverse Analysis dialog box

```
File Edit Format View Help
                    RAW    TRAVERSE              COMPASS RULE
        Point         Coordinates              Coordinates         Delta
          1      N     1000.0000      N     1000.0000        0.0000
                 E     1000.0000      E     1000.0000
N 45-02-20 W  Dist:500.3633
          3      N     1353.5534      N     1353.5696        0.4976
                 E      646.4466      E      645.9492
N 44-47-30 E  Dist:499.5610
          4      N     1708.0628      N     1708.0953        0.9952
                 E      998.8996      E      997.9049
S 45-07-40 E  Dist:499.6360
          5      N     1355.5394      N     1355.5881        1.4928
                 E     1353.4799      E     1351.9879
S 44-42-31 W  Dist:500.3382
          1      N      999.9351      N     1000.0000        1.9904
                 E     1001.9894      E     1000.0000
```

Figure 5-11   Traverse analysis-Compass rule applied report

```
File Edit Format View Help
                    RAW    TRAVERSE                NO RULE
        Point         Coordinates              Coordinates         Delta
          1      N     1000.0000      N     1000.0000        0.0000
                 E     1000.0000      E     1000.0000
N 45-00-00 W  Dist:500.0000
          3      N     1353.5534      N     1353.5534        0.0000
                 E      646.4466      E      646.4466
N 44-50-00 E  Dist:499.9000
          4      N     1708.0628      N     1708.0628        0.0000
                 E      998.8996      E      998.8996
S 45-10-00 E  Dist:500.0000
          5      N     1355.5394      N     1355.5394        0.0000
                 E     1353.4799      E     1353.4799
S 44-40-00 W  Dist:500.0000
          1      N      999.9351      N      999.9351        0.0000
                 E     1001.9894      E     1001.9894
Error North    : 0.0649
Error East     : -1.9894
Absolute error : 1.9904
Error Direction: N 88-07-51 W
Perimeter      : 1999.9000
Precision      : 1 in 1004.7602
Number of sides : 4
```

Figure 5-12   Traverse analysis, balanced angles report

File Edit Format View Help

```
Error North      : 0.0649
Error East       : -1.9894
Absolute error   : 1.9904
Error Direction  : N 88-07-51 W
Perimeter        : 1999.9000
Precision        : 1 in 1004.7602
Number of sides  : 4
Area             : 250678.1 sq. ft. , 5.7548 Acres
```

Figure 5-13   Traverse analysis report

22. This shows the Compass rule being applied. Note that Point 1 starts at 1000,1000 and returns to 1000,1000 at the end of the processing.

Exercise 5-6: Computing a Traverse Reduction in Civil 3D—2

In this exercise, you execute the field books described earlier in the traverse loop and cross check example. Use the field books constructed based on the field notes and run them through the Civil 3D software.

1. Open the drawing Chapter 5-b.dwg.
2. In the **Toolspace**, click on the **Survey** tab.
3. Right-click on the **Survey Databases** item; select **New local survey database....**
4. Name it **Chapter 5-b** when the dialog box appears to name the database.
5. Right-click on **Networks** and choose **New...**; when the dialog box for naming appears, type in **Chapter 5-b**.
6. Expand **Networks**, right-click on **Chapter 5-b**, and select **Import> Import field book...**; select **Chapter 5-b.fbk** from where your files are stored for the textbook. Accept any defaults that appear on executing.
7. There may be a dialog box asking: **Do you wish to abort import process?**, say **No**. The loop traverse will import.
8. Right-click on **Networks** and choose **New....**
9. Name the new network **Chapter 5-b cross check**. Hit **OK**.
10. Expand **Networks**, right-click on **Chapter 5-b cross check**, and select **Import> Import field book...**; select **Chapter 5-b-crosscheck.fbk** from where your files are stored for the textbook.
11. When the **Import Field Book** dialog box appears, hit **OK**. If you receive errors, say **Cancel**.
12. A dialog box may appear that warns that Point 1 exists. Select **Ignore**.
13. The cross check traverse computes. Note that it is an open traverse.
14. Expand the **Network** called **Chapter 5-b**. Right-click on the **Traverses** item and hit **New...**; name it **Chapter 5-b** and hit **OK**.
15. Click on **Traverses** and fill in the following data: the Initial Station (1), Initial Backsight (4), Stations (2,3,4,1), and Final Foresight (1).
16. Then a dialog box may appear that indicates you have made changes and not applied them. Hit **Yes** to apply the changes now.
17. Right-click on the traverse **Chapter 5-b** and select **Traverse Analysis....**
18. When the **Traverse Analysis** dialog box appears, accept the defaults and hit **OK**.
19. You may get a dialog box that reads, **First Occupied Point does not have known coordinates**. Hit **OK**.
20. The Notepad files for the Compass rule, a balanced angle analysis, and the traverse analysis display, as shown in Figures 5-14, 5-15, and 5-16. Again note in the Compass rule how Point 1 returns to 2000,2000 after balancing.

To access student data files, go to www.pearsondesigncentral.com.

```
File Edit Format View Help
                   RAW   TRAVERSE                COMPASS RULE
         Point           Coordinates                Coordinates            Delta
           1      N       2000.0000        N       2000.0000            0.0000
                  E       2000.0000        E       2000.0000
N 81-54-54 W  Dist:513.4309
           2      N       2072.2098        N       2072.2107            0.0011
                  E       1491.6732        E       1491.6725
N 29-50-13 E  Dist:440.5203
           3      N       2454.3366        N       2454.3382            0.0021
                  E       1710.8466        E       1710.8452
S 69-45-10 E  Dist:308.1994
           4      N       2347.6774        N       2347.6794            0.0028
                  E       2000.0024        E       2000.0005
S 00-00-00 W  Dist:347.6794
           1      N       1999.9974        N       2000.0000            0.0035
                  E       2000.0024        E       2000.0000
Area              : 155303.0 sq. ft. , 3.5653 Acres
```

Figure 5-14   Traverse analysis report—Compass rule applied report

```
File Edit Format View Help
                   RAW   TRAVERSE                 NO RULE
         Point           Coordinates                Coordinates            Delta
           1      N       2000.0000        N       2000.0000            0.0000
                  E       2000.0000        E       2000.0000
N 81-54-54 W  Dist:513.4300
           2      N       2072.2098        N       2072.2098            0.0000
                  E       1491.6732        E       1491.6732
N 29-50-13 E  Dist:440.5200
           3      N       2454.3366        N       2454.3366            0.0000
                  E       1710.8466        E       1710.8466
S 69-45-10 E  Dist:308.2000
           4      N       2347.6774        N       2347.6774            0.0000
                  E       2000.0024        E       2000.0024
S 00-00-00 W  Dist:347.6800
           1      N       1999.9974        N       1999.9974            0.0000
                  E       2000.0024        E       2000.0024
Error North      : 0.0026
Error East       : -0.0024
Absolute error   : 0.0035
Error Direction  : N 42-16-02 W
Perimeter        : 1609.8300
Precision        : 1 in 454175.0004
Number of sides  : 4
Area             : 155302.9 sq. ft. , 3.5653 Acres
```

Figure 5-15   Traverse analysis, balanced angles report

```
File Edit Format View Help
Error North      : 0.0026
Error East       : -0.0024
Absolute error   : 0.0035
Error Direction  : N 42-16-02 W
Perimeter        : 1609.8300
Precision        : 1 in 454175.0004
Number of sides  : 4
Area             : 155302.9 sq. ft. , 3.5653 Acres
```

Figure 5-16   Traverse analysis report

Reduce the cross check traverse.

21. Expand the network called **Chapter 5-b-crosscheck**. Right-click on the **Traverses** item and hit **New...**; name it **Chapter 5-b-crosscheck** and hit **OK**.
22. Click on **Traverses** and fill in the following data: the Initial Station (1), Initial Backsight (2), Stations (101,102), and Final Foresight (3).
23. Right-click on **Chapter 5-b-crosscheck** and choose **Traverse Analysis...**.
24. You may get a dialog box that reads, **First Occupied Point does not have known coordinates**. Hit **OK**.
25. Then a dialog box may appear that indicates you have made changes and not applied them. Hit **Yes** to apply the changes now.
26. Then click **Chapter 5-b-crosscheck** and right-click again. From the choices, select **Traverse analysis...**.

27. The Notepad files for the traverse analysis, a balanced angle analysis, and the Compass rule display, as shown in Figures 5-17, 5-18, and 5-19.

```
                  RAW    TRAVERSE              COMPASS RULE
        Point        Coordinates              Coordinates          Delta
        1        N      2000.0000       N      2000.0000         0.0000
                 E      2000.0000       E      2000.0000
N 28-26-40 W  Dist:204.1164
        101      N      2179.4782       N      2179.4755         0.0037
                 E      1902.7758       E      1902.7783
N 58-12-42 W  Dist:198.5366
        102      N      2284.0668       N      2284.0615         0.0072
                 E      1734.0176       E      1734.0224
N 07-45-04 W  Dist:171.8474
        3        N      2454.3464       N      2454.3387         0.0103
                 E      1710.8380       E      1710.8449
```

Figure 5-17   Traverse analysis report-Compass rule applied report

```
                                              RAW    TRAVERSE              NO RULE
                                     Point        Coordinates             Coordinates         Delta
                                     1        N      2000.0000      N      2000.0000         0.0000
                                              E      2000.0000      E      2000.0000
                            N 28-26-41 W  Dist:204.1200
                                     101      N      2179.4782      N      2179.4782         0.0000
                                              E      1902.7758      E      1902.7758
                            N 58-12-41 W  Dist:198.5400
                                     102      N      2284.0668      N      2284.0668         0.0000
                                              E      1734.0176      E      1734.0176
                            N 07-45-07 W  Dist:171.8500
                                     3        N      2454.3464      N      2454.3464         0.0000
                                              E      1710.8380      E      1710.8380
```

```
Error North      : -0.0077              Error North      : -0.0077
Error East       : 0.0069               Error East       : 0.0069
Absolute error   : 0.0103               Absolute error   : 0.0103
Error Direction  : S 42-01-51 E         Error Direction  : S 42-01-51 E
Perimeter        : 574.5100             Perimeter        : 574.5100
Precision        : 1 in 55593.6396      Precision        : 1 in 55593.6396
Number of sides  : 3                    Number of sides  : 3
```

Figure 5-18   Traverse analysis report   **Figure 5-19**   Traverse analysis, balanced angles report

When importing field books containing field collected data, the approach is exactly the same except, of course, that you may not reduce the traverse. You will simply see the data import into the Civil 3D drawing.

Exercise 5-7: Performing a Field Book Reduction in Civil 3D

You now execute a field book that will import an example of field-collected planimetric features. It will draw linework for an edge of pavement that was collected using a total station.

1. Open the drawing Chapter 5-c.dwg.
2. In the **Toolspace**, click on the **Survey** tab.
3. Right-click on the **Survey Databases** item; select **New local survey database....**
4. Name it **Chapter 5-c** when the dialog box appears to name the database.
5. Right-click on the **Chapter 5-c database** and select **Open database**. If the right-click menu has only **Close survey database**, then it is already open.
6. Right-click on **Networks** and choose **New...**; when the dialog box for naming appears, type in **Chapter 5-c**.
7. Expand **Networks**, right-click on **Chapter 5-c**, and select **Import> Import field book...**; select **Chapter 5-c.fbk** from where your files are stored for the textbook. Accept any defaults that appear on executing.
8. You may get a dialog box asking, do whether you wish to abort; say **No**.
9. The processing begins, and a roadway edge of pavement and two associated buildings will be drawn.

To access student data files, go to www.pearsondesigncentral.com.

Note:
In the **Toolspace** within the **Survey** tab, there is a button at the top of the **Prospector** that displays the **Survey User Settings** dialog box shown in Figure 5-20.

Figure 5-20 Survey User Settings dialog box

You have just imported the field book and automatically drawn the points and linework collected in the field. The previous exercises illustrate how powerful this aspect of the Civil 3D software is. The entire survey department can now use Civil 3D to develop existing ground base information that the engineering design team can use directly. The surveyor will, of course, receive the data from the engineers at the back end of the project for checking and stakeout preparation or 3D/GPS data preparation for the contractor. The formatting of this data is covered in Appendix A on data sharing.

CHAPTER SUMMARY

This chapter introduced you to surveying in Civil 3D. The technology allows you to develop the entire base required for a project, from the initial designs to quality control and data preparation.

CHAPTER TEST QUESTIONS

Multiple Choice

1. The survey features added to the 2007 release include which of the following?

   a. Traverse entry, editing, and management
   b. Traverse balancing
   c. Importing filed data collector files
   d. All of the above

2. The interface for the surveying capabilities includes which of the following?

a. Importing of SRTM satellite data

b. Automatically pounding hubs and stakes into the ground

c. Enabling the software to set up total stations so field crews are no longer needed

d. None of the above

3. The survey functionality allows users to create the formats required for 3D/GPS Machine Control equipment. Which manufacturers are supported?

a. Topcon, Trimble, Leica

b. Caterpillar, Komatsu, VanNatta

c. Mercedes, Range Rover, Ford

d. All of the above

4. Survey functions include which of the following?

a. Collecting planimetric and 3D data of existing conditions

b. Quality control of engineering data and preparation of stakeout data for construction

c. Computing property boundaries

d. All of the above

5. The types of data surveyors prepare includes which of the following?

a. Proposed finished ground engineering, drainage improvements, stormwater retention facilities

b. Surface data, geometric data, and control data

c. Site improvements for dams, airport, or highways

d. Design of subdivisions, harbors, and treatment plants

6. Which of the following pertains to traverse data established by surveyors?

a. They are often tied into control monuments.

b. They are repeatedly occupied and used in surveying and perhaps construction and provide a constant location from which to compute additional point data.

c. They are usually corrected for errors caused by human, ambient, or instrument lapses.

d. All of the above

7. When a traverse is corrected and balanced, what components are corrected?

a. The area within the closed traverse is corrected and rounded.

b. The control points governing the traverse are moved to new and more accurate locations.

c. The points or vertices of the traverse figure with its incorrect distances and angular errors are corrected.

d. All of the above

8. Surveyors also work in which of the following areas?

a. Aerial photogrammetry, GIS research, and GPS surveying

b. Hydraulic drainage computations for custom drainage structures

c. Designing beams and columns for standard building structures

d. None of the above

9. Why are VIOs (Visually Identifiable Objects) used in aerial photogrammetry?

a. They can be seen in the photographs.

b. They have horizontal and vertical control associated with them.

c. They assist in calibrating everything in the photo to a known coordinate.

d. All of the above

10. What makes Imaginary Reference Stations an interesting technology for surveyors?

a. They eliminate the need for base stations for many surveyors.

b. They create virtual stations that interpolate errors and corrections.

c. They are being developed by both public and private concerns.

d. All of the above

True or False

1. True or False: Civil 3D can create, edit, and balance traverses; import field shot data; and draw linework and points.

2. True or False: 2D and 3D control points are often established randomly and are never tied to anything official.

3. True or False: In photogrammetry, a VIO is a Vertical Interference Obstacle that interferes with the airplane's flight path.

4. True or False: We use the Compass rule to find North when we are in the field.

5. True or False: A polygon with six sides should have the sum of the interior angles equal to 750 degrees.

6. True or False: There are several files produced when balancing a traverse. They include analysis files, which display horizontal closure and angular error, a file showing raw and adjusted elevations; a file showing the balancing of the angular error; and the final adjusted coordinates.

7. True or False: The survey language can be customized so that the order of the data entry can be changed to the user's preferences.

8. True or False: The survey language can be customized so that the actual names of the commands (such as AD or BS) can be changed to what the user prefers.

9. True or False: An interface specifically developed for the surveyor exists in Civil 3D.

10. True or False: Civil 3D will perform the Compass rule only when balancing traverses.

CHAPTER EXERCISES

1. What functions do surveyors perform on engineering projects? Do surveyors work in two dimensions or three?
2. Why is establishing project control important?
3. How many degrees does a 16-sided closed traverse have inside it?
4. How might the following table be adjusted to correct the angular error in this traverse?

Adjustment of Angles			
Point	Measured Interior Angle	Average Correction (Degrees)	Adjusted Angle (Degrees)
A	120.5		
B	110.0		
C	110.5		
D	99.5		
E	100.0		
	———	———	———
Result:			

5. When speaking of traverse misclosure, what is the latitude and departure?
6. What is the relative precision for a 1000′ traverse that has a linear misclosure of 0.1?
7. If a traverse has a departure of 0.2 and a latitude of 0.3, what is the linear misclosure?
8. When using the survey language in Civil 3D, what do the following commands indicate: STA 10, BS 5?
9. When using the survey language in Civil 3D, what do the following commands indicate: NE 10 1000 1000, NE 5 1500 1000?
10. When shooting a traverse, why does it not close perfectly?

Civil 3D—The Modern Curvilinead

6

Chapter Objectives

- Understand the mathematics behind the Civil 3D geometry tools.
- Understand distances; bearings; information on traverses used for establishing control on projects; and formulas for circles, arcs, triangles, and lines.
- Use Civil 3D for creating and editing these geometry items.
- Use the many **Transparent** commands that are in Civil 3D.
- Understand how to develop, label, and edit alignments and parcels.

INTRODUCTION

Civil 3D is a modern curvilinead. What is a curvilinead? It is an instrument that draws curvilinear and rectilinear objects. The "3D" in Civil 3D could stand for Design, Delineation, Depiction because of its strengths in developing curvilinear and rectilinear geometry objects. This chapter begins with some of the formulas needed to design geometry and discusses curvilinear linework generation; roadway alignment; and parcel creation, editing, and drafting. The ability to modify these data and the development of curvilinear 2D geometry (Lines, Arcs, Spirals), parcels, alignments, and labels are discussed in detail.

REVIEW OF FUNCTIONS AND FEATURES TO BE USED

This chapter uses engineering functions to compute angles, slopes, and distances. Civil 3D has many tools for creating lines and curves, and this chapter examines how these are then used to create disciplinary objects such as alignments and parcels.

COMPUTATIONS OF LINES AND THEIR ANGLES

In a vector-based program, points create lines. Points occupy a position consisting of only an X coordinate, a Y coordinate, and a Z coordinate. A linear connection of the dots occurs with a clear start, a distance, and direction. Refer to Figure 6-1 for a line starting at 0, 0 and continuing through a point of 7.5, 2.5.

The points can be Civil 3D points or simply just AutoCAD points or picks on the screen, but they are points nevertheless. When drawing lines in AutoCAD, you can easily find out information about them by using the **LIST** command. But where does the **LIST** command compute its results from? Can these results be accomplished by hand, using manual techniques? You certainly should be able to reproduce these results using manual techniques just in case you want to check the computer. One of the worst things that someone using a computer can do when asked, "How do you know that the value is correct?" is to say, "Because the computer said so." A better response would be, "I know this is a correct estimate of the value based on my knowledge of the

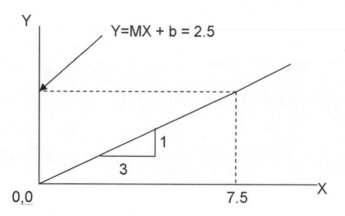

Figure 6-1   A vector

software's algorithms and the data I developed." It is necessary to know the engineering and mathematical formulas behind these algorithms, and each chapter in this text explores them. This chapter discusses linear and curvilinear computations.

Example 6-1: Find the Angle of a Two-Dimensional Line from the X Axis

To find the angle from the X axis of the two-dimensional line with the same coordinate values as shown in Figure 6-1, follow this process:

Slope $= \Delta Y/\Delta X = (20 - 15)/(10 - 5) = 5/5 = 1$

The angle then is computed as: $(\text{ATAN}((\text{ABS})\text{slope})) = \text{ATAN}(1) = 45°$

Example 6-2: Find the Angle of a Three-Dimensional Line from the X Axis

To find the angle from the X axis of the three-dimensional line with the same coordinate values as shown in Figure 6-1, follow this process:

Slope $= \Delta Z/\sqrt{A^2 + B^2} = (5 - 10)/(7.0710678) = 0.70710678$

The angle then is computed as: $(\text{ATAN}((\text{ABS})\text{slope}) = \text{ATAN}(0.70710678) = 35.254°$
The formula for a line, $Y = mX + b,$ was discussed in Chapter 3 under Point Basics.
The Y coordinate equals the slope of the line times the X coordinate plus the y intercept.
Therefore, in Figure 6-1, $m = .333, X = 7.5,$ and $b = 0; Y = 2.5.$

DISTANCES AND BEARINGS

Distances and bearings are used to show course and lengths for many items such as parcel lines, boundaries, alignments, pipelines, and so forth. The bearing has four quadrants, each no larger than 90 degrees. It always starts at either north or south and is followed by the angle and then the direction to which it turns, which is either east or west. See Figure 6-2.

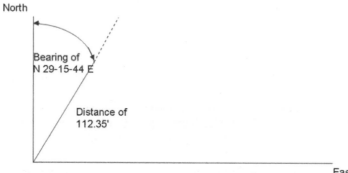

Figure 6-2   Bearing quadrants

3D Linework Uses Slope Distances
for Distance Measurement

Distances measured can include horizontal lengths, vertical lengths, **slope distances**, or vertical angles. Figure 6-3 shows what these are in establishing data connecting Point *A* to Point *B*.

slope distances: The distance measured from Point *A* to Point *B* along an incline. It will always be longer than the horizontal distance when the slope is not horizontal or vertical.

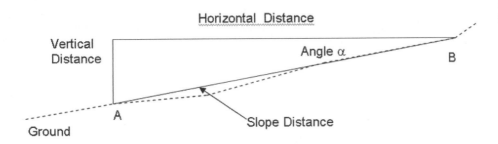

Figure 6-3   Slope distances

Example 6-3: Computing the Difference in Height Between Rods

As shown in Figure 6-4,

Rod reading = 7.21'
Rod reading = 2.63'
Difference in Elevation = 7.21 − 2.63 = **4.58'**

Figure 6-4   Computing the difference in height between rods

Control Surveys

Control surveys establish reference points and reference lines for preliminary and construction surveys. Vertical reference points called benchmarks are also established. These are then tied into state coordinate systems, property lines, road centerlines, or arbitrary grid systems. The various types of tie-in methods are shown in Figure 6-5.

• Type A, rectangular tie-in, is also known as a right angle offset. Remember in Chapter 3 how many commands assisted us in developing these Perpendiculars?

control survey: Sets the "monumentation" for the project. All survey shots and references typically come from or tie back to this monumentation.

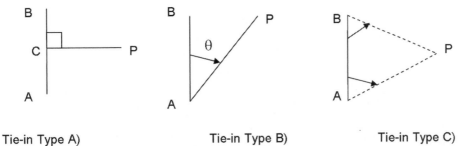

Tie-in Type A)   Tie-in Type B)   Tie-in Type C)   **Figure 6-5**   Tie-in methods

- Type B, polar tie-in, is also known as the angle/distance technique.
- Type C, intersection tie-in, uses two angles from a baseline to locate a position.

Example 6-4: Stationing

Distances along baselines are called stations, as in Figure 6-6. Right angles can be achieved from the baseline. The distance along this right angle is called an offset.

Station 2 + 36.517 is 236.517′ from the intersection of Elm and Pine. The left corner of the building is 236.517′ from Elm and 40.01′ at a 90 degree angle from Pine.

Figure 6-6   Stationing

Example 6-5: Doubling the Angle

A surveying technique to enhance precision when shooting data in the field is called Doubling the Angle. The angles are effectively shot and computed twice for each interior angle. Due to human error, ambient condition error, or equipment error, these measures are often slightly different. So the surveyor often creates a mean of the two angles, anticipating that the mean angular error is less than any one of the angles independently.

Station	Direct Angle	Double Angle	Mean
A	101-24-00	202-48-00	101-24-00
B	149-13-00	289-26-00	149-13-00
C	80-58-00	161-57-00	80-58-30
D	116-20-00	232-38-00	116-19-00
E	92-04-00	184-09-00	92-04-30
		Total Degrees	538-119-00 = 539-59-00
			(Is this correct?)

The total number of degrees within a closed polygon depends on the number of sides and is computed using the following formula. ANGULAR CLOSURE = $(N - 2) \times 180$; therefore, our polygon = $3 \times 180 = 540$-00-00. So subtracting these yields 540-00-00 minus 539-59-00 = 01′-00″ ERROR. See Figure 6-7.

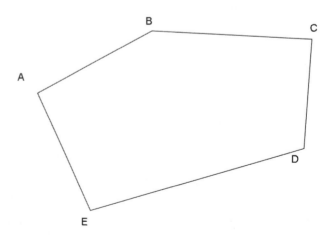

Figure 6-7   Polygons

Vector Data and Formulas

As a refresher, to fully understand the computations that the Civil 3D software performs, the following information is provided along with examples. Formulas for computing the data manually are also included.

Circles

- Radius, Perimeter, Area

Right Triangles

- Lengths of sides, Interior angles

Curvilinear Objects Including Arcs, Circular Curves, and Spirals

- Arc definition, Chord definition
- Define the components of an arc
- Formulas for computing Arc Length (L), Radius (R), Chord length (C), Mid-ordinate chord distance (M), External *secant* (E), and Tangent length (T)
- Define the components of a spiral
- Types of horizontal curves

secant: A line that intersects a circle twice. An external secant is the part of the secant that is outside the circle or arc.

Circle Formulas

Radius = 1/2 × Diameter
Pi radians = 180°
1 radian = 180/π
2 Pi radians = 360
Perimeter = 2 × π × r or, π × Diameter
Area = π × r^2

Right Triangle Definitions and Formulas

$a^2 + b^2 = c^2$
$a^2 = (c^2 - b^2)$
$b^2 = (c^2 - a^2)$
$c^2 = (a^2 + b^2)$

Sides

Tan = Opposite/Adjacent
Sin = Opposite/Hypotenuse
Cos = Adjacent/Hypotenuse
$A + B + C = 180°$

Note

$A° = 180° - 90° - B°$ or, $90° - B° \rightarrow B° = 90° - A°$
$A° = Tan^{-1}(b/a)$ or $Sin^{-1}(b/c)$ or $Cos^{-1}(a/c)$
$B° = Tan^{-1}(a/b)$ or $Sin^{-1}(a/c)$ or $Cos^{-1}(b/c)$

Example 6-6: Triangles

If the right triangle in Figure 6-8 has a 27.5′ base and a height of 38.7′, how would you find:

1. The angle B.

$B = Tan^{-1}(opp/adj) = Tan^{-1}(38.7/27.5) = 54.60261522$

$0.60261522 × 60 = 36.1569$

$0.1569 × 60 = 9.414 = 54 - 36 - 9$

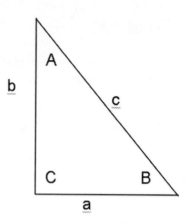

Figure 6-8   Triangles

2. The remaining angle of the triangle:

   $90 - 54.6026 = 35.40$

3. The length of the hypotenuse:

   $c = \sqrt{((27.5)^2 + (38.7)^2)} = 47.48'$

4. The area of the triangle:

   $(27.5 \times 38.7)/2 = 532.13 \text{ ft}^2$

5. What is the closest distance from *C* to any point along the hypotenuse?

   We know angle $B = 54.6026°$

   We know that Sin $(54.6026) = $ opp/hyp

   If $X = Y/Z$, then $Y = X \times Z$ and $Z = Y/X$, then $27.5 \times \text{Sin} (54.6026) = 22.42'$

6. Where does the shortest distance line intersect the hypotenuse in relation to point *A*?

   We know two sides of the new triangle so,

   $a^2 + b^2 = c^2$ and that $c = 22.42$ and $b = 27.5$

   $a = \sqrt{(c^2 - b^2)} = \sqrt{((27.5)^2 - (22.42)^2)} = 15.92'$

Because a right triangle is being divided into smaller right triangles, the interior always remains the same as with the original triangle.

Example 6-7: A Practical Problem

See Figure 6-9. A homeowner wants to remove the existing tree and put a well there. County regulations say the well must be 50′ from the drain field and 25′ from the house. Does it work?

   The measured distance from the tree to the house = 26′; OK. The distance from the drain field to the house is 32.5′. Distance from the tree to the drain field = $\sqrt{(32.5^2 + 26^2)} = 41.60$; not OK. See Figure 6-10.

   Suggested new location for well could be:

   An alternative #1 might be: $a = \sqrt{(c^2 - b^2)} = \sqrt{(50^2 - 32.50^2)} = 38'$
   An alternative #2 might be: $b = \sqrt{(50^2 - 26^2)} = 42.71$, say, 43′

From the corner of the drain field looking at the corner of the house, what is the angle to locate the proposed well?

   For alternative #2,

$A = \text{Tan}^{-1} (40/32.5) = 50.9°$
$ = \text{Sin}^{-1} (40/50) = 53.13°$
$ = \text{Cos}^{-1} (32.5/50) = 49.45°$

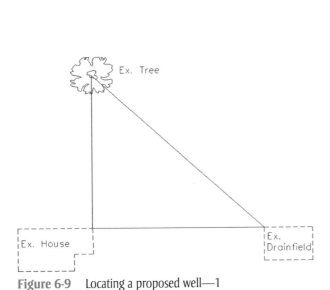

Figure 6-9   Locating a proposed well—1

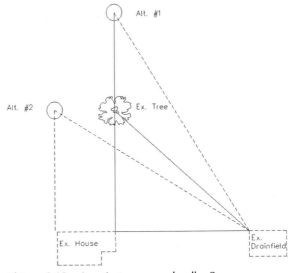

Figure 6-10   Locating a proposed well—2

CURVILINEAR OBJECTS—ARCS, CIRCULAR CURVES, AND SPIRALS—DEFINITIONS AND FORMULAS

Another aspect of drawing is the ability to compute curves and arcs. Arcs are defined as those curvilinear objects that have a fixed radius, and curves are those objects that may have a fixed radius but may also be dynamic. Spirals and parabolas fall into the curve category.

Some specific formulas for computing arc data and spiral data need to be discussed in detail before moving toward automated solutions.

Arcs have two definitions: the Arc definition (Figure 6-11) and the Chord definition (Figure 6-12). The Arc definition is the most widely used and typically used by highway designers and other land development staff. It is also called the *Roadway definition*. The Chord method is called the *Railway definition*.

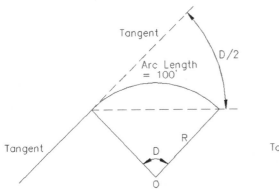

Figure 6-11   The Arc definition

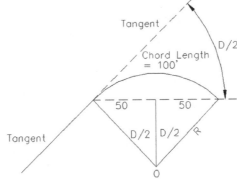

Figure 6-12   The Chord definition

The *Arc method* of curve calculation occurs where the degree of curve is measured over an arc length of 100′. The formulas are:

$D_a/100 = 360°/(2 \times PI \times R)$,
$D_a = 36000/(2 \times \pi \times R)$, or
$D_a = 5729.578/R$.
$R = 5729.578/D_a$. If $D_a = 1°$, then $R = 5729.578$ units and $\pi = 3.14159\ldots$
And $R = 5729.578/D_a$. If $D_a = 1°$, then $R = 5729.578′$ and $\pi = 3.14159\ldots$
And $R = 5729.578/D_a$. If $D_a = 1°$, then $R = 5729.578$ m and $\pi = 3.14159\ldots$

The *Chord method* of curve calculation occurs where the degree of curve is measured over a chord length of 100′. The formulas are:

$\text{Sin } (D_c/2) = 50/R$
$R = 50/\text{Sin } (1/2)D_c$, where D_c is in degrees.
If $D_c = 1°$, then $R = 5729.648$ units.

Circular Curves.   According to Figure 6-13,

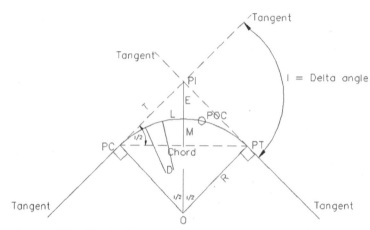

Figure 6-13   Circular Curves

PI = Point of Intersection
PT = Point of Tangency
T = Tangent length
L = Length of curve
E = External distance
$D = D_a$ degree of curve, arc definition
$D = D_c$ degree of curve, chord definition
POC = Point on Curve
PC = Point of Curvature
I = Deflection angle (Delta)
R = Radius
C = Chord length
M = Middle ordinate distance
PRC = Point of Reverse Curvature (not shown)
PCC = Point of Compound Curvature (not shown)

Arc Formulas.   Note in the formulas, the difference between the *letter I* and the *number 1*.

$L = 100 \times I°/D_a°$	$L = RI$ (where I is in radians), *or* $RI\pi/180$
$R = 5729.578/D_a°$	$T = R \times \text{Tan } (I/2)$
$C = 2R \times \text{Sin } (I/2)$	$R/(R + E) = \text{Cos } (I/2)$
$E = R((1/\text{Cos } (I/2)) - 1)$	$(R - M)/R = \text{Cos } (I/2)$
$M = R(1 - \text{Cos } (I/2))$	$E = T \times \text{Tan } (I/4)$
$M = E \times \text{Cos } (I/2)$	$R = 50/(\text{Sin } (D/2))$

Example 6-8: Basic Curve Formulas

If $I = 45$, $L = 75$, then $R = 95.49$, $T = 39.55$, $C = 73.09$, $E = 7.87$,
$M = 7.27$, $D_a = 60.0000$
$75 = (100 \times 45)/D_a$, therefore $D_a = (100 \times 45)/75 = 60.0000$
$R = 5729.578/60 = 95.49$; $E = 95.49((1/\text{Cos}(I/2)) - 1) = 95.49$
$\times 0.08239 = 7.867$
$M = 95.49 \times (1 - (\text{Cos }(I/2))) = 95.49 \times (1 - .92387) = 7.268$
$C = 2(95.49) \times \text{Sin }(45/2) = 73.08$

Example 6-9: Curve Application

Two highway tangents intersect with a right intersection angle $I = 12\text{-}30\text{-}00$ at station $0 + 152.204$ m. If a radius of 300 m is to be used for the circular curve, prepare the field book notes to the nearest minute in order to lay out the curve with 20 m staking.

Note:
The deflection angle for a chord length of 20 m from the PC is (20/L)(1/2). The field notes are set up in the following table.

Solution:

$T = R \times \text{Tan }(I/2) = 300 \times \text{Tan }(6°15')$
$\quad = 32.855$ m
$L = RI\pi/180 = (300)(12.50)(\pi)/180$
$\quad = 65.450$ m
Station of PI $= 0 + 152.204$
$-T = -(0 + 32.855)$
Station of PC $= 0 + 119.349$
$+L = +(0 + 65.450)$
Station of PT $= 0 + 184.799$ m

Station	Chord Dist from PC	Point	Deflection Angle
0 + 184.799	65.450	PT	6-15-00
0 + 180	60.651		5-47-30
0 + 160	40.651		3-52-55
0 + 140	20.651		1-58-19
0 + 120	0.651		00-03-44
0 + 119.349	0	PC	00-00-00
Procedure:	$180 - 119.349 = 60.651$		
	$(60.651/65.45) \times 6.25 = 5.7917° = 5\text{-}47\text{-}30°$		

Example 6-10: Centerline Curve

Find the arc distance for the roadway centerline shown in Figure 6-14.
If this were a complete circle, the perimeter would be:

$2\pi r = 2\pi 200 = 1256.64'$
Therefore, $27°/360° \times 1256.64 = 94.25'$.
Shortcut $= (\text{angle} \times R)/57.30 = 94.25'$
Partial area $= \text{angle}/360 \times \pi r^2$
Shortcut $= (\text{angle} \times R^2)/114.59 = 9424.91$ ft^2

Example 6-11: Miscellaneous Applications for Curve Solutions

These concepts can be used in widely varying problems. Here is an example of a pipe problem in which you need to compute flow through a pipe. A 48″ diameter RCP is flowing 14″ deep (Figure 6-15). What are the area of flow and wetted perimeter?

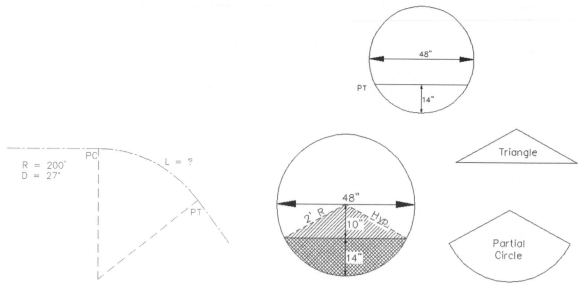

Figure 6-14   Arc distance

Figure 6-15   Flow through a pipe

Figure the angles of the triangle and base width (across water surface).

Cos angle = Adjacent/Hypotneuse
Angle = Cos − 1 (0.83′/2.0′) = 65.4807°

Then, the total angle across the water surface = 2 × 65.4807 = 130.9614°
The base width = $\sqrt{(c^2 - a^2)}$ = $\sqrt{(2^2 - 0.83^2)}$ = 1.82′
Then, the total width of the water surface = 2 × 1.82 = 3.64′
Figure the flow area. Area (triangle) = ((base × height)/2) × 2; the 2s cancel out.

3.64 × 0.83 = 3.02 ft^2
Area of water = angle × R^2/114.59 = 130.9614 × 2^2/114.59 = 4.57 ft^2

Flow area = 4.57 − 3.02 = 1.55
The wetted perimeter = angle × R/57.30 = 130.95614 × 2/57.30 = 4.57′

This information could be used in Mannings formula as follows:
The RCP is sloped at a grade of 5%. We know that the n = 0.013 for Mannings
friction coefficient. Then, $Q = A \times \left(\dfrac{A}{Wp}\right)^{2/3} \times \sqrt{S} \times \left(\dfrac{1.486}{n}\right)$

$Q = 1.55 \times \left(\dfrac{1.55}{4.57}\right)^{2/3} \times \sqrt{0.05} \times \dfrac{1.486}{0.013} = 19.26$ cfs.

Spiral Definitions and Formulas.   Spirals are used to create a smooth transition as one travels from a tangent to a curve and then back out to a tangent again. Figure 6-16 shows the parameters for coming into a spiral. The parameters are the same for leaving a spiral.

TS = Tangent to spiral point
SC = Spiral to Curve
CS = Curve to spiral
PI = Point of Intersection
D = Total deflection angle
D_s = Spiral delta angle
D_c = Circular curve delta
T = Total tangent length
R = Radius of circular curve
L = Length of spiral
LT = Long tangent
ST = Short tangent
X = Total "Horizontal" Spiral length

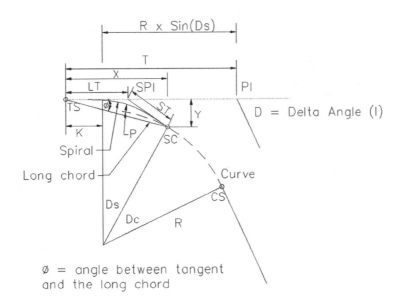

Figure 6-16   Spirals

Y = Total "Vertical" Spiral Length
P = Offset of the tangent line to the PC of the shifted curve
K = Abscissa of the PC of the shifted circular curve referred to the straight
   end of the spiral
SPI = Spiral PI

Formulas for Approximate Solutions to Spiral Problems

$$Y/L = \text{Sin} (\phi) \qquad\qquad Y = L \times \text{Sin} (\phi)$$

$$X_2 = L_2 - Y_2 \qquad\qquad X = \sqrt{(L_2 - Y_2)}$$

$$K = X/2 \qquad\qquad P = Y/4$$

$$LT = (\text{Sin} (2/3 \times \phi)) \times L/\text{Sin} (\phi) \qquad ST = (\text{Sin} (1/3 \times \phi)) \times L/\text{Sin} (\phi)$$

Types of Horizontal Curves.   The curves shown in Figure 6-17 illustrate the various types of curves that are in the civil engineering business. The ***broken back curve*** is usually not allowed by review agencies because the tangent is not tangent to the curve.

broken back curve: An alignment that has a linear segment either coming into or leaving an arc that is not tangent to the arc. This is usually not allowed in most jurisdictions.

Figure 6-17   Types of horizontal curves

CIVIL 3D'S DEFAULT ANGULAR SYSTEM

In Civil 3D, the default angle definitions occur using the Cartesian system, in which the positive X direction is to the right on the screen or monitor and negative X is to the left. Positive Y is up the screen, and negative Y is down. Positive Z is basically in the user's face with negative Z going into the monitor. Angles increase counterclockwise from $0°$ along the X axis to $360°$, back to the X axis. Figure 6-18 shows a $90°$ angle from the X axis.

Figure 6-18   Angles in AutoCAD

Another default in AutoCAD and Civil 3D is that the units for the angles tend to be set to decimal degrees and 0 places of precision. These should also be set up prior to usage so that the desired angles and criteria are to the company's liking. Some people prefer to use degrees, minutes, and seconds as the angle units type, and the precision is usually set to, at least, the nearest second. If you prefer to use decimal degrees, then the precision should be to at least four places. The software converts any output listings to the units the user sets. So if the units are set to decimal degrees and a **LIST** command is issued, the CAD system responds with decimal degrees as part of the listing. If the units are set to degrees, minutes, and seconds, then the system responds accordingly. These can be flipped at any point in the working session to achieve the desired units reporting.

CONVERTING DECIMAL DEGREES TO D-M-S

If the user must perform these computations manually, here are some examples of converting angular units from decimal degrees to degrees, minutes, and seconds.

Example 6-12: Angular Conversions Decimal Degrees to D-M-S

$49.5566°$ breaks down to $49°$ and 0.5566 of a degree. Then, multiply 0.5566 degree $\times$ 60 (minutes per degree) to get the number of minutes, which $= 33.396$ minutes. Now you have 33 minutes and 0.396 of a minute. Then multiply 0.396 minute $\times$ 60 seconds per minute to get the number of seconds, which is $= 23.76$ seconds. Therefore, $49.5566° = 49°-33'-23.76''$.

Example 6-13: Angular Conversions D-M-S to Decimal Degrees

To convert DMS $49°-33'-23.76''$ to decimal degrees, perform the following: $23.76''/60$ (seconds per minute) $= 0.396$ minute. Then add the $33'$ to the $0.396'$ to get $33.396'$. Then divide $33.396'$ by 60 (minutes per degree) and get 0.5566 degree. Then add the $49°$ to the 0.5566 to get $49.5566°$.

ANGLES IN CIVIL ENGINEERING

Now that you can compute the angles of linework manually and based on the Cartesian coordinate system, it is time to discuss in more depth how to talk about angles in terms that civil engineers and surveyors use. This industry uses angles to describe many things, such as property line directions, road centerline directions, and construction instructions for stakeout. Some of the types of important angles to understand are interior angles, azimuths, bearings, cardinal directions, deflection angles, and turned angles.

Interior angles (Figure 6-19) measure the angle between two linear objects. The angle can be acute or obtuse.

An azimuth can be measured from either the North or South. The North azimuth measures angles from the North axis, in a clockwise direction to 360°. The South azimuth measures angles from the South axis, clockwise to 360°.

Bearings (Figure 6-20) measure a heading and are broken into four quadrants: North, South, East, and West. Each quadrant has 90°. The quadrant usually referred to as quadrant 1 is the North-East quadrant and measures from North and turns toward the East. Therefore, a bearing of N 45°−30′−30″ E is located by facing North and turning toward the East an angle of 45°−30′−30″. Quadrant 2 is South-East and begins by facing South and turning the angle toward the East. Quadrant 3 is South-West and also begins by facing South but turns toward the West. Quadrant 4 is North-West, begins by facing North and turning the angle toward the West.

There are also angles known as cardinal directions, which are North, South, East, and West, routinely seen in describing the heading of a hurricane. "Hurricane Ivan is heading North-North-West," which is halfway between North and North-West. In degrees that would be N 22°−30′−00″ W.

Figure 6-19   Interior angles

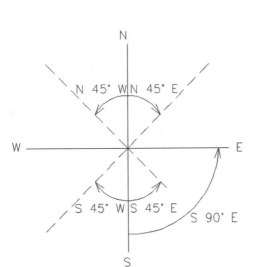

Figure 6-20   Bearings

Figure 6-21 illustrates a person standing at Point *B*, looking forward at the angle defined from Point *A* to Point *B* and then turning 28°−16′−51″ to the right to get to Point *C*. This shows deflection angles.

Figure 6-22 illustrates a person standing at Point *B*, looking back at Point *A*, and then turning 208°−16′−51″ to the right to get to Point *C*. This shows turned angles.

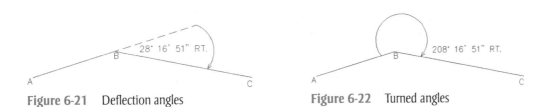

Figure 6-21   Deflection angles   **Figure 6-22**   Turned angles

On the subject of angles, there are two other types of angle measurement—one called Grads, and another called Radians. A Grad is 1/400th of a circle, where North is what would be zero, East is 100 g, South is 200 g, West is 300 g, and back to North is 400 g. This angular system is used in some international countries and by the United States Department of State. A Radian is 180°/π and is often used in computer programming and in the calculation of some arc formulas.

Exercise 6-1: Units

1. Begin the Civil 3D software. Be sure that the Dynamic UCS at the bottom of the screen is turned off.
2. Draw a line from **11,7** to **38,18** and terminate the command.
3. Then type **LIST** at the command prompt. The software responds as follows.

```
Select objects:
```

Select the object, hit **<Enter>**, and this listing will display:

```
LINE Layer: "0"
Space: Model space
Handle = 3F2
from point, X = 11.0000 Y = 7.0000 Z = 0.0000
to point, X = 38.0000 Y = 18.0000 Z = 0.0000
Length = 29.1548, Angle in XY Plane = 22
Delta X = 27.0000, Delta Y = 11.0000, Delta Z = 0.0000
```

Note the angle of 22 degrees. Is it an even 22°?

4. Next, at the command prompt, type **UN** for **Units** to bring up the **Units** dialog box. See Figure 6-23.

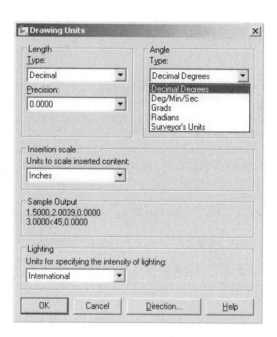

Figure 6-23   Units dialog box

5. Note under the **Angle Type** pop-down window are the supported angle types. **Decimal Degrees** is the default. The default **Precision** is set to 0; hence there is no precision for display beyond the nearest degree. Set the **Precision** to **4** and hit **OK**.
6. Type **LIST** again, select the line, and hit **<Enter>**. Notice that the angle shown now is 22.1663 degrees.
7. Next, at the command prompt, type **UN** again to bring up the **Units** dialog box.
8. Under the **Angle Type** pop-down window, choose **Deg/Min/Sec** and hit **OK**. Type **LIST** again, select the line, and hit **<Enter>**. Notice that the Angle in *XY* Plane = 22d9'59".
9. Next at the command prompt, type **UN** again to bring up the **Units** dialog box.
10. Under **Angle Type** pop-down window, choose **Surveyor's Units** and hit **OK**. Type **LIST** again, select the line, and hit **<Enter>**. Notice that the Angle in *XY* Plane is a bearing of N 67d50'1" E.

Many Geometry commands can be performed using the **Parcels** and **Alignments** menus. Discussion of other tools as well will follow but here is a brief explanation of the menu pull-downs for Parcels and Alignments.

The **Parcels** pull-down menu (Figure 6-24) commands include:

Create Parcel by Layout... invokes the **Parcel Layout Tools** toolbar.

Create Parcel from Object allows for creating new parcels from entities.

Create ROW allows for creating automatic offsets for Right of Way creation.

Edit Parcel includes Edit Parcel Segments, Edit Parcel Properties, and Renumber/Rename Parcels.

Edit Parcel Elevations offers many options for editing parcel elevations.

Add Parcel Labels adds specific labels to parcels.

Add Tables allows for creating property tables of lines, arcs, and so on.

The **Alignments** pull-down menu (Figure 6-25) commands are as follows:

Create Alignment by Layout... invokes the **Create Alignment - Layout** toolbar.

Create Alignment from Polyline allows for creating new alignments from polylines.

Edit Alignment Geometry... invokes the **Layout** toolbar for editing alignments that already exist.

Reverse Alignment Direction allows the same.

Design Criteria Editor... invokes the **Design Criteria Editor** dialog box.

Add Alignment Labels adds specific labels to alignments.

Add Tables allows for creating alignment tables of lines, arcs, and so on.

Figure 6-24   The Parcels pull-down menu

Figure 6-25   The Alignments pull-down menu

GEOMETRY COMPUTATIONS

Now that the chapter has covered the basic and fundamental mathematics behind curvilinear and rectilinear geometry, discussion proceeds with the capabilities of Civil 3D in these areas. Again, enormous functionality exists within AutoCAD alone, and because it is a prerequisite to know AutoCAD, coverage of those routines within Civil 3D follows.

In addition to investigating some of the primitive geometry tools, the tools for creating parcels and alignments are also explored.

THE TRANSPARENT COMMANDS TOOLBAR

You can use **Transparent Commands** within other commands that need data entry consisting of multiple points such as the AutoCAD **LINE** command. Figure 6-26 shows the **Transparent Commands** toolbar. These can be used just like the AutoCAD **Transparent Commands** by preceding them with an apostrophe. You can also pick them as needed from the toolbar. A user can

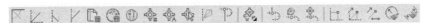

Figure 6-26   The Transparent Commands toolbar

set a series of points using that data entry format because it remains in that data entry mode until you change it or exit.

The Civil **Transparent Commands** are used to enter values based on information that can be supplied when you are prompted for a radius, a point, or a distance. Most of these commands are used to specify point locations within another operation, such as the creation of property lines for parcel data. These commands provide great flexibility of obtaining information from data already existing within the drawing without forcing you to accumulate the information ahead of time. This allows you to calculate the location for a point from a variety of angles and distances.

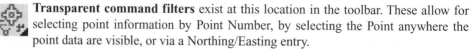
Job skills will benefit because these routines save hours of manual computation for designers.

They are fun to use and provide excellent visuals as you work with them. The command definitions from left to right across the toolbar are described as follows with the accompanying abbreviation that can be typed in as the command is being used.

'AD—Angle Distance

'BD—Bearing Distance

'ZD—Azimuth Distance

'DD—Deflection Distance

'NE—Northing Easting

'GN—Grid Northing Grid Easting

'LL—Latitude Longitude

'PN—Point Number

'PA—Point Name

'PO—Point Object

'SS—Side Shot

'SO—Station Offset

Transparent command filters exist at this location in the toolbar. These allow for selecting point information by Point Number, by selecting the Point anywhere the point data are visible, or via a Northing/Easting entry.

Three additional commands include: **Profile Station from Plan, Profile Station and Elevation from Plan**, and **Profile Station and Elevation** from COGO Point. These commands prompt for and allow for you to select information for the profile by referring to the plan view of the alignment. These can be beneficial in that an important location can be identified using plan view objects that cannot be seen when viewing the profile. This could be the location of a horizontal utility manhole, for instance.

'PSE—Profile Station Elevation

 'PGS—Profile Grade Station

 'PGL—Profile Grade Length

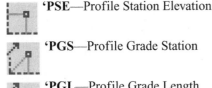 **'MR**—Match Radius

'ML—Match Length

Exercise 6-2: The 'AD Command

You now explore how these commands work. Let us begin with the **'AD** command. This command allows you to build linework using a turned angle and distance (Figure 6-27).

Angle: 128.0996 (d)

Figure 6-27   Turned angle and distance

 TIP   The **'AD** command can be used to describe a traverse based on an occupied point, a backsight, turned angles, and distances.

1. Open the drawing called Chapter-6-Geometry.dwg.
2. Using the **V** for **View** command, highlight the view called **Geom-A**, hit **Set Current**, and then hit **OK**. You draw linework using turned angles and distances from the line visible on the screen.
3. Type **L** for **Line**. Follow the prompts:
4. `LINE Specify first point:` Using an **Endpoint** Osnap pick the northern end of the line in the view.
5. `Specify next point or [Undo]` : Type **'AD** or select the first icon on the **Transparent Commands** toolbar.
6. `>>Specify ending point or [.P/.N/.G]` : Using an **Endpoint** Osnap pick the southern end of the line in the view.
7. `Current angle unit: degree, Input: DD.DDDDDD (decimal)`

To access student data files, go to www.pearsondesigncentral.com.

 TIP   If the prompt shows DD.MMSS then you can type 128d5'58.56" or change the drawing settings so it asks for DD.DDDDDD. This is done by going to the **Toolspace**, clicking on the **Settings** tab, right-clicking on the drawing name, and choosing **Edit Drawing Settings**. Choose the **Ambient Settings** tab and expand the **Angle**. Change the **Value for the Format** to the desired setting.

8. >>Specify angle or [Counter-clockwise] : Type **128.0996**
9. >>Specify distance: **75**
10. Resuming LINE command.
11. Specify next point or [Undo] : (922.68 1060.78 0.0)
12. Specify next point or [Undo] :
13. Current angle unit: degree, Input: DD.DDDDDD (decimal)
14. >>Specify angle or [Counter-clockwise] : **279.8302** (Figure 6-28).

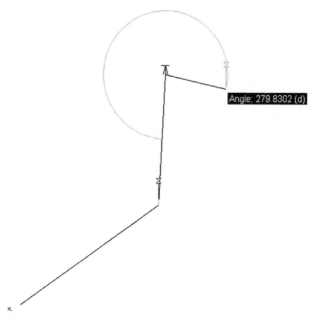

Angle: 279.8302 (d)

Figure 6-28   Turned angle of 279.8302

15. >>Specify distance: **100**

    Resuming LINE command.

16. Specify next point or [Undo] : (1020.15 1038.41 0.0)
17. Specify next point or [Close/Undo] :

    Current angle unit: degree, Input: DD.DDDDDD (decimal)

18. >>Specify angle or [Counter-clockwise] : **233.3313** (Figure 6-29).

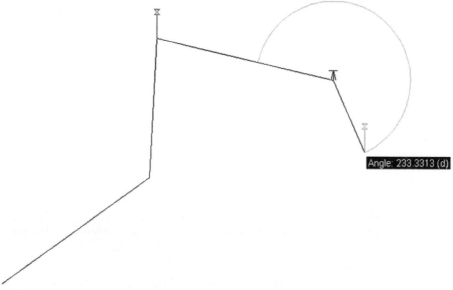

Angle: 233.3313 (d)

Figure 6-29   Turned angle of 233.3313

19. `>>Specify distance:` **75**
20. `Resuming LINE command.`
21. `Specify next point or [Close/Undo]:` (1050.34 969.758 0.0)
22. `Specify next point or [Close/Undo]:`
23. `Current angle unit: degree, Input: DD.DDDDDD (decimal)`
24. `>>Specify angle or [Counter-clockwise]:` **<Esc>**

    `Resuming LINE command.`

25. `Specify next point or [Close/Undo]:` **<Esc>** to terminate.
26. Save your file with the same name and a suffix of your initials.

Notice the almost video game–style graphics that appear to help you through the computations. The yellow marker simulates a station setup while the green "rodman" is placed at the backsight and the red "rodman" is placed at the foresight location. The red arc indicates that the computations are using a turned angle from the backsight to the foresight.

Exercise 6-3: The '**BD** Command

This command allows you to build linework using a bearing and distance.

Job skills will benefit from the use of the '**BD** command because surveyors routinely draw property and easement linework using distances and bearings.

1. Continue in the same drawing or open the drawing you just saved.
2. Using the **V** for **View** command, highlight the view called **Geom-A**, hit **Set Current**, and then hit **OK**. You draw linework using a bearing and distance from where you left off in the previous command. You can also use the line visible on the screen if you did not perform the last exercise. Of course, your results may vary from the figure somewhat.
3. `Command:` **L**
4. `LINE Specify first point:` Using an **Endpoint** Osnap, pick the end of the last line you drew in the previous exercise. It is near 1050, 969.
5. `Specify next point or [Undo]:` Type '**BD** or select the second icon on the **Transparent Commands** toolbar. A reminder displays: `Quadrants - NE = 1, SE = 2, SW = 3, NW = 4`
6. `>>Specify quadrant (1-4):` **1**, for Northeast quadrant (Figure 6-30).

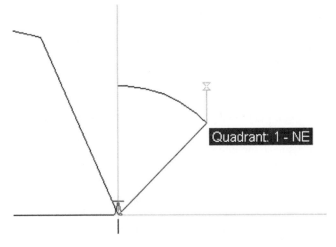

Quadrant: 1 - NE

Figure 6-30 The Northeast quadrant

7. A reminder displays: `Current direction unit: degree, Input: DD.MMSSSS (decimal dms)`
8. `>>Specify bearing:` **41.3329**, indicates a bearing angle of 41 degrees, 33 minutes, and 29 seconds.
9. `>>Specify distance:` **75**
10. `Resuming LINE command. Specify next point or [Undo]:` (1100.1 1025.88 0.0)

11. `Specify next point or [Undo]:` `Quadrants - NE = 1, SE = 2, SW = 3,`
    `NW = 4`
12. `>>Specify quadrant (1-4):` **3** `Current direction unit: degree, In-`
    `put: DD.MMSSSS (decimal dms)`
13. `>>Specify bearing:` **16.1907**
14. `>>Specify distance:` **80**
15. `Resuming LINE command. Specify next point or [Undo]:` `(1077.62`
    `949.102 0.0)`
16. `Specify next point or [Close/Undo]:` `Quadrants - NE = 1, SE = 2,`
    `SW = 3, NW = 4`
17. `>>Specify quadrant (1-4):` **<Esc>** twice to terminate.
18. Save your file with the same name and a suffix of your initials.

Exercise 6-4: The 'ZD Command

This command allows you to build linework using an azimuth (from North) and distance (Figure 6-31).

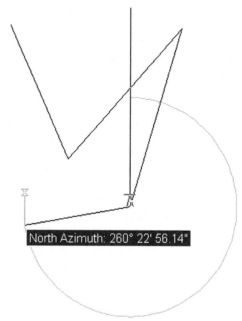

North Azimuth: 260° 22' 56.14"

Figure 6-31   Linework using a North Azimuth

TIP   If your jurisdiction requires the use of Azimuth (or South Azimuth), the **'ZD** command assists in laying out deed information.

1. Continue in the same drawing or open the drawing you just saved.
2. Using the **V** for **View** command, highlight the view called **Geom-A**, hit **Set Current**, and then hit **OK**. You draw linework using a bearing and distance from where you left off in the previous command. You can also use the line visible on the screen if you did not perform the last exercise. Of course, your results may vary from the figure somewhat.
3. `Command:` **L**
4. `LINE Specify first point:` Using an **Endpoint** Osnap, pick the end of the last line you drew in the previous exercise. It is near 1077,949.
5. `Specify next point or [Undo]:` Type **'ZD** or select the third icon on the **Transparent Commands** toolbar.

    `Current direction unit: degree, Input: DD.MMSSSS (decimal dms)`
6. `>>Specify azimuth:` **260.2256**
7. `>>Specify distance:` **100**
8. `Resuming LINE command. Specify next point or [Undo]:` `(979.023`
    `932.395 0.0)`

9. `Specify next point or [Undo]:` `Current direction unit: degree, In-put: DD.MMSSSS (decimal dms)`
10. `>>Specify azimuth:` **<Esc>** twice to terminate.
11. Save your file with the same name and a suffix of your initials.

Exercise 6-5: The 'DD Command

This command allows you to build linework using a deflection angle and a distance (Figure 6-32).

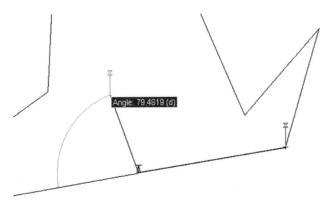

Figure 6-32   Deflection angle and a distance

1. Continue in the same drawing or open the drawing you just saved.
2. Using the **V** for **View** command, highlight the view called **Geom-A**, hit **Set Current**, and then hit **OK**. You draw linework using a bearing and distance from where you left off in the previous command. You can also use the line visible on the screen if you did not perform the last exercise. Of course, your results may vary from the figure somewhat.
3. `Command:` **L**
4. `LINE Specify first point:` Type in '**DD** or select the fourth icon on the **Transparent Commands** toolbar. Using an **Endpoint** Osnap, pick the end of the last line you drew in the previous exercise. It is near 979,932.
5. `>>Select line or [Points]:`
6. `Current angle unit: degree, Input: DD.MMSSSS (decimal dms)`
7. `>>Specify angle or [Counter-clockwise]:` **79.4819**
8. `>>Specify distance:` **75**
9. `>>Specify ending point or [.P/.N/.G]:` **<Esc>** twice to terminate.
10. Save your file with the same name and a suffix of your initials.

Notice that each of these commands keeps you in the data entry mode until you switch to another to terminate.

Exercise 6-6: The 'NE Command

This command allows you to build linework using a key-in of the Northing and Easting.

TIP   The nice part of the '**NE** command allows for data entry using the numeric keypad, which expedites the typing.

1. Continue in the same drawing or open the drawing you just saved.
2. Using the **V** for **View** command, highlight the view called **Geom-A**, hit **Set Current**, and then hit **OK**. You draw linework using a bearing and distance from where you left off in the previous command. You can also use the line visible on the screen if you did not perform the last exercise. Of course, your results may vary from the figure somewhat.
3. `Command:` **L**
4. `LINE Specify first point:` Using an **Endpoint** Osnap, pick the end of the last line you drew in the previous exercise. It is near 953,1003.

5. `Specify next point or [Undo]`: Type **'NE** or select the fifth icon on the **Transparent Commands** toolbar.
6. `>>>>Enter northing <0.0000>`: **960**
7. `>>>>Enter easting <0.0000>`: **950**
8. `>>>>Enter northing <0.0000>`: **<Esc>** twice to terminate.
9. Save your file with the same name and a suffix of your initials.

The 'GN Command

This command allows you to build linework using a key-in of the grid Northing and grid Easting. Again, a nice feature allows for data entry using the numeric keypad, which expedites the typing. This is similar to the geodetic calculator used earlier because it reads the geodetic zone when placing points.

The 'LL Command

This command allows you to build linework using a key-in of the latitude and longitude. This is similar to the geodetic calculator because it reads the geodetic zone when placing points.

Exercise 6-7: The 'PN Command

This command allows you to build linework using a key-in of the point number.

> This command is not limited to simply typing a point number; it can also connect multiple points using commas and apostrophes. For instance, you can draw a polyline by starting at a point number of, say, 100 and for the remaining vertices of the polyline you can refer to points in the file by 101-110, 100, which will draw linework through the consecutive points 101 through 110 and connect back to the starting point of 100.

1. Continue in the same drawing or open the drawing you just saved.
2. Using the **V** for **View** command, highlight the view called **Geom-A**, hit **Set Current**, and then hit **OK**. You draw linework using a bearing and distance from where you left off in the previous command. You can also use the line visible on the screen if you did not perform the last exercise. Of course, your results may vary from the figure somewhat.
3. `Command:` **L**
4. `LINE Specify first point`: Using an **Endpoint** Osnap, pick the end of the last line you drew in the previous exercise. It is near 950,960. Type **'PN** or select the eighth icon on the **Transparent Commands** toolbar.
5. `Specify next point or [Undo]`:
6. `>>Enter point number`: **2**
7. `Resuming LINE command. Specify next point or [Undo]`: (908.038 1000.71 0.0)
8. `Specify next point or [Undo]`:
9. `>>Enter point number`: **<Esc>** twice to terminate.
10. Save your file with the same name and a suffix of your initials.

Exercise 6-8: The 'PO Command

This command allows you to build linework using a pick of a point on the screen without snapping to it. You can pick any visible portion of the point or its text attributes.

1. Continue in the same drawing or open the drawing you just saved.
2. Using the **V** for **View** command, highlight the view called **Geom-A**, hit **Set Current**, and then hit **OK**. You draw linework using a bearing and distance from where you left off in the previous command. You can also use the line visible on the screen if you did not perform the last exercise. Of course, your results may vary from the figure somewhat.

3. Command: **L**
4. LINE Specify first point: Using an **Endpoint** Osnap, pick the end of the last line you drew in the previous exercise. It is near 908,1000. Type **'PO** or select the tenth icon on the **Transparent Commands** toolbar.
5. Select point object: Simply pick on the word **UNIT** for Point 2.
6. Resuming LINE command. Specify first point: (908.038 1000.71 0.0)
7. Specify next point or [Undo] :
8. >>Select point object: Hit **<Enter>**.
9. >>Specify next point or [Undo] : Type in **950,960**
10. Resuming LINE command.
11. >>Specify next point or [Undo] : **<Esc>** to terminate.
12. Save your file with the same name and a suffix of your initials.

Exercise 6-9: The **'SS** Command

This command allows you to build linework using side shot data. You pick an occupied point on which to establish your station and then a second point representing your backsight. Following that you provide an angle and distance to locate your object.

1. Continue in the same drawing or open the drawing you just saved.
2. Using the **V** for **View** command, highlight the view called **Geom-B**, hit **Set Current**, and then hit **OK**. You see an alignment in the view. You draw linework using a station and offset of this alignment.
3. Type **L** for **Line** or pick it from the **Draw** toolbar.
4. Command: 1 LINE Specify first point: Using a **Center** Osnap, pick the center of the circle near the alignment shown at the bottom of the drawing.
5. Specify next point or [Undo] : Type **'SS** or select the eleventh icon on the **Transparent Commands** toolbar.
6. >>Specify ending point or [.P/.N/.G] : **.P**
7. Current angle unit: degree, Input: DD.MMSSSS (decimal dms)
8. >>Specify angle or [Counter-clockwise/Bearing/Deflection/aZimuth] : **60.9261**, as in Figure 6-33.

Figure 6-33   Building linework using side shot data

9. `>>Specify distance:` **100**
10. `Resuming LINE command. Specify next point or [Undo]:` `(1010.87 699.428 0.0)`
11. `Specify next point or [Undo]: Current angle unit: degree, Input: decimal`
12. `>>Specify angle or [Counter-clockwise/Bearing/Deflection/ aZimuth] :` **<Esc>** to terminate.
13. Save your file with the same name and a suffix of your initials.

Exercise 6-10: The 'SO Command

This command allows you to build linework using a station and offset (positive for right and negative for left) from an alignment.

TIP This routine is useful because it also works inside other AutoCAD commands and references the alignment in question. It can be used to draw manholes at a station offset from an alignment.

1. Continue in the same drawing or open the drawing you just saved.
2. Using the **V** for **View** command, highlight the view called **Geom-B**, hit **Set Current**, and then hit **OK**. You see a shot alignment in the view. Draw linework using a station and offset of this alignment.
3. Type **C** for **CIRCLE** or pick it from the **Draw** toolbar.
4. `CIRCLE Specify center point for circle or [3P/2P/Ttr (tan tan radius)] :` Type **'SO** or select the twelfth icon on the **Transparent Commands** toolbar.
5. `>>Select alignment:` Pick the alignment in the view.
6. `>>Specify station along alignment:` **75**
7. `>>Specify station offset:` **25**
8. `Resuming CIRCLE command. Specify center point for circle or [3P/2P/Ttr (tan tan radius)] :` `(920.909 655.768 0.0)`
9. `Specify radius of circle or [Diameter] :`
10. `>>Specify station along alignment:` **<Esc>** to terminate the station, offset part of the routine.
11. `Resuming CIRCLE command. Specify radius of circle or [Diameter] :` **1.5**
12. Save your file with the same name and a suffix of your initials.

Exercise 6-11: The 'PSE Command

This command allows you to build linework using profile, station, and elevation criteria.

TIP When using this routine, notice that graphics appear to show you where the station you type is on the profile. A graphic then appears to show you the elevation that you type.

To access student data files, go to www.pearsondesigncentral.com.

1. Open the drawing called Chapter-6-Profile.dwg.
2. Using the **V** for **View** command, highlight the view called **Access Road-Profile View**, hit **Set Current**, and then hit **OK**. You see a shot profile in the view. You draw a bridge crossing over the road using a station and elevation data from this profile.
3. Type **L** for **Line** or pick it from the **Draw** toolbar.
4. `Command: 1 LINE Specify first point:` Type **'PSE** or select the seventeenth icon on the **Transparent Commands** toolbar.
5. `>>Select a Profile View:` Pick a grid line in the profile.
6. `>>Specify station:` **300**

7. >>Specify elevation: **364**
8. Resuming LINE command. Specify first point: (18300.0 21640.0 0.0)
9. Specify next point or [Undo]:
10. >>Specify station: **300**
11. >>Specify elevation: **355**
12. Resuming LINE command. Specify next point or [Undo]: (18300.0 21550.0 0.0)
13. Specify next point or [Undo]:
14. >>Specify station: **350**
15. >>Specify elevation: **355**
16. Resuming LINE command. Specify next point or [Undo]: (18350.0 21550.0 0.0)
17. Specify next point or [Close/Undo]:
18. >>Specify station: **350**
19. >>Specify elevation: **364**
20. Resuming LINE command. Specify next point or [Close/Undo]: (18350.0 21640.0 0.0)
21. Specify next point or [Close/Undo]:
22. >>Specify station: **<Esc>** twice to terminate.
23. Save your file with the same name and a suffix of your initials.

You see the outline of an overhead bridge in a thick linestyle (Figure 6-34).

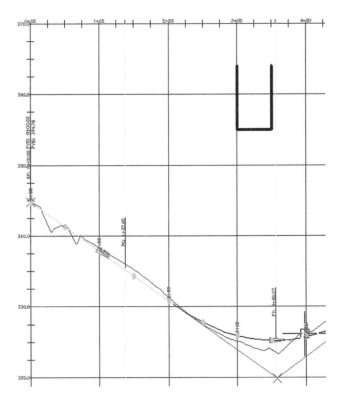

Figure 6-34   Using profile, station, and elevation criteria

Exercise 6-12: The '**PGS** Command

This command allows you to build linework using profile, grade, and station criteria (Figure 6-35).

Note that these commands can be used for almost any AutoCAD command. For instance, you can draw a pipe in profile while maintaining the grade of the pipe. You can draw the invert of the pipe, and the other invert can be established using a grade and station.

Figure 6-35   Using profile, grade, and station criteria

1. Continue on the same drawing, or open the drawing called Chapter-6-Profile.dwg.
2. Using the **V** for **View** command, highlight the view called **Access Road-Profile View**, hit **Set Current**, and then hit **OK**. You see a shot profile in the view. You draw a culvert from a point at −2% using the profile data.
3. Type **L** for **Line** or pick it from the **Draw** toolbar.
4. `Command: l LINE Specify first point:` **18217,21215**
5. `Specify next point or [Undo]:` Type **'PGS** or select the eighteenth icon on the **Transparent Commands** toolbar.
6. `>>Select a Profile View:` Pick a grid line in the profile.
7. `>>Specify grade <0.00>:` **−2**
8. `>>Specify station:` **285**
9. `Resuming LINE command. Specify next point or [Undo]:` (18285.0 21201.4 0.0)
10. `Specify next point or [Undo]:`
11. `>>Specify grade <-2.00>:` **<Esc>** twice to terminate.
12. Save your file with the same name and a suffix of your initials.

Exercise 6-13: The 'PGL Command

This command allows you to build linework using profile, grade, and length criteria.

1. Continue on the same drawing, or open the drawing called Chapter-6-Profile.dwg.
2. Using the **V** for **View** command, highlight the view called **Access Road-Profile View**, hit **Set Current**, and then hit **OK**. You see a shot profile in the view. You draw a culvert from a point at −2% using the profile data.
3. Type **L** for **Line** or pick it from the **Draw** toolbar.
4. `Command: l LINE Specify first point:` **18418,21222**
5. `Specify next point or [Undo]:` Type **'PGL** or select the nineteenth icon on the **Transparent Commands** toolbar.
6. `>>Select a profile view:` Pick a grid line in the profile.
7. `Current grade input format:` **percent**
8. `>>Specify grade <0.00>:` **−2**
9. `>>Specify length:` **100**

10. Resuming LINE command. Specify next point or [Undo]: (18518.0 21202.0 0.0)
11. Specify next point or [Undo]:
12. Current grade input format: percent
13. >>Specify grade <-2.00>: **<Esc>** twice to terminate.
14. Save your file with the same name and a suffix of your initials.

TIP You can continue drawing linework in the **'PGL** command if you have a series of pipe inverts to draw. This command can be used to draw anything in the profile that has a length and grade, such as the bottom of a ditch.

Exercise 6-14: The **'MR** and **'ML** Commands

These commands allow you to build linework by matching the radius or length of an object.

TIP The **'MR** and **'ML** commands are excellent for obtaining data from other criteria either known or within the file somewhere. Remember to use these as you create parcel and alignment data in the future.

1. Continue on the same drawing, or open the drawing called Chapter-6-Profile.dwg.
2. Using the **V** for **View** command, highlight the view called **Geom-D**, hit **Set Current**, and then hit **OK**. You see an arc and a line.
3. Type **C** for **Circle** or pick it from the **Draw** toolbar.
4. Command: **CIRCLE** Specify center point for circle or [3P/2P/Ttr (tan tan radius)]: **19135, 20050**
5. Specify radius of circle or [Diameter]: Type **'MR** or select the next to last icon on the **Transparent Commands** toolbar.
6. >>Select entity to match radius: Pick the arc on the screen.
7. Notice a circle shows up with the same radius of the arc.
8. Type **L** for **Line** or pick it from the **Draw** toolbar.
9. Command: 1 LINE Specify first point: **18530,20100**
10. Specify next point or [Undo]: Type **'ML** or select the last icon on the **Transparent Commands** toolbar.
11. >>Select entity to match length: Pick the line on the screen.
12. Notice a line shows up with the same length as the other line.
13. Resuming **LINE** command. Specify next point of [Undo]:
14. Specify next point or [Undo]: **<Esc>** to terminate.
15. Save your file with the same name and a suffix of your initials.

To access student data files, go to www.pearsondesigncentral.com.

PARCELS

This next section explores parcel information. You begin with the Parcel Settings and move toward generating parcels and see how Civil 3D handles them in a state-of-the-art manner.

Parcel Development in Civil 3D

Due to the potential complexities of laying out parcels, the Autodesk Civil 3D includes a wide range of tools to assist in the construction of the primitive components of the parcels; namely, the horizontal geometry, the lines, and the arcs. We have already seen the concepts in the earlier examples of the dynamic link that exists between the display styles for an object and the appearance of the object. The act of updating an object's style results in automatic changes to the appearance

Table Styles: A library of
styles for constructing tables that
report on point information.

of the object in AutoCAD. For example, if you update the label style for a parcel, the parcel linework annotation is updated. Open the file Chapter-6-Parcel.dwg from the student data files.

Open the **Settings** tab in the **Toolspace**. If you expand **Parcel**, notice Parcel Styles, Label Styles, *Table Styles*, and Commands. See Figure 6-36. Please note that although you are working with Chapter 6 drawings the styles in this chapter will refer to Chapter 4 styles that were created for a previous textbook.

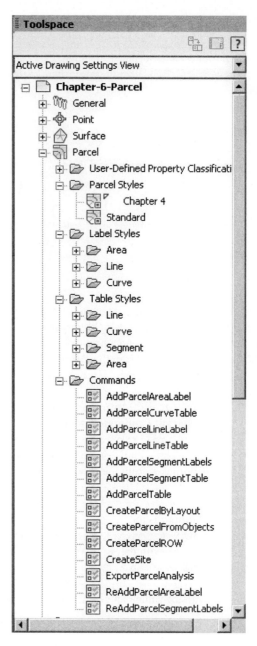

Figure 6-36   Parcel settings

These styles are discussed in detail, but generally the **Parcel Styles** handle how the parcel appears, what displays, and on which layers. The **Label Styles** control what annotation appears and how it looks for the components of the parcel; in other words, the area and the rectilinear and curvilinear linework. The **Table Styles** control how tables involving parcel data appear and which layers are involved. The **Commands** settings include preestablished settings for the details of building annotation and tables, such as units and precisions.

Exercise 6-15: Creating Parcel Styles

This exercise allows some serious practice in establishing styles for parcels. Civil 3D allows for some new features that are often used to add to the aesthetics of parcel drafting such as placing a hatch pattern around the edge of the parcels. You explore this and annotation styles as well in the next series of exercises.

To access student data files, go to www.pearsondesigncentral.com.

1. Open the file Chapter-6-Parcel.dwg.
2. Type **V** for **View** highlight the view called **Parcel – A**, hit **Set Current**, and then hit **OK**.
3. Then go to the **Settings** tab in the **Toolspace**; expand the items for **Parcel**.
4. Open **Parcel Styles**, and you see **Standard** and **Chapter 4**. These can be edited by right-clicking on them and choosing **Edit…**. Right-click on the **Chapter 4 Style** item and select **Edit…**.
5. In the **Information** tab, ensure that **Chapter 4** is the name of the style. Choose the **Design** tab in the dialog box. This is where the **Fill** setting is set. It defaults to 5′. This sets a 5′ hatch around the perimeter of the parcel, which is often found on engineering and surveying drawings as a highlighting method for parcels.
6. Choose the **Display** tab and turn **On** the **Parcel Area Fill** layer, so you can see the fill when it occurs. The **Parcel Segment** layer can be set under the **Layer** column. The layer **V-Prcl-Sgmt** is set to **red**, and the layer **V-Prcl-Htch** is set to color **254**. Hit **OK** to exit.

You now have a Parcel Style called Chapter 6 with layers set for the parcels.

Exercise 6-16: Creating an Area Label Style

Now create an Area Label Style for the parcels.

1. In the same drawing, expand **Label Styles**, expand **Area**, right-click on the **Chapter 4 Area Style** and choose **Edit…**.
2. In the **Information** tab, ensure that **Chapter 4 Area Style** is the name. Select the **General** tab and observe the settings.
3. Click in the **Value** column for **Text Style**, and you see a button with three dots (ellipses) on it. Click this button to see the available styles.
4. Select **Romans**.
5. Select the **Layout** tab next as in Figure 6-37. Note in the **Value** column for the **Property** of **Text** Contents. Click in the **Value** column for this item, and you see a button with three dots (ellipses) on it. Click this button and notice how the field and the related appearance of the area text can be altered. The **Preview** window on the right of Figure 6-38 can be edited by the user, and prefixes or suffixes can be typed in if needed. Hit **OK**.
6. Now select the **Dragged State** tab and observe the settings in here that control the properties for labels when they are dragged away from their initial insertion points. Hit **OK**.

Figure 6-37   Parcel Label Style Composer

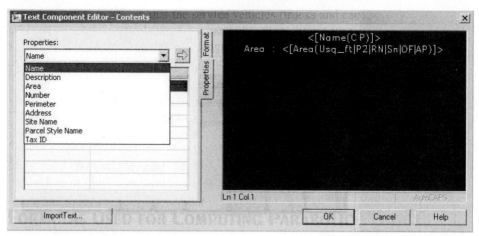

Figure 6-38   Text Component Editor

The **Summary** tab provides a single location to review and set all of the settings at once. This is a great destination for experts.

7. Go to the **Settings** tab in the **Toolspace**; under the **Label Styles**, you use the **Standard** Style for Lines and Curves, but you may want to take a moment to review these by selecting either **Lines** or **Curves**, right-clicking, and choosing **Edit....** Hit **OK** to depart the editing.

Although most of the settings are fairly routine and easy to understand, let us pause for a moment to explore some settings that may not be so self-evident. Expand the item for **Commands**. Right-click on the **CreateParcelbyLayout** setting and choose **Edit Command Settings....** An **Edit Command Settings** dialog box displays, shown in Figure 6-39. The interesting settings to

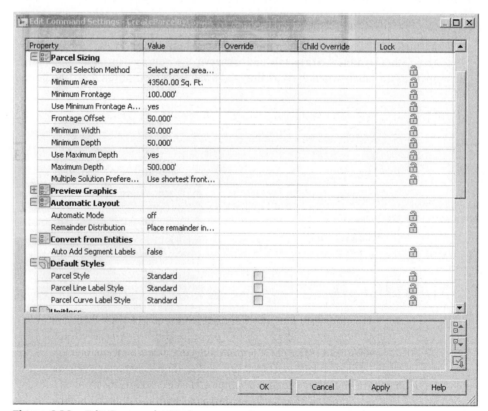

Figure 6-39   Edit Command settings

take note of are the blue icons. The blue icons, expanded in Figure 6-39, specify the default op-tions for **Parcel** commands.

At the bottom of this same dialog box, select the **Transparent Commands** settings, shown in Figure 6-40. A myriad of settings here control whether you have Northings/Eastings or *X*/*Y* prompts; whether you are prompted for the third dimension; the order in which latitude/longitude will be prompted, and the units in which slopes and grades will be set.

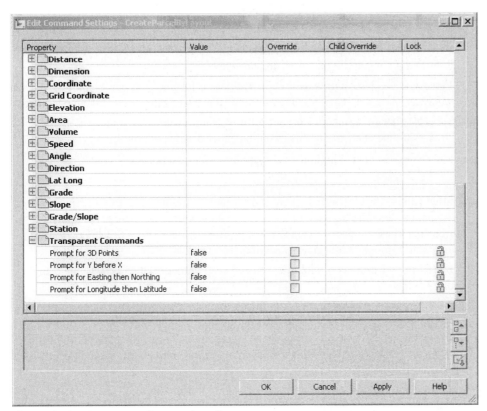

Figure 6-40   Transparent Commands settings

 Observe these settings carefully because they are similar to the **Command Settings** in other items.

TIP

Now that you have explored many of the settings controlling parcel development and display, let us create some using the commands provided.

In this same drawing and in the view provided earlier, **Parcel-A**, you will create some linework for a parcel.

From the **Parcels** pull-down menu, choose **Create Parcel by Layout....** A toolbar displays as shown in Figure 6-41. Note that it can be expanded/retracted by using the arrow at the far right of the toolbar.

Figure 6-41   Parcel Layout Tools

The commands available are described from the left and are referred to as Buttons 1 through 10 in their descriptions that follow:

Button 1:   **Create Parcel**

Button 2:   **Add Fixed Line—Two Points** draws a lot line as a line segment. Choose a starting point and an endpoint to create it.

Button 3:   **Add Fixed Curve:**

- **Fixed Curve (Three point)** draws a lot line as a curved component. You would define a starting point, a point on curve, and an endpoint.

- **Fixed Curve (Two points and radius)** draws a lot line as a curve component. You would define a starting point, a radius value, the curve's direction, and an endpoint.

Button 4:   **Draw Tangent-Tangent with No Curves** draws a connected series of lot line components. You would identify a series of points.

Button 5:   This button has several options to it including:

- **Slide Line—Create** creates one or more new lot lines defined with starting and ending points along the frontage of the lot or, at your option, using an angle relative to the frontage. These angles are measured in positive degrees, from 0 degrees (toward the endpoint) through 180 degrees (toward the start point).

- **Slide Line—Edit** moves a lot line. You can keep or modify the line's frontage angle in this routine.

- **Swing Line—Create** develops a lot line defined with starting and ending points along the frontage of the lot and a fixed swing point on the opposite side of the parcel. The size of the parcel can be modified by swinging the lot line to intersect a different point along the frontage. This is limited through minimum areas and frontage limits that you establish.

- **Swing Line—Edit** moves a lot line by pivoting it from one end. You can select which end to use as the swing point on the fly.

- **Free Form Create** develops a new lot line. You can define an attachment point to begin and then use bearings, azimuths, or a snap to a second attachment point to complete the command.

Button 6:   **PI Commands** for:

- **Inserting** creates a vertex at the point clicked on a parcel segment.

- **Deleting** eliminates a vertex that is selected on a parcel segment. It then redraws the lot line between the vertices on either side to repair the parcel line. This command can delete or merge parcels depending on how the vertex was deleted.

- **Breaking Apart PIs** separates endpoints at a vertex selected with a separation distance you specify. This command does not delete or merge parcels; it does, however, make them incomplete, and the components that are affected become geometry elements. These elements become parcels again once any loose vertices are reconnected to a closed figure.

Button 7:   **Delete Sub-entity** eliminates parcel components. If a sub-entity is eliminated when it is not shared by another parcel, the parcel is deleted. If a shared sub-entity is eliminated, the two parcels that shared it are merged together.

Button 8:   **Parcel Union** merges two adjacent parcels together where the first parcel selected determines the identity and properties of the joined parcel, similar to the AutoCAD **PEDIT** command.
Dissolve Parcel Union does the same.

Button 9: **Pick Sub-entity** selects a parcel component for display in the **Parcel Layout Parameters** dialog box. Use the **Sub-entity Editor** before choosing this command.

Button 10: **Sub-entity Editor** displays the **Parcel Layout Parameters** dialog box that allows for the review or editing of attributes of selected parcel components.

Undo and **Redo** buttons are used for creating and editing parcel data.

The graphics capabilities that accompany these commands are extraordinary. Following are some examples of how they work.

Exercise 6-17: Create Parcel By Layout

1. Remain in the same drawing. Type **V** for **View,** highlight the view called **Parcel-A,** hit **Set Current,** and then hit **OK.** In the **Prospector,** expand **Open Drawings,** expand the **Chapter-6-Parcel.dwg** expand **Sites,** expand **Site 1.**
2. Then right-click on **Parcels.** Choose **Properties....**
3. Under the **Composition** tab, set the **Site parcel style** to **Chapter 4,** which was created earlier. Set the **Site area label style** to **Chapter 4 Area Style,** also created earlier. Hit **Apply** and **OK.**
4. In the **Chapter-6-Parcel.dwg** drawing, select **Create Parcel By Layout...** from the **Parcels** pull-down menu.
5. When the **Parcel Layout Tools** toolbar displays, select the second from the left button **Add Fixed Line-Two Points** command. The dialog box for **Create Parcels-Layout** displays. Set the **Parcel Style** to **Chapter 4.** Set the **Area label style** to **Chapter 4 Area Style.** Turn **On** the toggle for **Automatically add segment labels.** Hit **OK.**
6. When it asks for a start point, use an **Endpoint** snap to select the point at **16000,19000,** which is a vertex of the parcel polyline already drawn in the file.
7. Then using Endpoint snaps, select the vertices of the polyline in a clockwise fashion. You must specify a start point for each line. Set the second and third vertex, and stop after selecting an endpoint at the third vertex at $X = 16268.9231$ $Y = 19285.9656.$

 TIP Note that after you draw one line, you must begin the next line again, unlike an AutoCAD line.

8. While staying in the command, select the third button in the toolbar, **Add Fixed Curve-Three Point.** Use an **Endpoint** snap to select the third vertex; use a **Nearest** snap to pick a point on the curve and an **Endpoint** snap to select the fourth vertex.
9. Then use the second button, **Add Fixed Line,** to select a first point at the endpoint at the fourth vertex and the second point at the beginning of the parcel where you started.
10. When the software asks for a new start point, hit **<Enter>** and then type **X** for **Exit,** as shown in the command prompt. You see a parcel, fully developed with annotation and hatching, as discussed in the setup of the settings earlier. Make sure that all layers are turned on.

If you look in the **Prospector** (Figure 6-42), you see this parcel listed there, with a **Preview** of the parcel.

Exercise 6-18: Editing Parcel Data

1. To edit the parcel, use the **Create Parcel by Layout...** from the **Parcels** pull-down menu again.
2. This time select button 6, **Insert PI.**

Figure 6-42   Preview of the Parcel

3. When prompted, pick the north parcel line. It requests that you pick a point for the new PI. Type **16100,19300** as the new PI location. Hit **<Enter>** twice to terminate and **X** to leave the routine.
4. You see the parcel updated with the new PI, new annotation, and a new area. The **Prospector** is updated if you select **Refresh** when right-clicking the parcel item. Refer to Figure 6-43.

Figure 6-43   Updated Preview of the Parcel

Exercise 6-19: Creating Parcel Data from Objects

A second option for creating parcel data is to select it directly from predrawn entities. Let us perform an example of this.

1. Type **V** for **View** and select the view called **Parcel—B**, hit **Set Current,** and then hit **OK**.
2. A copy of the same parcel data displays. Select **Create Parcel from Objects** from the **Parcels** pull-down menu.
3. `Select lines, arcs or polylines to convert into parcels or [Xref]:` Select the polyline displayed. Hit **<Enter>**.
4. The dialog box for **Create Parcels-From objects** displays (Figure 6-44). Set the **Parcel style** to **Chapter 4**. Set the **Area label style** to **Chapter 4 Area Style.** Turn **On** the toggle for **Automatically add segment labels.** Hit **OK**.

Figure 6-44   Create Parcels dialog box

5. Again the parcel is defined, hatched, labeled, and displayed in the **Prospector**. Note that you may need to choose **Refresh** from the right-click menu to see both parcels in the **Prospector** and make sure that all layers are turned on.

Exercise 6-20: Creating Rights of Way

Another command within the **Parcels** pull-down menu is the **Create ROW** command. This creates a right of way along an alignment. When a right of way is developed, adjacent parcel boundaries are offset by a user-specified distance from the right of way on each side of the alignment. Radii can be defined for end returns that exist along the right of way at intersections.

The **Right of Way** command works like a parcel, albeit a narrow variation of a parcel. When the **Create ROW** command is used, it prompts you to pick parcels. If an alignment is found on one of the edges of the selected parcels, a right of way is created in accordance with the preestablished parameters.

1. Type in **V** for **View** and select the view called **Parcel—C**, hit **Set Current,** and then hit **OK**. This shows an alignment and several parcels along the alignment.

2. Select **Create Parcel from Objects** from the **Parcels** pull-down menu.
3. `Select lines, arcs or polylines to convert into parcels or [Xref] :`
   Select the polylines of the three parcels in the view. Hit **<Enter>**.
4. The dialog box for **Create Parcel-From objects** displays. Set the **Parcel style** to **Chapter 4.**
   Set the **Area label style** to **Chapter 4 Area Style**. Turn **On** the toggle for **Automatically add segment labels**. Hit **OK**.
5. Again the parcels are defined, hatched, labeled, and displayed in the **Prospector.** Make sure that all layers are turned on.
6. Now choose the command **Create ROW** from the **Parcels** pull-down menu. When it asks you to select the parcels, choose the three parcels you just created, and hit **<Enter>**. Then the **Create Right of Way** dialog box, shown in Figure 6-45, displays to obtain the criteria for developing the ROW.

Figure 6-45   Create Right of Way dialog box

7. Set the value for **Offset from alignment** to **45**. Set the fillet radius for **Cleanup at parcel boundaries** to **35**. Set the fillet radius for **Cleanup at alignment intersections** to **35** as well. Hit **OK**.
8. The configuration should appear as shown in Figure 6-46.

Figure 6-46   Results of parcel layout

For the next step in this exercise, you will add a line table.

9. Type in **V** for **View** and select the view called **Parcel—C**. This shows an alignment and several parcels along the alignment.
10. Select **Add Tables** from the **Parcels** pull-down menu. Select **Add Line....**
11. The **Table Creation** dialog box displays, as shown in Figure 6-47.

In the selection window in the center of the dialog box, turn on the **Apply** button and make sure it is checked as in Figure 6-47. Then hit **OK**. A table is on your cursor and asks you to pick a point for the table.

Pick a point away from the parcel graphics. It appears as shown in Figure 6-48. Other tables can be brought in as well for curves and areas.

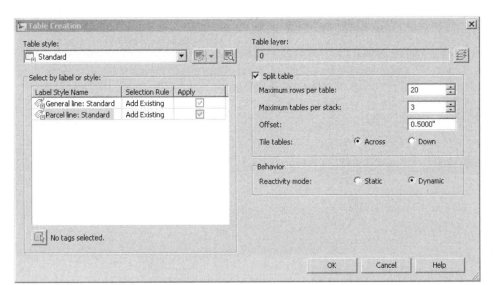

Figure 6-47   Table Creation dialog box

Line #	Length	Direction
L1	250.000	N0° 37' 57.21"E
L2	388.861	N72° 47' 09.54"E
L3	245.234	S16° 18' 58.54"E
L4	312.186	S72° 47' 09.54"W
L5	296.177	N87° 47' 36.99"W
L6	233.308	N1° 32' 20.88"E
L7	240.185	S2° 46' 36.64"W
L8	412.792	S85° 32' 05.26"E

Figure 6-48   Completed table

ALIGNMENTS

Alignments are developed to assist engineers, surveyors, and contractors in their computations and layout of projects. Alignments provide a common structure by which they can refer to the corridor, locate the positions easily, and be able to duplicate that location reliably. An alignment consists of *primitive elements,* such as lines, arcs, and spirals. Although each of these is an independent component, when strung together they create an alignment and can be thought of and referred to as a single object.

Alignments can be used in all corridor situations whether they are roadways, channels, aqueducts, or utilities such as waterlines.

The notion of *stationing* is what unifies thinking about alignments. Stationing (Figure 6-49) is a mathematical concept whereby the beginning of the alignment commences with a value, say 0, and this number increases by the lengths of the lines, arcs, and spirals until terminating at the end of the alignment. To make it a little easier to understand and work with, stationing also includes the concept of dividing the actual linear value by 100'. In other words, station 2 + 50 would be located 250' from the beginning of the alignment. Station 18 + 32.56 would be 1,832.56' from the beginning. The even stations are denoted on the left side of the plus sign and the leftover value is on the right side of the plus sign. Unless otherwise instructed, corridor alignments often begin with the station 10 + 00 or 1000'. This allows for changes to be made to the

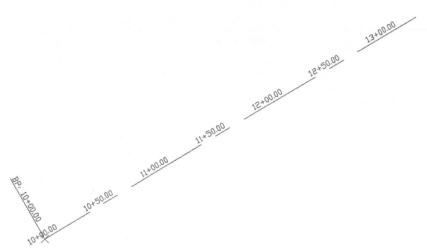

Figure 6-49   Stationing

alignment, and, within reason, you will at least remain in positive numbers when computing stationing. For example, if you began a roadway at station 0+00, it could happen that a superior would want to extend the roadway length 100′ from the beginning, thereby causing the beginning station to be −1+00. This causes potential confusion simply because of the addition of negative numbers. Anything designers can do to simplify the design and construction process pays off in the long run, and this is one of those things it is important to do.

In combination with stationing, a concept of offset values is also used in conjunction with alignments. Typically, a positive offset is to the right of the alignment, and a negative value is to the left, when looking forward toward increasing stationing. This additional concept allows users to locate objects, either existing or proposed, using the stationing for the alignment as the baseline for computations. For instance, it would not be difficult to locate a proposed fire hydrant with a station of 18+32.56 and an offset of 55′ (Right), or the corner of a drain inlet at station 9+55.32 and an offset of −14.5′ (Left).

One last item associated with alignments and their respective stationing is the concept of station equations or equalities. This is a situation in which the roadway begins, say, at station 10+00 and perhaps the alignment is 2000′ long. Thus, the ending station is 30+00. Now let us further say that a side road intersects the roadway halfway through it, at station 20+00. The hypothetical State Department of Transportation (DOT) has decided that the intersecting roadway is the predominant roadway and yours is not. Therefore, it decrees that your roadway will have your stationing from the beginning and will maintain your stationing until it intersects with the side road. At that point, the DOT wants the stationing of your road to pick up where the side street leaves off and continue on until your road ends.

This is where a station equation will exist. Our roadway stationing begins at 10+00 and progresses until station 20+00 where the side road enters the project, as in Figure 6-50.

If the side road has an ending station of, say, 11+96.32 when it intersects your road, then your road continues from that point onward accumulating its additional stationing values and adding them to the 11+96.32 from the side road. So your road would end at station 11+96.32

Figure 6-50   Side road intersecting main road

plus 10+00 remaining after the side road intersects your road for a total ending station of 21+96.32. To complicate things just a little further, note that the stationing could be decreasing instead of increasing. If it were, then your road could end at 11+96.32. It could also occur that there would be multiple stations on the alignment of the same value depending on how the station equations are applied to the alignment. See Figure 6-51.

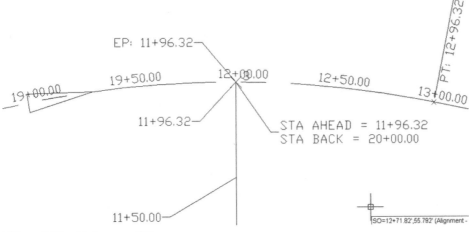

Figure 6-51   Station equation

In a subdivision corridor, items that reference horizontal alignments are gutters, sidewalks, and lot corners; water, sanitary, and storm sewers; catch basins; and manholes. This conversation is limited for the time being to roadway applications. However, they can be generalized to the other aforementioned project types.

The criteria used for the design of horizontal alignments for roadways are represented in terms of number of lanes, design speeds, and minimum curve radii. The minimum radius for curves increases with design speed such that large radius curves are required for high vehicle speeds. Correspondingly, there also tends to be a minimum radius once you go below a certain design speed, such as that found in residential subdivisions. A governmental agency, perhaps a DOT, usually specifies horizontal alignment design criteria for highways. For subdivision roads, it may be the county's highway department or the municipality that dictates the design criteria.

Horizontal Alignment Development in Civil 3D

Autodesk Civil 3D includes a robust toolset to assist in the construction of the primitive components of the horizontal alignment; namely, the horizontal geometry, the lines, arcs, and spirals. You have already seen the concepts in previous examples of the dynamic link that exists between the display styles for an object and the appearance of the object. The act of updating an object's style results in automatic changes to the appearance of the object in AutoCAD. For example, if you update a component within the alignment, a ripple-through effect updates profiles, sections, and annotations as well. There are similar tools for developing alignments as there are for creating parcel data. You can draw the alignment using polylines and convert them to alignment objects, or you can use the **Layout** toolbar to develop the design with alignment tools custom developed for use in design alignments.

Exercise 6-21: Alignment Settings

Alignment creation is explored in this section, beginning with the **Alignment Settings**. You see how Civil 3D handles them in a state-of-the-art manner.

1. Remain in the same drawing, Chapter-6-Parcel.dwg.
2. Open the **Settings** tab in the **Toolspace**. If you expand **Alignments**, notice **Alignment Styles**, **Design Checks**, **Label Styles**, **Table Styles**, and **Commands**. Each of these is discussed in detail, but generally the **Alignment Styles** handle how the alignment appears, what will display, and on what layers. The **Label Styles** control what annotation

To access student data files, go to www.pearsondesigncentral.com.

appears and how it will look for the components of the alignment; in other words, the stationing, equations, alignment components, station/offsets, and so on. The **Table Styles** setting (Figure 6-52) controls how tables involving alignment data appear and what layers are involved. The **Commands** settings, include preestablished settings for the details of building annotation and tables, such as units and precisions.

Figure 6-52 Table Styles setting

3. Right-click on the **Alignment Styles** item and select **New....** The **Information** tab allows for naming and optional descriptions. In the name field, type **Chapter 4—Alignments**.
4. The **Design** tab allows you to control the **Grip Edit Behavior**. This can be enabled or disabled as a toggle, and it controls whether the cursor snaps to a specified increment when grip editing the radius of a curve in the alignment. The **Radius snap value** specifies the curve's incrementing radius. Enable the **Grip edit behavior** and set the value to **25**.
5. In the **Display** tab, you can set the layers for individual components of the alignment if you want. For this example, set the color for **Lines** to **red** and the color for **Curves** to **green**.
6. Hit **Apply** and **OK**.
7. Now click on the **Label Styles** item, select **Station**, and then right-click on **Major Station**. Select **New....**

8. Click on the **Information** tab, type in the name of your style as **Chapter 4—Major Stations Label Style**.
9. Then in the **Layout** tab, Figure 6-53, under the **Text Property**, click in the **Value** column for **Contents**. Notice that a button appears on the right side of the field. Click on the button with the ellipsis (…).

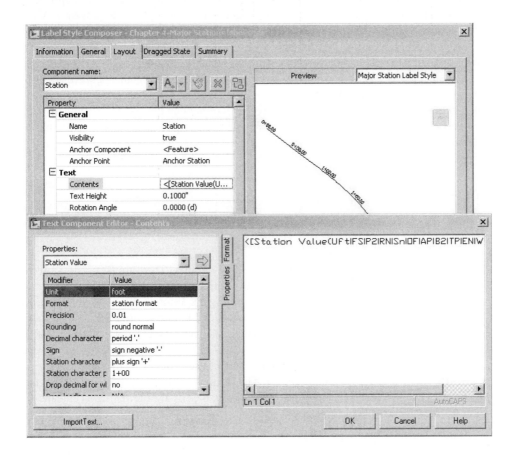

Figure 6-53   Text Component Editor—Label Text

10. A dialog box called **Text Component Editor—Contents** displays.
11. You see the formula in the window to the right. There is a parameter in the formula, **P2** for Precision to 2 decimal places. Click in there and delete the entire current formula.
12. In the **Modifier** column, notice the **Precision** item. Click in the **Value** column for this modifier. The default is 0.01. Change it to **1**.
13. *This next step is important.* Make sure you click the button with the **right arrow** on it to send the parameter change into the formula window to the right.
14. If you look in the formula, notice that the parameter **P** is now set to **0**.
15. Hit **OK**. The **Preview** in the **Label Style Composer** shows the stationing with no decimal places now.
16. Hit **Apply** and **OK** to exit.
17. Repeat this for the **Minor Stations** and call the label style **Chapter 4—Minor Stations Label Style**. Repeat Steps 8 through 15 for the **Minor Label Styles**.

This exercise should provide you with an idea of how the settings for alignments work. They are intended to be prebuilt into the Civil 3D product and then take effect on the creation of the alignment.

Now that you have gone through these basic examples, note that the dialog boxes for all the settings work essentially the same way and have the same types of parameters. This is true for the Label Styles for Label Sets; all the Stationing styles; the styles for lines, curves, spirals, and tangent intersections; and Table Styles.

The dialog boxes for the **Commands** section of the **Settings** were discussed under **Parcels, Command Settings**.

Fixed, Floating, and Free Lines and Curves

In getting started developing alignment objects, an important concept must be discussed first. That concept involves Constraint-based commands and the creation of fixed, floating, and free lines and curves. These objects can be edited dynamically, and the objects retain their tangencies.

A Fixed entity is fixed in its position and is defined by criteria such as a radius or located points. It is not dependent on other entities for geometry development or tangency. A Floating entity is always tangent to one entity and is defined by the parameters provided or is dependent on one other entity to define its geometry. A Free entity is always tangent to an entity before and after it and must have at least two other entities to which to attach that define its geometry.

Although a user can always develop polylines to create their alignments, there are also some state-of-the-art tools in the **Alignment Layout Tools** toolbar. They are called up by choosing the **Alignments** pull-down menu and selecting **Create Alignment by Layout**. The **Create Alignment— Layout** dialog box first displays asking you for some initial alignment style parameters, but then the **Alignment Layout Tools** toolbar displays (Figure 6-54). The commands available within it are described from the left and are referred to as Buttons 1 through 16 in their descriptions:

Figure 6-54 Alignment Layout Tools toolbar

Button 1:   This button has three choices. They are **Tangent-Tangent (No Curves)**, **Tangent-Tangent (With curves)**, and **Curve and Spiral Settings....** By using the **Tangent-Tangent** command, you can pick a series of points end-to-end in order to draw a fixed alignment in a fashion similar to drawing AutoCAD lines. The choices provide options to insert free curves automatically at each PI. These commands can be used effectively to create quick layouts of an alignment. The lines and curves can be modified by the user, and as the linework is edited, it always maintains tangency.

Button 2:   **Insert PI**.

Button 3:   **Delete PI**.

Button 4:   **Break-Apart PI**.

Button 5:   This button allows for creating **Fixed**, **Floating, and Free lines**. This concept is defined by the characteristics inherent within each type of line. These commands have several options tools, including:

- The **Fixed Line** commands allow you to enter a fixed line through two points, or you can enter a fixed line through two points where the line is tangent to the end of the selected fixed or floating entity.

- The **Floating Line** commands allow you to enter floating lines through points that are always tangent to fixed or floating curves, or you can enter a floating line tangent through a point. The lines drawn are always tangent to the end of fixed or floating curves.

- The **Free Line (Between two curves)** command allows you to enter a free line that is always tangent to a Fixed or Floating curve, either before or after the line.

Button 6:   This button has several options to it including:

- **Fixed Curve** and **More Fixed Curves** commands allow you to enter a fixed curve using 3 points, or you can enter a fixed curve using the following criteria to define the curves as shown in Figure 6-55.

Figure 6-55   FIXED CURVE and MORE FIXED CURVES commands

- The first three commands are performed by specifying two points and some additional criteria. They all achieve a fixed curve through three points.
- The next command develops a fixed curve tangent to the end of an entity and through a chosen point. This achieves a fixed curve through three points that is also tangent to the end of the entity you selected.
- Following that is the fixed curve developed by selecting a center point, providing a radius, and a curve direction, which achieves a fixed circle.
- The next command allows entering a fixed curve by specifying a center point, a pass-through point, and the curve's direction, which achieves a fixed curve that passes through the specified point.
- The last command enters a fixed curve by specifying a point, the curve's direction at the point, and a radius, which achieves a fixed circle with a center point and a radius.

Floating Curve and **More Floating Curves** commands allow you to enter floating curves using a variety of criteria that will be maintained on modification of those curves (Figure 6-56). The **Floating Curve** allows you to enter a floating curve that is attached to a fixed or floating line or curve entity, by specifying a radius, a pass-through point, and an angle range. This achieves a floating curve, which is always tangent to the entity to which it is attached. The submenu **More Floating Curves** is shown in Figure 6-56 and differs from the **Fixed** commands in that these entities are not pinned to any specific location in the drawing. These commands are described as follows:

- **Floating Curve (From entity end, through point)** which achieves a floating curve that is always tangent to the entity to which it is attached.
- **Floating Curve (From entity end, radius, length)** which achieves a floating curve entity that always starts at the end of the entity to which it is attached.
- **Floating Curve (From entity end, through point, direction at point)** which achieves a floating curve that remains tangent to the entity to which it was attached.

Figure 6-56   FLOATING CURVE and MORE FLOATING CURVES commands

The **Free Curve** commands allow you to enter free curves using a variety of criteria. **Free Curve Fillet (Between two entities, radius)** adds a curve between two entities with a specified angle range and radius.
Free Curve Fillet (Between two entities, through point) adds a curve between two entities with a specified pass-through point.

Free Curve (Best Fit) adds the most probable curve between two entities that remains tangent to the two entities.

Some new constraint-based tools have been added and, based on the information presented here, it should be obvious how to use them.

These next three button tools are for spiral design.

Button 7: **Floating Spirals**

- **Floating Line with Spiral (From curve, through point)** adds a floating spiral from an entity with a line at its end.

- **Floating Line with Spiral (From curve end, length)** adds a floating spiral from an entity with a line at its end.

Button 8: (More) **Floating Spirals**

- **Floating Curve with Spiral (From entity end, radius, length)** adds a floating spiral from an entity based on the radius and length provided.

- **Floating Curve with Spiral (From entity, radius, through point)** adds a floating spiral from an entity based on the radius and a point provided.

- **Floating Reverse Curve with Spirals (From curve, radius, through point)**

- **Floating Reverse Curve with Spirals (From curve, two points)**

- **Free Spiral-Curve-Spiral (Between two entities)** will prompt you to select the incoming and outgoing tangents and then prompt for spiral lengths and a radius for the curve.

- **Free Compound Spiral-Curve-Spiral-Curve-Spiral (Between two tangents)**

- **Free Reverse Spiral-Curve-Spiral-Spiral-Curve-spiral (Between two tangents)**

Button 9: Allows for a large number of sophisticated spiral geometry commands. These routines are summarized in the commands which follow:

- **Fixed Spiral** develops a spiral with a spiral in length and a curve radius.

- **Free Spiral (Between two entities)** requests length and radius information and then shows extraordinary graphics in the placement of the object.

- **Free Compound Spiral-Spiral (Between two curves)** develops two spirals back to back.

- **Free Reverse Spiral-Spiral (Between two curves)** develops two spirals back to back but in a reverse curve scenario.

- **Free Compound Spiral-Spiral (Between two tangents)**

- **Free Compound Spiral-Line-Spiral (Between two curves, spiral lengths)** develops two spirals back to back.

- **Free Reverse Spiral-Line-Spiral (Between two curves, spiral lengths)** develops two spirals back to back but in a reverse curve scenario.

- **Free Compound Spiral-Line-Spiral (Between two curves, line length)** develops two spirals back to back.

- **Free Reverse Spiral-Line-Spiral (Between two curves, line length)** develops two spirals back to back but in a reverse curve scenario.

Button 10: **Convert AutoCAD line and arc** creates a fixed two-point line or three-point curve alignment entity from an AutoCAD object.

Button 11: **Reverse Sub-entity Direction** does the same.

Button 12: **Delete Sub-entity** eliminates alignment components.

Button 13: **Edit best fit data for all entities** displays a table of data for all alignment sub-entities that were created by best fit.

Button 14: **Pick Sub-entity** selects an alignment component for display in the **Alignment Layout Parameters** dialog box. Use the **Sub-entity Editor** before choosing this command.

Button 15: **Sub-entity Editor** displays the **Alignment Layout Parameters** dialog box that allows for the review or editing of attributes of selected alignment components.

Button 16: **Alignment Grid View** brings up the **Panorama** view for reviewing the alignment.

Undo and **Redo** buttons are used for creating and editing data.

How to Design an Alignment

Now let us use some of the alignment development routines to check out the advantages that Civil 3D provides to its users. Begin with the first **Layout** tool in the toolbar.

Exercise 6-22: Tangent-Tangent (With Curves)

1. Open the file called Chapter 6 Alignments-2.dwg.
2. Type **V** for **View** and select **Align-A**, hit **Set Current** and then hit **OK**.
3. Set your current layer to **C-Road-Cntr**.
4. Turn **Off** the surface's contour layers on **C-Topo-Existing Ground**.
5. From the **Alignments** pull-down menu, select **Create Alignment by Layout...**.
6. Accept the defaults except choose the **Alignment Style** of **Chapter 4—Alignments** and set the site to **Site 1**. Figure 6-57 shows this dialog box. Hit **OK** when finished.
7. The **Alignment Layout Tools** toolbar now displays.
8. Using the **down arrow** next to the first button, select **Curve and Spiral Settings...** (Figure 6-58).

To access student data files, go to www.pearsondesigncentral.com.

Figure 6-57   Create Alignment dialog box

Figure 6-58   Curve and Spiral Settings...

9. In the **Curve and Spiral Settings** dialog box that displays, use the Clothoid type, which is the most commonly used, and hold the **200'** radius.

10. Now from the first button choose the command **Tangent-Tangent (With curves)**. At the command prompt when asked to provide the first point, type in the following coordinates: **14685,18545**. Then follow these instructions.

11. Specify next point: **15175,18510**
    Specify next point: **15250,18275**
    Specify next point: **15475,18175**
    Specify next point: **<Enter>** twice to terminate.

12. **Zoom** in on the **Alignment** and notice it has the component coloring as described earlier. Curves are already developed. Annotation is evident as well.

13. Now pick the **Alignment** and grips appear. Select a grip on the PI for the first curve. Drag it slightly to a new location while watching the curve. Do not move the PI so far that the curve cannot be computed and causes it to disappear. Cancel when finished moving the PI.

14. Now go to the **Alignments** pull-down menu and choose **Edit Alignment Geometry....** Select the alignment, and the **Alignment Layout Tools** toolbar appears. Choose the command on the right of the toolbar called **Alignment Grid View**, and the **Panorama** displays. Scroll through the **Panorama** and notice that the alignment held the radii of 200'.

Exercise 6-23: Insert PI

Now use the second tool called **Insert PI**.

1. Again, go to the **Alignments** pull-down menu and choose **Edit Alignment Geometry....** Select the **Alignment** in Figure 6-59, and the **Alignment Layout Tools** toolbar appears.

Figure 6-59   Select the alignment

2. Choose the second command, **Insert PI**.

3. Pick point near PI to insert: use the **Midpoint** snap and pick the first tangent **<Enter>**.

4. It places a new PI at 1+77.90, and a label appears.

5. Now pick the **Alignment** and notice that grips appear at keypoints on the alignment.

6. There are different types of grips denoted by their shape and include square, triangular, and circular grips. The Square grips are on alignment endpoints and allow the entire tangent component to be moved. The curves are the connecting segments and hold their radius as the tangent is relocated. The circular grips identify the curve geometry in the alignment. These can be slid along the tangents to lengthen or shorten the curve. The triangular grips are located at the PIs and can be moved to any other location as needed. When they are moved, they drag the curve along all the while holding the radius of the curves. Refer to Figure 6-60.

Figure 6-60   Edit with grips   **Figure 6-61**   Specifying a radius

7. Experiment with moving and relocating these grips. Move the PI grip for the PI you just added and observe how the alignment recomputes and redisplays.
8. Move that PI to a coordinate at or near an *X,Y* of **14865,18560**.
9. Then pick the **Alignment**, right-click, and select **Edit Alignment...** to redisplay the **Layout** toolbar.
10. Choose the **down arrow** on the sixth button from the left in the toolbar. When the menu drops down, select the command **Free Curve Fillet (Between two entities, radius)**.
11. `Select first entity:` Pick the tangent before the PI you just created.
12. `Select next entity:` Pick the tangent after the PI you just created.
13. `Is curve solution angle [Greaterthan180/Lessthan180] <Lessthan180>:` It is, so hit **<Enter>**.
14. `Specify radius in or [curveLen/Tanlen/Chordlen/midOrd/External]` : Type **250**.
15. `Select first entity:` **<Enter>** to terminate. Refer to Figure 6-61.

Notice that you now have a new curve in the alignment with a radius of 250′.

Exercise 6-24: Grips

Because you have seen several types of grips, let us take a moment to experiment further with these grips.

1. Pick the **Alignment** and notice that grips appear at keypoints on the alignment.
2. Move the circular grip for a curve and slide it along the tangent. Observe how the curve gets shorter or longer.
3. Grab a rectangular grip for an internal tangent segment and move it to a new location. Watch how the tangents and curves attached to it become relocated as well, while maintaining the curve radius.

Exercise 6-25: Using Spirals in Alignments

The software also supports spirals within the alignments. State DOTs use spirals in different ways. In some states, entrance and exit ramps for highways may be designed using spiral mathematics. Remember from the earlier description in this chapter that a spiral is a constantly changing radius. This differentiates spirals from simple arcs, which have a constant radius. You often need more physical space to build spiral ramps than those with arcs; hence you might find that the Texas DOT uses spirals more often than does the DOT in the Washington, DC, region, which has less available space. You may find that the DOT uses arcs for urban design but requires spirals for rural design for the same reasons.

For the alignment here, you will add a spiral to the end of the alignment.

1. Pick the **Alignment**, right-click, select **Edit Alignment Geometry…**, and the **Alignment Layout Tools** toolbar appears.
2. Choose the eighth icon from the left and from the pop-down menu options choose **Floating curve with Spiral (From entity end, radius, length)**.
3. `Select entity to attach to:` Use the **Endpoint** snap and snap to the right end of the alignment.
4. `Selected entity must be part of main entity. Select entity to attach to:` Select alignment.
5. `Specify radius <200.000'>:` **100**.
6. `Specify spiral in length or [A] <200.000'>:` **200**.
7. `Specify curve direction [Clockwise/cOunterclockwise] <Clockwise>:` Hit **<Enter>**.
8. `Specify length:` **200 <Esc>**.

Observe that a spiral curve has been added to the end of the alignment as expected; refer to Figure 6-62. Notice that the stationing is automatically continued from the previous length of the alignment.

When an alignment is being constructed, you may want to know detailed information about any of the components.

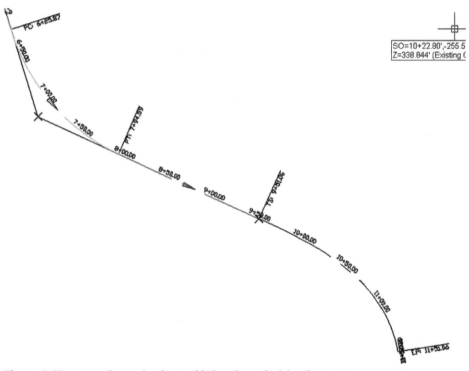

SO=10+22.80',-255.5
Z=338.844' (Existing (

Figure 6-62   A spiral curve has been added to the end of the alignment

Exercise 6-26: Spiral Information

Run through the following routine to obtain information about the spiral, which as you know can become quite complex in its mathematics.

1. Pick the **Alignment**, right-click, select **Edit Alignment Geometry…**, and the **Alignment Layout Tools** toolbar appears.
2. Pick the **Edit best fit data for all entities** the fourth icon in the toolbar from the right. Then select the command **Pick Sub-entity**, the third icon from the right.
3. Select the **Spiral Component**.
4. A **Criteria** window is populated with all of the spiral criteria for your inspection. See Figure 6-63.

Notice that you can pick any sub-entity to obtain its respective data as well.

Figure 6-63 Spiral criteria

Exercise 6-27: Fixed Lines and Curves

The next routine explores creating fixed lines and curves and shows what these features offer.

1. In the same file called Chapter 6 Alignments-2.dwg type **V** for **View** and select **Align-A**, hit **Set Current**, and then hit **OK**.
2. Set your current layer to **C-Road-Cntr**.
3. Turn off the surface's contour layers on **C-Topo-Existing Ground**.
4. From the **Alignments** pull-down menu, select **Create Alignment by Layout**. The **Create Alignment – Layout** dialog box appears. Select **Site 1** for the site, hit **OK**. This brings up the **Alignment Layout Tools** toolbar.
5. Select the black **down arrow** for the fifth icon from the left, and select the command called **Fixed Line (Two points)**. Enter the following data to construct that line and stay in the **Layout** toolbar when you are finished creating the line.
6. `Specify start point:` **15200,18700**.
7. `Specify next point:` **@200<30**. **Zoom** out to see it.
8. Now select the black **down arrow** for the sixth icon from the left, and select the command called **More Fixed Curves**. In the submenu, choose the **Fixed Curve (From entity end, through point)**.
9. `Select entity for start point and direction:`
10. Pick near the end of the line you just drew.
11. `Specify end point:` **15900,18800**. Notice the curve emerges from the end of the line and is also tangent. The alignment expands with the associated stationing.
12. Once again, stay in the **Layout** toolbar.
13. Now use a command to add another tangent from the end of the curve.

14. Select the black **down arrow** for the fifth icon from the left, and in the submenu, choose the **Floating Line (From curve end, length)**. Enter the following data to construct that line.
15. `Select start point`. Use the **Endpoint** snap and snap to the end of the curve you just drew.
16. `Specify length`: **400**.
17. Notice that a line emerges from the end of the curve that is also tangent to the end of the curve. See Figure 6-64.
18. Hit **<Enter>** to terminate the routine and leave the **Layout** toolbar.

Figure 6-64   Line emerges that is tangent to curve

If at some point you accidentally left the **Layout** toolbar, no problem. Just select the **Alignment,** right click, and choose **Edit Alignment...** to reenter the toolbar.

Do not pick **Create From Layout** when attempting to edit an alignment because this creates a **New alignment.**

There is a pull-down menu in Civil 3D 2010 shown in Figure 6-65, and it is called **Lines/Curves,** which will be familiar to Land Desktop users.

Several routines for establishing horizontal linework exist here and can assist in geometry computations.

Create Lines

These commands allow for drawing linework as follows (see Figure 6-66):

Figure 6-65   The Lines/
Curves pull-down menu

Figure 6-66   The Create
Lines commands

Line between 2 points, Lines between a list of points, Lines between Point Objects, Lines by Point Name, Northing/Easting or Grid Northing/Grid Easting, by Lat/Long, by directions such as Bearing and Distance or Azimuth, by Angle, by Deflection angle, by Station and Offset (great for right-of-way plats), by Sideshot, by Extension or trims a line by a specified distance from an object, off of the end of a curve, spiral, or another line, tangent to an object, or creates perpendiculars to a specified object.

Create Curves

These commands allow for drawing curvature as follows (see Figure 6-67):

> Curve between Two Lines
> Curve on Two Lines
> Curve through Point
> Multiple Curves
> Curve from End of Object
> Reverse or Compound Curve

Figure 6-67   The Create Curves commands

Curve between Two Lines draws curves between two tangents using other curve data.

Curve on Two Lines draws curve on two tangents, while leaving the tangent lines intact.

Curve through Point draws curve on two tangents, but passing through a P.O.C.

Multiple Curves draws curve on two tangents, using compound curves as you might see in an off-ramp of an interstate highway.

Reverse or Compound draws a reverse or compound curve from the end of existing curve.

Create Best Fit

These commands create best fit Lines, Curves and Parabolas using a least squares algorithm. (This works well with existing road centerlines.)

Attach Multiple

This is a great command for attaching arcs, lines, and spirals!

CHAPTER SUMMARY

In this chapter, you were introduced to drawing curvilinear and rectilinear objects. You learned the formulas needed to design the geometry, and you learned about curvilinear linework generation; roadway alignment; and parcel creation, editing, and drafting. The chapter also covered how to modify the data.

CHAPTER TEST QUESTIONS

Multiple Choice

1. Tie-in methods include which of the following?
   a. Rectangular tie-in
   b. Polar tie-in
   c. Intersection tie-in
   d. All of the above

2. The total number of degrees within a closed polygon depends on the number of sides and is computed using the following formula:
   a. ANGULAR CLOSURE = $(N) \times 180$
   b. ANGULAR CLOSURE = $(N - 2) \times 180$
   c. ANGULAR CLOSURE = $180/\pi$
   d. ANGULAR CLOSURE = $(N - 2)/180$

3. The Arc method of curve calculation occurs where:
   a. The degree of curve is measured over a chord length of 100′
   b. The degree of curve is measured at a radius of 100′
   c. The degree of curve is measured over an arc length of 100′
   d. None of the above

4. The following terms are associated with horizontal arcs:
   a. PVI, PVT, PVC
   b. ST, TS, SC, CS
   c. PI, POC, PRC, PC, PT
   d. All of the above

5. Some of the types of important angles to understand for civil design are:

   a. Interior angles, azimuths, bearings
   b. Cardinal directions
   c. Deflection angles, turned angles
   d. All of the above

6. For constraint-based design, there are:

   a. Fixed objects
   b. Free objects
   c. Floating objects
   d. All of the above

7. Constraint-based design includes the following objects:

   a. Splines and spirals
   b. Polylines
   c. Terrain models
   d. Civil 3D lines and curves

8. Civil 3D will:

   a. Automatically label alignments on creation
   b. Draft alignments based on styles
   c. Annotate stationing equations or equalities
   d. All of the above

9. Civil 3D **Parcel** commands will:

   a. Locate buildings on lots
   b. Fit structures into tight BRL line limits
   c. Warn when BRL lines are violated
   d. None of the above

10. In a subdivision corridor, items that reference horizontal alignments comprise:

   a. Gutters, sidewalks, and lot corners
   b. Utilities such as water, sanitary
   c. Storm drainage structures such as catch basins and manholes
   d. All of the above

True or False

1. True or False: **Transparent** commands occur without the user knowing about them.

2. True or False: A bearing has two quadrants: North and South.

3. True or False: Intersection tie-in uses two angles from a baseline to locate a position.

4. True or False: Distances along baselines are called stations.

5. True or False: The distance along the station and at a right angle to it is called an offset.

6. True or False: Arcs have a constantly changing radius.

7. True or False: Spirals and parabolas fall into the rectilinear category.

8. True or False: There are two type of arcs, and they are defined using the Roadway and Railway methods.

9. True or False: A PI for an arc is an abbreviation for Point of Interest.

10. True or False: A POC for an arc is an abbreviation for Point of Curvature.

11. True or False: Interior angles are measured only in buildings.

12. True or False: An azimuth angle can be measured from North, South, East, or West and cannot exceed 90 degrees.

13. True or False: Constraint-based design allows designers to embed certain parameters into objects that will be retained during modifications.

14. True or False: Free objects must have both incoming and outgoing objects to define them.

15. True or False: Floating objects must have an incoming object to define them correctly.

CHAPTER EXERCISES

1. What is the slope of a line with coordinates of 5000,5000 and 5100,5050?
2. What is the bearing of that same line in Problem 1?
3. What is a slope distance?
4. Describe the term *stationing* as used in alignment design.
5. How are station/offset values used?
6. Use the **Layout** toolbar to create fixed, free, and floating lines and fixed, free, and floating curves. Draw two unconnected fixed lines. Then add a floating curve to the two lines and note how it reacts after you leave the **Layout** toolbar and edit the grips.
7. Use the **Layout** toolbar to create fixed, free, and floating lines and fixed, free, and floating curves. Draw two unconnected fixed curves. Then add a floating line to the two curves and note how it reacts after you leave the **Layout** toolbar and edit the grips.

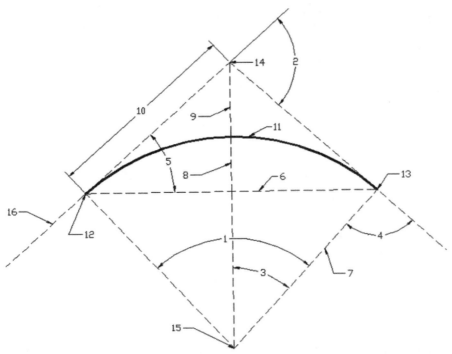

Figure 6-68

8. Name the parts of the arc shown in Figure 6-68.

   What is 1?   What is 2?

   What is 3?   What is 4?

   What is 5?   What is 6?

   What is 7?   What is 8?

   What is 9?   What is 10?

   What is 11?   What is 12?

   What is 13?   What is 14?

   What is 15?   What is 16?

9. Compute the missing values and the degree of curve for the following data. Use the formulas discussed in the chapter to solve these. Show your work.

   Curve 1: R = 93.55, L = XXX.XX, Tan = 44.46, Included angle (Delta) = 50-50-38, Chord Length = 80.32

   Curve 1: L = _____   Degree of Curve: _____

   Curve 2: R = 52.10, L = 46.01, Tan = XX.XX, Included angle (Delta) = 50-35-50, Chord Length = 44.53

   Curve 2: T = _____   Degree of Curve: _____

10. Fill in the missing blanks for the parts of the alignment (that is, PI, PC, etc.) in Figure 6-69. Note: A spiral, curve, spiral begins at 14+86.68.

    What is 1? _____ What is 2? _____ What is 3? _____

    What is 4? _____ What is 5? _____ What is 6? _____

    What is 7? _____ What is 8? _____

    What is the total length of this alignment?

11. Plot the following alignment into your CAD file. Plot the drawing at a scale of 1″ =50′.

Figure 6-69

Horizontal Alignment Station and Curve Report—Alignment			
Desc. Station	**Spiral/Curve Data**	**Northing**	**Easting**
PI	10+00 Length: 102.81	17405.34 Course: N 34-23-28 E	14810.53
PI	11+02.81 Length: 163.49 Delta: 34-22-39	17490.18 Course: N 68-46-06 E	14868.60

Circular Curve Data					
PC	10+71.88	17464.65 17408.17	14851.13 RP 14933.65		
PT	11+31.88 Delta: 34-22-39 DOC: 57-17-45 Mid-Ord: 4.47	17501.38 Type: RIGHT Length: 60.00 External: 4.68	14897.44 Radius: 100.00 Tangent: 30.93 Chord: 59.10	Es: 4.68 Course: N 51-34-47 E	
PI	12+64.43 Length: 157.56 Delta: 95-29-35	17549.39 Course: S 15-44-19 E	15021.00		

Circular Curve Data					
PC	11+81.88	17519.49 17449.58	14944.04 RP 14971.20		
PT	13+06.88 Delta: 95-29-35 DOC: 76-23-40 Mid-Ord: 24.57	17469.92 Type: RIGHT Length: 125.00 External: 36.54	15043.39 Radius: 75.00 Tangent: 82.56 Chord: 111.03	Es: 36.54 Course: S 63-29-06 E	
PI	13+81.88	17397.74	15063.74		

Advanced 3D Surface Modeling 7

Chapter Objectives

- Understand the mathematics needed for Civil 3D terrain modeling.
- Compute information about terrain models and contours manually using mathematical interpolation.
- Use Civil 3D to accomplish the same functions automatically and much faster than manually.
- Understand the TIN process and the components of the TIN data.
- Understand how to analyze surface data.

INTRODUCTION

This chapter introduces terrain modeling by discussing the various algorithms and methodologies used to develop Digital Terrain Models. A Digital Terrain Model is commonly known as a *DTM*. The DTM is the basis of most of the computations that occur in Civil 3D when it comes to the third dimension. These activities include road and utility profile creation, cross sections, earthwork calculations, contour representation, and other functions. The DTM may be one of the most important components to any project.

DTM: Digital Terrain Model

Several advanced terrain problems and related solutions are also explored. Terrain models are developed and edited. Several advanced techniques are deployed to analyze the models in 3D. Surfaces, contours, breaklines, and spot shots are discussed in detail.

To begin, an engineering project, whether it is a road design job or a site development project, almost always starts with an evaluation of the existing conditions. This can be done in a number of ways—for instance, by using a traditional survey crew with total stations or by commissioning a photogrammetist to obtain aerial photographs and stereodigitizing them into a CAD file. Control would be established in either case using local monumentation or Global Positioning Systems (GPS). The existing ground data are collected, processed, analyzed, and certified for use. In addition to the horizontal aspects of that data, the DTM would likely be developed as well.

REVIEW OF FUNCTIONS AND FEATURES TO BE USED

This chapter procedurizes how to create surfaces, how to create and modify Surface Styles to control the appearance of the surface, and how to display the surface data in a variety of different ways. Surface data are computed, the surface is analyzed, and a variety of display mechanisms are taught to view the site in innovative ways.

DTM Theory

In many cases, vertical geometry is developed from an original ground surface. In the "old" days engineers would manually interpolate contours that represented certain elevations on the ground surface.

In Figure 7-1, to plot a contour for every one foot of constant elevation change, you would locate where the contour enters the data set and plot that point. You would then locate where that same contour travels as it meanders through the data set. The following sequence illustrates how to do this manually. The method parallels that of Civil 3D in that it also uses linear interpolation to compute contour locations.

Figure 7-1   Surface spot shots

Example 7-1: Manually Compute Contour Locations

Let us identify where the 100′ contour would be. There are no data indicating that a 100′ contour exists in this data set because the lowest value is 100.3. See Figure 7-1. Therefore, locate the 101′ contour. It must be near the 100.3 ground shot, right? It appears that the 101′ contour will enter between Points 1 and 2 and exit between Points 1 and 5 (note that the direction of the contour is of no consequence to these calculations).

First compute the distance between Points 1 and 2, or because they may be on paper, scale it off the paper. This distance is 51′. Then the distance between Points 1 and 5 is scaled off. This distance is 75.4′.

Then compute the difference between the elevations of Points 1 and 2, which is 2.9′. The difference between the elevations of Points 1 and 5 is 1.5′. You now need to compute the difference from the 101′ contour to the elevation of Point 1, which is 0.7′. Compute the ratio of these elevations so that you can prorate the horizontal distance from Point 1 where the 101′ contour begins. Compute the ratio of the 101′ contour from the elevation at Point 1 with the elevation difference of Points 1 and 2. That would be 0.7/2.9, which equals 0.24. Therefore the 101′ contour begins at 24% of the total distance away from Point 1 toward Point 2. Therefore, 75.4*.24 equals 18.2′. You should scale and plot a point 18.2′ from Point 1 toward Point 2.

Let us compute the distance where the 101′ contour exits the data set. This must occur between Points 1 and 5, because no elevations exist anywhere else that would allow a 101′ contour to exit. Scale the distance from Point 1 to Point 5. You should get 75.3′. The elevation difference is 101.8 − 100.3 = 1.5. The elevation difference between Point 1 and the contour elevation of 101′

is $101 - 100.3 = 0.7$. The ratio of distance that the 101′ contour is from the 100.3 spot shot is $0.7/1.5 = 0.467$, which means that the 101′ contour is 46.67% of the distance from Point 1 to Point 5, which is $75.3*46.67 = 35.14'$.

Repeat this for any locations where the 101′ contour must pass related to the data you possess. In other words, the 101′ contour must pass between Points 1 and 3 and Points 1 and 4 on its way toward exiting between Points 1 and 5.

Continuing on with the computations in the same manner as just described, you need to be able to plot where the 101′ contour is relative to Points 1 and 3 and 1 and 4. Then you can sketch the probable path that the contour takes as it winds through the data set.

Distance from Point 1 to Point 3 = 103.48.

Positive Elevation difference between Points 1 and 3 = $105.6 - 100.3 = 5.3$.

The elevation difference between Point 1 and the 101′ contour = 0.7.

Therefore, the ratio of $0.7/5.3 = 0.13$, or 13% of the distance from Point 1 to Point 3, is established as the location of the 101′ contour, which is $0.13*103.48 = 13.67'$.

Distance from Point 1 to Point 4 = 101.18.

Positive Elevation difference between Points 1 and 4 = $104.1 - 100.3 = 3.8$.

The elevation difference between Point 1 and the 101′ contour = 0.7.

Therefore, the ratio of $0.7/3.8 = 0.184$, or 18.4% of the distance from Point 1 to Point 4, is established as the location of the 101′ contour, which is $0.184*101.18 = 18.64'$.

Now compute the location for the 102′ contour.

Distance from Point 1 to Point 2 = 51.

Positive Elevation difference between Points 1 and 2 = $103.2 - 100.3 = 2.9$.

The elevation difference between Point 1 and the 102′ contour = 1.7.

Therefore, the ratio of $1.7/2.9 = 0.586$, or 58.6% of the distance from Point 1 to Point 2, is established as the location of the 102′ contour, which is $0.586*51 = 29.89'$.

It can be seen that the 102′ contour does not exit between Points 1 and 5 because the elevation of the point is less than 102′. It must exist between Points 5 and 4.

Distance from Point 5 to Point 4 = 49.1.

Positive Elevation difference between Points 5 and 4 = $104.1 - 101.8 = 2.3$.

The elevation difference between Point 5 and the 102′ contour = 0.2.

Therefore, the ratio of $0.2/2.3 = 0.086$, or 8.6% of the distance from Point 5 to Point 4, is established as the location of the 102′ contour, which is $0.086*49.1 = 4.26'$

Distance from Point 1 to Point 3 = 103.48.

Positive Elevation difference between Points 1 and 3 = $105.6 - 100.3 = 5.3$.

The elevation difference between Point 1 and the 102′ contour = 1.7.

Therefore, the ratio of $1.7/5.3 = 0.32$, or 32% of the distance from Point 1 to Point 3, is established as the location of the 102′ contour, which is $0.32*103.48 = 33.19'$

Distance from Point 1 to Point 4 = 101.18.

Positive Elevation difference between Points 1 and 4 = $104.1 - 100.3 = 3.8$.

The elevation difference between Point 1 and the 102′ contour =1.7.

Therefore, the ratio of $1.7/3.8 = 0.447$, or 44.7% of the distance from Point 1 to Point 4, is established as the location of the 102′ contour, which is $0.447*101.18 = 45.26'$.

Now compute the location for the 103′ contour.

Distance from Point 1 to Point 2 = 51.

Positive Elevation difference between Points 1 and 2 = $103.2 - 100.3 = 2.9$.

The elevation difference between Point 1 and the 102′ contour = 2.7.

Therefore, the ratio of 2.7/2.9 = 0.93, or 93% of the distance from Point 1 to Point 2, is established as the location of the 102′ contour, which is 0.93*51 = 47.48′.

It can be seen that the 103′ contour exits between Points 5 and 4.

Distance from Point 5 to Point 4 = 49.1.

Positive Elevation difference between Points 5 and 4 = 104.1 − 101.8 = 2.3.

The elevation difference between Point 5 and the 103′ contour = 1.2.

Therefore, the ratio of 1.2/2.3 = 0.52, or 52% of the distance from Point 5 to Point 4, is established as the location of the 103′ contour, which is 0.52*49.1 = 25.6′.

Distance from Point 1 to Point 3 = 103.48.

Positive Elevation difference between Points 1 and 3 = 105.6 − 100.3 = 5.3.

The elevation difference between Point 1 and the 103′ contour = 2.7.

Therefore, the ratio of 2.7/5.3=0.509, or 50.9% of the distance from Point 1 to Point 3, is established as the location of the 103′ contour, which is 0.509*103.48 = 52.7′.

Distance from Point 1 to Point 4 = 101.18.

Positive Elevation difference between Points 1 and 4 = 104.1 − 100.3 = 3.8.

The elevation difference between Point 1 and the 102′ contour = 2.7.

Therefore, the ratio of 2.7/3.8 = 0.71, or 71% of the distance from Point 1 to Point 4, is established as the location of the 103′ contour, which is 0.71*101.18 = 71.89′.

Exercise 7-1: Manually Compute Contours

Compute the locations for where the 104′ and 105′ contours exist in the data set.

ANSWER TO EXERCISE 7-1

Distance from Point 2 to Point 3 = 78.8.

Positive Elevation difference between Points 2 and 3 = 103.2 − 105.6 = 2.4.

The elevation difference between Point 2 and the 104′ contour = 0.8.

Therefore, the ratio of 0.8/2.4 = 0.33, or 33% of the distance from Point 2 to Point 3, is established as the location of the 104′ contour, which is 0.33*78.8 = 26.26′.

Distance from Point 1 to Point 3 = 103.48.

Positive Elevation difference between Points 1 and 3 = 105.6 − 100.3 = 5.3.

The elevation difference between Point 1 and the 104′ contour = 3.7.

Therefore, the ratio of 3.7/5.3 = 0.698, or 69.8% of the distance from Point 1 to Point 3, is established as the location of the 104′ contour, which is 0.698*103.48 = 72.2′.

Distance from Point 1 to Point 4 = 101.18.

Positive Elevation difference between Points 1 and 4 = 104.1 − 100.3 = 3.8.

The elevation difference between Point 1 and the 104′ contour = 3.7.

Therefore, the ratio of 3.7/3.8 = 0.97, or 97% of the distance from Point 1 to Point 4, is established as the location of the 104′ contour, which is 0.97*101.18 = 98.14′.

It can be seen that the 104′ contour exits between Points 5 and 4.

Distance from Point 5 to Point 4 = 49.1.

Positive Elevation difference between Points 5 and 4 = 104.1 − 101.8 = 2.3.

The elevation difference between Point 5 and the 104′ contour = 2.2.

Therefore, the ratio of 2.2/2.3 = 0.956, or 95.6% of the distance from Point 5 to Point 4, is established as the location of the 104′ contour, which is 0.956*49.1 = 46.9′.

Distance from Point 2 to Point 3 = 78.8.

Positive Elevation difference between Points 2 and 3 = 103.2 − 105.6 = 2.4.

The elevation difference between Point 2 and the 105' contour = 1.8.

Therefore, the ratio of 1.8/2.4 = 0.75, or 75% of the distance from Point 2 to Point 3, is established as the location of the 105' contour, which is 0.75*78.8 = 59.1'.

Distance from Point 3 to Point 4 = 47.8.

Positive Elevation difference between Points 3 and 4 = 105.6 − 104.1 = 1.5.

The elevation difference between Point 3 and the 105' contour = 0.6.

Therefore, the ratio of 0.6/1.5 = 0.4, or 40% of the distance from Point 3 to Point 4, is established as the location of the 105' contour, which is 0.40*47.8 = 19.1'. See Figure 7-2.

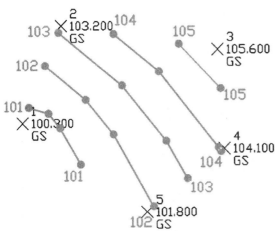

Figure 7-2   Hand-drawn contours

Today, many engineers use a computer and its software to perform this interpolation. Computers create and use Digital Terrain Models (DTM). The source data for this DTM can be composed of various types of data ranging from spot shots or ground shots, breaklines, and contours. A DTM is a digital approximation (that is, a model) of the data collected to represent the 3D conditions of the site. At various stages, assumptions, interpolations, and computations occur to prepare the "terrain surface." The user must study and understand what the software is trying to do in order to interact with the model. The user may make changes to override interpolations and assumptions made by the system, if desired.

The DTM TIN algorithm is based on Delauney's criteria, which create triangular planes that define the terrain surface. This is typically the method most manufacturers use and is one in which a triangle is created between the closest three points in the site. The triangle is a planar face from which computations can be performed. For instance, a profile of a roadway centerline can be computed from a TIN using linear interpolation. A new and increasingly used methodology for developing DTMs is topologically triangulated networks, or TTNs. This algorithm enables the user to segregate the data used as source data for the TIN processing.

Once a TIN is prepared, computations can be "sampled" or calculated from it. These might produce spot elevations interpolated from the triangle face, contours, a profile, or a cross section. A profile is the graphical intersection of a vertical plane, along the route in question, with the Earth's surface. Profiles are covered in detail in Chapter 8.

Cross sections are shorter profiles made perpendicular to the route in question. Two types of cross sections are often used: one for roadways or corridors and the other for borrow pits, landfills, and detention ponds.

THE TIN PROCESS

Figure 7-3 shows four spot shots, Figure 7-4 shows a resulting TIN, and Figure 7-5 shows contouring and depicts a hill or a rise. How do you know this is not a stream or ditch? If the algorithm had placed the interconnecting TIN line so that it connected the 100' elevations, there would be a different condition to be solved.

Figure 7-3   Four simple spot shots   **Figure 7-4**   A TIN from the four shots

Figure 7-5   Contours from the TIN

This example shows that the software can easily produce a seriously incorrect interpretation of the data, if controls are not put into place to prevent it. The contours generated in Figure 7-6 differed by almost 90 degrees from those in Figure 7-5! Only a technician who knew that the area contained a swale would be able to estimate contours properly for the data given. Of course, the software had no way of knowing whether to connect the points to produce a swale or a highpoint (ridge) condition. That information was not available from the data set of points alone. This situation typically occurs in low areas, hilltops, and ridges. The answer is to place breaklines at the

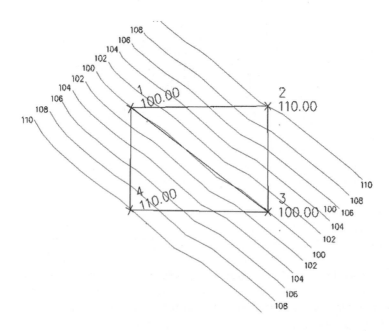

Figure 7-6   Same TIN, different contours

tops of ridges and in the centerlines of swales, at the tops of banks and in the toes of slopes, and every place a "break" exists that must be retained.

Ground Information

A contour is a linestring that represents a single elevation along a surface. It is a coplanar object that always has a consistent elevation at each vertex of the object. It is an imaginary linestring that connects points of equal elevation.

Contours usually have a primary interval and a secondary interval. Some call these index and intermediate, whereas others call them high and normal contour intervals, respectively. Some typical intervals might be 2′ and 10′ intervals where the 10′ intervals' linework is designated as a more dominant lineweight and perhaps a different linestyle than the 2′ contours. In high terrain areas, the interval might jump to 5′ and 25′ intervals. In flat areas, the interval might be 1′ and 5′ intervals, whereas metric projects may use .5 m and 2.5 m intervals.

The interval is important so that enough data are shown to convey an understanding of the site. Some interesting facts about contours follow. Refer to Figure 7-7.

- Contours were first introduced in 1729 by a Dutch surveyor named Cruquius in connection with depth soundings of the sea. Laplace then used the concept to represent terrain in 1816.
- Water flows perpendicular to the contour.
- Contours bend or point upstream when they cross creeks or rivers.
- Evenly spaced contours represent a fairly uniform or constant slope condition.
- Closed contours that end on an intermediate elevation should be identified with hachures or spot shots to indicate whether the ground is rising or dropping.

Figure 7-7   Contours speak to us

What Method Is Used to Calculate the Contours for the Site?

Let us review the contouring processing. In a particular set of data, the contours may be drawn as shown next. Please note that the algorithms for calculating contour lines vary from manufacturer to manufacturer. One general means for generating contours is straight-line interpolation from the TIN surface.

The calculations interpolate where the desired contour crosses the TIN line. In this manner, you can find out where the contour enters and leaves the triangle. As can be seen in Figure 7-8, this kind of processing is quite exact. Notice the 105′ contour. It must touch the 105′ spot shot.

Figure 7-8   An accurate contour

However, because the ground tends to roll in natural conditions, the contour must usually be "smoothed" to represent this rolling. When the software smoothes a contour, it adds error to it. See Figure 7-9.

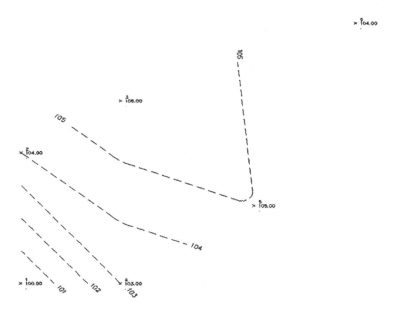

Figure 7-9   A smoothed contour

This error can be noticed in Figure 7-9 because the 105′ contour no longer touches the 105′ spot shot. The smoothing process sacrifices the sharp vertices while trying to retain the shape and location of the remaining contour. This is only one of several variations that can occur in contour generation.

The data in Figure 7-10 show a 140-acre site with breaklines and mass points. Breaklines represent a break in the surface where one plane changes slope from the plane adjacent to it. Mathematically, the breakline serves the TIN creation algorithm in that no triangle will ever be allowed to cross a breakline. This rule allows the user to control how a TIN is developed. This is more efficient than depicting it with contour data. The contour file for this project was around 20 MB whereas this file is less than 1 MB. The resulting contours for this site are shown in Figure 7-11.

With the accuracies attained by breaklines and mass point data, you can compute profiles and sections with more precision than that which is possible with contours.

Figure 7-10   Breaklines and mass points

Figure 7-11   Resulting site contours

Civil 3D has the industry's leading terrain modeling capabilities. Now that the theories and algorithms involving DTMs have been discussed, you now explore how Civil 3D handles these computations.

SURFACES IN CIVIL 3D

Next you run through an exercise that sets some basic settings, and then you create an Existing Ground Style and generate a surface. The **Surfaces** pull-down menu, Figure 7-12, contains the following commands:

Figure 7-12   The Surfaces pull-down menu

Create Surface... allows for the user to create and name a new surface and choose its surface type, TIN, Grid, and Volume.

Create Surface from DEM... allows for creating a surface from a Digital Elevation Model. These are available from several sources, including the U.S. Geological Survey at www.usgs.org.

Create Surface from TIN... allows for importing a TIN from Land Desktop. It requires a .tin and its associated .pnt file.

Edit Surface offers many options for surface editing.

Add Surface Labels allows for labeling the surface or its contours.

Add Legend Table... allows for bringing in a legend table for a variety of surface analyses that can be generated in Civil 3D.

Utilities is where you perform volume computations and use the **WATER DROP** command to check for drainage flow directions.

Exercise 7-2: Open Drawing and Inspect Source Data

To access student data files, go to www.pearsondesigncentral.com.

1. Launch Civil 3D and open the file called Chapter-7-DTM.dwg. Type **V** for **View**, select the view called **DTM-A**, hit **Set Current**, and hit **OK**.
2. Notice that there are breaklines and mass points in the file. The mass points are actually AutoCAD blocks floating at the correct elevation. The breaklines were developed by an aerial photogrammetist using stereodigitizing techniques. The breaklines are three-dimensional and have elevations at each vertex. The mass points are placed in the data set to densify the surface data. Together the breaklines and mass points represent the existing ground conditions.
3. Click on a breakline somewhere in the file and notice the grips. Place your cursor in one of the grips, but do not click it. Simply look at the lower left corner of the screen and observe that the X, Y, Z coordinates are shown for the grip. Notice the Z coordinate or elevation has a value representing the elevation of the surface at that location.

Now that you have observed the data set, prepare a Civil 3D surface for existing ground. First you must inspect some important surface-related settings. The first one you change is the **Precision of the Contour** label. Because you are labeling even contours that are multiples of 2, there is no need to have thousandths place precision on the annotation when whole numbers suffice. The precision is unneeded, and the extra decimal places tend to clutter up the drawing. Additionally, you create a layer for the annotation to reside on.

Exercise 7-3: Develop Surface Settings

1. Go to the **Toolspace**. Click on the **Settings** tab.
2. In the **Master View**, expand **Drawings**. Then expand **Surface**. Then expand **Label Styles**.
3. Choose the **Contour** label style, and note that one exists called **Standard**.
4. Click on the **Standard** label style, right-click, and choose **Edit....**
5. The **Label Style Composer** dialog box displays. Click on the **Information** tab and observe the contents of the panel. Click on the **General** tab and observe the contents of the panel.
6. Click the **Layout** tab. Several properties exist in the **Properties** column.
7. Click on **Text**; expand **Text**. Choose **Contents** and then refer to the **Values** column. Click on the value for **Contents**. Choose the button with the ellipsis (...).
8. This brings up the **Text Component Editor—Contents**.
9. Click in the **Preview** window on the right side of the dialog box; highlight the data there and erase them so that the window is blank.
10. Click on **Precision** in the **Modifier** column.
11. The value for the **Precision** is **0.001**, which is not appropriate for your contour label because you do not wish to have decimal points on even contours. Click on **0.001** and select **1** from the pop-down window in the **Values** column.
12. Then click the **blue arrow** at the top of the dialog box to populate the **Preview** window with the new data settings.
13. Look on the **Preview** window and see some code indicating that new settings exist. Hit **OK**.
14. In the **General** tab for the **Layer** property, click on the value where it shows **Layer 0** and notice that a button with an ellipsis (...) exists. Choose the button, and a **Layer** dialog box appears. Choose **New**. In the **Create Layer** dialog box, click on the value for **Layer** property where it says **Layer 1** and type in a new layer name of **C-Topo-Labl**. Hit **OK**, and hit **OK** again.
15. In the **Label Style Composer-Standard** dialog box under the **General** tab, there is a property for **Plan Readability**. Set **Anchors with Text**; set it to **True**.
16. Hit **Apply** and **OK**.

You need to set one more setting. When executing the procedure to label contours, several technicalities are established by the software that will provide benefits later on. One of those has to do with a Contour Label Control Line. This linework appears in the center of the contour label and can be placed on its own layer so it will be nonintrusive to the user when plotting or negotiating through the drawing.

Exercise 7-4: Set Up a Surface

Now allocate a surface for the project. Develop a surface name and set the type of surface you will have.

1. From the Civil 3D pull-down menu, choose **Surfaces**.
2. Select **Create Surface....**
3. The **Create Surface** dialog box appears.
4. Several types of surfaces can be created: a TIN surface, a Grid surface, and two types of Volume surfaces. The Volume surfaces are created during earthwork take-off computations. The Grid surface is used when a surface of evenly spaced rectangular data whose elevations are interpolated from the data is desired.
5. You want a **TIN** surface. In the window is the informational item that includes the name of the surface. Click on the **Value** column for the **Surface** name.
6. The **Surface** name is incremental so the first surface will be **Surface 1**, the second surface is **Surface 2**, and so on. Click in this field and type **Existing Ground** as your name or select the ellipses (...) to bring up the **Name Template** dialog box.
7. To the right of the type is the **Surface layer** field. Select the button on the right side of the dialog box for **Surface Layer**. An **Object Layer** dialog box appears. Where it says **Base layer name**, choose the button on the right for **Layer**, and the **Layer Selection** dialog box opens.
8. Hit the button for **New** layer and enter **C-Topo** in the field for **Layer 1**, hit **OK**, hit **OK** again. Then where it says **Modifier**, select **Suffix** from the pop-down window.

9. When the field to the right becomes available, type in a dash and an asterisk (**-***). This creates a layer with the name of the surface as a suffix to the layer name. You should get a layer called **C-Topo-Existing Ground**, as can be seen in the **Preview**.
10. Type **Existing Ground** for the **Description** also.
11. Leave all else as default and hit **OK**.
12. Next go to the **Toolspace** and choose the **Prospector** tab.
13. Look under **Open Drawings** for your drawing. Expand **Surfaces** to show the new surface you just created for Existing Ground.

Exercise 7-5: Build a Surface

The next step is to identify the 3D surface data and build the surface.

1. Expand the **Existing Ground Surface** item. You see an item for **Definition**.
2. Expand **Definition**, and you see all the data types that can go into the preparation of the surface. These include **Breaklines**, **Contours, DEM Files**, and **Drawing Objects**.
3. Your data set contains breaklines and blocks, as discussed earlier. Therefore, use the commands for adding **Breaklines** and use **Drawing Objects** to add the blocks.
4. Begin by clicking on **Breaklines**, then right-click on **Breaklines** and select **Add....**
5. A dialog box for **Add Breaklines** displays. Add a **Description** of **EG**.
6. Use **Standard** breaklines as the type of breakline but notice that other choices exist in the pop-down list. The choices allow for **Proximity breaklines**, **Wall breaklines**, **Breaklines from a file**, and **Non-destructive breaklines**.

TIP Proximity breaklines are 2D polylines that have points with elevations at each vertex in the polyline. The software uses the point elevations in creating 3D breaklines from the 2D polylines. The **Wall breakline** option is used to represent vertical components of surfaces. In actuality they are not truly vertical as this would cause issues in the software relating to a divide by zero in the denominator for various slope computations. Therefore, the software allows for Wall breaklines that contain wall height data, but the top of the wall is slightly offset from the bottom of the wall to avoid the vertical computational issue. The last choice is to bring in breaklines from an external text file.

You use **Standard** breaklines, which are the 3D polylines in the file. The last setting is a **Mid-ordinate distance** field, which is available for creating 3D breaklines from 2D polylines that have curves in them. In this case if you use the default of 1′, a 3D polyline would be created so that small chords simulate the curve but do not deviate from the arc by more than 1′.

7. Hit **OK**, and the command prompt instructs you to Select objects: Place a window around the data. Do not worry if there are points mixed in with the selection set of breaklines because the software filters anything that is not a breakline.
8. A **Panorama** dialog box may appear that indicates there are two crossing breaklines. Coordinates are displayed so the user can check the severity of the issue. In this case, you have determined that this will not harm your surface integrity and so continue on. Click the checkmark in the top right of the **Panorama** to continue. On completion of this function, the software creates the surface as can be seen by a yellow boundary.
9. Now in the **Prospector**, choose **Drawing Objects** under **Surface >> Definitions** area. Right-click and choose **Add....**
10. For the **Object type**, choose **Blocks**.
11. Type **EG** as the **Description** field in the dialog box and hit **OK**.
12. Select objects: Place a window around the data. Do not worry if there are breaklines mixed in with the selection set of points because the software filters out the unnecessary data.
13. On completion, the yellow surface boundary is updated to include the blocks.

Now that the surface is created, you typically want to view contours representing the surface.

Exercise 7-6: Develop Contours for the Surface

1. In the **Toolspace**, choose the **Settings** tab. Choose **Surface >> Surface Styles >> Standard**. Right-click on **Standard** and choose **Edit....**
2. In the **Surface Style** dialog box, choose the **Display** tab.
3. With the view direction in the pop-down window set to **Plan**, click **On** the lightbulb to turn on the **Major** and **Minor contours** and turn **Off** the lightbulb for **Border**. Note the colors are preset and can be changed here if so desired. Hit **Apply** then hit **OK**.
4. On leaving the dialog box, the contours in Civil 3D are automatically updated to show the contours as defined in the Style.
5. The next step is to create contour labels on the contours. From the Civil 3D pull-down menu, choose **Surfaces >> Add Surface Labels >> Contour-Multiple at Interval**.
6. `Select a surface: Pick on surface. Existing Ground, Pick first point:` Place a point at the top of the site and place a second point to the bottom and outside of the site.
7. `Interval along contour <100.000'>:` **500 <Enter>**. On completion of the command, zoom in and inspect the data and the contour labels every 500′ across the site.
8. Save your file to a name with your initials as the suffix of the name, Chapter-7-DTM-YourInitials.dwg.

TIP   Use the contour labeling as often as is needed to obtain coverage across the site for all the desired contours that you wish to be labeled.

Job skills will benefit in that the drawing labels can be customized. If you have duplicate labels, notice that you can delete the **Contour Label Control Line** to delete the label. Notice also that you can move this **Contour Label Control Line** to relocate the label.

Congratulations! You have created a surface, displayed its contours, and labeled them. Note that you can also add other labels, as shown in Figure 7-13.

Figure 7-13   Add Labels dialog box

Exercise 7-7: Create a Surface from DEM Data

Now use another Civil 3D command to build a surface based on DEM data. A DEM is a Digital Elevation Model data set. DEM data can be found in a number of locations, but one source is the USGS.org website. This exercise uses a DEM data set for Norfolk-E, Virginia.

To access student data files, go to www.pearsondesigncentral.com.

1. Launch Civil 3D and open the file called Chapter-7-DEM.dwg.
2. Under the **Surfaces** pull-down menu, choose the option for **Create Surface From DEM....**
3. When prompted, select the file called **Norfolk-E.dem**. This file was downloaded from the USGS.org website with the filename Norfolk-E.gz, which is a WinZip file that produces a file called Norfolk-E. It was renamed to a .DEM file prior to using it in this exercise. No scaling or geoedetics have been applied to the file, and it is being used directly as it was downloaded from the USGS.org website.
4. At this point, the software reads the file, prepares the surfaces, and generates the contours for the area.
5. Use **ZOOM EXTENTS** to see the results on completion.

Exercise 7-8: Importing a Surface from Land Desktop

Now use another Civil 3D command to import a TIN surface from a Land Desktop project. This file, specifically the .TIN file, can be found in the DTM folder of a Land Desktop project.

To access student data files, go to www.pearsondesigncentral.com.

1. Launch Civil 3D and open the file called Chapter-7-importtin.dwg.
2. Under the **Surfaces** pull-down menu, choose the option for **Create Surface from TIN....**
3. When prompted, select the file called **OSI-INTX.TIN**.
4. At this point, the software reads the file, prepares the surface for Civil 3D usage, and displays it based on the Style in effect.
5. Use **ZOOM EXTENTS** to see the result on completion.

Note:

You must have the associated OSI-INTX.PNT file for this to work. It is provided but is not requested in the process.

Exercise 7-9: Surface Labeling

This exercise explores some of the surface labeling features in Civil 3D. Zoom into the side road in the file you just imported. Let us evaluate the slopes of the roadway. See Figure 7-14.

Figure 7-14   Roadway contours with labels

1. Under the **Surfaces** pull-down menu, choose the option for **Add Surface Labels....**
2. A dialog box appears requesting information on the type of label you want to create.
3. Use a **Surface Feature;** the **Label type** will be a slope (as opposed to a spot elevation label), and you use a **Standard** slope label style. Hit the **Add** button.
4. The prompt requests you to choose whether you want a one-point or two-point label.

TIP A one-point label computes the slope at the point you pick based on the triangle slope of the TIN triangle. The two-point option allows you to pick two points where it computes the elevations of the two points, the distance between the two points, and the average slope between them.

5. Hit **<Enter>** for **One Point** and pick points inside the surface of the side road. Slope labels appear, and you can repeat this as often as needed.

Surface Analysis

The next item of discussion is how to perform analyses on the surface. Civil 3D has many types of analyses that can be computed. They include:

Contour renders surface triangles according to the range into which a contour falls.

Directions renders surface triangles according to the direction they face.

Elevations renders surface triangles according to the elevation range into which they fall.

Slopes renders surface triangles according to the slopes they have.

Slope Arrows places directional vector arrows based on the flow direction that a triangle has.

User-Defined Contours draws the location for user-specified contour elevations.

Watersheds draws the perimeters of drainage divides.

Exercise 7-10: Performing Slope Analysis

Quite often, there is concern with the slopes occurring across a site, so it is important to perform a slope analysis. Perform a slope analysis of the roadway as in Figure 7-15.

Figure 7-15   Surface analysis

1. Select the surface in the file. Right-click and choose **Surface Properties....**
2. A **Surface Properties** dialog box appears. Set the **Analysis** type to **Slopes**.
3. Set the **Number** of **Ranges** to **4**.

4. Turn off the **Scale scheme to fit** option. Click the **gray down** arrow.
5. For ID1, set the **Maximum Slope** to **3%**.
6. For ID2, set the **Minimum Slope** to **3%** and the maximum slope to **5%**.
7. For ID3, set the **Minimum Slope** to **5%** and the maximum slope to **20%**.
8. For ID4, set the **Minimum Slope** to **20%** and the maximum slope to **10000000%**. Hit **Apply** and **OK**.
9. The system sets the surface to display these data once the Style is set to do so.
10. Click on a contour and right-click. Choose **Edit Surface Style....**
11. Under the **Display** tab, turn **Off** the **Contour** components and turn **On** the **Slopes**. Hit **OK**.
12. The surface should display with red-colored faces.
13. Now from the **Surfaces** pull-down menu, choose **Add Legend Table....**
14. `Enter table type[ Directions/Elevations/Slopes/slopeArrows/Contours/ Usercontours/Watersheds] :` Type **S** for **Slope**.
15. `Behavior [ Dynamic/<Static>] :` Hit **<Enter>** for **Dynamic**.
16. `Select upper left corner:` Pick a point below and out of the way of the surface data, and a table of the statistics appears. See Figure 7-16.

Figure 7-16   A Legend

Exercise 7-11: How to Edit a Surface

Now explore surface editing a little. You have identified that a low spot for an inlet is needed at the intersection of these roads. Add that low spot by editing the surface and dropping the desired location by 1'.

1. Start by selecting the surface, right-click, and choose **Edit Surface Style....**
2. In the **Display** tab, turn **On** the **Contours** and **Points** and turn **Off** the **Slopes** from the last exercise.
3. Hit **OK** to see the contours for the surface.
4. Type **V** for **View**, select a view called **DTM-B**, hit **Set Current,** hit **OK**. This places your view near the intersection of the two roads.
5. In the **Prospector**, expand your drawing file. Expand the **Surfaces** item. Expand the surface called **osi-intx**. Expand **Definition.** Right-click on **Edits**, and a menu displays Surface editing commands.
6. Choose **Modify Point**, shown in Figure 7-17.
7. `Select points:` Type **15700,18843.5** and hit **<Enter>** twice.
8. `New elevation:` Type **441.8**.
9. Notice that a new contour appears immediately at the intersection of the roads, indicating that the point has dropped 1', thereby creating a new contour. That new contour shows up just above the cursor in Figure 7-18.

Figure 7-17 Surface editing

Z=442.799' (osi-intx)

Figure 7-18 Contour updating

Exercise 7-12: Adding Surface Boundaries

In the last surface-related exercise, you explore the concept of surface boundaries. Boundaries allow you to curtail surface computations based on the boundaries that you define.

1. Zoom into the view of the same file where you imported the **osi-intx** surface of the two roads. Zoom into the side road.
2. Draw a polyline around the outside edge of the side roadway, as shown in Figure 7-20.
3. In the **Prospector**, expand your drawing file. Expand the **Surfaces** item. Expand the surface called **osi-intx**. Expand **Definition**. Right-click on **Boundaries** and select **Add...** as in Figure 7-19.

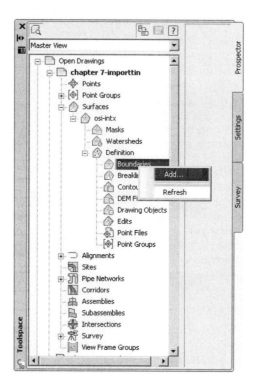

Figure 7-19   Add Boundary

4. When the **Add Boundaries** dialog box appears, type **B1** for the name of the boundary.
5. Choose **Outer** for the type of boundary. Leave the mid-ordinate distance at **1.0′**. Hit **OK**.
6. `Select object(s):` Pick the polyline you drew.
7. The surface is instantly reduced to exist within the boundary drawn. Notice that the adjacent road is now gone. See Figure 7-20.

To continue exploring with the surfaces features, take some time to change the **Surface Styles** and turn on or off various items to change how the surface can display itself.

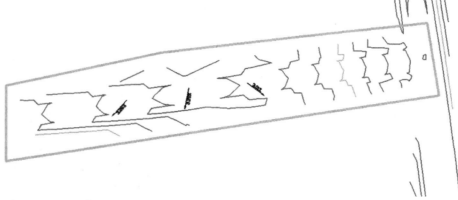

Figure 7-20   Effect of surface boundary

CHAPTER SUMMARY

This chapter introduced terrain modeling and discussed the mathematics needed to develop Digital Terrain Models. The DTM is the basis of most Civil 3D three-dimensional computa- tions, including road and utility profile creation and contour rep- resentation. Terrain models were developed and edited, and sev- eral advanced techniques were used to analyze models in 3D.

CHAPTER TEST QUESTIONS

Multiple Choice

1. Which of the following acronyms pertain to surface models?
   a. TIN
   b. DTM
   c. TTN
   d. All of the above

2. A DTM can represent which of the following?
   a. Caves and escarpments
   b. Existing and finished ground surfaces
   c. Roadway profiles
   d. None of the above

3. DTMs can be created by using the following as source data:
   a. Points, breaklines
   b. Roadway profiles and alignments
   c. DEMs combined with utility data
   d. All of the above

4. The following computations usually use surface data:
   a. Profiling
   b. Earthworks
   c. Cross sections
   d. All of the above

5. Contour intervals can be which of the following?
   a. 1′ and 5′ intervals
   b. 2′ and 10′ intervals
   c. 5′ and 25′ intervals
   d. All of the above

6. The following information items are attributed to contours:
   a. Laplace used the concept to represent terrain in 1816.
   b. Water flows perpendicular to the contour.
   c. Contours bend or point upstream when they cross creeks or rivers.
   d. All of the above.

7. What method is used to calculate the contours for a site?
   a. Straight-line interpolation from the TIN surface
   b. Slope analysis
   c. Delauney's method
   d. None of the above

8. Surfaces in Civil 3D can be:
   a. TIN surfaces
   b. Grid surfaces
   c. Volume surfaces
   d. All of the above

9. Proximity breaklines are:
   a. Breaklines near other breaklines
   b. Polylines that have points with elevations near their vertices
   c. Breaklines that are in the proximity of mass points
   d. None of the above

10. Civil 3D can analyze surfaces according to which of the following:
    a. Triangle direction
    b. Slope
    c. Elevation
    d. All of the above

True or False

1. True or False: A DTM stands for Digital Terrain Method- ology.

2. True or False: A contour with a value of 101.5 can never be a legitimate contour elevation.

3. True or False: A DEM is a legitimate source data type for a surface.

4. True or False: Contours can be used in conjunction with spot shots to develop surfaces.

5. True or False: The TIN theory is based on Descartes' methods.

6. True or False: Most of the computations for the third di- mension emanate from the surface model.

7. True or False: Cross sections are usually computed or- thogonally from the centerline.

8. True or False: The TIN algorithm computes triangle ver- tices based on the closest three points.

9. True or False: A contour is a linestring that represents a single elevation along a surface.

10. True or False: Contours may have primary and secondary intervals.

CHAPTER EXERCISES

1. Draw the 5′ contours where they fall on this map of spot elevations shot by a surveyor in the field (Figure 7-21). The tick marks designate where the actual spot shot is located. Use manual interpolated techniques to determine where the contours fall.

X 427.52 X 422.27 X 430.02 X 429.44 X 428.53 X 430.36 X 431.70 X 425.28 X 414.89 X 407.92 X 402.45

X 422.40 X 418.86 X 428.16 X 427.08 X 424.56 X 427.98 X 430.27 X 426.69 X 417.42 X 406.51 X 401.28

X 417.91 X 420.07 X 425.48 X 422.56 X 422.33 X 426.26 X 428.90 X 425.74 X 416.24 X 407.08 X 401.63

X 415.39 X 412.61 X 420.19 X 417.10 X 419.57 X 425.70 X 428.31 X 427.93 X 421.14 X 410.72 X 401.71

X 410.87 X 409.28 X 410.60 X 413.67 X 421.79 X 426.95 X 431.14 X 427.78 X 417.31 X 407.79 X 406.03

X 405.64 405.48 X 407.95 X 415.10 X 421.30 X 426.62 X 431.22 X 430.56 X 421.27 X 411.25 X 411.57

X 399.67 X 409.32 X 415.52 X 420.04 X 424.90 X 429.92 X 433.73 X 429.64 X 419.44 X 415.3 X 415.49

Figure 7-21 Surface Data—spot shots

X 404.73 409.59 X 415.65 X 420.97 X 426.32 X 425.35 X 432.04 X 431.25 X 424.36 X 422.29 X 419.74

2. Show the drainage for the site in Problem 1. Draw six arrows representing the drainage across the site.
3. Circle the high and the low points on the site in Problem 1.
4. What is the slope in Figure 7-22 from the 434 contour to the 424 contour, the 426 to the 424 contour, and the 422 contour to the 420 contour?
5. How many 2′ contours would exist on the side sloping of a retention pond if the top of the pond elevation were at 500′ elevation, the side sloping were at 3:1 down, and the existing ground tie-out were at 485?

Figure 7-22 Computing slope from contours

Advanced Profiles and Sections

8

Chapter Objectives

- Understand the algorithms and formulas involved in computing existing and proposed profiles.
- Understand how profiles and sections build on what was learned in the previous chapter on surfaces.
- Understand how existing ground profiles and cross-sectional data are associated with horizontal alignments.
- Design, label, and edit a proposed vertical alignment.
- Produce, label, and edit sections.

INTRODUCTION

This chapter begins with some of the theory involved in designing roads, moving you into the third dimension with creating roadway profiling; developing vertical tangents, vertical curves, and vertical alignments; and the editing and labeling of these. Roadway vertical tangents, vertical curves, vertical alignments (profiles), and profile views are discussed in detail. Cross sections are also covered in this chapter because they are closely related to profiles.

REVIEW OF FUNCTIONS AND FEATURES TO BE USED

There are three main requirements for designing a roadway. The first is the development of an alignment, covered in Chapter 6. The second is the roadway profile, covered in this chapter. The third is the road's cross-sectional *template*, to be discussed in Chapter 9 on corridor design. Here you learn how to produce existing ground profiles, how to place them into profile views, and how to develop *proposed profiles* and annotate them. This chapter explores the link between horizontal alignments, existing ground profiles, and cross sections and how they are updated when modifications are made to the data. Similar material will be procedurized for section-based views of the roadway as well.

In some locations across the country, road design can be accomplished with the alignment, the profile, and a simple cross-sectional detail outlining the typical cross section for the road. The contractor follows the alignment for horizontal control, the profile for vertical control, and then inputs the cross-sectional data into the paving machinery.

template: A template consists of one or more typical examples of how the roadway will appear for varying conditions, such as a roadway with a curb and gutter at the edge of the pavement or perhaps a shoulder treatment at the edge of the pavement. It is shown in a cross-sectional view and shows the road from left to right looking into the profile grade line (PGL).

proposed profile: The vertical alignment for the roadway as defined by the proposed vertical tangents and vertical curves.

THEORY OF VERTICAL ALIGNMENTS

Before getting into the Civil 3D approach for developing profiles, some of the rudimentary mathematics involved with the vertical alignments for roadways must be discussed.

Figure 8-1   A horizontal alignment

Profiles are created by sampling the elevation at intervals along a horizontal alignment (see Figure 8-1). The existing profile is shown as the heavy line in Figure 8-2. For tangent sections, this is often accomplished by computing the elevation wherever the alignment crosses the TIN lines in the terrain model. In curved locations, a chord-based system is often used to simulate the curve. The location of the chord is where the computation occurs as it crosses TIN lines in the model. Figure 8-2 shows an alignment lying on the terrain model.

Figure 8-2   An existing profile

PVI: The Point of Vertical Intersection of the incoming and outgoing vertical tangents. This is also referred to as the *VPI* for Vertical Point of Intersection.

PVC: The Point of Vertical Curvature where the vertical curve begins and departs the tangent. Also called *BVC* for Begin Vertical Curve.

PVT: The Point of Vertical Tangency where the vertical curve ends and returns to the tangent. Also called *EVC* for End Vertical Curve.

The proposed vertical alignment, shown as the light linework in Figure 8-2, is comprised of vertical tangents and vertical curves. Two tangents meet at a ***PVI (Point of Vertical Intersection)***. Usually if there is a grade break between the two longitudinal tangents that is considered slight, a vertical curve is not required. Slight differences between agencies may range from 0.5% to 2.5%. Anything beyond these values requires a vertical curve to smooth out the transition between the tangents. Figure 8-2 shows a dark, thick existing ground line, a light thin line for proposed tangents, and vertical curves. There are elevations on the vertical axis, and it is usually exaggerated to show vertical detail. There are stations along the horizontal axis that match the alignment. There are three proposed tangents and two vertical curves. The tangents are denoted by a beginning station and elevation and a grade. It ends at the ***PVC (Point of Vertical Curvature)***, where the vertical curve begins. The curve ends at the ***PVT (Point of Vertical Tangency)***. A short tangent exists, and then another PVC begins the next curve.

In Figure 8-3, a vertical curve is shown emboldened with annotation for the PVC and the PVT. The PVI is shown as a triangle. The back tangent is before the curve, and a forward tangent occurs after the curve. Once these are known, the only other criterion is the length of the curve because a parabolic equation governs the remaining computations.

Figure 8-3   A vertical curve

In Figure 8-4, criteria are identified with the curve data. A completed proposed profile shows the incoming tangent slope is 5.44%, the outgoing is −9.15%, and the vertical curve length is 400′.

Figure 8-4   Vertical Curve data

THE PROPERTIES OF PARABOLIC CURVES

Following are the properties of parabolic curves:

- A curve's elevation at the midpoint of the curve is halfway from the elevation at the PVI to the elevation at the midpoint of a straight line from the PVC to the PVT.
- The tangent offsets vary as the square of the distance from the points of tangency.
- For points spaced at equal horizontal distances, the second differences are equal, which is useful when checking the vertical curve computations. The differences (or subtractions) between the elevations at equally spaced stations are called first differences. The differences between the first differences are called the second differences.

The design of a vertical alignment is usually specified in terms of a maximum grade and the minimum length for the vertical curve. The maximum allowable grade is a parameter that considers whether the service vehicles can negotiate the grade easily and safely. In other words, trucks would have considerable difficulty in climbing a road with a 12% grade. It would be clearly unsafe for trucks to be descending this grade should the brakes fail. Therefore, a highway might limit the maximum grade to 8%, so that the service vehicles (trucks and cars) could negotiate the grade safely. Because the vertical curves are parabolic, their criteria are represented as a K factor. The K factor is computed by dividing the length of the curve by the grade break at the PVI. The relationship here is that a smaller K factor means a sharper curve and a larger K factor designates a flatter curve.

Cross-sectional design criteria depend on the service classification for the roadway. Subdivision roads may have four lanes for high-density areas and two lanes for less dense areas. They may be bounded by a curb and gutter and sidewalks for drainage and pedestrian traffic. Highways, on the other hand, usually have several lanes and are bounded by shoulders. Often there is a center median to divide the bidirectional traffic.

FORMULAS USED FOR COMPUTING PARABOLIC VERTICAL CURVE DATA

Where L = the Length of curve, the PVC station = PVI station $- (L/2)$.

The PVT = PVI $+ (L/2)$. The PVT = PVC $+ L$.

The general equation for a vertical curve is a parabolic equation, which derives as follows:

$Y_p = a + bX_p + cX_p^2$, where Y_p is any point on the parabola located X_p from the origin. And a, b, and c are constants.

For a vertical curve,

$a = Y_{BVC}$
$bX_p = g_1X$
$c = (g_2 - g_1)/2L$

Therefore:

$Y = Y_{BVC} + g_1X + ((g_2 - g_1)/2L)*X^2$

A useful term is the rate of change of grade. This is defined as r. Therefore:

$r = (g_2 - g_1)/L$

Combining the expressions results in the formula for a vertical curve of a roadway:

$Y = Y_{BVC} + g_1X + (r/2)*X^2$

Example 8-1: A Manually Computed Vertical Curve Problem

With a back tangent of 2%, a forward tangent of -2.5%, and a vertical curve length of $800'$, compute the starting and ending stations of this vertical curve and its accompanying table if the PVI station is 36+70 and the PVI elevation is 813.53.

$R = (g_2 - g_1)/L \rightarrow (-2.5 - 2)/8 = -.5625\%/\text{station}$
VPI $= 36 + 70$
$-L/2 = 4 + 00$
BVC $= 32 + 70$
$+L = 8 + 00$
EVC $= 40 + 70$

The Elevation at BVC $= 813.53 - (2.00)(4) = 805.53$

The Elevation at EVC $= Y_{BVC} + g_1X + (r/2)x^2 = 805.53 + (2)(8) + (-.5625)(64)/2$
$= 805.53 + 16.0 + (-18.054) = 803.53$

The Elevation at the midpoint of the chord of the curve $= (805.53 + 803.53)/2 = 804.53$

The Elevation at midpoint of curve $= (813.53 + 804.53)/2 = 809.03$

A table, such as in Table 8-1, can be established to compute the elevations along the vertical curve. You may select an interval for the information you are interested in computing, say every 20 or 25 feet. You would use Vertical Curve Property #3 described above, to ensure that you have computed the correct answers. You simply break down the formula for the vertical curve into its parts and make each part a column in the spreadsheet. The second to last column will compute the first difference between the elevations. The last column will compute the second difference (or the difference between the first differences). Note it equals r.

Table 8-1	Table for Computing Elevations Every 100′ Along a Vertical Curve					
Sta	X(Sta)	g_1X	$rX^2/2$	Curve Elev.	1st Diff	2nd Diff
40+70	8	16	−18	803.53		
40+00	7.3	14.6	−14.99	805.14		
39+00	6.3	12.6	−11.16	806.97	−1.83	
38+00	5.3	10.6	−7.9	808.23	−1.26	−.57
37+00	4.3	8.6	−5.2	808.93	−.7	−.56
36+00	3.3	6.6	−3.063	809.067	−.137	−.56
35+00	2.3	4.6	−1.488	808.642	.425	−.56
34+00	1.3	2.6	−.475	807.655	.987	−.56
33+00	.3	.6	−.025	806.105	1.55	−.56
32+70	0	0		805.53	.575	

The High/Low points of a vertical curve are computed as such:

$$X = g_1L/g_1 - g_2 \rightarrow -g_1/r \rightarrow -2/-.5625 = 3.555 \text{ stations} = X$$

The High point $= 32 + 70 + (3.555) = 36 + 25.5$
The Elevation $= 805.53 + 2(3.555) + (-.5625/2)(3.555)^2$
$= 805.53 + 7.11 - 3.554 = \mathbf{809.086}$

Another method for computing vertical curves for roads is by using the K factor, where $K = L/A$. L is the length of the vertical curve, and A is the algebraic difference between the outgoing and incoming vertical tangents. Therefore the Length of vertical curve can be computed based on a required K minimum value such that $L = KA$.

Tables 8-2 and 8-3 provide examples of the American Association of State Highway Transportation Officials (AASHTO) criteria for vertical curves for both crest and sag conditions with

Table 8-2	AASHTO Stopping Sight Distances for Crest Curves	
Design Speed	Minimum Stopping Distance (ft)	K Value for Crest Curve
30	200	19
35	250	29
40	305	44
45	360	61
50	425	84
55	495	114
60	570	151
65	645	193
70	730	247

Table 8-3   AASHTO Stopping Sight Distances for Sag Curves

Design Speed	Minimum Stopping Distance (ft)	K Value for Crest Curve
30	200	37
35	250	49
40	305	64
45	360	79
50	425	96
55	495	115
60	570	136
65	645	157
70	730	181

regard to being able to stop the vehicle. There must be enough sight distance for the driver to realize a problem and then apply the brakes. This information can be found in the AASHTO publication, *A Policy on Geometric Design of Highways and Streets*.

Very often designers need to design a vertical curve so that it meets a minimum K value as established by the transportation authority with jurisdiction over the design. The curve can exceed the minimum K value but must not be less than the required value. Engineers usually compute the length of curve needed to meet this condition and then round it up to the next even 50′ value to make it easier for others to check the work and stake it out for construction.

Another method for determining lengths of vertical curves has to do with passing sight distance. When a driver is in a sag curve, oncoming traffic can be observed easily because both cars are in the concave portion of the curve. However, when the driver is approaching a crest curve, eyesight is obscured by the crest of the hill. Therefore, there must be enough forward sight distance for the driver to see an oncoming vehicle before making a decision to pass another vehicle. Table 8-4 provides an indication of the AASHTO passing sight distances required for a roadway.

Table 8-4   AASHTO Passing Sight Distances

Design Speed	Minimum Passing Distance (ft)	K Value for Crest Curve
30	1090	424
35	1280	585
40	1470	772
45	1625	943
50	1835	1203
55	1985	1407
60	2135	1628
65	2285	1865
70	2480	2197

Sections.   Roadway sections (Figure 8-5, showing SL-1) are similar to profiles in that they represent conditions before and after design. They are three-dimensional in what they are representing and are denoted with axes similar to profiles.

Figure 8-5   Roadway sections

There are elevations on the vertical axis, which is usually exaggerated to show vertical detail, and there are distances along the horizontal axis that equate to the length of the cross section to the left and to the right of the centerline. Typically where the centerline crosses the section is denoted with zero (0), whereas the distances are shown positive leaving the centerline to the right and negative to the left.

The section information is shown in Figure 8-6 for the existing ground section.

Figure 8-6   An existing ground section

Applications Using Civil 3D for Profiling

Profiles and sections in Civil 3D are intelligent objects, similar to the point groups, parcels, terrain models, and alignments already discussed. Profiles and cross sections are dynamically linked to horizontal alignments and surfaces. When the horizontal alignment is edited, the profile and cross section associated to it automatically update. If the surface is modified, the profile and cross-sectional data also update automatically. The related annotation updates as well, thereby saving time in drafting functions. Styles in Civil 3D are defined to control the display of this profile and cross-sectional data as well as the related annotation. These Styles represent the standards of your company or agency or your client. They are developed and stored in prototype Civil 3D drawings and within the project drawings.

In Civil 3D, existing ground profiles and cross sections are related to horizontal alignments. Changes to the alignment result in automatic updates to the profile and to the sections. This is referred to as a *dynamic model*, the *ripple-through effect*.

The process to be followed in the next steps is:

1. Compute the data and plot existing ground profile data in a **Profile View**. The **Profile View Style** controls the display of the profile grid, the title, and the horizontal and vertical axes annotation for stations and elevations. The **Profile View Label Styles** control the display of the annotation inside the **Profile View**.

A step-by-step procedure for designing a road right through profiles and sections and then sending it to construction would involve the following tasks:

1. Create and, if needed, edit the horizontal alignment.
2. Compute and plot the existing ground profile in the **Profile View**.
3. Develop and, if needed, edit the vertical alignment.
4. Compute and analyze the existing ground cross sections.
5. Develop roadway template(s) or assemblies.
6. Process the Corridor.
7. Plot the proposed roadway design cross sections. Repeat Steps 1 through 7 as needed.
8. Develop construction stakeout information for traditional staking, or 3D digital data for 3D Machine Control using Trimble Link, Carlson Connect, or Leica XChange. Compute earthwork takeoffs.

2. Develop the finished ground profile using vertical tangents and vertical curves.

3. For the cross sections, compute and plot the existing ground cross-sectional data.

4. Civil 3D simplifies the modification process for existing ground profiles and cross sections due to the dynamic link to the horizontal alignment. To experience this, modify the source data and again observe the ripple-through effect.

You will begin by opening a drawing that has a surface and an alignment prepared so that your profiling activities can be expedited. Then you will use the **Profiles** pull-down menu, shown in Figure 8-7, with its commands described.

Create Profile from Surface... allows you to develop a profile of an alignment from the surface object, normally Existing ground.

Figure 8-7   The Profiles pull-down menu

Create Profile by Layout... opens the **Layout** toolbar for designing profiles using criteria.

Create Profile from File... allows the creation of a profile from an external file with data in it.

Quick Profile... creates a temporary profile view for a selected object such as a feature line.

Create Profile View... allows for creating a **Profile View** for use later.

Create Multiple Profile Views... allows for split profiles so they fit on multiple sheets.

Create Superimposed Profile... allows for superimposing multiple profiles into a **Profile View**.

Edit Profile Geometry... invokes the **Layout** toolbar for editing design profiles criteria.

Design Criteria Editor... allows making modifications to the design criteria XML file.

Add Profile View Labels allows for adding specific profile labels.

Exercise 8-1: Create Profile from Surface Data

Go to the **Prospector** and expand **Sites >> Site 1 >> Alignments >> Alignment—Chapter 6 >> Profiles**. You will see three existing ground profiles. Right-click on them and select **Delete...** for each. This is how to delete unwanted profiles.

1. Launch Civil 3D and open the file called Chapter-8-a.dwg.
2. Type **V** for **View** and select the view called **Plan-A**, hit **Set Current**, then hit **OK**.
3. From the **Profiles** pull-down menu, select the command **Create Profile from Surface...**. See Figure 8-8. Please note that although you are working with Chapter 8 drawings the alignments refer to Chapter 6 that were created for a previous textbook.

To access student data files, go to www.pearsondesigncentral.com.

Figure 8-8   Create Profile from Surface dialog box

4. The **Alignment** of **Alignment—Chapter 6** should be set. Now select the **Existing Ground** under the **Select surfaces** window and hit the **Add>>** button.
5. Then turn on the **Sample offsets**, type **45** into the **Sample offsets** field, and hit **Add>>**. In the **Profile list** window at the bottom, click on the second row where the offset of **45**

exists and double-click on the value in the **Style** column. The **Pick profile style** dialog box appears. From the selection options, choose **Existing Ground BRL Right** for the style of this offset profile (because 45 is positive and therefore to the right). You want to differentiate it from the centerline so as not to confuse it with the centerline profile.

Job skills benefit in that it is often desired to compute and draw the profile for the BRL (Building Restriction Line), so the reviewer can see what the ground is doing where a structure might be built.

6. Then type **−45** into the **Sample offsets** field and hit **Add>>**. In the **Profile list** window at the bottom, click on the third row where the offset of **−45** exists and double-click on the Value in the **Style** column. From the selection options, choose **Existing Ground BRL Left** for the style of this offset profile. Again, you want to differentiate it from the centerline and the other BRL linework so as not to confuse it. The values should appear as indicated in Figure 8-8.
7. Click on the button that says **Draw in profile view**.
8. Then the **Create Profile View** dialog box displays, as shown in Figure 8-9.

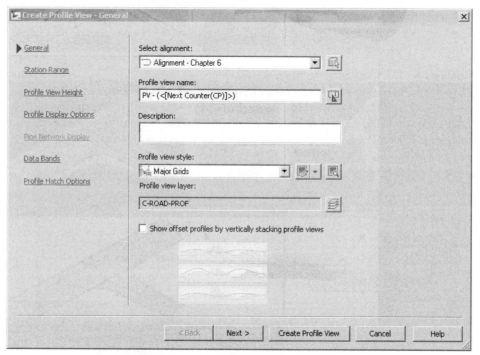

Figure 8-9   The Create Profile View dialog box

9. In the dialog box, check the name of the **Profile view name** field. Accept the automatic naming **PV - (<[Next Counter(CP)]>)**, which is 1. Provide a description of Chapter 8. From the **Alignment** pop-down window, **Alignment—Chapter 6** should be selected. Notice the profiles you computed in the previous box are shown.
10. As you have done several times in the previous chapters, create a layer for the **Profile View** called **C-Road-Prof-View**. Hit **Create Profile View** and place the location of the view to the right of all of the plan view data, say, at a coordinate of **18800,19500**.

Now you have an existing ground profile for your alignment. It also shows left and right offset profiles, which are often required by reviewing jurisdictions so they can observe the ground activity near where buildings might be constructed. The centerline profile should be red, the left profile is green, and the right profile is blue. The engineer also uses this information to analyze the impact that a proposed roadway or corridor might have near the BRL line.

Develop a Finished Grade Profile

The next task is to develop a proposed profile for the roadway. Use the Civil 3D commands to execute the formulas discussed earlier in this chapter. Create vertical tangents with PVIs between them and vertical curves at these PVIs. To begin, open a drawing containing the existing ground profile.

1. Launch Civil 3D and open the file called Chapter-8-b.dwg.
2. **Zoom** in to view the profile.
3. From the **Profiles** pull-down menu, select the command **Create Profile by Layout...**.
4. The prompt asks you to select the **Profile View** in which you will be working. Select the grid of the profile.
5. A **Create Profile** dialog box displays, requesting information about your profile. Set it up as shown in Figure 8-10, with a **Description**, a new layer for the proposed profile, and a style called **Design Style**. Use the **Complete Label Set** for the **Profile label set**. Hit **OK**.

To access student data files, go to www.pearsondesigncentral.com.

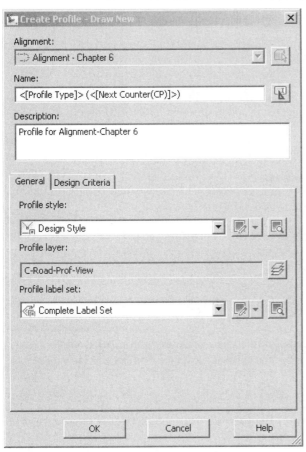

Figure 8-10   Profile information

PROFILE LAYOUT TOOLBAR

On hitting **OK**, the **Profile Layout Tools** toolbar displays. It is shown in Figure 6-11 and a description of the commands follows.

Figure 8-11   The Profile Layout Tools toolbar

This command has a pop-down arrow that allows you to draw vertical tangents with or without curves. A **Curve Settings** icon allows you to set the curve settings that will be used for the **Curves** option.

This command allows for the insertion of a PVI.

This command allows for the deletion of a PVI.

This command allows for moving a PVI.

These two commands bring Constraint Based Design to vertical geometry. These are similar to what was discussed in Chapter 6, except these control vertical computations. These two commands allow for the creation of Fixed, Free, and Floating Lines and Vertical Curves.

This command allows for the creation of a fixed tangent or three-point vertical curve from an AutoCAD line or spline.

This command allows for the insertion of a PVI using numeric table input. It requires station, elevation, and curve values if they are to be added here as well.

This command allows for the raising and lowering of a PVI.

This command allows for copying a profile.

This command allows for the display of PVI-based data in a pop-up window.

This command selects a PVI.

This command deletes an entity.

This command allows for editing best-fit data for all entities.

The first icon is a command that opens or closes the **Profile Layout Parameters** dialog box. The second icon opens or closes the **Profile Grid View** dialog box.

Exercise 8-3: Create a Proposed Profile

So, continuing on using the **Profile Layout Tools** toolbar that appears, create a proposed profile. The software prompts you to Select a command: from the **Layout** tools.

1. Using the pop-down arrow for the first icon, select the **Curve Settings...** command.
2. The **Vertical Curve Settings** dialog box displays, as shown in Figure 8-12. In the **Select curve type** drop-down window, use **Parabolic**, although circular and asymmetrical curves are available. Use a curve length of **400′**, so set the sag and crest curve lengths to **400**. Hit **OK**.

A crest curve goes over a hill whereas a sag curve goes into a depression.

3. From the **Profile Layout** toolbar, choose the first icon from the left to **Draw Tangents With Curves**. The software prompts you to select a start point for the vertical tangents with curves. Specify start point: Use the **Endpoint** snap to pick the left edge of the red existing ground centerline profile. It should be around 0+00 and elevation 324.5.
4. Specify end point: it is asking for the end of the tangent segment.

Figure 8-12   The Vertical Curve Settings dialog box

TIP Notice that as you move the cursor around the profile, the cursor tip will appear, telling you the SZ of the point where you are. The SZ is the station and elevation of your current location.

5. Locate the station of 9+00 and an elevation near 339.0 by reading the axis information. When you find that approximate location, use the **Nearpoint** snap and pick it on the vertical gridline.
6. `Specify end point`: Locate the station of 15+00 and an elevation near 327.0 by using these cursor tips. When you find that approximate location, use the **Nearpoint** snap and pick it on the gridline.
7. `Specify end point`: Locate the end of the **red** existing ground profile and use the **Endpoint** snap to pick it, thereby completing the development of the vertical tangents. This should be close to 21+56 and elevation 343.0. Feel free to **Zoom** in when needed to snap to these locations.

It is usually a smart move to place your PVIs at even stations to make it easier for surveyors or contractors to build the road without having to worry about odd station numbers. Nice, even 25, 50, or 100′ stations accommodate this.

8. **Zoom** out to view the profile and notice that curves exist automatically at the PVIs. Guess what the curve lengths are?
9. Take a moment to inspect the profile. Notice that the vertical tangents are one color whereas the curves are another color. This is to help you visualize when lines end and curves begin.

Exercise 8-4: Re-create Profile with Different Styles

Now let us assume that this profile is ready for plotting. Re-create this profile view with a different set of styles to make it more appropriate for a plot.

1. From the **Profiles** pull-down menu, choose **Create Profile View....** The **Create Profile View** dialog box appears, as shown in Figure 8-13. Provide the **Description** shown in the figure.

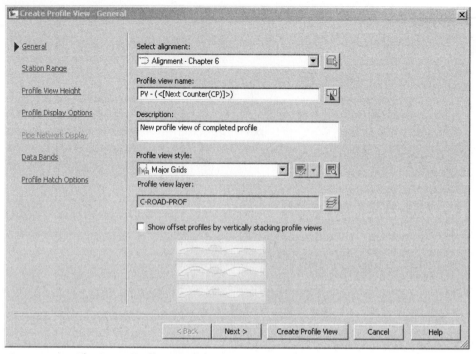

Figure 8-13   The Create Profile View dialog box

2. Click on **Data Bands** and change the **Band set** to **Profile Data & Geometry**.

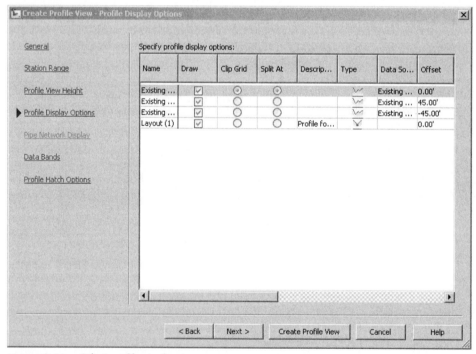

Figure 8-14   Select profiles to draw

3. Click on **Create Profile View**, the software prompts for a point to place the new profile. Pick a point somewhere well above the original profile.

TIP Notice that if you do not want to draw a particular profile, you can turn off the check mark in the **Create Profile View** properties dialog box using the **Profile Display Options** tab as shown in Figure 8-14.

4. Inspect the profile when it comes in and notice that curves are labeled and data bands come in at the bottom. Notice that one shows the horizontal geometry relative to the profile. This is a wonderful analysis tool to compare the horizontal and vertical geometries.
5. In order to acquire some additional experience in editing these Styles, notice that there is a band of information at the bottom representing the existing ground that is too verbose and unneeded. Now if this represented the finished ground, that could be useful in seeing that the vertical geometry is a single rapid observation.
6. Click on a grid for the **Profile View**. Right-click and select **Profile View Properties....** You can also access the **Profile View Properties** from the **Prospector**, as shown in Figure 8-15.

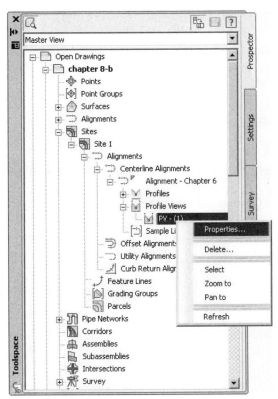

Figure 8-15   Access the Profile View Properties from the Prospector

7. Choose the **Bands** tab and select the last item in the **Band Type** column, vertical geometry.
8. In the column labeled **Profile 1**, set the value to **Layout (1)** so it knows to display graphics for the finished ground profile.
9. Next, delete the first **Profile View** used to construct the profile. Open the **Toolspace** and go into the **Prospector**.
10. Expand the items for the Current Drawing, **Sites**, **Site 1**, **Alignments, Alignment—1**, and **Profile Views**. Right-click on **PV – 1** and select **Delete...** to remove it from the project and drawing. Click **Yes** to the confirmation. Notice that when it is complete, the second "final" **Profile View** remains while the first is removed.

You can also just simply delete the graphics of the **Profile View** in AutoCAD.

This exercise illustrates how to develop an Existing Ground profile, what the **Profile Views** offer, how to alter the **Profile View Styles**, and how to develop a proposed roadway profile and alter its appearances and display capabilities.

Job skills will benefit from reviewing the bands showing the horizontal and vertical geometry so that an engineer or manager can easily review the design data without having to hunt through the profile or alignment data.

The next exercise explores what happens in Civil 3D when modifications are made.

Exercise 8-5: Modify the Label Style

You may have noticed that the vertical tangents are not labeled. Add these now as they and other labels can be affected on the fly or from the start.

To access student data files, go to www.pearsondesigncentral.com.

1. Launch Civil 3D and open the file called Chapter-8-c.dwg.
2. Notice that the previously developed plan and profile are visible.
3. **Zoom** into the **Profile** and notice that there are no grades on the vertical tangents. You want to add those to the **Profile**.
4. In the **Toolspace**, click on the **Settings** tab. Expand the **Profile** item, the **Label Styles** item, and the **Line** item.
5. Right-click on the label style **Finished Ground** and choose **Edit...**. See Figure 8-16.

Figure 8-16   Edit Label Styles

6. In the **Layout** tab, change the **Text Height** to **0.2** and the **Y Offset** to **0.2**. Set the color to **green**. Hit **OK** to exit.
7. Next, select the proposed profile linework in the Profile View, right-click, and choose **Edit Labels....**
8. The **Profile Labels** dialog box appears.
9. Under the **Type** pop-down, choose **Lines**.
10. Under **Profile Tangent Label Style**, choose **Finished Ground**.
11. Then hit the **Add>>** button. It should appear as shown in Figure 8-17.

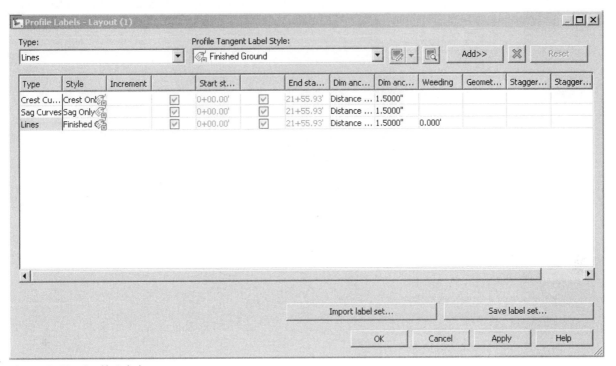

Figure 8-17   Profile Labels

12. Hit **OK** and notice that you now have grade labels on the vertical tangents.

THE RIPPLE-THROUGH EFFECT

Civil 3D has state-of-the-art capabilities in updating the design model. Because many of the objects are linked, they sense whether modifications have been made to the data that affect their display and computations.

Exercise 8-6: Try the Ripple-Through Effect

Next you open a drawing and make some changes to the data to observe how the ripple-through effect works and its potential to save enormous time and effort on the project.

1. Continuing on in the same drawing Chapter-8-c.dwg, discussion will concern making modifications.
2. **Zoom** into the beginning of the profile and notice that the existing ground elevation is around **324.5**.
3. Now type **V** for **View**, select the view called **Plan-A**, hit **Set Current**, and hit **OK**. Notice some contour activity and the alignment.
4. Select the alignment with the mouse. Notice that grips show up. Square grips appear on tangents, circular grips show up on the curves, and triangular grips appear on the **Pls (Points of Intersection)**.

To access student data files, go to www.pearsondesigncentral.com.

5. Using **Grip-edit** features, select the grip at station 0+00 and move it to another location within the contoured surface, say, near an *X, Y* of 14600,18750. The alignment relocates, recomputes, and redrafts its annotation.

6. Now type **V** for **View** and select the view called **Profile-A**, hit **Set Current**, and hit **OK**. Notice that the **red** Existing ground linework has changed up to around elevation 320, which is where the alignment now begins.

7. If you **Zoom** out to see the whole profile, notice that it actually became longer to compensate for the increased length created when the beginning of the alignment was moved. Normally, the proposed profile would need to be "stretched" to relocate its beginning and endpoints. This would be accomplished using the grip-edit features of the profile in exactly the same manner that you just moved the alignment.

In order to expand your skills, an optional exercise is to relocate the proposed profile using this method.

8. When you are finished experimenting, either open this drawing again, without saving it, or type **U** for **Undo** and repeat until the alignment returns to its original location.

9. Now type **V** for **View** and select the view called **Profile-A**, hit **Set Current**, and hit **OK**. Notice that the **red** Existing ground linework has changed back to what it was, around elevation 324.5.

10. This is a major feature of the Civil 3D software, which we call the *ripple-through effect*.

11. Feel free to experiment with this file and save it as another name so you can return to it in the future.

Job skills benefit from this feature in that "value engineering" can be performed in identifying the best design for the issues at hand. By experimenting with various design alternatives, the engineer can focus on the most cost-effective solution. Many firms are now offering value engineering to their clients as an added benefit to their services.

Exercise 8-7: Numerical Editing of Profiles

The next function you explore is the numerical editing of a profile. Sometimes designers feel it is advantageous to edit a profile using a tabular view that allows them access to the elevations, slopes, and grades. Civil 3D allows for this in addition to visual or graphical edits.

To access student data files, go to www.pearsondesigncentral.com.

1. Launch Civil 3D and open the file called Chapter-8-d.dwg. It opens with the profile in the view.

2. From the **Profiles** pull-down menu, choose **Edit Profile Geometry**. When prompted, select somewhere on the **blue** proposed profile. The **Profile Layout Tools** toolbar displays.

Note that you can also simply grip the proposed profile, right-click, and select **Edit** to achieve the same result.

3. Pick the command near the end of the toolbar called **Profile Grid View.** This will display the **Panorama** with all of the profile data in it, shown in Figure 8-18.

4. The fields that cannot be edited are screened back and inaccessible. Fields that can be altered are accessible by double-clicking in the cell.

5. For PVI 2, change the **Profile Curve Length** to **500**. Hit **<Enter>** and close the **Panorama**.

6. Then **Zoom** into PVI 2 and notice the annotated curve length is now 500. The graphics and text have been automatically updated.

No.	Lock	PVI Station	PVI Elevation	Grade In	Grade Out	A (Grade Change)	Profile Curve Type	K Value	Sub-Entity Type	Profile Curve Length
1	🔒	0+00.00'	324.519'		1.61%					
2	🔒	9+00.00'	338.991'	1.61%	-2.02%	3.63%	Crest	110.195	Symmetric Parabola	400.000'
3	🔒	15+00.00'	326.859'	-2.02%	2.48%	4.50%	Sag	88.837	Symmetric Parabola	400.000'
4	🔒	21+55.93'	343.130'	2.48%						

Figure 8-18   Profile Panorama

Exercise 8-8: Delete a Profile Component

Sometimes it is necessary to use an asymmetrical vertical curve that occurs when there is not enough incoming or outgoing tangent length to accommodate a symmetrical curve. For instance, you might be required to have a 500′ curve; however, there is only 200′ of incoming tangent available. Therefore, an asymmetrical curve where the first portion of the curve is 200′ and the second portion of the curve is 300′ would satisfy the overall length requirement. You will now perform an example of this. Begin by deleting the second curve and notice how Civil 3D automatically drafts it up. Follow that up by adding an asymmetrical curve to that same PVI.

1. In the same file called Chapter-8-d.dwg, choose **Edit Profile Geometry...** from the **Profiles** pull-down menu. When prompted, select somewhere on the **blue** proposed profile. The **Profile Layout Tools** toolbar displays.
2. Choose the fourth button from the right, the command to **Delete Entity**.
3. Pick point near PVI to delete: Pick a point near the PVI for the second curve at station 15+00.
4. Hit **<Enter>** to complete the sequence.
5. Notice that the curve is gone, but the PVI remains.

Exercise 8-9: Create an Asymmetrical Curve

Now add in an asymmetrical curve.

1. In the same file called Chapter-8-d.dwg, choose **Edit Profile Geometry...** from the **Profiles** pull-down menu. When prompted, select somewhere on the **blue** proposed profile. The **Profile Layout Tools** toolbar again displays.
2. Choose the command **More Free Vertical Curves >> Free Asymmetrical Parabola (PVI Based)** from the pop-down arrow in the toolbar. It is associated with the sixth button from the left.
3. `Pick point near PVI or curve to add curve:` Pick a point near the PVI at station 15+00.
4. The software asks you to specify **Length 1** of the asymmetrical curve. Type **200**.
5. The software asks you to specify **Length 2** of the asymmetrical curve. Type **300**.
6. Hit **<Enter>** to complete, and notice the new curve and the related annotation, shown in Figure 8-19. Notice the center of the curve does not exist at the PVI as it would for a symmetrical curve. This asymmetrical curve can be very useful in road design.

To access student data files, go to www.pearsondesigncentral.com.

Figure 8-19   Curve data

Asymmetrical vertical curves are often used as a last resort in road design. They might be used in situations in which a standard symmetrical vertical curve just does not work. For example, let us say you are designing a curve near an intersection and there is a PVI that requires a vertical curve approaching that intersection. The prevailing DOT code may require a vertical curve length of, say, 600′. It could be that you have only 200′ to the left of the PVI before you enter the intersection, but you have plenty of space to the right side of the PVI. This is where you might place an asymmetrical curve such that 150′ occurs to the left side of the PVI and 450′ occurs to the right side. In this fashion, you have accommodated the requirement to establish a 600′ curve without encroaching on the intersection.

SUPERIMPOSING PROFILES

Another powerful feature within the profiling functions of Civil 3D is the ability to superimpose one profile into another. This is useful when you wish to compare how one profile relates to another.

Exercise 8-10: Superimpose One Profile onto Another

To access student data
files, go to
www.pearsondesigncentral.com.

1. Launch Civil 3D and open the file called Chapter-8-e.dwg. There is an additional alignment and another profile in this file. They were prepared in the same manner as the one you just completed and are included here in order to expedite this command usage.
2. **Zoom** into the two profiles so they can be seen.
3. From the **Profiles** pull-down menu, choose **Create Superimposed Profile….** Select source profile: select the red linework in the shorter profile.
4. `Select destination profile view:` select a gridline in the longer **Profile View**.
5. The **Superimpose Profile Options** dialog box appears. You can restrict the length of the profile to be computed if you wish or just hit **OK**.
6. The superimposed profile appears in the longer profile.
7. Notice that it is longer than it was in the source profile. That is because the profile is projected into the destination orthogonally. The source alignment is not parallel to the destination alignment.
8. **Zoom** into the plan view and inspect how the source alignment is drawn. It is on the **C-Road** layer.

CIVIL 3D SECTIONS

The last part of this chapter delves into sections. As discussed earlier, sections are typically, but not always, orthogonal to the alignment and are created at intervals, that travel along the alignment. Sections provide you with more information on what is occurring adjacent to your alignment. Civil 3D develops cross-sectional data in **Sample Line Groups**, and, as we have seen already, Styles control the appearance of the **Sample Line Groups**. Next you will use the **Sample Line Tools** toolbar, Figure 8-20.

Figure 8-20   Sample Line
Tools toolbar

The window on the left side of the **Sample Line Tools** toolbar provides the ability to name the sample lines. The icon to its right brings up a dialog box that allows you to change the template naming, which is automatic and sequentially increments the name.

The pop-down window near the center of the toolbar displays the current **Sample Line Group** with which the sample line is associated. The icon to its right allows you to create or modify the **Sample Line Group**. The options within this icon include **Create sample line group, Edit group defaults, Delete current group**, or you can be prompted to select a group from the drawing, which then becomes the current Sample Line Group.

The fifth button from the right displays the various sample line creation methods used to create the sample line(s). The pop-down arrow allows for other actions such as creating sample lines **By range of stations...**, along the alignment. In this case, a perpendicular transient graphic appears in Civil 3D that you can move along the alignment to witness the current location. The other methods for creating sample lines include **At a station, From corridor stations**, **Pick points on screen**, and **Select existing polylines**.

The fourth button from the right prompts you to select a sample line from the screen.

The third button from the right toggles the select or edit sample line functionality. When the button is down, the **Edit Sample Line** dialog box is displayed.

The last two buttons are **Undo** and **Redo**.

Exercise 8-11: Create Sample Lines for Sections

Next you explore the abilities of sections.

1. Open a file called Chapter-8-f.dwg.
2. From the **Sections** pull-down menu, select **Create Sample Lines...**. When prompted, select the **Alignment** in the plan view.
3. The **Create Sample Line Group** dialog box opens, as shown in Figure 8-21. Hit **OK**.

To access student data files, go to www.pearsondesigncentral.com.

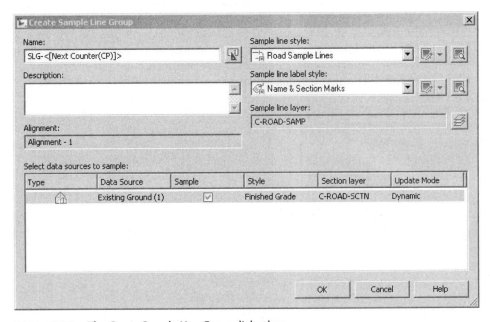

Figure 8-21   The Create Sample Line Group dialog box

4. The **Sample Line Tools** toolbar displays.
5. Using the pop-down arrow associated with the fifth button from the right, select the **By range of stations** icon. The **Create Sample Lines—By Station Range** dialog box appears. See Figure 8-22.

Figure 8-22   The Create Sample Lines—By Station Range dialog box

6. Notice that by default the cross-sectional data are sampled 30′ to the left and right of the alignment and data are sampled at 50′ increments along the alignment.
7. Change the **Left** and **Right Swath Width** to **50′**.
8. Change the **Increment Along Curves** and **Spirals** to **25′**.
9. For the **Additional Sample Controls**, turn all the options to **True**. So, **At Range Start and End**, **At Horizontal Geometry Points**, and **At Superelevation Critical Stations** are all marked **True**. This way you obtain additional sections at these locations as well.
10. Hit **OK**.
11. `Specify station along alignment`: hit **<Enter>**. Notice that sample lines appear along the alignment with 50′ lines on tangents and 25′ lines on curves.
12. You will notice in the **Prospector**, under **Sites**, **Site 1**, **Alignments**, **Center Alignments Alignment 1**, and **Sample Line Groups** that a number of sections now appear.

Note that in the **Plan View**, linework has shown up illustrating where the sections were cut.

Exercise 8-12: Create Sections

In the next steps, you create existing ground cross section views for each of these locations. In order to view these cross sections to evaluate what is occurring to the side of your alignment, you need to develop cross section views, similar to profile views.

1. From the **Sections** menu, click **Create Multiple Section Views...**, which displays the **Create Multiple Section Views** dialog box, as shown in Figure 8-23. In the **General** tab, change the **Group plot style** to **Plot All** and hit **Create Section Views**.

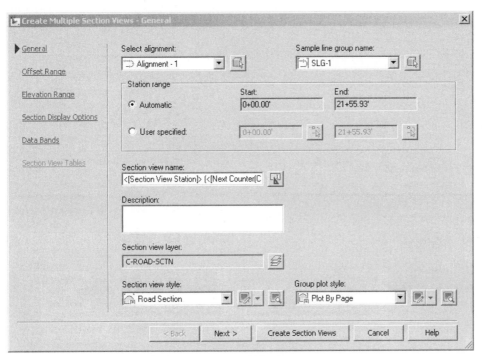

Figure 8-23   The Create Multiple Section Views dialog box

2. When prompted to identify the *section view* origin, pick a point to the right of the profile for the cross sections to be placed, say at **21000,21000**. **Zoom** in and notice that Section sample lines are shown on the alignment in Figure 8-24 and sections should be in your drawing similar to those shown in Figure 8-25.

> **section view:** A Civil 3D term for the location in Civil 3D where sections are displayed. Each section view must be related to an alignment. The section view displays new or existing sections.

Figure 8-24   Section sample lines are shown on the alignment

These cross section views are objects that are dynamically linked to the horizontal alignment in much the same manner that the profile view was when you were making modifications. If the horizontal alignment is relocated, the existing ground cross-section views automatically update to reflect those modifications.

3. **Zoom** into one section (Figure 8-26) and notice that there is too much information for the grade breaks of the existing ground. You do not really need this density of data, so turn it off.
4. Click on the gridline for a section, right-click, and select **Section View Properties...** to invoke the dialog box.
5. Select the **Sections** tab. In the **Labels** column, select the cell for the grade breaks where it says **<Edit...>**.
6. A **Section Labels** dialog box appears. Click on the grade breaks row and hit the button with the red **X** to delete. Hit **OK**. Hit **OK** again. The labels are gone and the section is easier to read.

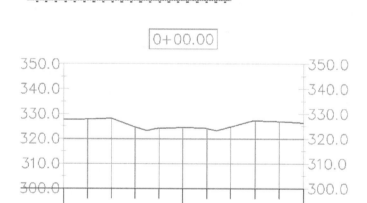

Figure 8-25 Plotted sections

Figure 8-26 One section

TIP

To turn these off prior to computing the sections and to effect this change on all sections, you can access the settings in the **Toolspace Settings** tab. Go to the **Section View** parameter and right-click. Select **Edit Feature Settings...** to access the **Edit Feature Settings** dialog box. Expand **Default Styles**, click on **Section Label Set**, click on the value of **EG Section Labels.** This allows you to select the button for the **Value**. This invokes the **Section Label Set** dialog box. Click on the middle icon and choose **Edit Current Selection** from the pop-down arrow. The same dialog box appears and you can hit the same red **X** to delete the grade breaks as you did earlier. Import your sections again to see the results.

CHAPTER SUMMARY

This chapter addressed the theory involved in designing roads, then moved into creating roadway profiles. You learned how to develop and annotate your proposed profiles. The chapter explored the link between horizontal alignments, existing ground profiles, and cross sections, looking at how they are updated when modifications are made to the data. Next we look at corridor design.

CHAPTER TEST QUESTIONS

Multiple Choice

1. There are three main requirements for designing a roadway. They are:
   a. Alignments, sections, and templates (or assemblies)
   b. Profiles, sections, and earthworks
   c. Alignments, corridors, and parcels
   d. Alignments, profiles, and a proposed section

2. Proposed vertical alignments can be developed from:
   a. Horizontal tangents, curves, and spirals
   b. Vertical tangents and vertical curves that do not exceed 8%
   c. Vertical tangents and vertical curves
   d. None of the above

3. Which of the following vertical curve properties are true?
   a. A tangent ends at the PVC, and a vertical curve begins at a PVC.
   b. A vertical curve begins at a PVT, and a vertical tangent begins at a PVT.
   c. Two tangents meet at a PVC.
   d. None of the above

4. Which of the following are properties of a vertical curve?
   a. The tangent offsets vary as the square of the distance from the points of tangency.
   b. For points spaced at equal horizontal distances, the second differences are equal.
   c. A curve's elevation at the midpoint of the curve will be halfway from the elevation at the PVI to the elevation at the midpoint of a straight line from the PVC to the PVT.
   d. All of the above

5. The design of a vertical alignment is usually specified in terms of:
   a. A maximum grade and the minimum length for the vertical curve
   b. A minimum grade and the minimum length for the vertical curve
   c. A maximum grade and the maximum length for the vertical curve
   d. Always being dictated by the State Department of Transportation

6. Civil 3D has a ripple-through effect:
   a. Where profiles and cross sections are dynamically linked to horizontal alignments and surfaces
   b. If the surface is modified, the profile and cross section data also update automatically
   c. Where related annotation updates as changes are made
   d. All of the above

7. A proposed profile can be edited using which of the following features?
   a. By graphically selecting grips for PVIs
   b. By using the numerical editor in the **Edit Profile** toolbar
   c. By graphically selecting grips for vertical tangents
   d. All of the above

8. Which of the following modifications can be accomplished by using the **Edit Profile** commands?
   a. Inserting and deleting PVIs
   b. Inserting and deleting alignment segments
   c. Inserting and moving PVIs, but not deleting them
   d. All of the above

9. Which of the following vertical curves are supported?
   a. Parabolic
   b. Circular
   c. Asymmetrical
   d. All of the above

10. Cross sections can be created in the AutoCAD drawing in which of the following ways?
    a. Individually
    b. By sheet
    c. All sections can be imported at once
    d. All of the above

True or False

1. True or False: Profiles are created by sampling the elevation at intervals along a horizontal alignment.

2. True or False: Profiles computed along tangent sections usually sample the elevation wherever the alignment crosses the TIN lines in the terrain model.

3. True or False: A profile cannot be developed if the alignment has horizontal curves or spirals.

4. True or False: A PVI is the intersection of two vertical tangents.

5. True or False: A PVC is the intersection of two vertical curves.

6. True or False: Sometimes a grade break may occur that does not require any vertical curve at all.

7. True or False: A vertical curve is usually parabolic with an ever-changing radius.

8. True or False: The K value for profile computations is derived from empirical results of roadway friction factors.

9. True or False: Roadways are designed for safety and never use subjective parameters such as passing sight distances or stopping sight distances.

10. True or False: In Civil 3D, profiles are linked to the alignment and can react to changes made to the alignment.

CHAPTER EXERCISE

1. With a back tangent of −2%, a forward tangent of 1.6%, and a vertical curve length of 800′, compute the starting and ending stations of this vertical curve and its accompanying table if the PVI station is 87+00 and the PVI elevation is 743.24.

Advanced Corridor Development 9

Chapter
Objectives

- Understand corridor design, in which the proposed section or template for the roadway is created.
- Develop assemblies.
- Customize subassemblies.
- Create and edit simple roadways.
- Create multiple assembly roadways.
- Understand a safety technique used by engineers to assist motorists in handling curves called superelevating the roadway.
- Create multiple baseline roadways.

INTRODUCTION

This chapter commences with discussions and algorithms for roadway superelevations and then moves into corridor development. Civil 3D offers state-of-the-art capabilities for developing roadways and corridors in general.

At this point the text has discussed developing alignments, existing, and proposed profiles, and cross sections. This chapter covers corridor design, which is the creation of the proposed section or template for the roadway. The objectives should be generalized because a corridor can include not only roadways but many other projects as well. If a project has a beginning, an end, limitations to the right and left, and standardized cross-sectional components, it may be a corridor. Think of stream improvements and railroads as examples of this, perhaps even tunnels and aqueducts. The chapter also delves into a safety technique used by engineers to assist motorists in handling curves called superelevating the roadway.

REVIEW OF FUNCTIONS AND FEATURES TO BE USED

This chapter provides instruction in the functions for corridor design. These include using **Tool Palettes** to access subassemblies and how to configure them for use in almost any scenario. These subassemblies are used to build assemblies for the sections to be designed. The discussion then walks through examples of how to build both simple and sophisticated corridors. The chapter also covers viewing the resulting cross sections of the design and various outputting strategies.

CORRIDOR THEORY

Once the section is developed, considerations are then made for safety as the driver negotiates curves in the road. According to the laws of mechanics, when a vehicle travels on a horizontal curve, it is forced outward by centrifugal force. Therefore, engineers use a method called *superelevation*

superelevation: Refers to the cross slope introduced into a cross section of a roadway in order to compensate for the centrifugal forces created by horizontal curves. According to the laws of mechanics, when a vehicle travels on a curve it is forced outward by centrifugal force. On a superelevated roadway, this force is resisted by the vehicle weight component parallel to the superelevated surface and the side friction between the tires and pavement. The pavement is essentially tilted to counter the forces described above.

by which they tilt the pavement lanes to counteract the centrifugal force. The two figures presented here indicate a template in normal conditions (along the tangent of a road) in Figure 9-1 and in the superelevated condition (around a curve, in this case, turning to the left) in Figure 9-2.

Figure 9-1   A normal template

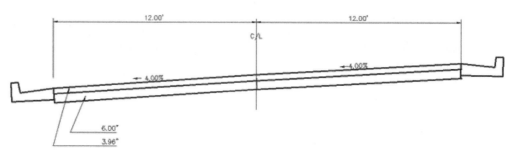

Figure 9-2   A superelevated template

Civil 3D performs DOT-level highway design because it allows for corridors with multiple baselines and multiple assemblies, all operating under a variety of conditions. Many subassemblies are included for roadway, curb, and sidewalk design.

SUPERELEVATION OF ROADWAYS—BASIC CRITERIA

On a superelevated highway, this centrifugal force is resisted by the vehicle's weight parallel to the superelevated surface and the friction between the tires and pavement. Centrifugal force cannot be balanced by superelevation alone, because for each curve radius a specific superelevation rate must be selected for a particular driving speed. In other words, the ***rate of superelevation*** varies based on the radius of the curve. Any side thrust must be offset by side friction. If the vehicle is not skidding, these forces are in equilibrium. Figure 9-3 illustrates the trigonometry involved in computing superelevation problems. Refer to the *AASHTO Green Book: A Policy on Geometric Design of Highways and Streets,* 5th Edition, for an authoritative reference on this subject.

rate of superelevation: The rate of banking a roadway. AASHTO (American Association of State Highway and Transportation Officials) provides examples of design superelevation rates based on the design speed, the radius of curve, and the superelevation rate.

Variables and terms for superelevations include:

e = Superelevation slope

e_{max} = Maximum superelevation rate for a given condition

R = Curve radius

v = Velocity

$P = mv^2/R$

B = Horizontal lane width

A maximum superelevation (SE) is required when the radius (R) is a minimum:

$\tan(a) = P/mg$ $\tan(a) = (mv^2/R)/mg$ $\tan(a) = v^2/gR$

$SE = B*\tan(\alpha)$ $SEmax = Bv^2/gR$

This model is theoretical and is usually guided by the state DOT or AASHTO.

Superelevation transitions are used to define the pavement rotation up to a maximum superelevation and are also used to bring a superelevated section back to the normal crown state. At a reverse curve, the section is often flat at the **PRC** as the superelevation in one direction transitions to the other direction.

PRC: Point of Reverse Curvature

Two components make up the total transition for a superelevated section: the Tangent runout and runoff (Figure 9-4). The Tangent runout defines the length of highway needed to bring a normal crown section to a section where the outside lane has a zero percent slope instead of normal crown. The superelevation runoff defines the distance needed to bring a section from flat to fully superelevated, or vice versa.

Figure 9-3   Superelevation trigonometry

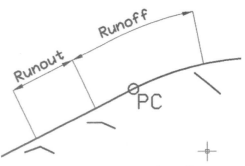

Figure 9-4   Tangent runout and runoff

TIP   The superelevation criteria for entering a curve are usually mirrored as the driver leaves a curve.

Figure 9-5 shows how the edge of pavement rises and drops based on the tilting of the road before and after the **PC** or **PT** of a curve.

PC: Point of Curvature
PT: Point of Tangency

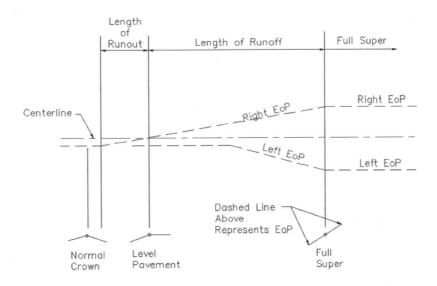

Figure 9-5   The edge of pavement in superelevation

Standard superelevation rates are usually provided by the Department of Transportation that oversees roadway design in the jurisdiction. A typical chart from which to obtain these values, shown in Figure 9-6, comes from the Virginia Department of Transportation (VDOT). For a specific curve radius and a design speed, the superelevation rate can be easily determined. For example, for a 3000′ radius curve and a design speed of 40 mph, the state requires a minimum of 2.5% superelevation rate.

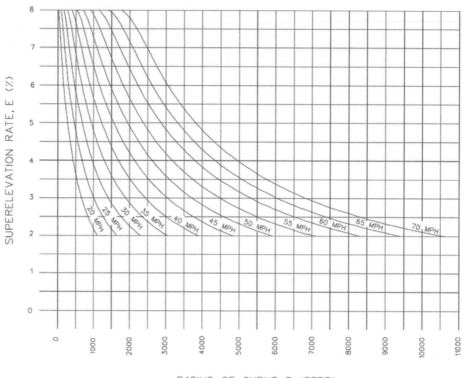

Figure 9-6   Superelevation rates for VDOT

For more information on design standards for roadway design, the American Association of State Highway and Transportation Officials (AASHTO) studies and recommends criteria to engineers. It can be located at www.aashto.org. Consult with your local state, county, or city DOT for its respective requirements as well.

Now that sections and superelevations have been discussed, you will use Civil 3D to develop a corridor.

CREATE A CORRIDOR FOR A ROAD

Remember that a corridor is a Civil 3D object and as such is linked to the horizontal and vertical alignments, surfaces, and assemblies that were used to create it. If one or more of these components are altered, the corridor is correspondingly modified.

> **TIP** For the rebuild to be automatic, you must right-click on the corridor and select **Rebuild-Automatic**. Otherwise, a rebuild can be executed at your choice by right-clicking on the corridor and selecting **Rebuild**.

The next step is to modify subassembly properties for design criteria, create an assembly from the subassemblies, and then create the Corridor model.

Subassemblies are the primitive components of assemblies, and they instruct the software on how to handle lanes, curbs, guardrails or shoulders, related side sloping, and tie-out. Civil 3D provides many subassemblies to begin with, which you can access from the **Tool Palettes**. The assemblies, on the other hand, are stored in the drawing and can be accessed from the **Project Toolspace** under **Assemblies**. They contain the definition of the typical section being designed and are developed by piecing together subassemblies.

This corridor has the following design requirements: The road will be a crowned section with a pavement width of 12′. The cross slope of the lane is −2.0% from the crown. A 6″ curb and 2′ gutter are used, located at the edge of pavement. Add on a 2′ grass strip, a 4′ sidewalk, and another 2′ grass strip, respectively. Then the side sloping will be 3:1 until it hits existing ground.

The **Corridors** pull-down menu is shown in Figure 9-7.

Create Assembly... allows you to develop a roadway template, now called an assembly. It is constructed from subassemblies selected from the **Catalog** or **Tool Palettes**.

Create Assembly Offset allows you to develop a controlling offset on an assembly. This is used for roads that have other paths that will define the design, such as a service road.

Create Subassembly from Polyline allows you to develop new subassemblies from polylines that you draw in AutoCAD.

Subassembly Tool Palettes allows you to open the **Tool Palettes** window where you can access subassemblies.

Subassembly Catalog... allows you to access catalogs of metric and imperial tools.

Create Simple Corridor... designs the corridor from an alignment, a profile, and an assembly.

Create Corridor designs a corridor for a sophisticated roadway including such items as station frequency and controlling offsets, multiple baselines, and regions.

View/Edit Corridor Section allows you to view the corridor sections and edit them interactively.

Utilities allows you several options for creating objects and importing subassemblies.

Exercise 9-1: Set Up Toolspace and Subassembly Settings

1. Open the drawing called Chapter-9a.dwg.
2. Under the **General** pull-down menu, click on the **Tool Palettes** window command. See Figure 9-8 for an example of the **Tool Palettes**. Choose the **Imperial-Basic** tab.

To access student data files, go to www.pearsondesigncentral.com.

Figure 9-7 The Corridors pull-down menu

Figure 9-8 The Tool Palettes window

3. Note that right-clicking at the bottom of the tabs brings up a list of the many **Tool Palettes** available including metric roadway design.

MODIFY SUBASSEMBLIES FOR THE ROAD

This **Tool** palette can be used to develop the roadway corridor, and it will remain in place for future jobs as well.

You will now modify the properties of the subassemblies needed for the road. The modifications occur as the subassemblies are placed into the assembly. These include the **BasicLane**, the **BasicCurbandGutter**, the **BasicSidewalk**, and the **DaylightStandard** subassemblies.

You can create the assembly from the subassemblies on the **Tool Palette**. The assembly contains the design control for the proposed typical section of the road.

Exercise 9-2: Create the Assembly

1. Type **Z** for **Zoom** at the command prompt and hit **<Enter>**. Type **C** for **Center** and type **17000,20000**. When asked for a height, type **50**.
2. This has placed you in a location where you can create the assembly. There is nothing special about this location; it is simply out of the way and zoomed to a height of 50′.
3. From the **Corridors** pull-down menu, select **Create Assembly....** The **Create Assembly** dialog box opens.
4. Accept the default name and set the name of the layer to **C-Road-Assm.** Leave the remaining settings as default and hit **OK**.
5. Specify assembly baseline location: Pick a point in the middle of the screen and a small symbol with a **red** line shows up. This indicates the assembly location to which you will attach subassemblies.

If you look in the **Prospector** and expand the tree for **Assemblies**, you see the assembly name. You now attach the subassemblies to both the left and right sides of the assembly location.

Exercise 9-3: Attach Subassemblies to an Assembly

1. From the **Imperial-Basic** tool palette, click the **BasicLane** subassembly. The properties for the subassembly can be altered at that time. Look in the **Properties** palette under **Advanced Parameters** and ensure that the parameter for **Side** is set to **Right**. Set the **Depth** to **0.67**. Ensure that the **Width** is set to **12.0** and the **%Slope** is **−2.0**.
2. Select marker point within assembly: Pick the assembly baseline location, which is the circular symbol in the middle of the assembly that you created. The lane should show up on the right side of the assembly marker.
3. From the **Imperial Basic** tool palette, click the **BasicCurbandGutter** subassembly. Look in the **Properties** palette under the **Advanced Parameters** and ensure that the parameter for **Side** is **Right**. Change the **Gutter width** to **2.0**. Change the **Gutter %Slope** to **−2.0**. Change the **Curb Height** to **0.5** and the **Curb Width** should be **0.5** as well. The **Curb Depth** should be **1.5**.
4. Select marker point within assembly: Click on the upper right circle of the lane you just placed and the **BasicCurbandGutter** subassembly appears connected to the lane.
5. From the **Imperial Basic** tool palette, click the **BasicSidewalk** subassembly. Look in the **Properties** palette and ensure that the parameter for **Side** is **Right**. Change the **Width** to **4.0**. Change the **Depth** to **0.33**, and change both of the **Buffer widths** to **2.0**.
6. Select marker point within assembly: Click on the upper right circle of the **Basic-CurbandGutter** subassembly, and the sidewalk appears connected to the back of the Curb.
7. Now repeat this process, but select the parameter for **Side** being **Left**, place the left side of the assembly, and connect it up as you did the right side.
8. When finished, the assembly should have a left and right travel lane, curb and gutter, and a sidewalk on both sides.

9. Next, you handle the tie-out of the road to the existing conditions. Using the **ImperialDaylight** tab in the **Tool** palette, click the **DaylightStandard** subassembly. Check the **Properties** dialog box and ensure that the side is **Right**, the **Ditch width** is **0.0**, the **Flat Cut Max Height** is **5.0**, the **Flat Cut Slope** is **6.0**, the **Flat Fill Max Height** is **5**, and the **Flat Fill Slope** is **6.0**.

10. Place it on the top rightmost circle on the sidewalk. Repeat for the left side by setting the **Side** parameter to **Left**.

11. Press **<Enter>** twice to finish the command.

You have now created the assembly. Figure 9-9 shows how it should appear.

Figure 9-9   A completed assembly

Job Skills benefit in that the designer can build the right side independently of the left if he or she chooses. The assembly does not have to be symmetrical.

The assembly for the Access Road is now complete. Save the file. You now move forward to create the roadway. In this task, the pieces to the corridor puzzle come together. You have all the components for the corridor. Let us summarize. The primitive geometry for the alignment is developed, and a completed alignment is defined. The **Profile View** is established with an existing ground profile. From there a finished ground profile (or **PGL**) was developed for the corridor. Then you set the settings for some subassemblies and created an assembly.

PGL: The profile grade line is the proposed profile.

Note that you can edit any particular subassembly by selecting it, right-clicking, and choosing **Subassembly Properties...** from the menu. Parameters can be altered as needed. You now create the corridor and the finished design surface.

Exercise 9-4: Create a Corridor

1. Open the drawing called Chapter-9b.dwg. Notice the assembly.
2. Restore a presaved view to place the view around the centerline.
3. Type **V** for **View** at the command prompt to obtain the **View** dialog box. Select the **Plan** view, hit **Set Current**, then hit **OK**. You are placed at the centerline of the Access Road. A view is set up for the profile as well in the event that you need it.
4. From the **Corridors** pull-down menu, select **Create Simple Corridor....**
5. Accept the default name and hit **OK**.
6. `Select a baseline alignment:` Pick the **red** centerline in the view.
7. The command prompt then asks you to `select a profile <or press enter key to select from list>`:
8. Hit **<Enter>**, and the **Select a Profile** dialog box appears. Choose **Layout (5)** and hit **OK**. Note that the other options are the offsets created in a previous chapter.
9. The command prompt then asks you to `select an assembly <or press enter key to select from list>`: Hit **<Enter>** and select **Assembly 1**.
10. A large window of data displays for **Target Mapping**.

To access student data files, go to www.pearsondesigncentral.com.

If you recall from Chapter 2, **Target Mapping** is a technical way of assigning the particular alignments, profiles, and surfaces required by the subassemblies to create the complete assembly. For instance, the **DaylightStandard** subassembly needs to know to which surface to compute, and so the **Target Map** for this would be the **Existing Ground** surface. See Figure 9-10.

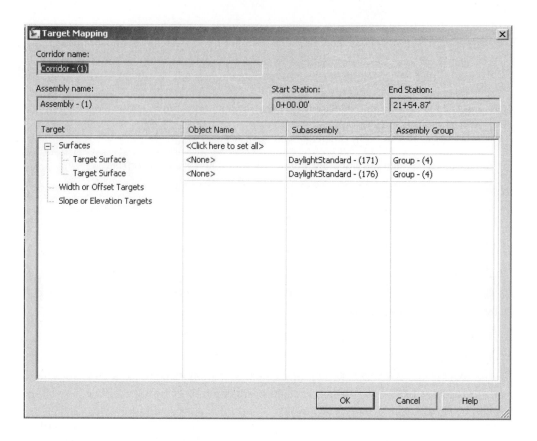

Figure 9-10 The Target Mapping dialog box

11. In the second column and in the row for **Surfaces** is a cell that says **<Click here to set all>**.
12. When you click on the cell, a dialog box called **Pick a Surface** displays. Choose the **Existing Ground** and click **OK**. You see the **Target Surface** is now **Existing Ground**. Click **OK**, and the corridor generates.
13. Close the **Panorama** if it appears and inspect the results of the processing. A Corridor model is evident in the drawing.

Let us learn how to control the appearance of the corridor data.

14. Click and select the roadway corridor. Then right-click and choose **Corridor Properties...** shown in Figure 9-11.
15. In the **Surfaces** tab, click the button on the left to **Create a corridor surface**.
16. After you choose this button, a **Corridor (1) Borders & Contours** is created and appears in the window below.
17. In the **Data type** pop-down window, select **Links** if it is not already selected.
18. In the **Specify code:** pop-down window, choose **Top**. Then hit the **+** button to the right to add it to the matrix. The **Top** surface then appears under the **Name** column.
19. In the **Surface Style** column, click on the style that defaults, typically **Borders & Contours**.
20. A **Pick Corridor Surface Style** dialog box displays with a pop-down menu. Select **Borders & Contours**. Click on the pop-down arrow to the right of **Borders & Contours** and select **Edit Current Selection**. A **Surface Style** dialog box appears. Select the **Contours** tab. Set the **Contour interval** to **2** and **10** for the intermediate and index contours, respectively. Hit **OK**. Hit **OK**.
21. Now choose the **Boundaries** tab at the top.
22. Right-click on **Corridor (1) Surface (1)**. Choose **Add Automatically**.
23. Select **Daylight** from the menu that displays.
24. The **Name** column now shows a boundary item. Hit **OK**.
25. You should see contours for the corridor in AutoCAD when it is finished processing.

Civil 3D automatically creates a surface object upon creating a Corridor surface. You can see it in the **Prospector** under **Surfaces**.

Let us continue controlling the appearance of the corridor data and visualize it with faces and shading. To set the data up so they can be viewed in 3D, perform the following exercise.

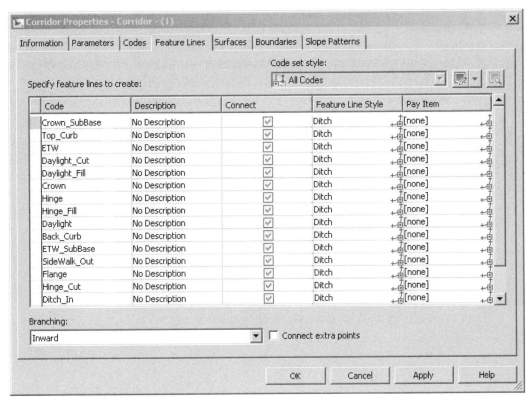

Figure 9-11 Corridor Properties

Exercise 9-5: Set Up Corridor for 3D Shading

1. Click and select the roadway corridor. Then right-click and choose **Corridor Properties....** A **Corridor Properties** dialog box appears. Select the **Surfaces** tab.
2. In the **Surface Style** column, click on the style that defaults, typically **Borders & Contours**.
3. A **Pick Corridor Surface Style** dialog box displays with a pop-down menu. Select **Borders & Triangles and Directions**. Hit **OK**.
4. Use AutoCAD's **3DOrbit** command to view the corridor in a bird's-eye perspective to help you see the road in 3D. In the event it is not rendered, while in the **3DOrbit** command, right-click, choose **Visual Styles**, and select **Conceptual** shading to shade the view. You see the road is 3D, complete with representation of the gutters and sidewalks.
5. If you have already left the **3DOrbit** command and the view is not shaded, use the **View** pull-down menu, and select **Visual Styles** and **Conceptual** shading.
6. Type **PLAN <Enter> <Enter>** to return to the plan view when you are finished viewing.
7. Save and close the file.

SUPERELEVATING A ROADWAY

The next step is to walk through a procedure for superelevating a roadway. Civil 3D has some excellent and very easy-to-use tools for computing superelevations. You will open another file and create a different template, which is for a more sophisticated highway condition. The specifications for this roadway are as follows: 12′ pavement lane, a curb and gutter, a sidewalk with a slope to drain into the roadway, and a multiple side slope configuration for tying out to daylight. These are multiple subgrade surfaces on this template for a base and subbase situation. You use AASHTO's superelevation criteria, and should the roadway design violate these criteria, the software provides a warning.

Exercise 9-6: Create an Assembly for Superelevations

1. Open the drawing called Chapter-9c.dwg.
2. Restore a presaved view to place your view around a location where you build a new corridor assembly.
3. Type **V** for **View** and select the view called **Assembly**, hit **Set Current**, then hit **OK**.

To access student data files, go to www.pearsondesigncentral.com.

4. Under the **Corridors** pull-down menu, choose **Create Assembly....** When the **Create Assembly** dialog box appears, accept the defaults by hitting **OK**.
5. `Specify assembly baseline location:` Choose a point in the middle of the screen. Notice that a marker appears for **Assembly—1**.

Using the **Tool Palettes** for **Civil 3D**, you will select a variety of subassemblies from which to create the overall assembly.

6. From the **Imperial-Roadway** tab, select the icon for **LaneOutsideSuper**. Before placing it, note that the **Properties** dialog box opens, allowing you to make changes to the parameters. Make the following changes: Select **Right** because you will do the right side first. The width is **12′**. The **Pave1 Depth** is **0.167** for a 2″ asphalt top surface. The **Pave2 Depth** will be **0.0**. The **Base Depth** will be **0.33′**, and the **Sub-base Depth** will be **1′**.
7. `Select marker point within assembly:` Pick a point on the right side of the circle on the assembly marker. A pavement lane with subgrades appears.
8. Look back in the **Properties** dialog box and change the side to **Left**.
9. Pick a point on the left side of the circle of the assembly marker. A pavement lane with subgrades appears.
10. Now pick the **Imperial—Structures** tab in the **Tool Palettes**. Notice many structures for assembly creation in this area.
11. Choose the **UrbanCurbGutterGeneral** structure.
12. Set the settings for this dialog box as shown in Figure 9-12.

TIP   Note that if you click on any of the settings in the dialog box for **Dimension A—G**, the bottom of the dialog box provides an explanation of what these dimensions represent.

13. Do the left side of the template first.
14. Once these parameters are set, click a point on the upper left **Edge of Pavement** circle of the pavement.
15. Change the **Properties** dialog box to the **Right** side, and place the curb and gutter on the circle at the top right of the **Edge of Pavement**.
16. You now see curb and gutter on the left and right of the template.
17. Now, choose the **UrbanSidewalk** from the **Imperial—Structures** tab in the **Tool Palettes**.
18. Note in the **Properties** dialog box that settings now exist for the sidewalk. Set the **Side** to **Right**. Set the **Inside boulevard width** to **2′**. Set the **Sidewalk width** to **4′**. Set the **Outside boulevard width** to **1′**. Set the **Slope** to **2%**. Set the **Depth** to **0.33′**.
19. Now pick a point on the circle at the upper right, top, back of curb. You see a sidewalk. Change the **Properties** setting for **Side** to **Left** and select a point on the circle at the upper left, top, and back of curb. Sidewalks now exist on both sides of the template.
20. Now, choose the **DaylightStandard** from the **Imperial—Daylight** tab in the **Tool Palettes**. Set the settings as shown in Figure 9-13.
21. Then pick a point on the circle at the left edge of the sidewalk extension. A cut/fill subassembly appears.
22. Change the **Side** to **Right** in the **Properties** dialog box and place the subassembly on the right side as well.

This completes your assembly development. The assembly should appear as shown in Figure 9-14. Save your file.

Exercise 9-7: Establish Superelevation Criteria

You must now set the superelevation characteristics for the roadway. To do this, you inspect the alignment properties. You will now run through this procedure and set alignment properties for superelevations.

ADVANCED	▲
Parameters	▲
Version	R2009
Side	Left
Insertion Point	Gutter Edge
Gutter Slope ...	Outside Lane Slope
Gutter Slope	-2.000%
Subbase Depth	1.500'
Subbase Ext...	1.000'
Use SE	Use outside lane s...
Subbase Slope	-2.000%
Dimension A(...	7.000"
Dimension B(...	24.000"
Dimension C(...	2.000"
Dimension D(...	6.000"
Dimension E(...	6.000"
Dimension F(...	5.000"
Dimension G(...	13.000"

Figure 9-12   Urban Curb Gutter— General settings

Figure 9-13   The DaylightStandard subassembly parameters

Figure 9-14   Completed assembly

1. Open the drawing called Chapter-9d.dwg.
2. Restore a presaved view to place your view around the centerline.
3. Type **V** for **View** and select the view called **Plan**, hit **Set Current**, then hit **OK**.
4. Select the roadway and right-click. Choose **Alignment Properties...** from the menu.
5. Go to the **Design Criteria** tab and click the button labeled **Add Design speed....**
6. Click in the **Design Speed** cell for that station number **1** and type **45** for the speed.
7. Then click on the **Superelevation** tab to the right. See Figure 9-15 and notice that there are three buttons on the upper left side of the box. Click on the third button, labeled **Set Superelevation Properties**.
8. The **Superelevation Specification** dialog box appears, as shown in Figure 9-16. Hit **OK**.
9. The superelevation rate table can be changed for the eMax rate, whether the roadway is two or four lanes, whether the roadway is crowned or planar (such as in a divided highway). Take a moment to address the other parameters to see how they can be selected. Hit **OK**.
10. A clean, well-laid-out dialog box appears showing parameters that dictate the superelevation of the roadway. See Figure 9-15 where each curve is broken into regions that can be addressed individually.
11. Any grayed-out items cannot be changed because they are set elsewhere, such as the design speed. Other parameters can be changed simply by selecting the item.
12. When finished inspecting, hit **OK**.

The computations occur for the superelevation data. Refer to Figure 9-16 showing the computations. All the critical and most often needed stations are computed and shown in the table.

To access student data files, go to www.pearsondesigncentral.com.

Figure 9-15 Superelevation specifications

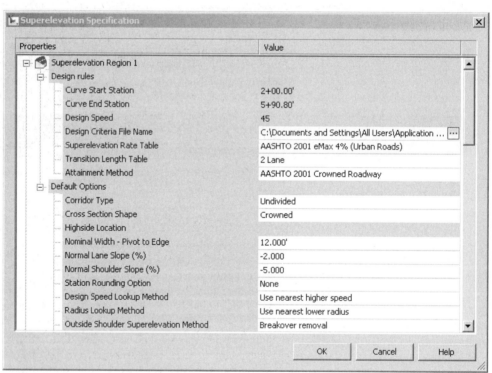

Figure 9-16 Superelevation computations

Civil 3D computes these data. If there are any errors or notifications of which the user needs to be aware, they appear in the **Panorama**. These might include warnings that curve radii are not up to par. Close the **Panorama** when you are through inspecting its contents.

Exercise 9-8: Build a Simple Corridor

1. Select **Create Simple Corridor...** from the **Corridors** pull-down menu.
2. The **Create Simple Corridor** dialog box appears and requests a name for the corridor. Hit **OK** for the default name and layer.

3. `Select a baseline alignment:` Click on the centerline for the road.
4. `Select a profile:` **Zoom** out and select the proposed profile in the profile view in the upper right part of the drawing.
5. `Select the Assembly:` Pick the **Assembly** marker in the assembly you created.
6. The **Target Mapping** dialog box shown in Figure 9-17 then appears so that Civil 3D can identify which surfaces are involved in the computations.

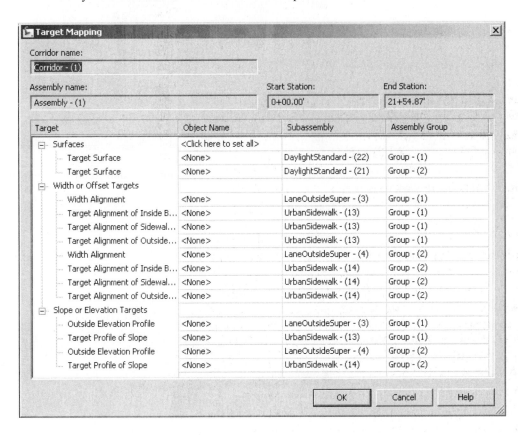

Figure 9-17 The Target Mapping dialog box

7. In the **Object Name** column, in the first row it says to **<Click here to set all>**. Click in that cell and choose the **Existing ground** surface. That will be the surface to which you tie out. Hit **OK**. Hit **OK** to execute.

Exercise 9-9: Use View/Edit Corridor Sections

The corridor is now complete. Let us inspect it. If you **Zoom** back to your centerline, it should appear as shown in Figure 9-18.

Figure 9-18 Completed corridor

1. The daylight limits are shown around the perimeter of the site.
2. To inspect the cross section of the proposed road, choose **View/Edit Corridor Section** from the **Corridors** pull-down menu. You are prompted to Select a corridor, pick the corridor object.
3. A **Section Editor** tab appears at the top of the screen. Click on it and choose the **Parameter Editor** command. A table appears showing all the pertinent data for the cross section at station 0+00. Refer to Figure 9-19.
4. Take a moment to review this information. It should reflect a normal cross slope for the road.

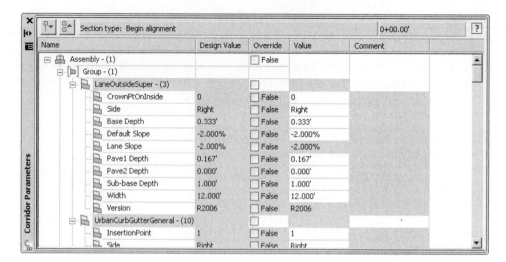

Figure 9-19 View/Edit Corridor Section Tools

5. A view of the road section also appears in AutoCAD. **Zoom** and **pan** freely to inspect it visually. See Figure 9-20.

Figure 9-20 A view of the road section

6. In the **Section Editor** use the drop-down menu for stations and select other stations, for instance, 2+50. Notice that the roadway is now superelevated.
7. A view of the superelevated roadway is also displayed in AutoCAD. See Figure 9-21.

When through inspecting the sections, terminate the command by closing the toolbar.

Figure 9-21 A view of the superelevated roadway

CODES AND FEATURE LINES

Two additional items that should be mentioned with regard to corridor design are codes and feature lines.

Codes represent specific three-dimensional locations on the Corridor model that are identified with descriptions. They are defined with the subassemblies and are used to create and organize the assemblies. Codes can be exported for the corridor as point objects and uploaded to data collectors, or made available to 3D Machine Control for automated construction. Corridor section labeling is supported through the introduction of Code, Point, Link, and Shape label styles. Corridor assemblies and sections can be annotated with the new label styles.

Exercise 9-10: Review These Codes

1. In the same drawing, look in the **Prospector**. Expand **Corridors** and right-click on **Corridor - (1)**. Choose **Properties** from the menu. When the dialog box appears, select the **Codes** tab. Refer to Figure 9-22.
2. Change the **Code set style** to **All Codes**.
3. Look through the **Name** column and note that there are **Link** codes, **Point** codes, and **Shape** codes. Hit **OK** when finished observing.

A brief explanation of these items follows:

Link codes are the codes assigned to each of the links that are part of the assembly definitions for the roadway. A link is a straight-line segment between endpoints on any cross section.

Figure 9-22   Corridor Codes

Shape codes are closed cross-sectional areas created by the subassembly. Shape codes can be used to visualize different materials within the assembly, in order to view the assembly more clearly.

Feature lines represent the linear elements of corridors such as centerlines, edge of pavement, ditch components, and daylight cut/fill lines. These can be used for visualizing the corridor but can also be exported as alignments or as **Grading Feature Lines**.

Exercise 9-11: Change the Aesthetics of the Corridor

This next procedure walks you through how to assign a feature line style for an element of the corridor.

1. In the same drawing, look in the **Prospector**. Expand **Corridors** and right-click on **Corridor - (1)**. Choose **Properties...** from the menu. When the dialog box appears, select the **Feature Lines** tab.
2. Look through the **Code** column and note that there are descriptions for items such as **Top_Curb**, and so on.
3. Click on the **Top_Curb**, look in the **Feature Line Style** column, and you see it defaults to **Ditch**. Click on the icon in the cell for that row. Refer to Figure 9-23.
4. A **Pick Feature Line Style** dialog box with a drop-down menu appears. Select the **Curb Line** style in the drop-down menu.
5. There is a button just to the right of the **Curb Line** item in the drop-down menu. Click on the triangle and select **Edit Current Selection Style**. A **Feature Line Style—Curb Line** dialog box displays. Click on the **Display** tab and note that you can control how this item appears in AutoCAD. In **Model**, it appears as a magenta color. Hit **OK** when finished observing. Hit **OK** and you are in the **Corridor Properties** dialog box again.
6. Click on **Daylight_Fill** and change the **Feature Line Style** for this to **Daylight Line—Fill**.
7. Click on **Daylight_Cut** and change the **Feature Line Style** for this to **Daylight Line—Cut**.
8. Hit **OK** to exit.
9. The corridor recomputes. When it is complete, **Zoom** in and notice that the corridor shows a magenta line where the **Top of Curb** exists. Look just outside of the flowline for the curb.
10. Also observe that the **Daylight Lines** for **Cut** and **Fill** have changed color.

The next powerful feature is to export these items to AutoCAD for additional functionality. This linework can be sent to AutoCAD in 2D or 3D, which allows for customization.

11. Look in the **Corridors** pull-down menu and select the **Utilities** command.

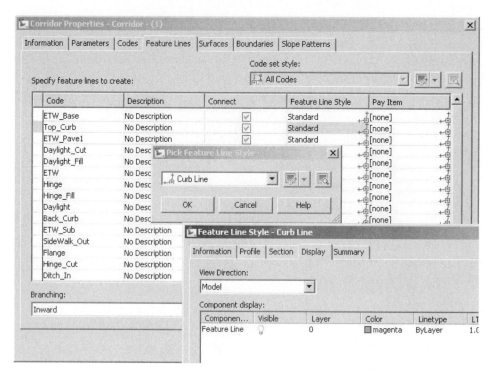

Figure 9-23 Corridor Properties, Feature Line Styles

12. You can export these objects as Polylines, Feature Lines, Alignments, or Profiles. Select **Create Grading Feature Line from Corridor**.

13. `Select a corridor feature line:` **Zoom** in and select the magenta **Top of Curb** object. A **Create Feature Line from Corridor** dialog box appears. Hit **OK**.

14. `Select a corridor feature line:` **Zoom** out and select the **Cut/Fill** linework. **Select a Feature Line** dialog box appears. Hit **OK**. Hit **<Enter>** to complete.

15. When finished, notice that these objects are now in AutoCAD as separate entities and in three dimensions!

One more concept to explore has to do with a major transportation corridor. This area of engineering warrants its own independent textbook; however, it needs to be touched on here.

The Civil 3D **Corridors** pull-down menu has another function for creating corridors called **Create Corridor** You have used the **Create Simple Corridor** up to this point. The **Create Corridor** command is for high-level roads that have multiple alignments, ramps, gores, multiple assemblies, and so on. It is in this function that multiple assemblies are assigned and act together in roadway design.

MULTIPLE BASELINES

The software makes more in-depth use of regions in this methodology. Although you have already seen regions used in the design of superelevations, these regions are used to expand that functionality.

Exercise 9-12: Multiple Baselines

To access student data files, go to www.pearsondesigncentral.com.

1. Open the file called Chapter-9-e.dwg. It has the same alignment and profile you have been working with but has two assemblies. One is a four-lane, rural assembly with a shoulder, and the other is a two-lane urban assembly with curb and gutter. A wide, white boundary is drawn for a surface to be created later. Type **V** for **View** and select the **Assembly** view, hit **Set Current**, then hit **OK**. **Zoom** out a little, and you see both assemblies.

2. Look in the **Corridors** pull-down menu and select the **Create Corridor** command.

3. Select **Alignment—1** when asked by hitting **<Enter>** to access the library of alignments.

4. Select **Profile—Layout (5)** when asked by hitting **<Enter>** to access the library of profiles.

5. Select **Assembly—(1)** when asked by hitting **<Enter>** to access the library of assemblies.

6. A **Create Corridor** dialog box appears, showing that the software already assumes a **Region 1**.

7. For **Baseline 1—Region 1**, change the ending station to **1000** for the use of **Assembly—(1)**.

8. Then right-click on **Baseline 1**, and a shortcut menu appears allowing you to **Add Region....**
9. First a **Create Corridor Region** dialog box appears, asking you to select the appropriate assembly for the second region. Select **Assembly—(2)**. See Figure 9-24.

Figure 9-24 Multiple Baselines—Corridor Properties

10. Now change the starting station to **1000** for **Region 2**.
11. Click the button at the top right of the dialog box that says **Set all Targets**; a **Target Mapping** dialog box appears. Click on **Surfaces <Click here to set all>**. Select **Existing Ground** and hit **OK**.
12. Hit **OK** and the system reprocesses the corridor.
13. When it is finished, click on the corridor, right-click, and select **Corridor Properties....**
14. In the **Surfaces** tab, click the button on the left to **Create a corridor surface**.
15. After you choose this button, a **Corridor—(1) Surface—(1)** is created and appears in the window below.
16. In the **Data Type** pop-down window, select **Links** if it is not already selected.
17. In the **Specify Code** pop-down window, choose **Top**. Then hit the + button to the right. The **Top** surface appears under the **Name** column.
18. In the **Surface Style** column, click on the style that defaults, typically **Borders & Contours**.
19. A **Pick Corridor Surface Style** dialog box displays with a pop-down menu. Select **Borders & Contours** as the style. Click on the pop-down arrow to the right of **Borders & Contours**. Choose **Edit Current Selection** and go to the **Contours** tab. Set the **Contour interval** to **2** and **10** for the intermediate and index contours, respectively.
20. You should see contours for the corridor in AutoCAD when it is finished processing.
21. Zoom in and identify station 10+00 and notice that the software has built a corridor using the multiple assemblies. It has transitioned between the urban template and the rural template along the common edges, that is, the pavement. A 336′ contour runs through the transition between 10+00 and 10+25.

Exercise 9-13: Create a Corridor Surface

The next option to discuss is creating a corridor surface that will be evident in the **Surfaces** area of the **Prospector**.

1. In the same file, look under the **Corridors** pull-down menu. Select **Utilities >> Create Detached Surfaces from Corridor....**

2. Pick your corridor when requested.
3. A **Create Corridor Surfaces** dialog box displays, confirming your surface naming and the styles to use. Use the defaults or change them here and hit **OK**.
4. Look under the **Prospector** and notice a new surface representing the corridor.
5. Expand **Corridor—(1)**, **Surface—(1)**. Expand **Definitions**.
6. Right-click on **Boundaries** and select **Add....**
7. Give it a name of **Corridor Boundary** in the name field that displays in the **Add Boundaries** dialog box. Hit **OK**.
8. Pick the white polyline around the corridor as a boundary.
9. This can be used to perform surface-related functions such as pasting it into the existing ground to create a monolithic surface and the like.

Exercise 9-14: Earthworks on a Corridor Surface

Let us perform earthworks on the corridor surface and compare it to the existing ground surface.

1. From the **Surfaces** pull-down menu, choose **Create Surface....**
2. In the **Create Surface** dialog box, in the upper left pop-down menu for **Type**, choose **TIN volume surface**, shown in Figure 9-25.

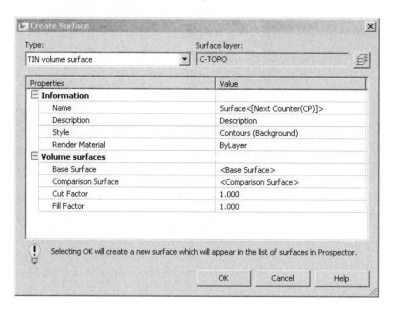

Figure 9-25 Create Surface dialog box

3. Under the **Value** column for the **Name** field, provide a name of **TIN Volume EG vs. Corridor**.
4. In the **Volume surfaces** field, there are fields for selecting the comparison surfaces.
5. Select **Existing Ground** for the **Base Surface** and select **Corridor (1)—Surface (1)** for the **Comparison Surface**. Hit **OK**.
6. Look in the **Prospector** and you see a surface called **TIN Volume EG vs. Corridor**. Right-click on it and select **Surface Properties....**
7. Choose the **Statistics** tab in the dialog box for **Surface Properties** and expand the **Volume** item. Volumes are automatically computed for the two surfaces. See Figure 9-26.
8. If these two surfaces change, the volumes recompute if the **Rebuild—Automatic** item is checked in the surface parameters.

Exercise 9-15: Corridor-Related Quantity Takeoffs

Now let us use the **Quantity Takeoff** commands under the **Sections** pull-down menu to compute some quantities from the corridor.

This task is often used due to the requirement to estimate the costs for providing certain quantities of material for a project. Contractors and engineers must be able to ascertain the cost of the project before it goes to construction.

Figure 9-26   Quantities from surface calculations

1. Open Chapter-9-f.dwg; you will notice that the **Sample Line Group** has already been created as discussed in the earlier chapter on **Sections** in order to expedite this exercise. Right-click on **Corridor 3** to rebuild it.
2. Look under the **Sections** pull-down and select **Compute Materials...**.
3. A dialog box will display called **Select a Sample Line Group**; select the SLG-1 group. The **Compute Materials** dialog box then displays.
4. In the top left of the dialog box is a pop-down window; select the option called **Earthworks**.
5. For the **EG Criteria**, **Object name**, select **Existing ground (1)**.
6. For the **Datum**, select **Corridor (3) Corridor (3)—Surface (1)**.
7. Hit **OK**.
8. Look under the **Sections** pull-down and select **Generate Volume Report...**.
9. The **Report Quantities** dialog box will display. Use **Alignment—1**, **SLG-1**, **Material List—1** and the **Earthwork** style sheet. See Figure 9-27. Hit **OK**.
10. A volume report is generated and should appear similar to that in Table 9-1.

To access student data files, go to www.pearsondesigncentral.com.

Figure 9-27   Report Quantities dialog box

Table 9-1   Volume Report

Project: chapter 9-f.dwg   Alignment: Alignment—1   Sample Line Group: SLG-1
Start Sta: 0+00.000   End Sta: 21+54.874

Station	Cut Area (sq. ft.)	Cut Volume (cu. yd.)	Re-usable Volume (cu. yd.)	Fill Area (sq. ft.)	Fill Volume (cu. yd.)	Cum. Cut Vol. (cu. yd.)	Cum. Reusable Vol. (cu. yd.)	Cum. Fill Vol. (cu. yd.)	Cum. Net Vol. (cu. yd.)
0+00.000	230.93	0.00	0.00	12.77	0.00	0.00	0.00	0.00	0.00
0+50.000	249.93	445.24	445.24	19.05	29.47	445.24	445.24	29.47	415.77
1+00.000	237.50	451.33	451.33	24.24	40.08	896.57	896.57	69.55	827.02
1+50.000	149.15	358.01	358.01	29.75	49.99	1254.58	1254.58	119.53	1135.05
2+00.000	23.37	159.74	159.74	62.78	85.67	1414.32	1414.32	205.20	1209.11
2+25.000	12.87	15.88	15.88	68.78	61.40	1430.20	1430.20	266.61	1163.59
2+50.000	5.73	8.17	8.17	93.73	75.71	1438.37	1438.37	342.32	1096.05
2+75.000	4.94	4.69	4.69	88.94	85.13	1443.06	1443.06	427.45	1015.61
3+00.000	4.28	4.03	4.03	90.46	83.70	1447.09	1447.09	511.15	935.94
3+25.000	0.26	1.99	1.99	93.74	85.58	1449.08	1449.08	596.73	852.36
3+50.000	0.88	0.51	0.51	115.93	97.19	1449.59	1449.59	693.92	755.67
3+75.000	0.34	0.53	0.53	164.63	129.83	1450.12	1450.12	823.74	626.38
4+00.000	0.00	0.15	0.15	226.89	181.29	1450.27	1450.27	1005.03	445.24
4+25.000	0.00	0.00	0.00	313.84	249.79	1450.27	1450.27	1254.82	195.45
4+50.000	0.00	0.00	0.00	392.70	325.78	1450.27	1450.27	1580.60	−130.33
4+75.000	0.00	0.00	0.00	402.37	368.14	1450.27	1450.27	1948.74	−498.47
5+00.000	0.02	0.01	0.01	446.26	394.79	1450.28	1450.28	2343.53	−893.25
5+25.000	0.00	0.01	0.01	424.96	404.87	1450.29	1450.29	2748.39	−1298.10
5+50.000	0.00	0.00	0.00	372.11	369.68	1450.29	1450.29	3118.07	−1667.78
5+75.000	0.25	0.12	0.12	352.70	336.44	1450.42	1450.42	3454.51	−2004.10
5+90.799	0.01	0.08	0.08	327.22	199.01	1450.50	1450.50	3653.52	−2203.02
6+00.000	0.00	0.00	0.00	333.64	112.50	1450.50	1450.50	3766.02	−2315.52
6+25.000	0.00	0.00	0.00	256.94	272.76	1450.50	1450.50	4038.78	−2588.28
6+50.000	2.44	1.05	1.05	191.42	207.30	1451.55	1451.55	4246.08	−2794.53
6+75.000	7.60	4.33	4.33	136.95	152.02	1455.88	1455.88	4398.10	−2942.21
7+00.000	0.30	3.41	3.41	69.75	96.36	1459.30	1459.30	4494.46	−3035.16
7+25.000	9.11	4.55	4.55	14.39	39.40	1463.84	1463.84	4533.86	−3070.02
7+50.000	105.75	52.55	52.55	2.55	7.93	1516.39	1516.39	4541.79	−3025.39
7+75.000	119.49	102.62	102.62	1.34	1.86	1619.01	1619.01	4543.65	−2924.64
8+00.000	126.91	112.51	112.51	0.16	0.72	1731.52	1731.52	4544.37	−2812.85
8+25.000	205.70	152.86	152.86	0.00	0.08	1884.37	1884.37	4544.44	−2660.07
8+50.000	251.87	211.86	211.86	0.00	0.00	2096.24	2096.24	4544.44	−2448.21
8+75.000	212.69	215.08	215.08	0.00	0.00	2311.32	2311.32	4544.45	−2233.13
9+00.000	161.94	171.23	171.23	4.43	2.11	2482.55	2482.55	4546.56	−2064.01
9+25.000	141.41	136.40	136.40	28.53	15.66	2618.95	2618.95	4562.22	−1943.27
9+50.000	126.50	119.50	119.50	69.13	46.48	2738.45	2738.45	4608.70	−1870.26
9+75.000	114.29	107.19	107.19	81.12	71.59	2845.64	2845.64	4680.29	−1834.65
9+77.881	113.05	11.67	11.67	82.87	9.03	2857.31	2857.31	4689.32	−1832.01
10+00.000	105.83	89.66	89.66	89.62	70.65	2946.97	2946.97	4759.97	−1813.01

Station	Cut Area (sq. ft.)	Cut Volume (cu. yd.)	Re-usable Volume (cu. yd.)	Fill Area (sq. ft.)	Fill Volume (cu. yd.)	Cum. Cut Vol. (cu. yd.)	Cum. Reusable Vol. (cu. yd.)	Cum. Fill Vol. (cu. yd.)	Cum. Net Vol. (cu. yd.)
10+50.000	111.45	201.19	201.19	146.94	219.04	3148.15	3148.15	4979.01	−1830.86
11+00.000	80.40	177.64	177.64	218.61	338.47	3325.79	3325.79	5317.48	−1991.69
11+50.000	0.00	74.44	74.44	337.46	514.87	3400.23	3400.23	5832.36	−2432.13
11+77.881	0.03	0.01	0.01	411.42	386.66	3400.25	3400.25	6219.02	−2818.77
12+00.000	3.63	1.41	1.41	349.49	315.25	3401.65	3401.65	6534.27	−3132.62
12+25.000	68.19	31.24	31.24	297.95	302.94	3432.90	3432.90	6837.20	−3404.31
12+50.000	93.19	70.44	70.44	199.92	234.39	3503.34	3503.34	7071.59	−3568.25
12+75.000	124.56	95.33	95.33	103.30	144.29	3598.67	3598.67	7215.88	−3617.21
13+00.000	161.55	125.55	125.55	71.53	83.39	3724.22	3724.22	7299.27	−3575.05
13+25.000	165.57	144.57	144.57	42.22	54.33	3868.79	3868.79	7353.60	−3484.81
13+50.000	170.90	150.11	150.11	32.50	35.93	4018.89	4018.89	7389.53	−3370.63
13+75.000	164.95	150.21	150.21	39.50	34.70	4169.11	4169.11	7424.23	−3255.12
14+00.000	154.41	141.83	141.83	54.28	44.93	4310.93	4310.93	7469.16	−3158.22
14+25.000	146.96	132.16	132.16	64.48	56.67	4443.10	4443.10	7525.83	−3082.74
14+50.000	137.18	124.11	124.11	71.30	64.89	4567.20	4567.20	7590.72	−3023.52
14+75.000	131.24	117.92	117.92	77.86	71.27	4685.12	4685.12	7662.00	−2976.87
15+00.000	113.28	107.56	107.56	67.47	69.18	4792.69	4792.69	7731.18	−2938.49
15+25.000	85.00	87.11	87.11	149.85	103.33	4879.80	4879.80	7834.51	−2954.71
15+50.000	55.72	61.52	61.52	165.29	148.59	4941.31	4941.31	7983.09	−3041.78
15+66.536	83.55	40.22	40.22	91.67	79.73	4981.53	4981.53	8062.82	−3081.29
15+66.537	83.55	0.00	0.00	91.67	0.00	4981.53	4981.53	8062.82	−3081.29
15+75.000	103.49	30.84	30.84	64.06	23.89	5012.37	5012.37	8086.71	−3074.35
16+00.000	211.75	151.20	151.20	2.13	29.93	5163.56	5163.56	8116.64	−2953.08
16+25.000	390.31	281.89	281.89	0.00	0.94	5445.45	5445.45	8117.58	−2672.13
16+50.000	516.35	420.90	420.90	0.00	0.00	5866.36	5866.36	8117.58	−2251.23
16+75.000	630.68	530.89	530.89	0.00	0.00	6397.25	6397.25	8117.58	−1720.33
17+00.000	621.03	580.18	580.18	0.00	0.00	6977.42	6977.42	8117.58	−1140.16
17+25.000	588.40	563.78	563.78	0.00	0.00	7541.21	7541.21	8117.58	−576.38
17+50.000	533.25	524.78	524.78	0.00	0.00	8065.99	8065.99	8117.58	−51.59
17+75.000	470.20	469.74	469.74	0.00	0.00	8535.73	8535.73	8117.58	418.15
18+00.000	411.09	411.08	411.08	0.00	0.00	8946.81	8946.81	8117.58	829.22
18+25.000	317.45	341.69	341.69	0.34	0.15	9288.50	9288.50	8117.73	1170.76
18+50.000	263.18	275.74	275.74	18.36	8.29	9564.23	9564.23	8126.02	1438.21
18+75.000	204.76	223.36	223.36	49.05	29.65	9787.59	9787.59	8155.67	1631.92
19+00.000	160.84	174.42	174.42	45.20	41.30	9962.01	9962.01	8196.97	1765.04
19+25.000	153.34	149.21	149.21	34.24	34.92	10111.22	10111.22	8231.90	1879.32
19+50.000	162.22	149.78	149.78	25.34	26.34	10261.00	10261.00	8258.24	2002.76
19+54.873	163.99	30.23	30.23	22.97	4.16	10291.23	10291.23	8262.40	2028.83
20+00.000	133.33	248.46	248.46	22.59	38.08	10539.70	10539.70	8300.48	2239.22
20+50.000	275.76	378.79	378.79	10.66	30.79	10918.49	10918.49	8331.26	2587.22
21+00.000	218.93	458.05	458.05	8.29	17.55	11376.54	11376.54	8348.81	3027.73
21+50.000	153.64	344.97	344.97	19.36	25.61	11721.51	11721.51	8374.42	3347.09
21+54.874	0.00	13.87	13.87	0.00	1.75	11735.37	11735.37	8376.16	3359.21

In computing earthworks, a section-based method is used whereby the amount of cut and fill is computed between each section of the corridor. The volume of cut between station 0+00 and station 0+50 is 445.24 c.y. and the volume of fill between those same stations is 29.47 c.y. The difference between those two figures is 415.77 c.y., which is referred to as a Net Volume of 415.77 c.y. cut. Notice that the entire amount of cut and fill is assumed to be reusable, such that the earth cut from one area of the project can be used to fill another area.

The entire project's volumes are shown in the last row of Table 9-1. In the last row, the fourth column from the right shows the accumulated amount of cut removed from the existing ground. It is 11,735.37 c.y. of earth. The second column from the right shows the accumulated amount of fill needed to achieve the proposed conditions above existing ground. It is 8,376.16 c.y. of fill. Therefore, the entire project must dispose of 3,359.21 c.y. of the earth that was cut; hence, there is a net volume of 3,359.21 c.y. of cut. Typically it must be trucked off the site because it is excess earth. Clearly this is not a balanced site or all of the earth would have been used somewhere on the site.

ROADWAY DESIGN FOR REHABILITATION AND RECONSTRUCTION—

The next exercise delves into roadway rehabilitation and reconstruction. This part of the software is new to most Autodesk users because the Land Desktop software could not perform this function as elegantly as Civil 3D can. The idea is that not all roads are new roads; in fact, far more roads are maintained each year than built new. Civil 3D provides tools to assist engineers responsible for roadway maintenance, and these include subassemblies for asphalt overlays, median reconstruction, sidewalk rehabilitation, milling and overlaying, and curb and gutter replacements. There are parametric values that can even compute how much of a stripped material can be reused for the new overlay.

Exercise 9-16: Roadway Design for Rehabilitation and Reconstruction

To access student data files, go to www.pearsondesigncentral.com.

1. Open Chapter-9-g.dwg; notice that you have already created an alignment and an existing ground profile. A new assembly has been created called **Assembly—Rehab**. This mill and overlay subassembly was used to place a crowned surface over another, worn, existing crowned surface.
2. The method to perform these computations is to use the alignment in the drawing, which has been prepared to coincide roughly with the asphalt crown of the existing road. The profile used is the existing ground profile for the existing roadway because it already has reasonable grades on it. Then use the new assembly for rehabilitation of the new overlayed surface.
3. Select **Create Corridor** from the **Corridors** pull-down menu. Select the only **Alignment** available. Then select the existing ground profile for the proposed profile and select the **Assembly—Rehab** assembly for the new surface.
4. When the dialog box displays, choose the button for **Set all Targets** and then click in the cell for **<Click here to set all>**. Choose the **Existing Ground** surface and hit **OK**. Hit **OK** to compute.
5. Then **Zoom** into the plan view of the road and notice a corridor exists.
6. From the **Corridors** pull-down menu, select **View/Edit Corridor Section** and browse to stations 0+00, 4+00, and 17+00 and inspect the sections. Notice that milling and overlaying has occurred per your specifications. Refer to Figures 9-28, 9-29, and 9-30.

Figure 9-28   Milling and Overlaying Result 1

Figure 9-29   Milling and Overlaying Result 2

Figure 9-30   Milling and Overlaying Result 3

Exercise 9-17: Designing a Bifurcated Highway

This last roadway-related exercise explores a situation in which there are two baselines. This can occur in many projects, such as a mainlane with an off-ramp or a mainlane with a frontage or a potentially bifurcated highway.

This next design has an eastbound and westbound set of mainlanes. Although the alignments are parallel, the profiles are not the same. This is a ***bifurcated highway***. This exercise uses multiple baselines to show how a DOT-level roadway might be designed.

1. Open Chapter-9-h.dwg; notice that you have already created two alignments and two profiles. Two new assemblies have been created called **Assembly—Eastbound** and **Assembly—Westbound**. There is also a third profile called **Profile—Middle** to guide the center of the median between the two mainlanes.
2. From the **Corridors** pull-down menu, select the **Create Corridor** command. You are asked to select an alignment, so pick the **Alignment—Eastbound**, either from the screen or by hitting **<Enter>** and choosing it from the library. Then select the profile called **Layout–Rt side** from the library as well. Last, select the **Assembly—Eastbound**.
3. This displays the **Create Corridor** dialog box. Click the **Add Baseline** button in the top left of the dialog box to add a baseline to your computations. Choose **Alignment—Westbound** when prompted.
4. Then right-click on the **Baseline 2** and select **Add Region....** Select the **Assembly—Westbound** when prompted. Set the **Profile for Baseline 2** to **Layout—Left**.
5. Click the button for **Set All Targets**. See Figure 9-31.
6. Click the cell where it says to **<Click here to set all>** and select the **Existing Ground (1)** surface for any tie-outs.
7. Then in the **Target Profile** row, under **Object Name**, select **Layout middle** and hit **Add** for both of the **Target Profile** items. This guides the center of the median between the two baselines. Click **OK**. Click **OK** to compute.
8. When the processing is completed, select **View/Edit Corridor** sections from the **Corridors** pull-down menu. Notice how the center of the median now follows the **Layout middle** profile established. Refer to Figure 9-32.
9. Then feel free to establish the surface and view it using the **3DOrbit** command. You can see the two baselines interconnected, each with its own alignment and profile activity. Refer to Figure 9-33.

Exercise 9-18: Designing an Intersection

Perhaps the most requested topic during our training sessions is intersection and cul-de-sac design. Civil 3D has the ability to create integrated intersections and cul-de-sacs, but it is a somewhat advanced topic.

bifurcated highway: Where one direction of traffic has an independent PGL from the opposite direction of traffic. The profile may go uphill in one direction and downhill in the opposite direction.

To access student data files, go to www.pearsondesigncentral.com.

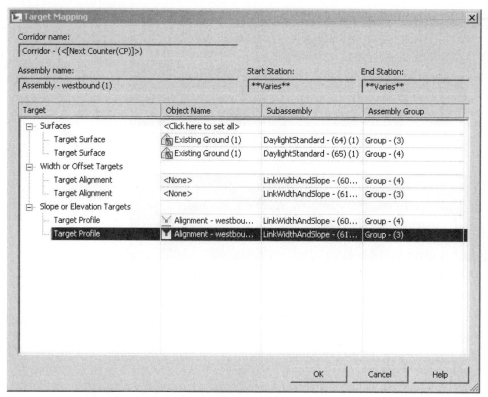

Figure 9-31   Target Mapping for a bifurcated roadway

Figure 9-32   Cross section of resultant bifurcated roadway

Figure 9-33   Isometric view of bifurcated roadway

roadway assembly fragments:
Pieces of cross-sectional templates that are applied to locations on alignments where they can be controlled from and then stretched to various targets elsewhere in the corridor.

The concept is to use ***roadway assembly fragments***, tie them onto one or more alignments, and allow the floating side of the fragment to stretch to any one of many targets that can be identified elsewhere in the corridor. In the simplest sense, you use a typical assembly for the portions of the corridor that are fairly uniform and standardized. At the point when nonstandard conditions occur, such as the intersection of two or more alignments or in cul-de-sac situations, then you can use this fragment methodology. This is a topic that we usually spend significant time on in the classroom; in order to abbreviate it for this text, we will analyze an existing, already designed intersection and cul-de-sac. From this information, you should be able to observe the concepts described and reproduce them on a project fairly easily.

1. Open Chapter-9-i.dwg; you will notice that you already have some alignments and pro-files developed. This is a T-intersection with a cul-de-sac on the east end. The roads are called **Primary Road** and **Side Road**. You will notice that we have additional alignments. The alignment around the cul-de-sac is called **Culdesac ep**. For the intersection, the alignments are called **l-ep**, which is the left edge of pavement for the primary road; **small ep**, which is the edge of pavement directly within the intersection; **l-return**, which is the left end return of the side road as it connects with the primary road; and **r-return**, which is the right end return of the side road as it connects with the primary road.

2. Inspect these alignments by using the **Toolspace**, locating them in the **Prospector** under **Sites**, **Site 1**, **Alignments**, and **Centerline Alignments**. Right-click on each alignment and select **Zoom To** to inspect it visually.

3. Note that there are also existing ground and proposed ground profiles developed for each of the alignments. Inspect these profiles by using the **Toolspace**, locating them in the **Prospector** under **Sites**, **Site 1**, **Alignments, Centerline Alignments**, and **Profile Views**. Right-click on each **Profile View** and select **Zoom To** to inspect them visually. You will see profiles for the Primary road, the Side road, the Left Ep inside the intersection (be-tween the returns), the two curb returns, and the cul-de-sac. Refer to Figure 9-34.

To access student data files, go to www.pearsondesigncentral.com.

Figure 9-34   Profiles for intersection and cul-de-sac design

4. Next, notice the assemblies that have been created. **Assembly-3** is the main assembly for the primary and side roads. **CDS** is the assembly that will "spin" around the right end return of the side road as it connects. **CDS (1)** is the assembly that will "spin" around the left end return of the side road as it connects. The **CDS** is also the assembly that will be used to design the cul-de-sac and it will also be "spun" to create the pavement and tie-outs. See Figure 9-35.

Figure 9-35   Assemblies for intersection and cul-de-sac design

5. Now that you have inspected the components of the alignments, profiles, and assemblies, let us examine how they are compiled into a corridor. Notice that Corridor (1) is the Pri-mary Road, Corridor (2) is the Side Road, Corridor (3) is the Left Curb Return (looking into the Side Road from the Primary Road), and Corridor (4) is the Right Curb Return (looking into the Side Road from the Primary Road). Notice that the cul-de-sac is part of the Primary Road. Select the Primary Road Corridor; right-click and select **Corridor Properties**. The **Corridor Properties** dialog box will display as shown in Figure 9-36.

6. Notice that the **Parameters** tab shows how to prepare the intersection for the incoming side road. The name indicates that **Assembly (3)** will be used; however, regions are estab-lished that allow differing tie-out conditions from station 0+00 up to the intersection, through the intersection, and then after the intersection. The conditions that differ are that the road will be tied to existing ground on both the left and right up to the intersection,

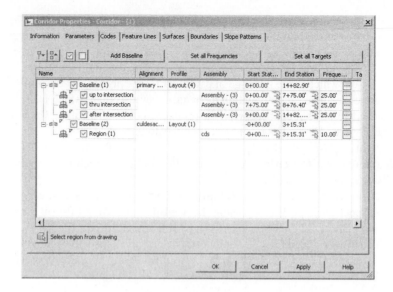

Figure 9-36   Corridor properties for primary road

only on the right through the intersection, and again on both left and right after the intersection. Verify this by clicking the button that says **Set All Targets** in the dialog box as shown in Figure 9-37. The Target Surface whose **Object Name** is set to **<None>** is the left side through the intersection.

Figure 9-37   Set All Targets

7. Also examine how the cul-de-sac is developed. Notice in **Corridor Properties** for **Corridor (1)** that another alignment exists in the dialog box called **culdesac** and it uses a profile called **Layout (1)**, which is the profile for the unwrapped cul-de-sac around the EP of the cul-de-sac. The assembly used is **CDS**, and it is applied to the entire spin-out of the cul-de-sac. To inspect the targets for just the cul-de-sac, click the button on the right side of the dialog box in the **Target** column for the **CDS** assembly. It has three dots on it. This invokes the targets for the cul-de-sac specifically, shown in Figure 9-38.

8. The Surface target shows a tie-out to existing ground on the right side of the assembly, an Alignment target of the Primary Road (where the assembly will be stretched to for horizontal control), and to Layout (4) (where the assembly will be stretched to for vertical

Figure 9-38   Target Mapping dialog box

control). The frequency was increased to 10′ for the cul-de-sac to create a more granular computation for this smaller area.

9. In the plan view of the drawing, you can see that the assembly ties to the primary road centerline and then to the end of the centerline as it spins. Refer to Figure 9-39, where dashed linework shows the intervention of the cul-de-sac over the primary road computations.

10. For the intersection, click the side road; right-click and select **Corridor Properties**. Notice that we begin the corridor at the PC of the curb return. Close the dialog box.

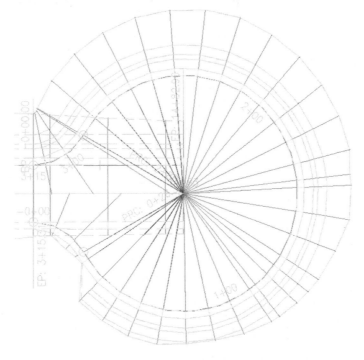

Figure 9-39   Completed cul-de-sac

11. Now click the **Corridor (3)**. Right-click and select **Corridor Properties**. There are two regions: one from station 0+00 along the left EP of the Primary Road to the intersection of the Side Road with the EP of the Primary Road, and another from the intersection to and along the centerline of the Side Road.

12. Hit the button to **Set All Targets**. You will see that Surface targets is the existing ground for tie-out. The alignment targets are the Small EP for the region from 0+00 to 0+27, and the Side Road for station 0+33 to the end stationing for the curb return. The profiles are controlled by tying the target to the profile called **Small EP PGL-2** for the region from 0+00 to 0+27 and to the profile called **Sideroad PGL** for the stationing of 0+33 to the end stationing for the curb return.

13. Repeat this inspection for the right curb return and notice similar targeting there. Inspect the plan view of the intersection to see how the assemblies tie to the targets to complete the design.

You may notice that the roadway continues up to the center of the cul-de-sac. Therefore your next step might be to end the processing of that part of the road at the PC of the EP of the beginning of the cul-de-sac. Explore these possibilities.

TIP

This is certainly not the only way to prepare intersections and cul-de-sacs! Experiment with concepts and realize that everything can be placed into a single corridor, or items can be pieced together. The idea here is that by making changes to alignments, assemblies, or profiles, the entire corridor will update with new computational results.

At this point you have developed basic roads as well as a more sophisticated roadway with subgrades and superelevations. There are many more structures for building assemblies within the software, and now you have a strong foundation to explore them.

Begin to combine the concepts you have learned. For instance, a powerful feature of the software is that after a corridor is developed, very often changes occur to the design. You have already seen the ripple-through effect that occurs when modifications are made to the various object components. If the existing ground surface is modified, that change ripples through the corridor and re-develops the corridor. If the profile is changed, it ripples through the design and affects the sections. Take some time to try out these features similar to what has been accomplished in previous chapters.

NEW CORRIDOR INTERSECTION CAPABILITIES

This is the main new feature of note (in our opinion) in the 2010 release of Civil 3D. Before this function was introduced, each roadway corridor was independent of the others. Although the corridors could have multiple baselines, it was impossible to create corridors that crossed each other as the streets would in three-way and four-way intersections.

Earlier in this chapter, we had an exercise on designing intersections. This was the method we were forced to use prior to Civil 3D 2010. Keep this example; it may still come in handy because you may still need to custom craft some corridors together using this technique.

For most corridors and intersections, however, we can use the new **CreateIntersection** wizard. This is an easy-to-use set of dialogs that walk you through the parameter setup for automatically designing these difficult 3D solutions. Intersections are a new object type in the software and can be seen in the Prospector as an intersection icon.

To invoke this routine you can type **Createintersection** or use a ribbon by selecting **Home** tab **>> Create Design** panel **>> Intersection**. If you follow the steps in the dialog, you will be able to create intersections in 3D more rapidly than ever.

In our exercise on how this function works, you will open a drawing already prepared for performing an intersection design. This simply means that two corridors have already been built. They intersect at a "T" or three-way confluence. The software can also handle four-way confluences, but this example will get the concept across.

Exercise 9-19: Creating an Intersection

To access student data files, go to www.pearsondesigncentral.com.

1. Open Chapter-9-Intersection.dwg. Type in V for View and select the view called Intersection to navigate to the corridors in question.
2. Type **Createintersection** at the command prompt. You can also use the ribbon by selecting the **Home** tab, **Create Design Panel**, and **Intersection**.
3. The prompt asks for the intersection. Select the intersection of the centerlines of the two corridors. Note that the intersect snap should be on already; if it isn't, turn it on. (Just to be sure you are at the correct location; the intersection X,Y coordinate is at 15941.6547, 18335.6246. Don't type the value; we are simply providing this value so you can be sure you are at the correct location.)
4. The prompt responds with `Select main road alignment <or press enter key to select from list>:` Hit **<Enter>**
5. When the Select alignment dialog displays, choose the **Horizontal Road** and hit **<Enter>**.
6. The **Create Intersection** dialog then comes up. See Figure 9-40. The intersection name will default; use the Standard intersection marker style, leave the layer at 0 for now, and use the Standard intersection label style, and the intersection corridor type will be primary road crown maintained. Hit **<Next>**.

Figure 9-40

7. The next screen within the wizard displays. See Figure 9-41. Click the button for **Offset Parameters** and Figure 9-42 displays. Inspect the values in the fields to observe that the primary road will be 15′ by default to the left and right of the main alignment. Change this to **12′**. Note the secondary road parameters and change these to **12′** too. Hit **<OK>**.

Figure 9-41

TIP   Civil 3D 2010 supports intersections with up to four quadrants. This is sufficient for three-way and four-way intersections.

8. Now click the **Intersection Curb Return Parameters** and that dialog will display as shown in Figure 9-43. Note that there is a drop-down menu for the **Intersection** quadrant at the top of the dialog. The parameters for each quadrant can be controlled individually if needed. Click in the **Curb Return Type** drop-down and note that it supports three types of returns: chamfer, circular, and 3-centered arcs. Leave it on circular. Note that if you click the **Widen turn lane for incoming road** toggle, a new set of parameters shows up in the dialog. These would be used to set the widening criteria. Turn off the **Widen turn lane for incoming road** toggle, accept the default values, and hit **<OK>**.

9. Staying within the **Create Intersection** dialog, click on the button for **Offset Profile Parameters**. This feature allows the user to create profiles to guide the **Edge of Pavement** or

Figure 9-42

Figure 9-43

compute it based on the cross slope of the roadway. Again, we will use the defaults shown in Figure 9-44 and hit **<OK>**.

10. Again, staying within the **Create Intersection** dialog, click on the button for **Curb Return Profile Parameters** and the dialog in Figure 9-45 displays. Note how the **Regions** can be controlled separately. Following your inspection of the values, hit **<OK>**.

11. Hit **Next** in the **Create Intersection** dialog and Figure 9-46 shows. We will take the default of **Create New Corridor** in the upper left of the dialog and we will daylight to the **Corridor (1) Surface** in the upper right corner.

12. In the middle of the dialog is a screen with several options. The following graphics provide an idea of the options for connecting the two roadways together. Inspect your options by reviewing the figures shown here.

   • Curb Return Fillets—Figure 9-47

   • Primary Road Full Section—Figure 9-48

   • Primary Road Part Section—Daylight Left—Figure 9-49

   • Primary Road Part Section—Daylight Right—Figure 9-50

   • Secondary Road Full Section—Figure 9-51

   • Secondary Road Half Section—Daylight Left—Figure 9-52

   • Secondary Road Half Section—Daylight Right—Figure 9-53

13. Following your observations of the **Corridor Region Section Types**, we will leave the defaults as they are; in other words, we will use **Assembly (1)**. Hit the **Create Intersection** button.

14. Upon completion notice the resulting intersection as shown in Figure 9-54. Note that this was created as a new corridor and can be viewed under **Corridors** in the **Prospector**.

Figure 9-44

Figure 9-45

Figure 9-46

Figure 9-47

Figure 9-48

Figure 9-49

Figure 9-50

Figure 9-51

Figure 9-52

Figure 9-53

Figure 9-54

Exercise 9-20: Creating an Intersection as Part of an Existing Corridor

1. Open Chapter-9-Intersection.dwg. Type in **V** for View and select the view called Intersection to navigate to the corridors in question.

2. Type **Createintersection** at the command prompt. You can also use the ribbon by selecting the **Home** tab, **Create Design Panel, Intersection**.

3. The prompt asks for the intersection; select the intersection of the centerlines of the two corridors. Note that the intersect snap should be on already; if it isn't, turn it on. (Just to be sure you are at the correct location; the intersection X,Y coordinate is at 15941.6547, 18335.6246. Don't type the value; we are simply providing this value so you can be sure you are at the correct location.)

4. The prompt responds with: `Select main road alignment <or press enter key to select from list>:` Hit **<Enter>**

5. When the **Select alignment** dialog displays, choose the **Horizontal Road** and hit **<Enter>**.

6. The **Create Intersection** dialog then comes up. See Figure 9-40. The intersection name will default; use the Standard intersection marker style, leave the layer at **0** for now, use the **Standard** intersection label style, and the intersection corridor type will be primary road crown maintained. Hit **<Next>**.

7. The next screen within the wizard displays. See Figure 9-41. Click the button for **Offset Parameters** and the dialog displays. Inspect the values in the fields to observe that the primary road will be 15′ by default to the left and right of the main alignment. Change these values to **12′** for the primary and secondary roads as shown in Figure 9-42. Hit **<OK>**.

To access student data files, go to www.pearsondesigncentral.com.

TIP Civil 3D 2010 supports intersections with up to four quadrants. This is sufficient for three-way and four-way intersections.

8. Now click the **Intersection Curb Return Parameters** and that dialog will display as shown in Figure 9-43. Note that there is a drop-down menu for the **Intersection** quadrant at the top of the dialog. The parameters for each quadrant can be controlled individually if needed. Click in the **Curb Return Type** drop-down and note that it supports three types of returns: chamfer, circular, and 3-centered arcs. Leave it on circular. Note that if you click the **Widen**

turn lane for incoming road toggle, a new set of parameters shows up in the dialog. These would be used to set the widening criteria. Turn off the **Widen turn lane for incoming road** toggle, accept the default values, and hit **<OK>**.

9. Staying within the **Create Intersection** dialog, click on the button for **Offset Profile Parameters**. This feature allows the user to create profiles to guide the Edge of Pavement or compute it based on the cross slope of the roadway. Again, we will use the defaults shown in Figure 9-44 and hit **<OK>**.

10. Again, staying within the **Create Intersection** dialog, click on the button for **Curb Return Profile Parameters** and the dialog in Figure 9-45 displays. Note how the **Regions** can be controlled separately. Following your inspection of the values, hit **<OK>**.

11. Hit **Next** in the **Create Intersection** dialog and Figure 9-55 shows. Change the default from **Create New Corridor** in the upper left of the dialog to **Add to Existing Corridor** and select the **Horizontal Road Corridor**. We will daylight to the **Surface (1)** in the upper right corner.

12. Hit the **Create Intersection** button.

13. Upon completion notice the resulting intersection. Note that this was created as part of the **Horizontal Road** corridor and can be viewed under **Corridors** in the **Prospector**.

Note that chapter-9-intersection-complete.dwg and chapter-9-intersection-ex-corridor-complete.dwg are the completed versions for this exercise.

Figure 9-55

Chapter Summary

Civil 3D offers state-of-the-art capabilities for developing roadways. This chapter looked at corridor design, with algorithms for superelevations to ensure motorist safety. In corridor design, the proposed template for the roadway or corridor is completed. The chapter also covered intersection and cul-de-sac design.

Chapter Test Questions

Multiple Choice

1. According to the laws of mechanics, when a vehicle travels on a horizontal curve:

   a. It is forced outward by centrifugal force
   b. It is forced inward by centrifugal force
   c. It is unaffected
   d. None of the above

2. Engineers use which method(s) to counteract centrifugal forces that are trying to send the car off the road on curves?

   a. Superelevation where the pavement lanes are tilted
   b. Vertical curves where the pavement is curved in crests and sags

c. Tapers and widenings of pavement

d. None of the above

3. The rate of superelevation varies:

a. Based on the vertical curves in the profile

b. Based on the radius of the horizontal curve

c. Based on the tangent lengths of the alignment

d. Based on the centrifugal forces involved

4. Variables and terms for superelevations include:

a. e, e_{max}, R, V

b. R, K, L

c. PVC, PRC, PI

d. All of the above

5. A maximum superelevation (SE) is required:

a. When the radius (R) is a minimum

b. When the radius (R) is a maximum

c. In all cases

d. Never

6. At a reverse curve, the roadway section is often:

a. At e_{max} because the roadways are fluctuating the most at that point

b. Flat at the PRC as the superelevation in one direction transitions to the other direction

c. In a tangent; therefore, there is no need to address it

d. None of the above

7. The Tangent runout defines:

a. The length of highway needed to bring a normal crown section to a section where the outside lane has a zero percent slope instead of normal crown

b. The distance needed to bring a section from flat to fully superelevated, or vice versa

c. The length of vertical curve needed to negotiate the arc

d. All of the above

8. Using the Virginia DOT superelevation chart in Figure 9-6, what superelevation rate would be appropriate for a 2500' radius curve and a design speed of 60 mph?

a. 5%

b. 6%

c. 6.5%

d. 5.5%

9. Civil 3D provides subassemblies for which of the following?

a. Tunnels

b. Lanes, curbs, guardrails, and shoulders

c. Bridge trusses and cable stayed bridges

d. All of the above

10. Corridors can be checked for quality assurance using the following methods:

a. **3DOrbit**

b. View/Edit Sections

c. Surface Styles

d. All of the above

True or False

1. True or False: Horizontal alignments, profiles, and subassemblies are used to build corridors.

2. True or False: Assemblies are created by drawing polylines to represent the proposed roadway conditions.

3. True or False: Centrifugal forces act on the vehicle as it negotiates through horizontal curves.

4. True or False: Superelevated roadway sections are always used when the roadway goes through turns.

5. True or False: Superelevations are used to counter the centrifugal forces acting on vehicles as they go in and out of curves on roadways.

6. True or False: The *AASHTO Green Book* is a good reference for highway design.

7. True or False: e_{max} is the maximum to which a road can be superelevated before the car will leave the pavement on an arc.

8. True or False: Two components used in superelevating a roadway are runout and runoff.

9. True or False: Subassemblies are the primitive components of assemblies, and they instruct the software in how to handle lanes, curbs, guardrails or shoulders, related side sloping, and tie-out.

10. True or False: Civil 3D provides many subassemblies to begin with, and you access them from **Tool Palettes**.

CHAPTER EXERCISES

1. Describe the process that a superelevated roadway goes through as it moves from normal crown to a fully superelevated section.

2. If a roadway has a −2.08% cross slope, how many feet will it take to superelevate to flat or 0% if it has a superelevation rate of 6%?

3. If a roadway has a −2.08% cross slope, how many feet will it take to superelevate to a fully a superelevated roadway if it has a superelevation rate of 5%?

4. If a roadway is fully superelevated to 4% and needs to go back to a normal crown of −2.08%, how many feet will it take to reduce its superelevation to a crowned section roadway if it has a superelevation rate of 4%?

5. Using the Virginia DOT superelevation chart shown in Figure 9-6, what superelevation rate would be needed to counteract a curve radius of 5000′ and a speed of 65 mph?

6. Using the Virginia DOT superelevation chart shown in Figure 9-6, what curve radius would be appropriate for a superelevation rate of 3.0% and a design speed of 40 mph?

7. Using the Virginia DOT superelevation chart shown in Figure 9-6, what superelevation rate would be appropriate for a 3500′ radius curve and a design speed of 55 mph?

8. Using the Virginia DOT superelevation chart shown in Figure 9-6, what design speed would be allowable for a superelevation rate of 5% and a curve radius of 2800′?

Chapter Objectives

- Understand the grading capabilities of Civil 3D.
- Understand feature lines and gradings.
- Understand earthworks theories and applications using Civil 3D.

INTRODUCTION

This chapter discusses Civil 3D grading capabilities pertinent to site grading and subdivision design. This is often the next logical step in the design process. Once the roadway is developed, the site can be accessed, and the 3D layout of the site can be developed. The roadway usually plays a major part in the site design because the site drainage is often dictated or influenced by the roadway around it.

REVIEW OF FUNCTIONS AND FEATURES TO BE USED

It is important for you to understand some of the grading capabilities of Civil 3D. These tools can also create object-oriented entities that can perform powerful design functions that are interactive and react to the conditions about them. A large percentage of an engineering project involves grading and, for many reasons, a chief concern is drainage. Other concerns are landscaping, aesthetics, security, and safety. These functions use elevations, slopes, and grades and tie out to the natural ground conditions.

This chapter provides instruction in the functions for grading and includes feature lines, breaklines, and grading objects.

In Chapter 2 you went through the design of a basic commercial site. The discussion here covers the commands that allow you to design almost any type of site from subdivisions to commercial to landfill and retention ponds. Grading objects and feature lines are discussed in detail.

VIRTUAL (3D) SITE DESIGN™

Methods of creating proposed topographic grading data include Developing Zones of Slope Influence, Contour digitizing, Developing 3D breaklines, and Developing 3D spot shots. 3D points should be used in these designs, not so much for their ability to influence the TIN, but rather as "thinking points." Thinking points are set to locate critical locations in 3D. If you are wondering whether you can establish a drain inlet 200 feet away if you slope the ground at a −2% grade, you may set a thinking point at that location using those exact criteria. Once you see the elevation of the point, you can decide whether to use those criteria. If you do use them, you then have a 3D location from which you can traverse to other locations on the site. If you decide not to use them, you can easily erase them and try an alternative criteria set.

A Zone of Influence is a plane or group of planar objects that are set by the designer in 3D using elevations, slopes, or grades. The intent is to create a basic, fundamental base surface on which the designer would add more surface objects as the site design matures.

Figure 10-1 shows a site developed 100% in three dimensions. This site contains an underground detention pond, which sets some of the minimum proposed elevations due to hydraulic requirements. An existing roadway sets the criteria for the southern edge of the site. An adjacent property is being built to the north of the site, and its proposed elevations are considered as the existing elevations to which to tie in. The plan is to tie in to existing ground on the east and the west sides of the site. The black linework shows the 3D breaklines, and the markers shown indicate the spot elevations that "tied out" the site.

Figure 10-1   Site developed in three dimensions

Figure 10-2 shows the resulting computer-generated contours for the site.

Figure 10-2   Resulting computer-generated contours for the site

Figure 10-3 shows a cross section through the site with impeccable detail. Notice the section cut through the truck loading dock, the building finish floor, and the parking lot islands.

Figure 10-3   A cross section through the site

Notice the detail in the truck loading dock and the drainage divides in the parking lot in Figure 10-4. The section below is cut through the building, the dock, the drive lane, and the curb.

Figure 10-4   A section showing a truck loading dock

Note the renderings of the site in 3D in Figures 10-5 and 10-6. Each island, drainage divide in the parking lot, and loading dock comes to life.

Figure 10-5   Renderings of the site—1

Figure 10-6   Renderings of the site—2

Requirements for quality control for this project were very high due to the visibility of the site. Drainage could not go into the street and had to be self-contained and directed into the underground storage ponds beneath the site. Notice the bird's-eye view and rendered depiction of the site. The curbs, gutters, and loading docks are all evident (see Figure 10-6).

Earthworks for the project were also accomplished using these data. Figure 10-7 shows a subdivision developed in 3D. The profile for the site had a very high level of terrain activity with roadway grades of up to 10%. Some of the residential houses had 50′ of drop from the front of the lot to the back of the lot. Preliminary and final grading design were performed for this subdivision. The plan view of a piece of the subdivision is shown here.

Figure 10-7   A subdivision developed in 3D

Three-dimensional houses were developed for the housing styles to be used. Examples of the houses are shown in Figure 10-8. The house on the left has no walkout basement, has a garage on the left side of the house, and can be used on lots that are fairly flat. The house on the right does have a walkout basement and a garage on the right side of the house. This can be used on lots that have a good fall toward the back of the house. Once the houses were situated, the task of designing the driveways had to be done.

Figure 10-8   A 3D house template

This was a major component of the project because earthworks had a major impact on cost. Figure 10-8 shows the two houses in plan view: one with a walkout basement, one without. The bottom of Figure 10-8 shows the elevation view of a house template. With the road and houses laid out in 3D, it was fairly easy to design the driveways. See Figure 10-9.

Figure 10-10 shows a section of the design completed. The houses float in 3D, and the point data represent the tie-out to the existing ground. It should be noted here that the tie-out can be seen immediately when performed. The benefit here is that if the tie-out projects into the adjacent property, the designer can adjust the side slopes at that point to rectify it.

Figure 10-9 Subdivision driveways

Figure 10-10 A section of the design

The graphics in Figures 10-11 through 10-15 show other sites that are readily developed as 3D models. This methodology plays very strongly into the rapidly growing 3D/GPS Machine Control market. This is a GPS-based technology by which the earthmoving equipment is located on the

Figure 10-11 A TIN model of a commercial site

Figure 10-12   A rendered view of the commercial site

Figure 10-13   A TIN model of an office building site

Figure 10-14   A rendered view of an office building site

Figure 10-15 A rendered view of a "big box" site

existing ground based on GPS. An on-board computer stores the Digital Terrain Model for the proposed surface(s), which may include subgrade surfaces. Robotics handle the hydraulic movement of the earthmoving blade. This technology requires an accurate 3D model from which to operate. If engineering firms do not learn to work in 3D, they will lose more and more work to those that do work in 3D. Civil 3D provides add-on software that can convert the Civil 3D data into a formatted data conducive for use by Topcon, Trimble, and Leica equipment. They are Carlson Connect, which addresses Topcon; Trimble Link from Trimble; and Leica X-Change.

The concept of engineers designing their sites in three dimensions is called Virtual Site Design, which is designing a site in the computer using slopes, grades, and elevations. The contouring, labeling, and analyses should be computer generated from that point on. With the site in 3D, some very visual viewpoints can be established to verify quality control, and all editing of the surface would be done to the 3D elements, which consist of breaklines, points, and grading objects.

Once a designer has a surface, one of the quality assurance functions to be performed is earthworks. You need to know how much earth you are moving or cutting or filling. There are several methods for earthworks computations, some of which are explored next.

EARTHWORKS ALGORITHMS

In order to discuss the validity of results from an earthworks computation, you should know which algorithms were used in the processing because the results can vary based on the method selected. Some of the common methods are as follows:

- Section method
- Grid method
- Composite method

Each of these methods has positive and negative aspects. Please review the next set of graphics. The Section method entails computing a cross section through the existing ground and the proposed surface. The area of cut is computed as well as the area of fill for that section. Then, at some interval away, another section is computed, and the area of cut and fill in that section is computed. Then the two areas of cut are averaged together to obtain an average end area of cut. Similarly, the two areas of fill are averaged together to obtain an average end area of fill. These numbers yield a square footage of material. Then the average cut is multiplied over the interval distance yielding the cubic footage of material between the two sections. Divide that by a factor of 27 to obtain the number of cubic yards. Repeat this for each section in the project.

TIP Divide by 27 to obtain cubic yards from cubic feet because 1 cubic yard is 3′ × 3′ × 3′.

Example 10-1: The Section Method Done by Hand

In this example problem computed by hand, refer to Figure 10-16. Here is a simple situation in which you have a road section with two 12′ lanes and 6′ of 3:1 embankment.

Figure 10-16   A roadway section in fill

In order to compute this earthwork, you do not need to compute the amount of cut because there is none; this entire section is in fill. Therefore, the fill area is computed using a series of triangle and rectangular area formulas as follows:

Fill in embankment:

(6′ × 2′)/2 = 6 s.f.; there are two embankment areas, so the fill in the embankment is 12 s.f.

Fill under the pavement is computed using a rectangular area formula for the 2′ of fill and then a triangular area formula for the fill above the 2′ but under the grade of the road.

12′ × 2′ = 24 s.f.; there are two lanes, so 24 s.f. × 2 = 48 s.f.
Then: 12′ × .5′ = 6 s.f.; there are two lanes, so 6 s.f. × 2 = 12 s.f.
Summing, we have 48 s.f. + 12 s.f. + 12 s.f. = 72 s.f. of material.

For the second section, which was cut 50′ away from the first, please refer to Figure 10-17. This section has both cut and fill. Let us compute the fill first.

Figure 10-17   A roadway section in cut and fill

Fill in embankment:

(3′ × 1′)/2 = 1.5 s.f.; there are two embankment areas, so the fill in the embankment is 3 s.f.

Fill under the pavement is computed using a rectangular area formula for the 1′ of fill and then a triangular area formula for the fill above the 1′ but under the grade of the road.

12′ × 1′ = 12 s.f.; there are two lanes, so 12 s.f. × 2 = 24 s.f.
Then: 12′ × .5′ = 6 s.f.; there are two lanes, so 6 s.f. × 2 = 12 s.f.
Summing, we have 24 s.f. + 12 s.f. + 3 s.f. = 39 s.f. of material.

Now compute the amount of cut.
Cut in embankment:

(3′ × 1′)/2 = 1.5 s.f.; there are two embankment areas, so the fill in the embankment is 3 s.f.

Cut under the pavement is computed using a rectangular area formula as well.

12′ × 1′ = 12 s.f.; there are two lanes, so 12 s.f. × 2 = 24 s.f.
Summing, we have 24 s.f. + 3 s.f. = 27 s.f. of cut for the second section.

Computing the average fill between the two sections we have

39 s.f. + 72 s.f. = 111/2 = 55.5 s.f.

Computing the average cut between the two sections we have
0 s.f. + 27 s.f. = 27/2 = 13.5 s.f.
The volume of fill between section 1 and section 2 is 72 s.f. × 50′ = 3600 s.f./27
    = 133 c.y.
The volume of cut between section 1 and section 2 is 27 s.f. × 50′ = 1350 s.f./27
    = 50 c.y.

Therefore, a net fill of 83 c.y. exists between the two sections.

Example 10-2: The Grid Method Done by Hand

The next type of earthworks is the Grid method. In this case, a grid is identified and laid across the site. The grids are uniform, and the elevations of the proposed surface and the existing surface are computed for each corner of each grid. The difference between the proposed and existing elevations are computed for each corner. The four corners of each grid are averaged and multiplied by the area of the grid to obtain the cubic feet of material. This is then divided by 27 to obtain c.y. This example contains 4 grids, each 50′ × 50′; see Figure 10-18.

Figure 10-18   The Grid method

Beginning with the grid in the upper left, compute as follows:

−1 + −5 + −2 + −2 = −10′/4 corners = −2.5′ of average cut.
With a grid area of 2500 s.f., that grid contains 2500 × 2.5′
    = 6250 c.f. of cut. Divided by 27 yields 231.5 c.y. of cut.

The grid in the upper right corner computes as follows:

−5 + 0 + −2 + 0 = −7′/4 = −1.75′ of cut. There is also some fill in this grid of
    0 + 1 + 0 + 1 = 2′/4 = .5′ fill.

Therefore, the cut for the grid is $2500 \times 1.75 = 4375$ s.f., divided by 27 = 162.0 c.y. of cut. The fill for the grid is $2500 \times .5$
= 1250 s.f. divided by 27 = 46.3 c.y. of fill. The net is 162 − 46.3
= 115.7 net cut.

The lower left grid computes as follows:

$-2 + -2 + -1.5 + -3 = -8.5/4 = -2.125'$ net cut. With a grid area of 2500 s.f., that grid contains $2500 \times 2.125' = 5312.5$ c.f. of cut. Divided by 27 yields 196.8 c.y. of cut.

The grid in the lower right corner computes as follows:

$-2 + 0 + -3 + 0 = -5'/4 = -1.25'$ of cut. There is also some fill in this grid of
$0 + 1 + 0 + 1.5 = 2.5'/4 = .625'$ fill.
Therefore, the cut for the grid is 2500×1.25
= 3125 s.f., divided by 27 = 115.7 c.y. of cut. The fill for the grid is $2500 \times .625$
= 1562.5 s.f. divided by 27 = 57.8 c.y. of fill.
The net is 115.7 − 57.8 = 57.9 net cut.

The earthworks for the site then is:

Cut = 231.5 + 162 + 196.8 + 115.7 = 706.0 c.y.
Fill = 0 + 46.3 + 0 + 57.8 = 104.1 c.y.
The net is 601.9 c.y. of cut.

The last method is the Composite (in Land Desktop terminology) or Prismoidal method. Civil 3D uses this method for its site-based earthworks, and it is a TIN comparison-based method. It is more math intensive than the others, but Civil 3D can rapidly perform it. It produces a more accurate volume than the Average End Area or the Grid method.

Pros and Cons of Earthworks Algorithms

Section Method

- Pro: It is a traditional method, is understood by all, and produces good results.
- Con: Accuracy varies according to interval and can be enhanced by running the section computations twice, where the second run is perpendicular to the first run.

Grid Method

- Pro: It is also a traditional method, is understood by all, and produces good results.
- Con: Interpolation occurs. Hence, some loss of accuracy exists; the perimeter can be lost if the grid falls off the surface; highs and lows inside of each grid can be lost; and accuracy varies according to grid size.

Composite Method

- Pro: It is the best theoretical method, uses all surface data, and no interpolation is involved.
- Con: It seems to be sensitive to vertical faces (which you should not have anyway).

Now that grading capabilities have been discussed, let us explore some of Civil 3D's functions. The **Grading** pull-down menu (Figure 10-19) has several commands that are critical to 3D site design. These are described next.

Create Grading... invokes the toolbar for performing grading functions.

Create Grading Infill inserts a grading face with no criteria inside an area bounded by feature lines or lot lines.

Draw Feature Line allows for the creation of feature lines used in many grading functions. The options for creating them include slope, grade, and elevational data combined with horizontal distances.

Create Feature Lines from Objects allows selecting existing AutoCAD objects and converting them to feature lines.

Create Feature Lines from Alignment creates a feature line from the geometry of an alignment and the elevations of a specified profile.

Figure 10-19   The Grading pull-down menu

Figure 10-20   The Edit Grading submenu

Quick Profile... draws a temporary profile based on linework selected and surfaces chosen. These profiles are deleted on saving and are used for quality assurance/control.

Edit Grading (see Figure 10-20) allows for a submenu that contains the following routines:

- **Grading Editor...** allows for editing grading objects in a **Panorama**.
- **Edit Grading** allows for editing the grading parameters for objects such as the **Stepped Offset** command.
- **Delete Grading** deletes a selected grading object.
- **Change Group** allows for changing the grading group that an object resides in.

Edit Feature Line Elevations (see Figure 10-21) submenu has several commands that are critical to 3D site design. These commands include:

- **Elevation Editor...** is a dialog-based command that allows for making changes to the elevations of objects.

Figure 10-21   The Edit Feature Line Elevations submenu

- **Quick Elevation Edit** allows for quick, on-the-fly alterations to the slopes/grades of feature lines.
- **Edit Elevations** is a prompt–based command that allows for making changes to the elevations of objects.
- **Set Grade/Slope between Points** is a command prompt system for altering the grades and elevations of feature lines at user-selected locations.
- **Insert/Delete Elevation Point** inserts/deletes vertices. These points do not alter the horizontal geometry of the object; they affect only the third dimension.
- **Insert High/Low Elevation Point** inserts a point elevation based on the incoming and outgoing user-selected grades.
- **Raise/Lower** raises or lowers an object.
- **Set Elevation by Reference** sets the elevation based on a referenced 3D elevation from another location.
- **Raise/Lower by Reference** raises or lowers an object at a given slope/grade from a specified location.
- **Adjacent Elevations by Reference** specifies the elevations of an object based on a grade, slope, or elevation difference from points on another feature.
- **Grade Extension by Reference** specifies the elevations of an object by extending the grade of a segment on another feature.
- **Elevations from Surface** sets the elevations of feature line vertices based on surface sampling.

Edit Feature Line Geometry (see Figure 10-22)

- **Insert/Delete PI** inserts/deletes vertices. These do affect the geometry of the feature line.
- **Break** breaks a feature line or parcel line.
- **Trim** trims feature lines or parcel lines.
- **Join** joins feature lines similar to AutoCAD's PEDIT.
- **Reverse** reverses the direction of the feature line.

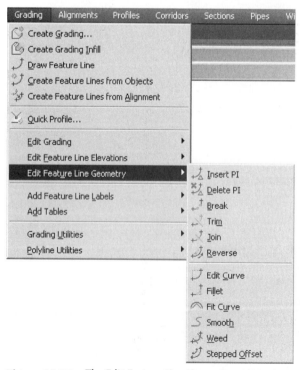

Figure 10-22   The Edit Feature Line Geometry submenu

- **Edit Curve** edits the radius of a feature line arc, parcel line arc, or survey figure arc.
- **Fillet** places a curve at the PI of a feature line.
- **Fit Curve** fits the PI with a curve similar to PEDIT's **FIT** command.
- **Smooth** smooths the PI with a curve similar to PEDIT's **SMOOTH** command.
- **Weed** deletes unneeded vertices.
- **Stepped Offset** offsets the feature line and raises or drops it. Think curb faces or retaining walls here!

Add Feature Line Labels labels slopes on feature lines.

Add Tables allows you to add tables for lines, curves, and segments.

Grading Utilities

- **Grading Volume Tools...** invokes the toolbar to adjust cut/fill volumes for grading groups.
- **Create Detached Surface...** detaches the surface from the grading group so it no longer updates.

Polyline Utilities

- **Convert 2D to 3D Polylines** converts polylines to allow them to be used to set different elevations on each vertex.
- **Convert 3D to 2D Polylines** converts polylines to flatten them.
- **Edit Polyline Elevations** edits elevations at vertices.

The Grading Creation Tools

The **Grading Creation Tools** are described next (see Figure 10-23).

Figure 10-23   The Grading Creation Tools toolbar

 Set the **Grading Group**.

Sets the **Target Surface**.

Sets the **Grading Layers**.

 Sets the **Criteria Set**.

 Develops **Grading** with one of five commands:

- **Create Grading** creates a grading object based on the criteria.
- **Copy Create Grading** copies the criteria and style from an existing grading and applies it to a grading you wish to create.
- **Create Transition** allows for transitions around objects.
- **Create Infill** connects the interior of grading objects such as on the top of a berm of a detention pond where one grading develops the inside of the pond and the other grading develops the outside of the pond.

 Edit Grading allows for absorbing elevations from the surface and some management commands.

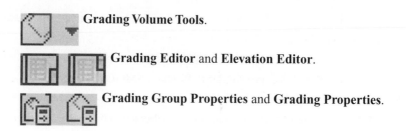

Grading Volume Tools.

Grading Editor and **Elevation Editor**.

Grading Group Properties and **Grading Properties**.

Exercise 10-1: Laying Out a Basic Parking Lot in 3D

Now explore Civil 3D and run through some procedures using the grading objects.

To access student data files, go to www.pearsondesigncentral.com.

1. Open Chapter-10-a.dwg.
2. Type **V** for **View**, select the **Plan** view, hit **Set Current**, then hit **OK** and you see some existing ground contours.
3. There is a white object on the **C-Site-Grad-3D** layer. Use this as the construction limits for this site.
4. Let us set it to the existing ground elevation and drape it on the existing ground in order to guarantee that no grading occurs outside these limits.
5. From the **Grading** pull-down menu, select the command **Create Feature Lines from Objects**. Choose the white polyline object on the **C-Site-Grad-3D** layer, accept the defaults in the **Create Feature Lines** dialog box, hit **OK**, and one feature line is added to **Site 1**. Turn on the **C-Topo-Grad-Flin** layer to see it.
6. From the **Grading** pull-down menu, choose the **Edit Feature Line Elevations** command and then choose **Elevations from Surface**.
7. Select the **Existing Ground** surface.
8. Turn on the toggle to insert intermediate grade break points. Hit **OK**.
9. Select the feature line and hit **<Enter>**. Notice it processes and places small markers where it has inserted intermediate breaks.
10. This object is now "draped" onto the existing ground data with a 3D vertex at each TIN crossing. Click on the feature line, and notice all the vertices that now have the elevations of the existing ground embedded into them.
11. Turn on the layer called **C-Site-Grad-Text** for the design parameters for this site.
12. These parameters indicate a Finished and Basement floor elevation for the building in the upper right of the site and a 4' sidewalk with a 2% cross slope draining toward the parking lot. It has a 6" high curb on it. The parking lot drains to the Southwest at −2%.

Next you will create the 3D objects that meet these specifications.

13. **Zoom** into the **cyan** building polylines and notice two lines: one representing the outside building wall and the inside linework representing the building's basement. From the **Grading** pull-down menu, select **Create Feature Lines from Objects**. `Select lines, arcs, polylines or 3d polylines to convert to feature lines or [Xref]:` Select the two **cyan** building polylines and hit **<Enter>**.
14. Accept the defaults in the **Create Feature Lines** dialog box, and hit **OK**.
15. Choose **Edit Feature Line Elevations >> Elevation Editor** from the **Grading** pull-down menu.
16. When asked, select the outside cyan polyline representing the building pad. This is the outermost **cyan** linework.
17. In the **Panorama** that displays, set the elevations to **362.0** for all vertices. Click the green checkmark.
18. Repeat the command and select the inside cyan polyline representing the building basement.
19. Set the elevations to **353.0** for all vertices.
20. Draw a **3D** polyline along the west and southern edge of the building by snapping to the edge of the finished floor of the building. This inherits the elevations of the finished floor.
21. From the **Grading** pull-down menu, select **Edit Feature Line Geometry >> Stepped Offset**. The following prompts and responses should occur:

```
Specify offset distance or [Through/Layer] : 4
Select an object to offset:
Specify side to offset or [Multiple] : Pick a point outside the building.
Specify elevation difference or [Grade/Slope/Elevation/Variable]
<0.000>: g
Specify grade or [Slope/Elevation/Difference/Variable] <0.000>: −2
```

TIP You can use the **<Shift>** **<Space>** keys to select objects on top of other objects if needed.

22. Hit **<Enter>** to terminate. This object represents the top, face of curb.
23. Repeat this command, and the following prompts and responses should occur.

```
Specify offset distance or [Through/Layer] <4.0000>: .1
Select an object to offset: Select the top, face curb.
Specify side to offset or [Multiple] : Pick a point outside the building.
Specify grade or [Slope/Elevation/Difference] <−2.000>: d
Specify elevation difference or [Grade/Slope/Elevation/Variable]
<−0.080>: −.5
```

24. `Select an object to offset:` Hit **<Enter>** to terminate. This represents the flowline of the curb.

The building and the sidewalk are established. Let us work on the parking lot now.

25. Draw a pline that represents the drainage divide in the parking lot from the edge of sidewalk at the northwest corner of the building diagonally to the southwest corner of the parking lot.
26. Then use **Grading >> Draw Feature Line** to draw a feature line from the flowline of the curb at a **−2%** grade to the lower left corner of the parking lot designated by the **red** polyline. Accept the defaults in the dialog box when it displays. Refer to Figure 10-24 for the location of the swale. Then the following prompts and responses should occur: Specify start point: Snap to the flowline of the curb near the northwest corner of the building. This is shown in Figure 10-25. It should have an elevation of 361.40.

```
Specify elevation or [Surface] <361.420>: <Enter>
Specify the next point or [Arc] : Distance 426.778', Grade −84.597,
Slope −1.182:1, Elevation 0.000'.
```

Figure 10-24   Parking lot swale

Snap to the lower left corner of the red polyline in the southwest corner of the parking lot.

```
Specify  grade  or  [SLope/Elevation/Difference/SUrface/Transition]
<0.000>: −2
```

```
Specify the next point or [Arc/Length/Undo] : <Enter>.
```

This elevation should be 352.51 when you are finished.

27. Next draw a pline by snapping to the flowline of the edge of sidewalk, which is the same spot that Figure 10-25 indicates. Then snap to the upper left corner of the **red** polyline depicting the parking lot. Snap to the end of the swale drawn at −2% to the lower left corner of the parking lot. This will draw a polyline from the curb flowline near the northwest corner of the building around the north and west perimeter of the parking lot to the southwest corner of the parking lot.

Figure 10-25 Snap location

28. From the **Grading** pull-down menu, select the command **Create Feature Lines from Objects**. Choose the **white** polyline object that you just drew around the north and west side of the parking lot, accept the defaults in the **Create Feature Lines** dialog box, hit **OK**, and one feature line is added to **Site 1**.

29. Choose **Edit Feature Line Elevations >> Elevation Editor...** from the **Grading** pull-down menu. Select the new feature line you just converted. When the **Panorama** displays, set the elevation for the second vertex to **356.387**. The three elevations for the vertices should then be **361.043**, **356.387**, and **352.508,** respectively. Close the **Panorama**. This will be the polyline shown in Figure 10-26.

Now set the perimeter of the east and southern edge of the parking lot.

Use the same command sequence to establish both grade and elevation along this object. From the flowline of the sidewalk beginning at the southeastern edge of the building, design a −1% grade drop to the southeastern corner of the parking lot, and then tie into the drainage divide in the southwest corner of the parking lot at an elevation of 352.8861.

30. Draw a pline from the flowline of the sidewalk beginning at the southeastern edge of the building to the southeastern corner of the parking lot, and then end it at the drainage divide at the southwestern corner of the parking lot. Refer to Figure 10-27 for the location of this polyline.

31. From the **Grading** pull-down menu, select the command **Create Feature Lines from Objects.** Choose the polyline object that you just drew around the east and south side of the parking lot, accept the defaults in the **Create Feature Lines** dialog box, hit **OK**, and one feature line is added to **Site 1**.

Figure 10-26 Polyline on the north and west perimeter

Figure 10-27 Location of south and east perimeter of parking lot

32. Choose **Edit Feature Line Elevations >> Elevation Editor** from the **Grading** pull-down menu. Select the new feature line you just converted. When the **Panorama** displays, set the grade for the first vertex to **−1.0%**. The three elevations for the vertices should then be **361.043**, **360.596**, and **352.508**, respectively. Close the **Panorama**. Save your file.

   This object now represents the southern edge of the parking lot and is designed to achieve a −1% drop from the sidewalk to the southeastern corner and tie into the diagonal divide at the southwest corner.

33. Open Chapter-10-b.dwg.
34. Select **Create Grading...** from the **Grading** pull-down menu.
35. The **Grading Creation Tools** toolbar appears.
36. Move from left to right across the toolbar, setting or verifying the settings as you go.
37. Choose the first button on the left to set the **Grading Group** for the next step. A **Create Grading Group** dialog box displays.
38. Accept the default name of **Grading Group <Next Counter>**. Turn **On** the **Automatic Surface Creation**. The **Use the Group Name** toggle should be **On**. The **Surface Style** should be set to **Borders & Contours**. Accept **10.0** for tesselation spacing and **3** degrees for angle. This sets intermediate computations. Turn **Off** the **Volume base surface**. Hit **OK**.
39. When the **Create Surface** dialog box appears, hit **OK** for the defaults.
40. Next click on the second button, set the **Target Surface**, and choose the **Existing ground**.

To access student data files, go to www.pearsondesigncentral.com.

41. Click on the third button to set the **Grading Layers** and accept the default layers.
42. Click on the fourth button to set the **Criteria Set**. Select **Basic Set** as the criteria set to use.
43. In the pop-down window, choose **Surface @ 2-1 Slope**. With the **Details** button enabled (the chevron icon on the right of the toolbar), notice that details for the **Grading Method** and **Slope Projection** are shown in Figure 10-28.

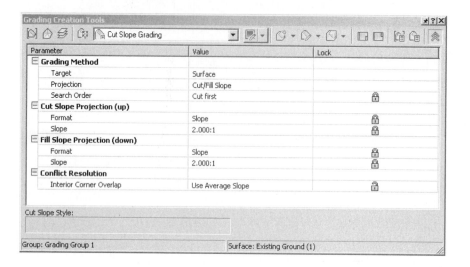

Figure 10-28 The Grading Creation Tools dialog box

44. Next choose the second button to the right of the pop-down window that says **Surface @ 2-1 Slope**. It should default to **Create Grading**.
45. Select the feature: Pick the feature line at the north edge of the parking lot.

    Select the grading side: Pick a point to the outside of the parking lot.

    Apply to entire length? Hit **<Enter>** for **Yes**. Grading appears along the north side of the parking lot.
46. Select the feature: again, assuming that you will repeat this sequence. Pick the feature line along the southern edge of the parking lot.

    Select the grading side: Pick a point to the outside of the parking lot.

    Apply to entire length? Hit **<Enter>** for **Yes**. Grading appears along the south side of the parking lot. Hit **<Enter>** to exit.
47. Pick on a contour and right-click. Select **Edit Surface Style....** In the **Contours** tab, expand the **Contour intervals** item and change the minor and major intervals to **2** and **10**, respectively.

Notice that the grading ties out to existing ground along the north, west, and southern sides. See Figure 10-29.

Now tie the north and eastern sides of the building out to the northeastern corner of the site.

48. Explode the outside cyan building feature line.
49. Use the **BREAK AT POINT** AutoCAD command to place a break on the outside cyan polyline at the northwest corner of the building. Use the same command to place a break on the outside **cyan** polyline at the southeast corner of the building. By doing this, you can project the top and right sides of the building toward the existing ground.
50. Select **Create Grading...** from the **Grading** pull-down menu.
51. The **Grading Creation Tools** toolbar displays.
52. Click on the fourth button to set the **Criteria Set**. Select **Basic** as the criteria set to use.
53. In the pop-down window, choose **Surface @ 2-1 Slope**.
54. Once again, choose the second button to the right of the pop-down window that says **Surface @ 2-1 Slope**. It should default to **Create Grading**.
55. Select the feature: **Zoom** in and pick the outer edge of the building that you just broke. Hit **OK** to the **Create Feature Lines** dialog box that displays.

    Select the grading side: Pick a point well outside of the building.

    Apply to entire length? Type **Y** for **Yes**. Hit **<Enter>** to accept and terminate.

Figure 10-29   The grading tie-outs

56. Grading appears as shown in Figure 10-30, in which the entire perimeter is now tied to existing ground.

Figure 10-30   Resultant grading

57. Let us add in the sidewalk and drainage divide in the parking lot.
58. Look in the **Prospector** under **Surfaces**. Expand the surface called **Grading Group 1**. Expand **Definition**. Right-click on the **Breaklines** item and select **Add....**
59. Hit **OK** to accept all the defaults that come up in the **Add Breaklines** dialog box.
60. When asked to select objects, place a crossing window to include the sidewalk edges, basement, the left and southern edge of the building, and the drainage breakline in the parking lot.
61. If the **Panorama** appears with messages, close it.
62. You see now that the contours reflect the sidewalk and drainage divide. See Figure 10-31.
63. Using **3DOrbit**, rotate the view into a 3D bird's-eye perspective. The Surface style for 3D kicks in, and a 3D triangulation appears automatically.
64. Turn off the layer for the existing ground, **C-Topo-Existing Ground**, and you isolate the proposed parking lot. As discussed in Chapter 9 on corridors, you can select **View >> Visual Styles >> Conceptual** shading and then observe something like Figure 10-32. It shows the basement, the divide, and the sidewalk clearly.

In the next exercise, you will compute earthwork volumes for the site.

Figure 10-31   The contours reflect the sidewalk and drainage divide

Figure 10-32   Gouraud shading

Earthwork volumes, sometimes called takeoffs, are performed on projects in order to estimate the amount of earth being moved. This is important to the engineer in that the design goal is often to produce a "balanced site." This means that the earth that is cut or dug out is then used to lift or fill the site in areas where needed. Balancing means that you have no excess cut or fill material. Consider that a dump truck might have a capacity of 10 c.y., and you can estimate how many truckloads it would take to move excess earth on the site.

Exercise 10-2: A Quick Earthworks Volume

Now you will compute the earthworks for the site.

To access student data files, go to www.pearsondesigncentral.com.

1. Open Chapter-10-c.dwg.
2. Select **Utilities** from the **Surfaces** pull-down menu. Then choose **Volumes....**
3. When the **Panorama** appears, click the first button from the left to create a new volume entry. A row of data displays in the window.
4. Click in the cell for **Base surface** where it says to **<select surface>** and choose **Existing Ground**.
5. Then click in the cell for **Comparison Surface** where it says to **<select surface>** and choose **Grading Group 1**. Click somewhere in the **Panorama** to execute the processing. It should yield almost 12,000 c.y. of material in a net fill condition.

Exercise 10-3: "Popping Up" a Curbed Parking Lot Island

In order to provide another example of the power of the **Grading** tools in Civil 3D, you will now see how to pop a curbed island out of the asphalt paving area. The curb will be 6″ high and have a slight kilter to its face so as to avoid a vertical edge on the face of curb.

1. Open Chapter-10-c.dwg or stay in the drawing from the last exercise.
2. **Zoom** into the parking area to the west of the building. You see some plines representing the flowline of some parking islands.
3. From the **Grading** pull-down menu, select **Create Feature Lines from Objects**. Select the four parking lot islands in the parking lot. Hit **OK** to the **Create Feature Lines** dialog box.
4. From the **Grading** pull-down menu, select **Edit Feature Line Elevations** and then **Elevations From Surface**. When the **Set Elevations from Surface** dialog box displays, select **Grading Group 1** as the surface to compute to. Turn on the toggle to insert intermediate grade breaks. Hit **OK**.
5. `Select object or [Multiple/Partial]` : Pick all four islands one by one, and the software computes additional elevations from the asphalt pavement over and beyond the vertices in the plines. The pline islands are now "draped" onto the parking lot surface.
6. You are now ready to pop the islands up from the surface. From the **Grading** pull-down menu, select **Edit Feature Line Geometry >> Stepped Offset**. The following prompts and responses should occur:

   `Specify offset distance or [Through/Layer] <0.1000>:` **.1**

   `Select an object to offset:` Pick an island.

   `Specify side to offset or [Multiple]` : Pick a point inside the island.

   `Specify elevation difference or [Grade/Slope/Elevation/Variable] <-0.500>:` **.5**

7. Repeat this for each island. Inspect the results when complete and notice that the interior object is 0.5′ higher than the outside object, hence achieving the top of curb.
8. Now you will add the islands into the surface of the parking lot.
9. Look in the **Prospector** under **Surfaces**. Expand the surface called **Grading Group 1**. Expand **Definition**. Right-click on the **Breaklines** item and select **Add....**
10. Hit **OK** to accept all the defaults that come up in the **Add Breaklines** dialog box.
11. When asked to select objects, select the eight objects representing the islands.
12. If the **Panorama** appears with messages, close it. Hit **<Enter>**.
13. You see now the islands and the contours "jump" the curb as expected.
14. See Figure 10-33 for an example of the **3DOrbit** that you can perform.

To access student data files, go to www.pearsondesigncentral.com.

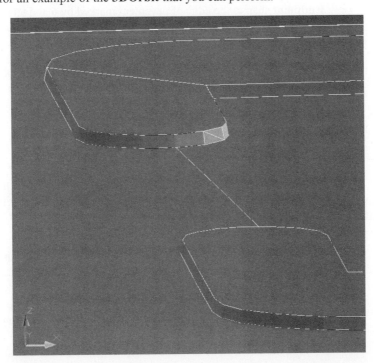

Figure 10-33   Parking lot islands

Exercise 10-4: A Brief Example of Intersection Design

One more example to introduce the gradings to readers is the age-old intersection design.

Intersections are one of the most often asked about design tasks that people want to automate. You open a file that has some edge of pavement in it. The linework is in 3D and can be achieved from the corridor design using the **Corridor >> Utilities >> Create Grading Feature Line from Corridor** command. The linework for each component of the corridor can be imported into AutoCAD. Then, using the **EXPLODE** command, explode the feature lines so that they can be trimmed, extended, or broken as needed to begin developing the desired site features. That is where the exercise begins. You add the intersection returns and illustrate an example of how intelligent feature lines can be. Note: Generalize on this example!

Note that intersections and cul-de-sacs can be graded using the **Corridor** tools as well, but these might be considered high-end skills. The approach in this chapter deals with "hand grading." Intersections have been automated in Civil 3D 2010.

To access student data files, go to www.pearsondesigncentral.com.

1. Open Chapter-10-d.dwg and note that a basic intersection has been developed as described previously. The edge of pavement and centerlines are in 3D. The **red** arcs denote where the returns are supposed to be and they are in 2D.
2. Under the **Grading** pull-down menu, select the **Create Feature Lines from Objects** command.
3. Select the four edges of pavement, identified with numbers 1, 4, 3, and 6, plus the one in the intersection between 3 and 6. Also select the two centerlines on **Layer 0**, and hit **<Enter>**. Hit **OK** for the dialog box that displays.
4. Now draw a polyline by snapping to the edge of pavement at the point marked by a number **1**. Make sure to select the **Endpoint** snap to the white edge of pavement and not the **red** arc. The **white** edge has a 3D elevation. Then type **A** for **arc** and then type **S** for **second point** (of the arc) and **Near** snap to a point on the **red** arc marked with a number **2**. Then **Endpoint** snap to the edge of pavement marked by a number **3** and terminate.
5. Repeat the **Polyline** command and perform this on the right side of the intersection. Snap to the edge of pavement at the point marked by **4**. Make sure to **Endpoint** snap to the **green** edge of pavement and not the **red** arc. Then type **A** for **arc** and then type **S** for **second point** (of the arc) and **Near** snap to a point on the **red** arc marked with a **5**. Then **Endpoint** snap to the edge of pavement marked by **6** and terminate.
6. Under the **Grading** pull-down menu, select the **Create Feature Lines from Objects** command. Select the two polylines that you just drew. Now use the **Grading** pull-down menu, and select **Edit Feature Line Elevations** and then **Edit Elevations** to check the elevations of the two arcs that you converted to feature lines. Notice that Civil 3D recognized that the plines were being connected to feature lines and automatically inherited the elevations at the endpoints.
7. From the **Surfaces** pull-down menu, select **Create Surface....** Provide a **Name** for the surface, call it **Intersection**, and use the **Borders & Contours** style.

This is a revolutionary function in case you did not realize it. This is the first time in AutoCAD history that there can be a 3D arc! Notice that there are no chords to simulate the arc as has been the case in the past using various routines.

8. In the **Prospector**, under **Surface**, expand the intersection surface that was just created. Expand **Definition** and right-click on **Breaklines** Select **Add....** Type **Intersection** in the description for the breaklines when the dialog box appears.
9. Select all the feature lines, including the edge of pavement, the arcs that you created at the intersection, and the centerlines. Do not forget the edge of pavement breakline in the intersection between the arcs.

10. A **Surface** generates showing contours inside the intersection. Use **3DOrbit** to inspect the intersection in 3D.

11. Now, generalize on this concept because if the intersection had a curb and gutter, it could be created just as easily within a minute or two. Refer to Figure 10-34 to see the contours created in the intersection.

Figure 10-34   Contours are created in the intersection

You could take a lot more time performing grading features but would likely need a separate textbook to cover all the situations. In the meantime, explore these commands and find that almost any type of site can be designed in 3D.

> **TIP**   Be aware that you can create your own grading criteria. Look in the **Toolspace Settings** under the **Grading** item. Expand **Grading Criteria Sets** and notice the **Basic** grading set. Right-click on **Basic** grading and select **New...** to create your own criteria. When the dialog box appears, click on the **Criteria** tab and explore how you can customize these tools.

Congratulations! You have graded a parking lot, a building with a basement, and its related tie-outs and sidewalks. You have also added parking lot islands and computed earthworks. You have even had a taste of modeling an intersection using **Grading** commands! Enormous powers exist in the grading objects and only experimentation can yield their true powers.

CHAPTER SUMMARY

This chapter covered Civil 3D capabilities for site grading and subdivision design. Once the roadway is created, the site can be accessed and its 3D layout developed. Much of an engineering project involves grading, and one of the chief concerns is site drainage. This chapter provided instruction in the functions for grading and included feature lines, breaklines, and grading objects.

CHAPTER TEST QUESTIONS

Multiple Choice

1. When grading a site, which of the following information items are useful?

   a. Elevations
   b. Slopes
   c. Grades
   d. All of the above

2. The **Elevation Editor** can be used to perform which design tasks?

   a. Establish profiles and vertical tangents grades
   b. Set grades and elevations
   c. Establish the elevations for superelevations
   d. All of the above

3. Methods of creating proposed topographic grading data include which of the following?

   a. Developing Zones of Slope Influence
   b. Contour digitizing
   c. Developing 3D breaklines and Developing 3D spot shots
   d. All of the above

4. You would consider using "thinking points" for which of the following design tasks?

   a. Annotating parcel lines
   b. Balancing traverses
   c. Establishing pipe inverts
   d. None of the above

5. The sites developed in Civil 3D can be made ready for use by 3D/GPS Machine Control equipment by using which of the following add-ons?

   a. Carlson Connect, which addresses Topcon
   b. Trimble Link
   c. Leica X-change
   d. All of the above

6. Understanding that the concept of engineers designing their sites in three dimensions is a "must achieve" goal, then what do they rely on the computer to do for them?

   a. Assisting in designing the site in the computer using slopes, grades, and elevations
   b. Creating the contouring objects and analyses
   c. Annotating the contour, spot shot, and grade labeling
   d. All of the above

7. What are some of the methods for performing earthworks takeoffs?

   a. Section method
   b. Grid method
   c. Composite method
   d. All of the above

8. In the Section earthworks method, there are the following computations: Section 1 has a cut area of 100 s.f., Section 2 has a cut area of 200 s.f., Section 1 has a fill area of 50 s.f., and Section 2 has a fill area of 150 s.f. The distance between Section 1 and Section 2 is 50 feet. What is the net value for cut or fill for the volume between Section 1 and Section 2 in cubic yards?

   a. 278 c.y. cut
   b. 185 c.y. fill
   c. 93 c.y. cut
   d. 463 c.y.

9. Which of the following earthworks algorithm properties are true?

   a. The Grid method is a traditional method; however, some loss of accuracy can occur for a variety of reasons.
   b. The Section method is a traditional method; however, some loss of accuracy can occur for a variety of reasons.
   c. The Grid method produces good results when used properly, but highs and lows that may occur inside individual grids may not be accounted for in the computations.
   d. All of the above.

10. When working with some of the **Grading** tools, what results can be achieved?

   a. Grading objects can be created according to our design criteria.
   b. Surfaces can be automatically created as we create grading objects.
   c. Contours for the surfaces can automatically be displayed.
   d. All of the above.

True or False

1. True or False: The civil engineering field should prepare its roadway and site designs using contours because they represent the proposed site conditions better than any other data type.

2. True or False: A Zone of Influence is a method of design, not a command in Civil 3D.

3. True or False: Once a proper 3D site is created, sections can be pulled to observe extraordinary detail such as loading docks and parking lot islands.

4. True or False: Civil 3D can use 3D house templates for grading purposes.

5. True or False: There are several types of earthworks algorithms available in Civil 3D.

6. True or False: The Grid method can be performed only manually by the user.

7. True or False: To convert cubic feet of earthworks into cubic yards, you multiply by 27.

8. True or False: The Grid method gets less accurate as the size of the grid becomes smaller.

9. True or False: The Section method becomes more accurate as the size of the interval between sections becomes smaller.

10. True or False: A "balanced site" means that whatever earth is cut or dug out is then used to lift or fill the site in areas where that needs to be done.

CHAPTER EXERCISES

1. What is the difference between slope and grade in the software's viewpoint?
2. What is a "tie-out"?
3. What is daylight?
4. What types of quality control can be used to check the proposed design?
5. What type of CAD data can be used for rendering the site?
6. What is a "thinking point"?
7. How can someone perform quality control on his or her grading?
8. What do the commands **Distance @ Grade**, **Distance @ Slope**, **Relative Elevation @ Slope**, **Surface @ 2:1**, **Surface @ 3:1**, **Surface @ 6:1**, and **Surface @ Slope** do?
9. Could you use the **Distance @ Grade** tool in the **Grading Layout** toolbar to create an island with a curb?
10. Compute the earthworks for the site in Figure 10-35 based on a 100′ × 100′ grid method. Show your work.

Figure 10-35

Piping for Storm Sewers and Drainage

11

Chapter Objectives

- Understand basic hydrology and hydraulic concepts.
- Perform piping layout and drafting for utilities and storm sewers.

INTRODUCTION

This chapter discusses developing storm sewer plan and profile data. This is part of a larger engineering task related to hydrology and hydraulics. Civil 3D performs some limited hydrologic computations. The hydraulics is also limited but does use object-oriented piping for storm sewers on your project. It extracts the rim elevations and develops inverts based on criteria established. This feature, although not a totally complete hydraulics design tool, is a welcome addition to the software's capabilities.

The purpose of this chapter is to introduce you to some basic hydrology and hydraulic concepts and provide some basic procedures for using Civil 3D toward these purposes.

REVIEW OF FUNCTIONS AND FEATURES TO BE USED

This chapter provides instruction in the functions for producing hydrologic watersheds from the surface object as well as producing pipes in plan and profile views. These will carry into sections should they be imported as well. The features for piping are objects and react to the environment around them. These functions can be used for typical drafting purposes as well as to react to design changes and conflict resolution. The piping of multiple networks can be imported into any number of profiles or sections to test for conflicts.

HYDROLOGY

Runoff

When rain or snow falls onto the Earth, it follows the laws of gravity and conveys to the lowest point. Part of the precipitation is absorbed by the ground and replenishes the groundwater reservoirs. Most of it, though, flows downhill and is called runoff. Runoff is extremely important in site design because it changes the landscape through erosion. Engineers typically must design retention facilities to detain the amount of additional runoff their design creates when they replace natural grass-covered ground with asphalt-paved parking lots and the like. If the additional runoff were not captured and held, it would likely flood or erode downstream properties.

A Definition of Runoff. Runoff is a portion of precipitation, snowmelt, or irrigation water that flows over ground in uncontrolled, above surface streams, rivers, or sewers. Computation factors include the speed of its arrival after a rainfall or a snowmelt; the sum of total discharges during a specific period of time; and the depth to which a drainage area would be covered if all the runoff for a given period of time were uniformly distributed over it.

Meteorological Factors Affecting Runoff.   The following meteorological factors affect runoff:

- Type of precipitation such as rain, snow, sleet, and so on
- Rainfall intensity, amount, and duration
- Distribution of rainfall over the watershed
- Other meteorological and climatic conditions that affect evapotranspiration, such as temperature, wind, relative humidity, and the season

Physical Characteristics Affecting Runoff.   The computations of hydrologic study often involve the type of land use, the vegetation on the land, the soil type evident in the area, the total drainage area involved, the shape of the watershed basin, elevations, slopes, drainage patterns, topography, bodies of water, and biogeomorphism, which accounts for the impedances that may exist that could alter the flow of water in the basin.

The watershed for Front Royal, Virginia, is shown in Figure 11-1.

- Rivers and streams in this watershed: 15 (provided by EPA's River Reach File, version 1)
- Lakes in the watershed: 68; total number of acres: 679.8
- River and stream miles:

  1358.7 total river miles

  988.9 perennial river miles

  % of total rivers and streams that have been surveyed

Figure 11-1   A simple watershed map

Software for Hydrologic Estimations and Computations.   Software for hydrologic estimations and computations includes TR-20—rainfall runoff calculations; HEC-1—water surface profiles; and TR-55—Technical Release 55 (TR-55). These present simplified procedures for small urbanizing watersheds to calculate storm runoff volume, peak rate of discharge, hydrographs, and storage volumes required for floodwater reservoirs.

In these computations there are some of the following items:

IDF (Intensity-Duration-Frequency) Curves.   These indicate the relationship between the intensity (I) and duration (D) of a rainfall event with a given return period (T).

The Rational Method for Predicting Runoff.   This may be used to predict the peak runoff with the equation

$q = CIA$, where:

q = Peak runoff (CFS) C = Runoff coefficient

I = Rainfall intensity (in./hr) A = Area (acres)

The method indicates that the units have been "rationalized" where 1 cubic foot per second (CFS) = 1.01 in.-acre/hr.

The rational method is dependent on the selection of C and I, where C is based on the soil, ground cover, and other factors, and I is obtained from the local IDF curve for a given return period and duration.

One of the challenges of the rational method is that of choosing the correct duration. The rational method is intended only to determine peak runoff.

SCS Storm Distributions

By studying the Weather Bureau's Rainfall Frequency Atlases, the Soil Conservation Service (SCS) determined that the continental United States could be represented by four dimensionless rainfall distributions each of a 24-hour duration. These distribution curves were developed from the same depth-duration-frequency data used for IDF curves.

The major advantage of the SCS storm distributions is that each curve contains depth information for storm events of all durations up to 24 hours. These distributions also provide the cumulative rainfall at any point in time, which makes them useful for volume-dependent routing calculations.

Determining the Time-of-Concentration

For overland flow computations related to storm activity, a time-dependent factor must be introduced in order to determine how the runoff is distributed over time. The time-of-concentration (T_c) is used for SCS methods. The T_c is usually defined as the time required for a theoretical drop of water to travel from the most hydrologically remote point in the watershed to the point of collection.

Some Important Equivalents

1 cfs = 448 gallons/minute
1 cfs-day/mi^2 = 0.03719″ of runoff
1″ of runoff/mi^2 = 26.89 cfs-day = 2,323,200 ft^3 = 53.33 acre-ft
1 acre = 43,560 sq. ft = 4047 sq. m = .4047 ha
1 sq. mi = 640 acres = 2.59 sq. km
Acceleration of gravity = 32.17 ft/s^2 = 9.806 m/s^2

Example 11-1: Watersheds

In Figure 11-2, delineate the watershed boundaries for the site.

Figure 11-2   Delineate the watershed boundaries

The graphic in Figure 11-3 shows an example of watershed boundaries.

Figure 11-3 An example of watershed boundaries

Exercise 11-1: Civil 3D Watersheds

You now explore Civil 3D and its ability to develop watersheds from the surface model.

To access student data files, go to www.pearsondesigncentral.com.

1. Open Chapter-11-a.dwg.
2. Type **V** for **View**, select the **Plan** view, hit **Set Current**, then hit **OK**, and you see existing ground contours.
3. These contours belong to a surface model. Watershed generation is built into every surface model. Click on and select the **Surface** in AutoCAD; right-click and select **Edit Surface Style....**
4. When the **Surface Style** dialog box comes up, click on the **Display** tab and deselect or turn **Off** the contours and border layers. Select the **Watersheds** layers and turn it **On**.
5. Then click on the **Watersheds** tab. Several types of watersheds are automatically computed as shown in Figure 11-4.

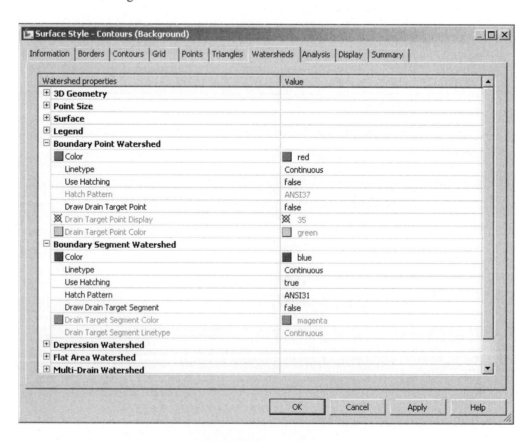

Figure 11-4 The Surface Style dialog box

6. Hit **OK** in the **Surface Style** dialog box, and the surface immediately represents itself as a watershed analysis, as shown in Figure 11-5.

Figure 11-5   A watershed analysis

TIP

The type of watersheds automatically computed include the following.

Boundary Point, a watershed in which water leaves the shed at a single location.
Boundary Segment, a watershed in which water leaves the shed over a levee or wall type object (technically it is likely to be the side of a TIN triangle).
Depression, a watershed in which water is in a basin and has no way out.
Flat Area, a watershed that is flat (this is interesting to observe in proposed roadways because flat areas are not desirable in the paved lanes due to safety reasons because they can cause hydroplaning).
Multi-Drain, a watershed in which water has multiple ways out of the shed.
Multi-Drain Notch, a watershed in which there is a flat area between two points on the surface, reminiscent of a trapezoidal channel.

Each of these watersheds can be colored or shaded differently so that it stands apart for analysis.

HYDRAULICS

Hydraulics, like hydrology, is a huge field within civil engineering. The word *hydraulics* comes from the Greek word *hydraulikos,* meaning water. This term comes from another term meaning water pipe. Hydraulics systems, whether retaining or conveying water, are designed to deal with water at rest or in motion. This discussion is concerned with the principles and methods of planning, controlling, transporting, conserving, and using water.

Basic Concepts Related to Flowing Water

Flow is classified into two conveyances: open channel and closed conduit flow. Open channel flow occurs when the flowing stream has a free or unconstrained surface that is open to the air. Flows in channels or in pipelines with partial flow and venting are examples. In open channels, the only force that can cause flow is the force of gravity on the fluid.

Hydraulically speaking, a pipe is a closed conduit that carries water under pressure. It can be of any shape but is often round for friction purposes.

Flow occurs in a pipeline when a pressure or "head" difference exists between the ends. The discharge Q that occurs depends mainly on the amount of pressure or head difference that exists from the inlet to the outlet; the friction or resistance to flow caused by pipe length, pipe material, bends, constrictions, changes in shape and size, and type of fluid; and the cross-sectional area of the pipe.

Discharge–Area–Velocity Relationships

Flow rate or discharge, Q, is the volume of water in cubic feet passing a flow section per unit time, usually measured in cubic feet per second (ft^3/s). To get the time rate of flow or discharge, Q, in cubic feet per second, use the equation: $Q = AV$, or $V = Q/A$.

Hydraulic Mean Depth and Hydraulic Radius

An irregular flow cross section often uses a hydraulic radius and depth for computing area. The hydraulic radius, R_h, is defined as the area of the flow section divided by the wetted perimeter, P_w: $R_h = A/P_w$. The wetted perimeter times the hydraulic radius is equal to the area of irregular section flow.

Velocity Head Concept

It is known that a dropped object gains speed as it falls due to acceleration caused by gravity (g), which is equal to 32.2' per second per second (ft/s^2). Measurements show that an object dropping 1' reaches a velocity of 8.02' per second (ft/s). An object dropping 4' reaches a velocity of 16.04 ft/s. After an 8' drop, the velocity attained is 22.70 ft/s.

If water is stored in a barrel and an opening is made in the barrel wall 1' below the water surface, the water shoots from the opening with a velocity of 8.02 ft/s, which is the same velocity that a freely falling object reaches after falling 1'. Similarly, at openings 4' and 8' below the water surface, the velocity of the shooting water is 16.04 ft/s and 22.68 ft/s, respectively. Therefore, the velocity of water shooting from an opening under a given head (h) is the same as the velocity that would be attained by an object falling that same distance. The equation that shows how velocity changes with head defines velocity head: $V = \sqrt{2gh}$, which is also written as $h = V^2/2g$.

CIVIL 3D STORM SEWERS

This chapter explores Civil 3D and its ability to draft storm sewer piping using the piping objects. The main menu for piping is the **Pipes** pull-down, shown in Figure 11-6. The first thing you must do is **Set Pipe Network catalog** and select either **Imperial** or **Metric** piping. Then you select the **Create Pipe Network by Layout...** tool, which invokes the **Layout** toolbar for placing pipes and structures. Editing can occur after the system is in place. **Draw Parts in Profile View** allows the network to be automatically drawn in the profile of your choice. **Add Pipe Network Labels** can be done afterward if the labeling style chosen did not perform labeling.

Figure 11-6   The Pipes pull-down menu

Several routines exist to aid design. They include the following:

- **Create Pipe Network by Layout...**, by which you can create a pipe network using Network Layout Tools.
- **Create Pipe Network from Object**, by which you can create pipe systems from pre-existing AutoCAD objects.
- **Change Flow Direction...**, which allows for changing the downhill flow of water.
- **Set Pipe Network Catalog...**, which allows you to set the default path for the pipe and structure catalog.
- **Parts List**, by which new pipe parts can be developed. This includes both structures and pipe types. They can be created or edited.
- **Part Builder...**, by which new graphic parts can be developed with a version of the **Dynamic Blocks Editor**.

Under **Utilities** are:

- **Create Interference Check**, by which you can visualize where conflicts exist between utilities. This allows you to solve for physical conflicts as well as tolerance conflicts. This is important for jurisdictions that have tolerance where, say, the water lines cannot be within 5′ of a sanitary line.
- **Create Alignment from Network Parts...**, by which you can create an alignment from connected pipe network parts.

Your job here is to place a storm structure network beginning at station 9+00 using a manhole. It connects with a 12″ concrete pipe to another manhole at station 12+00. Then a 12″ pipe is used to connect to a manhole at 15+00. This connects to a headwall just off the paving perpendicular to station 15+00. Use the **Network Layout Tools** toolbar (Figure 11-8) to create the network. The tools are described here:

 Pipe Network Properties, which is the first command.

 Select surface, which is used for scanning for the rim elevation.

 Select alignment if there is a need to relate the piping to a station/offset of an existing alignment.

 Parts List for pipe and structure components.

 Structure List allows for selecting a structure.

 Pipe List allows for selecting a pipe type.

 Places the Pipe, Structures, or both.

 Toggle upslope/downslope changes the sloping for the pipe from downhill to uphill.

 Deletes the pipe network object.

 Displays the Pipe Network Vista, tabular editing.

Exercise 11-2: Create Pipes by Layout

1. Open Chapter-11-b.dwg.
2. Type **V** for **View**, select the **Plan** view, hit **Set Current**, then hit **OK** and you see a corridor between station 9+00, a high point, and 15+00, a low point.

To access student data files, go to www.pearsondesigncentral.com.

3. From the **Pipes** pull-down menu, Figure 11-6, select **Set Pipe Network Catalog**.
4. Choose **Imperial** for each selection item.
5. Then choose **Create Pipe Network by Layout** from the **Pipes** pull-down menu.
6. A **Create Pipe Network** dialog box displays. Set the defaults as shown in Figure 11-7, where the **Surface name** is **Corridor—(1), Surface—(1)** and the **Alignment name** is **Alignment—1**. Hit **OK**.

Figure 11-7   The Create Pipe
Network dialog box

7. The **Network Layout Tools** toolbar displays.
8. Choose the first button on the left in Figure 11-8, **Pipe Network Properties**. It invokes a dialog box for **Pipe Network Properties**. Set the parameters for the **Layout Settings**, as shown in Figure 11-9.

Figure 11-8   The Network Layout Tools toolbar

9. Then pick the tab for **Profile**, and set the parameters for **Structure profile label style** to **Standard** and the **Pipe profile label style** to **Standard**. Hit **OK**.
10. In the pop-down **Structure List**, select **Concentric Structure 48 dia. 18 frame 24 cone 5 wall 6 floor**, from the **Concentric Cylinder Structure** item.
11. Pick **12 inch concrete pipe** from the **Pipe List**.
12. Pick on the command in the toolbar for **Draw Pipes and Structures,** choose **Pipes and Structures**. Specify the structure insertion point: Pick a point on the corridor near station 9+00.
13. Pick another point at station 12+00 while staying in the command.
14. Pick another point at station 15+00 while staying in the command.
15. Now in the pop-down **Structure List**, change the **Concentric Structure 48 dia. 18 frame 24 cone 5 wall 6 floor**, to a **38×6×48 inch Concrete Rectangular Headwall VH** from the **Concrete Rectangular Headwall Variable Height** item.
16. Place the last point near the end of the 3:1 side sloping (approximately 40′ right of the centerline for the corridor at station 15+00). Then hit **<Enter>** to complete the network.

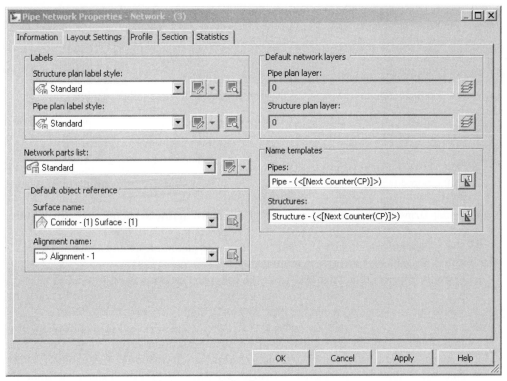

Figure 11-9   The Pipe Network Properties dialog box

On inspection, note that the piping is drawn in the plan view. Next, lay it into the profile and see how it appears. After that, move the piping around to refine it for your needs and observe how it recomputes itself.

Exercise 11-3: Create Pipes in the Profile

1. Type **V** for **View**, select the **Prof** pipe view, hit **Set Current**, then hit **OK** and you see a profile between station 9+00, a high point, and 15+00, a low point.
2. From the **Pipes** pull-down menu, select the command to **Draw Parts in Profile View**.
3. `Select network(s) to add to profile view or (Selected parts only):` **Zoom** out and select a pipe in the **Pipe Network** you just created and hit **<Enter>**.
4. `Select profile view:` **Zoom** back to the profile and select any grid line in your profile.
5. Observe your profile because the pipe system is then drawn into the profile for you. It appears something like Figure 11-10.

Figure 11-10   A Pipe Profile

Notice that the rim elevations are all automatically taken from the roadway's finished ground surface. The labeling appears as directed by the Standard labels selected in the styles chosen. You need to modify the label styles to reflect the way you want your plans to appear.

Exercise 11-4: Add a Structure

Take a few moments to edit and examine the system. You will add another manhole structure at station 11+00.

1. Choose **Edit Pipe Network...** from the **Pipes** pull-down menu. `Select part from pipe network:` Pick a pipe in the plan view.
2. The **Network Layout Tools** toolbar displays.
3. In the pop-down **Structure List**, change the current structure to **Concentric Structure 48 dia. 18 frame 24 cone 5 wall 6 floor**.
4. Under **Draw Pipes and Structures**, click the **down arrow** to choose **Structures Only**. `Specify the structure insertion point:`
5. Use a **Nearest** snap to pick a point on the pipe near station 11+00 and notice a new structure is placed. Hit **<Enter>** to terminate.
6. From the **Pipes** pull-down menu, select the command to **Draw Parts in Profile View**.
7. `Select network(s) to add to profile view or (Selected parts only):` **Zoom** out and select a pipe in the **Pipe Network** you just created and hit **<Enter>**.
8. `Select profile view:` **Zoom** back to the profile and select any grid line in your profile. Notice that the system added the new structure at station 11+00.
9. Now adjust the labeling for the profile to add more information. Choose the **Add Pipe Network Labels >> Add Pipe Network Labels...** (Figure 11-11) command from the **Pipes** pull-down menu.

Figure 11-11   Add Pipe Network Labels dialog box

10. Change the **Standard Structure** label style by clicking on the **down arrow** next to the **Structure label style** pop-down window and selecting **Edit Current Selection** style.
11. This brings up the **Label Style Composer** (Figure 11-12).
12. In the **Layout** tab, look in the **Value** column for the **Text Property Contents**. In that cell is a button with ellipses to enter the dialog. Click that button.
13. This causes the **Text Component Editor—Contents** dialog box to display.
14. Using the **Properties** pop-down window, add in the following data items for labeling: **Structure Station, Structure Offset**, and **Insertion Rim Elevation**. Click in the black window at the end of the existing text string and hit **Enter** to move the cursor down one line. From the pop-down menu select a new data item. Hit the **gray arrow** to the right of the **Properties** pop-down window after each selection to populate the window to the right. Hit

Figure 11-12   The Label Style Composer dialog box

Enter to move the cursor down one line and choose another data item. When complete as shown in Figure 11-13, hit **OK**, **OK**, and **OK** to exit. `Select part contained in the network to be labeled:`, Notice that the profile labeling has already been altered.

Figure 11-13   Text Component Editor dialog box

Exercise 11-5: Move Structures

Now you move the beginning structure from station 9+00 to station 8+50.

1. **Zoom** back to the plan view or type **V**, select **Plan** view, hit **Set Current**, then hit **OK**.
2. Click on the manhole structure and notice two **cyan** grips appear. See Figure 11-14.
3. Click on the square grip and stretch the grip to approximately station 8+50.
4. Notice that the structure and pipe move at the same time.
5. Now **Zoom** back to the profile, or type **V**, select **Prof** view, hit **Set Current**, then hit **OK**.
6. Notice that the pipe and structure are already relocated in the profile view.

Figure 11-14   Grips on a structure

Exercise 11-6: Create Pipes by Layout

You now perform a brief exercise in identifying pipe conflicts.

To access student data
files, go to
www.pearsondesigncentral.com.

1. Open Chapter-11-c.dwg.
2. Type **V** for **View**, select the **Plan** view, hit **Set Current**, hit **OK**, and you see two piping systems in the corridor between station 10+00, a high point, and 13+00. You will now examine whether a conflict occurs here.
3. Select **Utilities >> Create Interference Check** from the **Pipes** pull-down menu.
4. `Select a part from the first network:` Select the pipe that follows the corridor centerline.
5. `Select another part from the same network or different network:` Select the other pipe on the north side of the corridor centerline.
6. The **Create Interference Check** dialog box displays. See Figure 11-15. Click on the button at the bottom of the dialog box that says **3D proximity check criteria....**

Figure 11-15   The Create Interference Check dialog box

7. When the **Criteria** dialog box appears, turn **On** the **Apply 3D Proximity Check** button.
8. Then type in **5′** for the **Use Distance** field and hit **OK**. Hit **OK**.
9. You get a response that says 1 interference was found, which is correct.
10. To see the interference, type **V** for **View**, select **Pipe Conflict**, and set it current.
11. You see a sphere indicating the conflict. Figure 11-16 shows a 2′ sphere for a 5′ conflict. This is just one way to show conflicts. Try experimenting with the settings and identify other methods on your own.

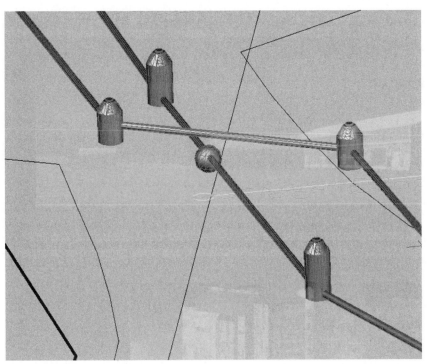

Figure 11-16   An interference of two pipes

With experimentation, you will notice that very powerful drafting features exist in the piping abilities of the Civil 3D product. The 2007 version added huge capabilities to the product, and its modeling and drafting features are unparalleled. The 2008 version added strong plan and profile drafting routines that have been much desired.

CHAPTER SUMMARY

This chapter looked at storm sewer plan development and introduced you to hydrology and hydraulic concepts. Civil 3D provides basic procedures to perform piping layout and drafting for utilities and storm sewers. The chapter also provided instruction in the functions for producing hydrologic watersheds from the surface object.

CHAPTER TEST QUESTIONS

Multiple Choice

1. Meteorological factors affecting runoff include which of the following?

    a. Type of precipitation such as rain, snow, sleet, etc.
    b. Rainfall intensity, amount, and duration
    c. Distribution of rainfall over the watershed
    d. All of the above

2. Physical characteristics affecting runoff include which of the following?

    a. Location such as the tropics, piedmonts, mountains
    b. Land use, vegetation, soil type, and total drainage area involved
    c. Shading of the watershed basin
    d. Sunlight strength

3. Various software is usually used to compute which of the following hydrological characteristics:

    a. Storm runoff volume
    b. Peak rate of discharge
    c. Hydrographs and storage volumes
    d. All of the above

4. Intensity-Duration-Frequency curves indicate which relationships?

    a. Between duration and area
    b. Between storage volumes and flows
    c. Between the intensity and duration of a rainfall event with a given return period
    d. Between erosion and siltation factors

5. The time-of-concentration is:

   a. Used for SCS methods
   b. Defined as the time required for a theoretical drop of water of water to travel from the most hydrologically remote point in the watershed to the point of collection
   c. Also called a T_c
   d. All of the above

6. Several types of watersheds are automatically computed in Civil 3D. They include:

   a. Boundary Profiles
   b. Boundary Points and Segments
   c. Weirs
   d. Low Flow Areas

7. The discharge of water depends mainly on:

   a. The amount of pressure that exists from the inlet to the outlet
   b. The friction or resistance to flow caused by pipe length
   c. Pipe material, bends, constrictions, the type of fluid, and the cross-sectional area of the pipe
   d. All of the above

8. The hydraulic radius, R_h, is defined as:

   a. The area of the flow section divided by the wetted perimeter
   b. The wetted perimeter divided by the area of the flow section
   c. $Q = AV$
   d. None of the above

9. Several terms associated with fluid flow include which of the following?

   a. Velocity head
   b. Hydraulic radius
   c. Discharge–area–velocity relationships
   d. All of the above

10. The word *hydraulics* comes from:

    a. The Greek word *hydraulikos*
    b. The English term *water*
    c. Hydrology
    d. Water at rest or in motion

True or False

1. True or False: Runoff is that part of precipitation that is absorbed by the ground, thereby replenishing our reservoirs.

2. True or False: Runoff can cause erosion.

3. True or False: Hydrologic study often involves such items as land use, vegetation, soil type, and total drainage area.

4. True or False: Meteorological factors affecting runoff include rainfall quality and contaminants.

5. True or False: As evidenced by the watershed for Front Royal, Virginia, watersheds tend to be small and usually less than one acre.

6. True or False: IDF curves can be found on the Internet and stand for Internet-Definable-Frequency curves.

7. True or False: The rational method for predicting runoff may be used to predict the peak runoff.

8. True or False: The rational method formula is $q = CIA$, where q is the peak runoff being computed.

9. True or False: Although the rational method appears straightforward, it is totally dependent on the "correct" selection of the area involved.

10. True or False: The time-of-concentration is usually defined as the time required for a drop of water to be absorbed into the ground.

CHAPTER EXERCISES

1. What is the volume of water in a full 24″ pipe if the velocity of the flow is 5 ft/s?

2. What is the velocity of water in a 48″ pipe, flowing full with a volume of 60 cfs?

3. What size of pipe is needed to convey 50 cfs at a velocity of 4 ft/s?

4. Develop a storm network in Civil 3D that uses different pipe sizes and structures as an exercise in placing the objects.

5. Edit these objects to increase, decrease, or change slopes of the pipes.

Plan Production Tools

12

- Turn an alignment and profile into a set of sheets immediately ready for plotting
- Create Frames
- Create Sheets

INTRODUCTION

This chapter introduces Plan Production Tools to the Civil 3D user. This technology was added to the 2008 release and offers the generation of plan over profile sheet layout. This function now provides a tool that is traditionally found in civil engineering software and assists the user in preparing what are typically called Plan/Profile plot sheets. Civil 3D will use a corridor alignment and its related vertical profile information to set up, rotate, scale and cut layout frames in Layouts automatically for direct plotting.

The Civil 3D Plan Production Tools functionality includes the following abilities.

- The **Prospector's** interface has a **View Frame Groups** collection.
- The **General** menu has the option, **Plan Production Tools**. See Figure 12-1.
- Two main functions are **Create View Frames...** and **Create Sheets...**.

The purpose of this chapter is to introduce you to the routines of "cutting P&P sheets" as they are called.

Figure 12-1 General pull-down menu

REVIEW OF FUNCTIONS AND FEATURES TO BE USED

The text provides instruction in the use of functions for generating plan and profile sheets for plotting purposes. When you lay your cursor on a tab, a preview of that layout appears.

TIP If the user adds Ortho-photos to the plan view, the resulting plot can be quite striking. Figure 12-2 shows a project where hundreds of P&P sheets were generated and aerial photos were included and set to precise geodetic coordinates.

Figure 12-2   P&P sheet

Exercise 12-1: Creating a P&P Sheet

You will open a Civil 3D drawing that has an alignment and profile designed. You will then run through a procedure that will create a set of frames and then a set of sheets for plotting the P&P drawings.

To access student data files, go to www.pearsondesigncentral.com.

1. Open the drawing Chapter 12-a-start.dwg. Note that the alignment, surface, profile, corridor, and assemblies are all created.

TIP If you place your cursor in the large profile and move it left to right, you will see a visual concurrence occurring in the plan view showing the corresponding location of the cursor in the profile related to the plan view. If you lay your cursor in the plan view, you will see some visuals in the profile as well.

2. Select **General >> Plan Production Tools >> Create View Frames**. The **Create View Frames** dialog displays. Set it up as shown in Figure 12-3.

Figure 12-3   Create View Frames - Alignment dialog box

3. Then click **Next**. The next dialog box appears as shown in Figure 12-4. Select **Plan and Profile** under **Sheet Settings**.

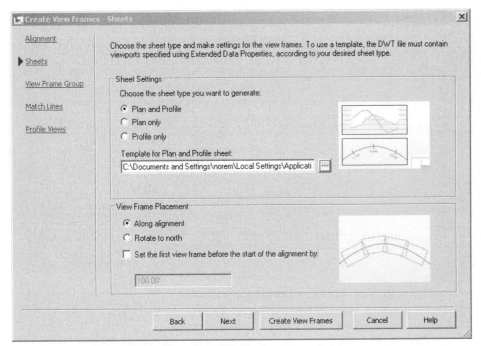

Figure 12-4   Create View Frames - Sheets dialog box

4. Select the template to use for the sheet creation as \Login\Local Settings\Application Data\Autodesk\C3D2010\enu\Template\Plan Production\Civil 3D (Imperial) Plan and Profile.dwt|ANSI D Plan and Profile 40 Scale.
5. Select **Along alignment** under **View Frame Placement**. Hit **Next**.
6. The **Create View Frames—View Frame Group** dialog box appears, shown in Figure 12-5.
7. Set as shown in Figure 12-5 and hit **Next**. This brings up the **Match Lines** settings.
8. The **Match Lines** dialog box is shown in Figure 12-6. Set the settings as shown. Click **Next**.

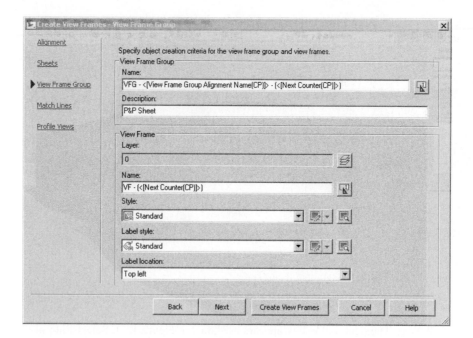

Figure 12-5 Create View Frames - View Frame Group dialog box

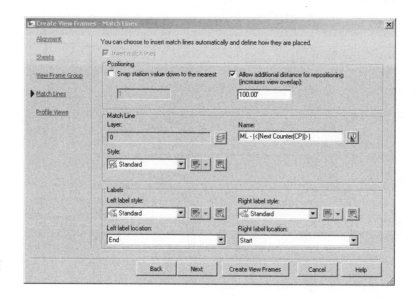

Figure 12-6 Create View Frames - Match Lines dialog box

9. When the **Create View Frames - Profile Views** dialog box appears, simply select **Standard** for the **Profile View Style** and the **Band Set** for now. Then click **Create View Frames**. See Figure 12-7 for an example of the Frames created.

10. Select from the pull-down, **General >> Plan Production Tools >> Create Sheets....** The **Create Sheets - View Frame Group and Layouts** dialog box displays as shown in Figure 12-8. Hit **Next**.

11. When the **Create Sheets – View Frame Group and Layouts** dialog box appears, choose **VFG - primary road - (1)** as the new sheet set name. Hit **Next**.

12. Accept the .DST Storage location offered.

13. Accept the sheet location offered as well as the Sheet File name. Hit **Next** and the **Create Sheets - Profile Views** dialog box appears.

Note:
The software will force a Save after Step 16 so prepare yourself accordingly.

Figure 12-7 View of Created Frames

Figure 12-8 Create Sheets - View Frame Group and Layouts dialog box

14. For the **Other profile view options**, select **PV - (1)**, which is the profile you wish to have plotted. Hit **Next**, and the **Create Sheets - Data References** appears. See Figure 12-9.

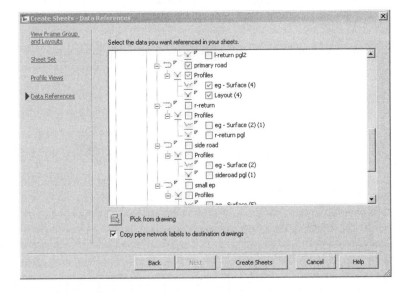

Figure 12-9 Data References

15. The primary road and its respective profiles should be selected.
16. Click on **Create Sheets**. Now you see that your current drawing will be saved. The prompt asks you to Select profile view origin: pick any point in your drawing.
17. The **Sheet Set** was created in your Temp folder as shown above in Step 13.

18. In the **Sheet Set Manager**, click **Open** and get the file called **VFG - primary road - (1).**dst in the Temp folder. This is shown in Figure 12-10.

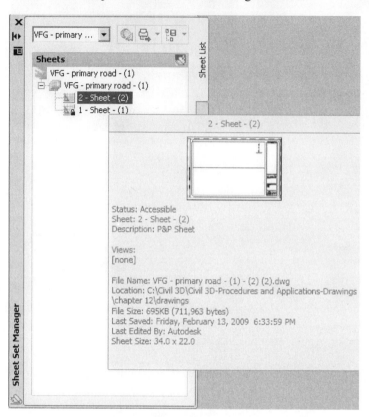

Figure 12-10   Sheet Set Manager

19. Then double-click the **Sheet** called **1 - Sheet - (1)**.
20. The file will open, and a **Plan and Profile** sheet will appear.

Sheet preparation is still a major function in the business. Note that the date, sheet number, and many other drafting items are in the drawing. See Figure 12-11 for the completed P&P sheet.

Feel free to open the second sheet in the **Sheet Set Manager**.

Figure 12-11   Completed P&P sheet

CHAPTER SUMMARY

This chapter introduced the Plan Production Tools to the Civil 3D user. You created Plan/Profile sheets as well as plan sheets ready for plotiing. A very important component of our busi-ness is in relaying our designs to others in a cohesive and easy to understand manner.

CHAPTER TEST QUESTIONS

Multiple Choice

1. Concerning Plan Production Tools, what does P&P stand for?

   a. Plan and profile
   b. Plan and production
   c. Profile and procedure
   d. None of the above

2. The expression "cutting P&P sheets" refers to which of the following?

   a. Creating sheets for preview purposes
   b. Generating plan and profile sheets for plotting purposes
   c. Separating drawings to export to another system
   d. None of the above

3. Why are plan and profile sheets created?

   a. To review design criteria
   b. To design an alignment and profile
   c. For plotting purposes to show the plan with the profile
   d. None of the above

4. Which of the following are the two main functions of the Plan Production Tools?

   a. **Create View Frames** and **Create Sheets**
   b. Create alignments and profiles
   c. Create the preview and layout
   d. None of the above

5. What happens when you place your cursor on a tab?

   a. A preview of the layout appears.
   b. A selection of options appears.
   c. Nothing
   d. None of the above

6. Which of the following happens when you place your cursor in the profile view and move it left to right?

   a. Only the profile view moves.
   b. Nothing

   c. You will see a visual concurrence happening in the plan view.
   d. None of the above

7. When creating P&P sheets, which of the following sheet settings are needed?

   a. **Plan** only
   b. **Profile** only
   c. **Plan and Profile**
   d. All of the above

8. Which of the following scale ratios might be more applicable to a plan profile sheet than the others?

   a. For the plan: $1'' = 10'$ horizontal,
      For the profile: $1'' = 10'$ horizontal and $1'' = 1'$ vertical.
   b. For the plan: $1'' = 10'$ horizontal,
      For the profile: $1'' = 10'$ horizontal and $1'' = 10'$ vertical.
   c. For the plan: $1'' = 50'$ horizontal,
      For the profile: $1'' = 50'$ horizontal and $1'' = 5'$ vertical.
   d. For the plan: $1'' = 1'$ horizontal,
      For the profile: $1'' = 1'$ horizontal and $1'' = 1'$ vertical.

9. Why would a designer add ortho-photos to a plot?

   a. To make it appear that more work was done than really was
   b. To add photographic detail to augment the CAD vectors in the plot
   c. To show existing conditions so a survey won't need to be done
   d. None of the above

10. Can the AutoCAD sheet manager be used with Civil 3D?

    a. Yes, but only if you leave Civil 3D and move to Auto-CAD.
    b. No, a plotting module would need to be purchased.
    c. No, it is not compatible.
    d. Yes

True or False

1. True or False: Plan production tools are rarely used.

2. True or False: Plan production tools reside in the **Plotting** menu.

3. True or False: Only one tab can be created per sheet.

4. True or False: Ortho-photos cannot be used with plan and profile sheets.

5. True or False: Sheet sets need to be created in AutoCAD.

6. True or False: Sheet preparation is a critical function required in almost every project.

7. True or False: Sheet sets can only be sent to a printer.

8. True or False: Sheet sets must be created before View Frames are created.

9. True or False: Aerial photos are always needed for the creation of plan and profile sheets.

10. True or False: Once created, views cannot be altered.

CHAPTER EXERCISES

Because this chapter has only one exercise (Exercise 12-1), we suggest that you run through it again and produce two additional types of production plots.

1. Run through Exercise 12-1 again but generate Plan Only Sheets.

2. Run through Exercise 12-1 again but generate Profile Only Sheets.

Data Sharing in Civil 3D

INTRODUCTION

You have worked with Civil 3D using AutoCAD drawings and have performed your design tasks using a single AutoCAD drawing each time. In a production atmosphere, this may not always be the case. Sometimes engineers work in an environment in which they need to share data among teammates. In order to provide an understanding of how this could work, this appendix addresses data sharing for several purposes: (1) to share data with others on your team, and (2) to share data with people external to Civil 3D users.

The 2007 version added a concept called the **Vault**, which allows for securities and protections of the project data. The user is asked to log in with a password. If the password is lost or the employee who sets it leaves the organization without communicating the password to others, issues can arise. If the employee had administrator privilege, then only Autodesk can break the password. Contact Autodesk and fill out the required legal paperwork to accomplish this. Otherwise, if the employee did not have administrator access, the system administrator can gain access to the **Vault** to clear the password.

DATA SHARING

The exercises you have worked on in this text have included the use of point data, parcel data, surfaces, alignment data, profile views and profiles, corridors, and section data. The main method for data sharing has traditionally been through passing AutoCAD files back and forth. This allows others to see and manipulate the graphical data involved but does not provide strong access to the actual design data.

Civil 3D allows some very effective methods for sharing that design data. It has the ability to share the data not only with other Civil 3D users but also with non–Civil 3D users. In fact, data can be shared with others who do not even have AutoCAD as a foundation CAD platform.

Many larger projects have subconsultants working on them whereby each party contributes its own specialized expertise, or perhaps projects are multidisciplinary. In any event, data need to be shared between these groups to maximize efficiency, avoid errors, and minimize redundancies. The surveyor's base conditions need to be shared with the designers so they can develop the proposed conditions. When the proposed design conditions are finished, these must be sent back to the surveyor for quality control and preparation of stakeout or 3D/GPS Machine Control data. If machine control data are involved, they must be shared with the contractor.

This appendix covers Civil 3D's four main methods of data sharing. The first method is by simply copying the AutoCAD file and sending it to others who have Civil 3D for their use. In this case, the data are inherently available. The second method is through the use of LandXML. The third method is performed through the use of data shortcuts, and the fourth method is accomplished through the use of Civil 3D's project abilities.

Method 1: Inserting or Copying a Drawing

As discussed, Civil 3D makes it easy to incorporate data into a drawing by inserting one drawing into another drawing or by simply using **Save As....** When you wish to obtain access to data within another drawing, you just need to insert the source drawing into the active drawing or open the copy. All the object data such as terrain models, alignments, and so on are immediately available to the working session. Note that there is no live link to the source drawing when using this procedure.

Method 2: LandXML

Civil 3D includes a simple methodology called LandXML, which works similarly to the way it did in Land Desktop. This feature is a data migration tool developed to send design data across operating systems (say, from Windows XP to Unix), across different versions of CAD systems (say, between AutoCAD or Microstation), or between systems that have different CAD standards (say, between a consulting firm and the State Department of Transportation). LandXML, which is being promoted by a nonprofit group, can be accessed via the Web at Landxml.org. It is supported by a group of software manufacturers interested in making their customers' data available to others in the interest of efficiency.

The ability to import or export LandXML makes use of a file format that is open, is text based, and is not software dependent. In other words, it uses a simple definition for each data type, and each software manufacturer can read it and reassemble its respective data into its software's definition. It is also an archival facility because the data are in a generic text-based format.

Let us look at some examples of how data are stored in LandXML. The following example involves an alignment, and this is how it appears in a LandXML file.

```
<?xml version="1.0"?>
<LandXML xmlns="http://www.landxml.org/schema/LandXML-1.0"
xmlns:xsi="http://www.w3.org/2001/XMLSchema-instance"
xsi:schemaLocation="http://www.landxml.org/schema/LandXML-1.0
http://www.landxml.org/schema/LandXML-1.0/LandXML-1.0.xsd"
date="2005-06-26" time="10:42:00" version="1.0" language="Eng-
lish" readOnly="false">
  <Units>
    <Imperial areaUnit="squareFoot" linearUnit="foot"
volumeUnit="cubicYard" temperatureUnit="fahrenheit"
pressureUnit="inchHG" angularUnit="decimal degrees"
directionUnit="decimal degrees"
/Imperial>

  </Units>
      <Project name="C:\Admin\prentiss-hall-civil 3d\civil
3dapplications\student files\appendix-a.dwg"
      /Project>
    <Application name="Autodesk Civil 3D" desc="Civil 3D" manu-
facturer="Autodesk, Inc." version="2007" manufact-
urerURL="www.autodesk.com" timeStamp="2005-06-26T10:42:00"
  /Application>
  <Alignments name="Site 1">
    <Alignment name="Alignment - 1" length="2154.87367186"
staStart="0." desc="Chapter 6 alignment">
      <CoordGeom>
        <Line dir="354.45437497" length="200.">
          <Start>18553.70716247
 14599.21456424</Start>
          <End>18534.37948987 14798.27847627</End>
        </Line>
          <Curve rot="cw" chord="386.34076129"
crvType="arc" delta="30.03271185" dirEnd="324.42166312"
dirStart="354.45437497" external="26.35954132"length="390.79932237"
midOrd="25.45941315" radius="745.55877333" tangent="200.">
            <Start>18534.37948987
14798.27847627</Start>
            <Center>17792.31025954
```

```
14726.22889691</Center>
              <End>18398.68871707 15160.00654818</End>
              <PI>18515.05181728 14997.3423883</PI>
            </Curve>
        <Line dir="296.56505118" length="0.">
            <Start>18398.68871707
15160.00654818</Start>
            <End>18398.68871707 15160.00654818</End>
        </Line>
            <Curve rot="ccw" chord="380.90154719"
crvType="arc" delta="35.55331015" dirEnd="359.97497326"
dirStart="324.42166312" external="31.2774218"
length="387.08193805" midOrd="29.78404589" radius="623.80018303"
tangent="200.">
            <Start>18398.68871707
15160.00654818</Start>
            <Center>18906.03838059
15522.94316422</Center>
            <End>18282.23825707 15522.67068898</End>
            <PI>18282.32561686 15322.67070806</PI>
          </Curve>
        <Line dir="359.97497326" length="200.">
            <Start>18282.23825707
            15522.67068898</Start>
            <End>18282.15089729 15722.6706699</End>
        </Line>
            <Curve rot="ccw" chord="383.19792514"
crvType="arc" delta="33.33121545" dirEnd="393.30618871"
dirStart="359.97497326" external="29.29379845"
length="388.65516287" midOrd="28.06330696"
radius="668.09146379" tangent="200.">
            <Start>18282.15089729
15722.6706699</Start>
              <Center>18950.24229735
15722.96249153</Center>
              <End>18391.88615615 16089.82026175</End>
              <PI>18282.06353751 15922.67065082</PI>
            </Curve>
        <Line dir="33.30618879" length="0.00099774">
            <Start>18391.88615615  16089.82026175</Start>
            <End>18391.88670402 16089.82109561</End>
        </Line>
            <Curve rot="cw" chord="382.73122679"
crvType="arc" delta="33.79240661" dirEnd="359.5137823"
dirStart="33.30618891" external="29.70487123" length="388.3352508"
midOrd="28.42259646" radius="658.43108381"
tangent="199.99900122">
            <Start>18391.88670402
16089.82109561</Start>
            <Center>17841.60420785
16451.37422662</Center>
            <End>18500.01158371 16456.96167135</End>
            <PI>18501.7087748 16256.96987144</PI>
          </Curve>
        <Line dir="359.5137823" length="200.00100003">
            <Start>18500.01158371
16456.96167135</Start>
          <End>18498.31437567 16656.95546999</End>
        </Line>
      </CoordGeom>
    </Alignment>
  </Alignments>
</LandXML>
```

The next example is of a surface definition. It begins with header information and then defines the coordinates of each point involved with a reference point number. It follows that with a triangle referencing those point numbers so that the exact triangulation is honored.

```
<?xml version="1.0"?>
<LandXML xmlns="http://www.landxml.org/schema/LandXML-1.0"
xmlns:xsi="http://www.w3.org/2001/XMLSchema-instance"
xsi:schemaLocation="http://www.landxml.org/schema/LandXML-1.0
http://www.landxml.org/schema/LandXML-1.0/LandXML-1.0.xsd"
date="2005-06-26" time="10:48:52" version="1.0"
language="English" readOnly="false">
  <Units>
  <Imperial areaUnit="squareFoot" linearUnit="foot"
volumeUnit="cubicYard" temperatureUnit="fahrenheit"
pressureUnit="inchHG" angularUnit="decimal degrees"
directionUnit="decimal degrees"
  /Imperial>
  </Units>
  <Project name="C:\Admin\prentiss-hall-civil 3d\civil
3dapplications\student files\appendix-a.dwg"
  /Project>
  <Application name="Autodesk Civil 3D" desc="Civil 3D"
manufacturer="Autodesk, Inc." version="2007" manufact-
urerURL="www.autodesk.com" timeStamp="2005-06-
26T10:48:52"<</Application>
  <Surfaces>
  <Surface name="Corridor - (1) Surface - (1)" desc="">
    <Definition surfType="TIN">
  <Pnts>
    <P id="1">18492.21916265 14593.24452217 325.96527275</P>
    <P id="2">18517.37799852 14595.68726399 321.75240699</P>
    <P id="3">18520.3639572 14595.97717908 321.75240699</P>
    <P id="4">18532.30779192 14597.13683944 324.75240699</P>
    <P id="5">18533.30311148 14597.2334778 324.73240699</P>
    <P id="6">18537.28438973 14597.62003125 324.65240699</P>
    <P id="7">18539.27502885 14597.81330798 324.61240699</P>
    <P id="8">18539.68974533 14597.85357396 324.61240699</P>
    <P id="9">18539.77268863 14597.86162716 324.11240699</P>
    <P id="10">18541.76332775 14598.05490389 324.27907366</P>
    <P id="11">18553.70716247 14599.21456424 324.51907366</P>
    <P id="12">18565.65099719 14600.3742246 324.27907366</P>
    <P id="13">18567.64163631 14600.56750132 324.11240699</P>
    <P id="14">18567.72457961 14600.57555452 324.61240699</P>
    <P id="15">18568.13929609 14600.61582051 324.61240699</P>
    <P id="16">18570.12993521 14600.80909723 324.65240699</P>
    <P id="17">18574.11121345 14601.19565068
    324.73240699</P>....
  ... </Pnts>
  <Faces>
    <F>679 117 116</F>
    <F>369 281 280</F>
    <F>735 73 734</F>
    <F>783 126 127</F>
    <F>693 131 130</F>
    <F>519 391 392</F>
    <F>693 3 2</F>
    <F>688 125 124</F>
    <F>690 5 4</F>
    <F>690 6 5</F>
    <F>689 7 6</F>
    <F>737 70 71</F>
    <F>687 8 7</F>
```

```
<F>229 174 175</F>
<F>685 122 684</F>
<F>528 403 404</F>
<F>739 68 69</F>
<F>741 65 66</F>
<F>317 227 228</F>
<F>683 119 682</F>
<F>742 64 65</F>
<F>681 118 117</F>
<F>675 674 21</F>
<F>230 175 176</F>
<F>707 34 706</F>
<F>716 56 715</F>
<F>682 13 12</F>
<F>463 357 356</F>....
```

By inspecting these data, one can see why this is a generic, simple, and text-based method for data sharing that can easily cross platform lines, CAD system lines, or CAD standards lines.

One company can send its LandXML data to another, and each organization's CAD system can invoke its respective CAD standards when the data are imported into the design software.

You can import the LandXML information using your own native CAD standards and be unaffected by the graphics used to generate the data because LandXML exports only design data, not the graphical appearance of it. The importation process then creates the data with the aesthetics or properties of the CAD system performing the import. The critical aspect of this process is maintaining the design data integrity.

Method 3: Data Shortcuts

Civil 3D provides a data collaboration tool called data shortcuts, which allows you to externally reference objects that are either inside or outside a project. Data shortcut users are one of the following types. Either they have the source object's drawing open and produce the data shortcut (which is an external XML file that contains the AutoCAD.DWG filename, path, and object name), or they are the users of the data shortcut. If they are the users, they can create a reference to the object or read it and obtain ownership of the copy of the object. The referenced object initially has read-only geometry properties and takes up less file space when the drawing is saved, because it is only referenced.

Data shortcuts can be used for obtaining access to surfaces, alignments, and profiles. Alignment and profile data shortcuts are closely tied to each other because a profile data shortcut's source drawing must be the same as the profile's alignment data shortcut.

One last note is that data shortcuts are visible and accessible to the next method of Civil 3D projects for data sharing.

Method 4: Civil 3D Projects

A method provided in Civil 3D to allow sharing of data between Civil 3D users that is somewhat similar to that used by Land Desktop users is the project method. The person who has the source data available attaches the drawing to a project and makes data available to the project. Other users can then obtain access to these data through a Check Out/Check In system.

The project object cannot be modified directly. To modify it, the object has to be checked out. Changes are made, and the object is then checked back in to the project. If you try to modify a local copy of the data without first checking it out, it cannot be checked back in to the project. The modifications made will exist only in the drawing in which they were made.

The next task is to perform some exercises using methods 2 through 4.

Exercise A-1: Using LandXML

1. Open the file called Appendix-a.dwg. There are several data types in this file including points, a corridor, surfaces, and a pipe network.
2. From the **File** pull-down menu, select the **Export>>Export to LandXML...** command. The **Export to LandXML** dialog box appears so that you can check one or more of the

To access student data files, go to www.pearsondesigncentral.com.

items for export. There is a **Pick from drawing** button at the bottom, which allows you to select an object directly from the AutoCAD file.

3. Check the **All Points** toggle under the **Point Groups** category as shown in Figure A-1. Check the **Alignment - 1** in the dialog box under **Site, Site 1, Alignments**, and all the individual profiles check automatically. Hit **OK**.

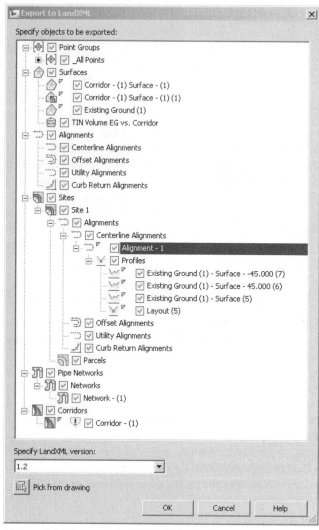

Figure A-1   Export to LandXML dialog box

4. Provide a name for the file in a location that you can locate later. Hit **Save**.
5. When that process is complete, select **File** from the pull-down menu, choose **New**, and create a new Civil 3D file, using the Autodesk **_AutoCAD Civil 3D (Imperial) NCS Base.dwt** file as a template.
6. From the **File** pull-down menu, select the **Import >>Import LandXML...** command. Locate the .xml file you just created and hit **Open**. The **Import LandXML** dialog box in Figure A-2 displays.
7. Accept that all the data are checked for import, and hit **OK**. You may get a **Panorama** box.
8. **Zoom Extents**, and you see the alignment and points in the new file.
9. Look in the **Prospector** and note that the alignment and points are visible here as well. If they are not, ensure that the button at the top left of the dialog box is toggled on. Right-click on **Alignments** and check the **Show Preview** option. Then right-click on **Alignment-1**. See Figure A-3.
10. The only thing that is left to be done is to set the **Styles** for the objects imported.

Figure A-2   Import LandXML dialog box

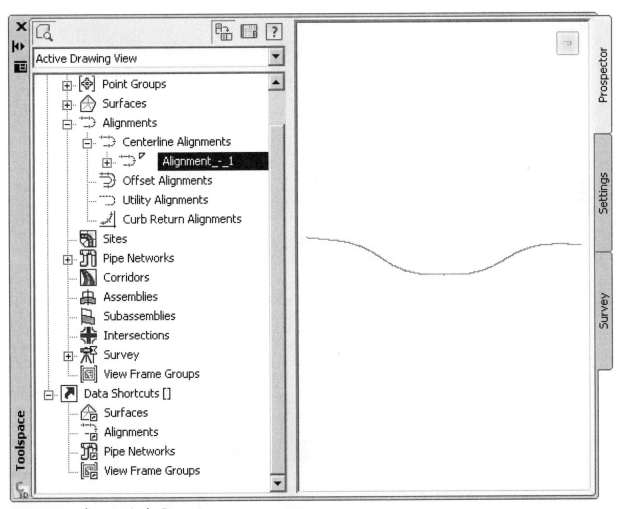

Figure A-3   Alignment in the Prospector

Exercise A-2: Using the Data Shortcuts Method

1. Open the file called Appendix-a.dwg. There are several data types in this file including points, a corridor, surfaces, and a pipe network.
2. Set a new working folder using the **Toolspace, Master View, Prospector** tab, right-click **Data Shortcuts**. Click **Set Working Folder...** and select the folder you want.
3. Then create a new data shortcut folder using the **Toolspace, Master View, Prospector** tab, again right-click **Data Shortcuts**. Click **New Data Shortcuts Folder....** In the **New Data Shortcuts Folder** dialog box, provide a name and text description. Click **OK**.
4. The next step is to create a data shortcut using the **Toolspace, Master View, Prospector** tab, right-click **Data Shortcuts**. Click **Create Data Shortcuts...** The **Create Data Shortcuts** dialog box will display.
5. Click an object type to include in the new data shortcut. In the dialog box, select the object that you want to reference in other drawings. The data shortcut is created.
6. Note that the **Surface** and **Alignment** shortcuts in the dialog box now can be expanded. Expand them and they should appear as in Figure A-4.

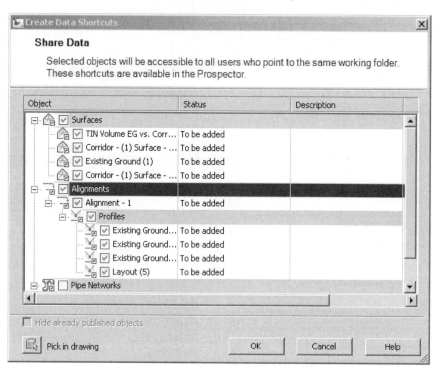

Figure A-4   The Create Data Shortcuts dialog box

You have created a data shortcut and saved it for use by others. Now let us explore how you or others who are on the project team can use these shortcuts.

7. From the Civil 3D pull-down menu, click **File** and then **New** and create a new drawing. Use the **_AutoCADCivil 3D (Imperial) NCS Base.dwt** template to create the new file.
8. Save it as a properly named AutoCAD file of your choosing. While in the new file, look at the **Prospector, Master View, Data Shortcuts**, and you will see the shortcuts available.
9. To create a reference in the new file, right-click on the **Corridor-(1)Surface (1)** shortcut and click **Create Reference....** See Figure A-5.

Figure A-5   Create Reference

10. Hit **OK** to the **Create Surface Reference** dialog box, taking the defaults. See Figure A-6.
11. Perform a **Zoom Extents** on the drawing, and you should see the contours for the corridor surface.
12. In the **Prospector**, right-click on the **Alignment 1** item. Click **Create Reference...**, and a **Create Alignment Reference** dialog box appears. Again, you do not really "own" this alignment but can use it and display it. See Figure A-7.

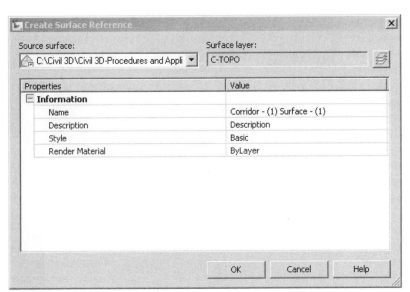

Figure A-6   Create Surface Reference dialog box

Figure A-7   Create Alignment Reference dialog box

13. Accept the defaults as shown in the figure, and hit **OK**. If a **Panorama** appears saying the alignment was created, close it.
14. You see the alignment in the file now.

TIP   If you click on the alignment and right-click, you see the typical commands to edit the alignment or the Style. If you select **Alignment Properties**, notice that nothing can really be modified because it is referenced. The Style, however, can be altered as needed.

15. While in the new file you created, in the Prospector under **Data Shortcuts** select **Alignment 1**. Right-click and choose **Open Source drawing....** The original file from which the data shortcut was created opens.
16. Click on the **Alignment** in the drawing, right-click, and choose **Edit Alignment Geometry....** When the toolbar displays, click on the **Alignment Grid View** on the right side of the toolbar. The **Panorama** opens with the numeric alignment data in it.
17. Scroll to the right until you can see the radius for the first curve in the alignment. Change it to **500**, hit **<Enter>**, and close the panorama. The alignment radius is now 500′ for the first curve.
18. Save the file.
19. Using the **Window** pull-down menu, switch to the new drawing.
20. When you do, the **Data Shortcuts** pop-up window will display, telling you that the data shortcut has been altered and you need to synchronize it.

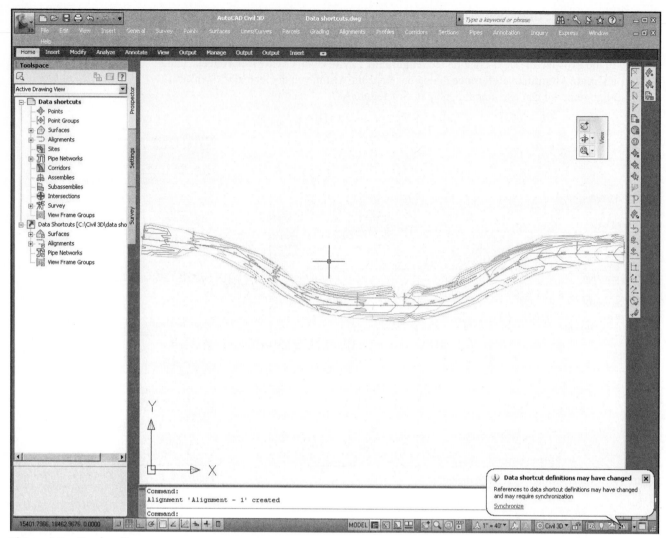

Figure A-8   Synchronize

21. Click on the **blue** hyperlink where it says **Synchronize**, shown in Figure A-8.
22. The command prompt notifies you that Alignment 'Alignment-1' created. **Alignment Alignment-1** is now up to date. **Surface Corridor-(1) Surface-(1)** is now up to date.

If you wish to take complete control of the data shortcut, then you can promote it. This detaches it from its source.

23. Click on the **Alignment**, right-click, and select **Promote**. The command prompt tells you that **1 Data References** successfully promoted.
24. Click on the **Alignment** now, and notice that grips appear, which allow you to edit the alignment, because you now "own" it.

This example shows how data shortcuts can be used. These shortcuts can be placed on a server for each member of the team to use in referencing the data that is in your drawing. They can be used to compute profiles, to change the appearances of data for different uses, or for report creation.

Exercise A-3: Using the Projects Method

To access student data files, go to www.pearsondesigncentral.com.

1. Open Appendix-a-projects.dwg.
2. Check in the **Toolspace Prospector,** and notice that there is a **Projects** item when the **Master View** is showing. See Figure A-9.
3. Right-click on **Projects** and you can **Set Working Folder....** This means that you can set the project path wherever you wish. Under the project path will reside the individual projects that you create.

Figure A-9   A projects item in the
Toolspace Prospector

Figure A-10   Check In

4. The system defaults to **\Civil 3D Projects**, and you can switch that to a more desired location for this exercise if you like.

5. In **Prospector**, right-click on the drawing name, select **Add to Project...** If the software asks you to log in to the **Vault**, do so.

6. Next, expand the drawing, expand **Surfaces** so you can see the **Corridor—(1) Surface—(1)**. Right-click on the **Corridor—(1) Surface—(1)**, and you see an option to **Attach to Project**. Select **Add to Project**.

7. An **Add to Project** dialog box displays, allowing you to attach the surface to the project, but it needs to know under what terms you are attaching it. The default is **Check in.** Click in the pop-down window where it says **Check in**. The other options are **Check in** and **Keep Checked in** and **Check in** and **Protect**. Leave the default. Hit **OK**. See Figure A-10.

8. You now see the **Corridor—(1) Surface—(1)** under the **Surfaces** item in the **Projects** area of the **Prospector**. It can now be used by others on the project team. You will see how in the next part of the exercise.

Close the file you are in. There is no need to save it.

9. Click **File >> New** and create a new drawing. Use the **_AutoCADCivil 3D (Imperial) NCSBase.dwt** template to create the new file.

10. Save it as a properly named AutoCAD file of your choosing.

11. In the **Prospector**, right-click on your AutoCAD file, and select **Attach to Project**.

12. Choose the project called **My Project**.

13. In the **Prospector**, expand **Surfaces**, and you will see the **Corridor—(1) Surface—(1)**. Right-click on the **Corridor—(1) Surface—(1)**, and you are able to **Check Out, Get from Project**, or **Protect the surface**. Choose **Check Out**.

14. **Zoom Extents** and you see the corridor surface in the default style. You also see the **Surface** in the **Prospector** under your file's **Surfaces**.
15. After using it or making modifications to the surface, you can right-click on the **Corridor— (1) Surface—(1)** in the **Prospector** under your file's **Surfaces** and choose **Check it In**.
16. Comments can be added and a log of who checked it in/out is maintained.

Check Out means that you can create an accessible read/write copy of a project object in your drawing. When you check an object out, it then overwrites equivalent objects in your file, thereby keeping the drawing updated with the project.

Get from Project means that you can create a read-only copy of the project object in your drawing.

Protect prevents others from checking out and changing a project object.

Check In means that you can update the project with changes you made to that object while it was checked out by you. This feature locks the local copy of the object in the drawing. See Figure A-10.

Unprotect means that you allow others to check out and change a project object.

These are the main methods for sharing data in Civil 3D. As the use of the software matures, the need to share the data will likely arise, and these exercises will assist in accomplishing that.

SHARING DATA WITH CONTRACTORS FOR 3D/GPS MACHINE CONTROL

Three software add-ons assist designers using Civil 3D in developing their 3D data for contractors using robotic earthmoving devices, commonly known as machine control. This technology has been growing very rapidly and can decrease the amount of time contractors need to construct a project. As a result, contractors increasingly want the data that engineers create, and they want them in 3D!

Autodesk has recognized this need and typically offers three manufacturer's add-ons into the Civil 3D software: Carlson Connect, which addresses Topcon, Trimble Link from Trimble, and Leica X-change. Topcon, Trimble, and Leica are the three main suppliers of machine control equipment in the world. These add-ons are of no cost to the user.

Carlson Connect

Carlson Connect (Figure A-11) is another solution that offers a collection of routines for transferring and converting data between Autodesk Land Desktop or Autodesk Civil 3D and several popular data collectors. Carlson Connect runs inside Civil 3D and uses the current project data.

Once engineers or designers have created their data in 3D, say, for a roadway or a site grading project, there will be a surface involved. By using the **Carlson Connect** pull-down menu and choosing the **Topcon** command and then **Export Surface to Topcon TN3 File**, the surface can

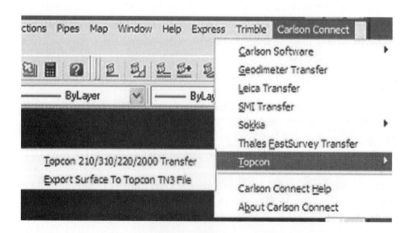

Figure A-11   Carlson Connect

be formatted into the appropriate binary file for Topcon equipment. The TN3 file can be copied to a flashcard for insertion directly into the equipment on site.

Trimble Link

Trimble's equivalent routine would be in two parts. The first is **Export Surface** file for Sitevision for sending your Civil 3D surfaces. The second is for roadway data whereby you would use **Export Road** file for Sitevision. See Figure A-12.

Figure A-12   Trimble Link

Leica X-change

Leica Geosystems released the Leica X-change for Autodesk Civil 3D, which is a group of tools running inside Autodesk Civil 3D that allows the import of data from and the export of data to a Leica System 1200 job. Points, lines, and areas as measured in the field with System 1200 (TPS and GPS) can be directly imported into an Autodesk Civil 3D drawing. Conversely, points created in Civil 3D can be exported to a System 1200 job for later usage in the field. The benefit for the user is seamless data transfer between the System 1200 and Autodesk's Civil 3D software, thereby eliminating intermediate conversion steps, avoiding loss of data, and taking full advantage of the linework capabilities of the System 1200.

SHARING CIVIL 3D CONFIGURATION DATA

Before leaving this topic of sharing data, the last to discuss is sharing data among fellow project teammates. Civil 3D shares its CADD standards, Styles, and assemblies using AutoCAD files. The product configuration largely is performed in an AutoCAD file in which the environment variables and profiles can be established like normal.

Then the Styles and assemblies should be configured for Civil 3D. The Styles are stored in the AutoCAD template for dissemination to other users. The assemblies can be simply placed inside the AutoCAD file or dropped into **Tool Palettes**.

Labeling in Civil 3D 2010

B

This appendix briefly discusses labeling methods. One of the main tools is the ability to label simple lines and curves. Many types of objects can be labeled automatically by choosing the **Add labels...** function available under several menu pull-downs. In the **Add Labels** dialog box that will appear, under the **Feature:** option you can select **Line and Curve**. Choose the label type of either **Single** or **Multiple** segment. Then select the style by which you want to label, and hit the **Add** button to perform the function.

To access student data files, go to www.pearsondesigncentral.com.

Another labeling tool is the **Notes** function. This can be performed by choosing the **Add labels...** function available under several menu pull-downs. In the **Add Labels** dialog box that will appear, under the **Feature:** option you can select **Note**. The label type is **Note**. Then select the style by which you want to label, and hit the **Add** button to perform the function. You will be asked to **Pick label location:** and then pick in the drawing where you wish the new label to be placed.

TIP

The Note is a free-form label whose main properties are that it will resize and rotate as described by the Style when plotted.

Exercise B-1: Expressions

Another important labeling function is the ability to add expressions to the labeling. A quick example follows.

1. Open a file such as chapter 2-k-complete.dwg. Expand the **Toolspace Settings**, and look under **Alignment, Label Styles**, and **Curve**. You see an option called **Expressions** in all the labeling style areas. Expressions can be created for all the labeling styles. They are then attached during Style creation.
2. Right-click on **Expressions** and select **New....**
3. Provide a name for your expression; call it **Half-Delta**.
4. Just to the right and below the **Expression** window is a button called **Insert Function**. Click it and select the function called **RAD2DEG**.
5. Then click in the **Expression** window to the right of the parenthesis. Now click on the **Insert Property** button just below the **Expression** window.
6. Select the **Delta Angle** property.
7. Then click in the **Expression** window and add another parenthesis to the right side of the {Delta Angle} term. Then type **/2** after the expression to divide the value in half.
8. It should say **RAD2DEG({Delta Angle})/2** on completion.
9. Hit **OK**.
10. Now right-click on the **Curve** style called **Standard**. Choose **Edit....**
11. In the **Label Style Composer** dialog box, choose the **Layout** tab.
12. Under the pop-down window called **Component name:** select **Delta**.
13. Now under the **Text Contents Value** field, click the button to the right of the field with the dots on it to enter the editing facility.
14. Click before the Δ = in the **Preview** window and hit **<Enter>** to open a blank line.

15. Move to the blank line and type **Half-Delta=**.
16. Now click under the **Properties** pop-down window, and select the property called **Half-Delta** that you just created.
17. Hit the **gray arrow** to the right to send it into the **Preview** window. Hit **OK** and you see the half delta in the **Preview** window of the **Label Style Composer**. Hit **OK** again to leave.
18. Now in Civil 3D, draw an arc by typing **Arc** and selecting three points somewhere on the screen. Type **PE** for **PEdit** and convert the arc to a **Pline**.
19. Then choose the **Alignment** pull-down menu, select **Create Alignment from Polyline**, choose the arc, and accept the defaults when creating the alignment.
20. Then choose **Alignments >> Add Alignment Labels >> Add Alignment Labels....**
21. An **Add Labels** dialog box appears.
22. Select **Alignment** for the **Feature:**.
23. Select **Single Segment** for **Label type:**.
24. Click the **Add** button and choose the **arc**. A label appears showing the Length, Radius Delta, and Half-delta for the arc. Mission accomplished!

This example shows how to create an expression and use it for augmenting the labeling capabilities of the software. Note: In the version of Civil 3D that we worked with this function did not work for us. However, it did work in the 2008 version, and we are hoping this problem will be recognized and rectified by the release of Civil 3D 2010.

Software and Hardware Versions

C

SOFTWARE VERSIONS AND SPECIFICATIONS

The software discussed in this text is Autodesk Civil 3D 2010.
Some of the major Civil 3D 2010 enhancements comprise the following items.

- Ribbons are a new interface tool that provides a new method for accessing Civil 3D commands.
- Users now have the ability to create alignments from objects, not just Plines.
- New alignment-based solutions:
- Alignments can now have "Types." Types include centerline, offset, utility, and curb return.
- Create offset alignments that are dynamic to the parent alignment.
- Create rule-based non-parallel offsets for bus turnouts and lane widenings.
- New corridor solutions:
- New tools for managing corridor data, the ability to edit a Region, geometric override cleanup tools, a new automated method of creating boundaries for corridors with multiple baselines, and creating a shrinkwrap boundary around the entire corridor.
- A new Create Intersection wizard automates roadway intersection design, including curb returns and widening, from specified main and side road alignments. This is currently limited to a four-way crossing.
- Hydrology improvements include the ability to launch the Hydraflow from within Civil 3D and support for metric units.
- Improved data sharing with Revit.
- Drafting improvements:
  - Masking of contour labels has been added.
  - Profile and section labels can be staggered to avoid overlaps.
- Draw and label projected objects in profile and section views.
- New parcel commands for Sliding Side Line and Swing Line layouts. These are similar to the old Land Desktop tools in function. Parcel previews can now be observed to see how a change will affect the parcels.
- Piping can now handle multiple pipe networks. HGL and EGL can now be computed and labeled. New pipe/structure part types are now available for Circular pipes such as: Corrugated Metal, High Density Polyethylene (HDPE), Corrugated HDPE, and Ductile Iron. For Elliptical pipes, Concrete Arch Pipes are now supported. And for Structures (Inlet\Outlet), Flared End Section, Trench Drain, Winged Headwall, Flexible Metal Rectangular End Section for Arc Corrugated Metal Pipe (CMP), and Flexible Metal Rectangular End Section for Round CMP. Additionally, several new sizes have been added to existing part families.
- A new Quantity Takeoff ability was added. You can access master pay item lists and assign pay items to drawing objects or closed areas.
- New Surface-related routines include a better memory management schema for large data sets. Although introduced in 2009, this feature maintains 2 million points in RAM.

Beyond this figure, however, the points are then sent to a paging file on the hard disk. The only limit here is practicality and hard disk size.

- Survey features include a new data import wizard for various data sources and a linework definition file for field collection.

Civil 3D 2009 enhancements comprise the following items: A hydraulic solution called Hydraflow from Intellisolve, a new **SIMPLIFY SURFACE** command that allows you to remove extra points from a surface without sacrificing accuracy, including points that are in an external point file or database, Breakline weeding, Expansion or compaction factors for volume computations, the ability to locate observation tolerance errors for angle, drawing settings support of International Foot or US Survey Foot for units in a drawing that are displayed in feet, a translate survey database tool, support for AASHTO criteria for design and analysis for alignments and profiles, and a new Design Check setting that allows for managing design criteria that are expressed as formulas. It also adds a variety of fixed, floating, and free linework to the constraint-based design tools, station tracking in multiple viewports, the ability to Mirror template subassemblies, better sharing of assemblies and four new subassemblies, the ability to generate labels from Civil 3D objects that exist within an Xref, a new wizard that improves the process of creating single or multiple section views, an external editor for data shortcuts, an improved eTransmit that includes Vault references and data shortcuts, render materials that can be displayed in Google Earth, and a changed status bar that shows a link to Vault and the addition of Survey Link Extension version 7.5.5 (from TDS).

Civil 3D 2008 added Plan Production tools as the main feature. Other enhancements comprised the ability to do more with Sub-Entities, added the old Land Desktop **Lines/Curves** menu, and the ability to extract AutoCAD objects from the Civil 3D objects. The Civil 3D 2007 version added significant labeling enhancements, corridor design improvements, new subassemblies, new piping tools, and an entire survey solution for data collectors and traverses. The Civil 3D 2006 version added the following enhancements to its feature set: corridor design enhancements, additional data sharing, and utility pipe drafting. The previous version, Civil 3D 2005, was the second iteration (but the first public release) of the Civil 3D solution and added Autodesk VIZ to the solution suite. The first version, a "pre-release" version called Civil 3D, was actually a preview of what was to come. The marketing philosophy of Autodesk was to release the software to its current clients in advance of it being made available to the public. In this fashion, Autodesk's goal was to build interest in the user population and persuade them to become acclimated to the revolutionary philosophies required to use the software successfully. It also wanted the customer to have time to consider the implementation expenses and compare them with the productivity improvements.

The Civil 3D software is provided to Autodesk Land Desktop users who have subscriptions for the Civil Design add-on as part of the subscription service. In 2005, it was formally introduced for sale to the general public.

HARDWARE SPECIFICATIONS

This section is included because very often an information technology department does the purchasing for the organization. These departments usually buy generic desktop PCs and laptops with little regard for the applications being used. CADD systems and visualization software are some of the most hardware-intensive applications available, and they deserve to be budgeted for accordingly.

Note:
Always check with the software manufacturer before making final decisions as specifications may change.

Autodesk Recommended System Requirements for AutoCAD Civil and AutoCAD Civil 3D

The following recommended configuration for Civil 3D 2009 is taken from the Autodesk website. There were no 2010 specifications available at the time of this writing, so it is assumed that the general architecture requirements have stayed about the same as they were for 2009.

- Intel® Pentium® 4 (3 GHz or higher); AMD Athlon™; multiple processors supported, dual-core supported
- 32-bit only: Microsoft® Windows Vista® Ultimate/Business/Enterprise, Microsoft® Windows XP (SP2)

Note: Windows XP 64 and Windows Vista 64 are supported in 32-bit compatibility mode only.

- 3 GB RAM
- 5 GB free disk space for installation
- 1,280 × 1,024 display with true color, 1,600 × 1,200 or greater recommended (OpenGL® accelerator with full OGL ICD support not required)
- Microsoft® Internet Explorer® 6.0 (SP1 or later)
- DVD drive

Recommended Vault Server Components.   The Autodesk® Vault server components can be installed on the same computer as AutoCAD Civil or AutoCAD Civil 3D 2009 if the computer complies with these recommended requirements:

- 3 GHz or higher: Intel Pentium 4, Intel® Xeon®, AMD Athlon 64, AMD Opteron™
- 32-bit: Microsoft Windows XP Home Edition (SP2), Microsoft Small Business Server 2003 Standard/Premium (SP2), Microsoft Small Business Server 2003 R2 Standard/Premium (SP2)
- 32-bit and 64-bit: Microsoft Windows XP Professional (SP2), Microsoft Vista Home Basic/Premium (SP1), Microsoft Vista Ultimate/Enterprise/Business (SP1), Microsoft Server 2003 Standard/Enterprise (SP2), Microsoft Server 2003 Standard/Enterprise R2 (SP2), Microsoft Server 2008 Standard/Enterprise
- 2 GB RAM
- 60 GB free disk space for installation
- Microsoft Internet Explorer 6.0 (SP1 or later)
- DVD drive

Identify the Civil Engineering Industry

Now that the software used in this text as well as the suggested hardware have been identified, discussion follows on the work you will be doing, the business of civil engineering, and the kinds of projects that would be appropriate to apply Civil 3D toward.

The types of work falling into an industry that provides civil engineering design typically include services such as Planning, Preliminary Design, Surveying, Final Design, Value Engineering, Plans Preparation and Construction Document Preparation, and Site Data Preparation. The goal is to define which industries can make use of the Civil 3D product at this time.

Civil engineering projects are generally performed for two types of clients: public clients and private clients. Public clients include governmental agencies such as municipal, county, state, and federal agencies. Private clients include landowners, developers, and industrial, commercial, and legal organizations.

The projects performed for the **public sector** often include corridor design such as roads, tunnels, channels, and aqueducts; construction management; environmental engineering; transportation (which includes traffic flows, evacuation planning, signage, and signalization); airport engineering; bridge design; waste management; wetlands delineation and mitigation; water supply (which includes treatment, distribution, and pump stations); sewage networks (which includes collection and effluent treatment); and water resources.

The project types performed for the **private sector** may be comprised of design of subdivisions, roads, commercial sites, and industrial sites. They may also include design, analysis, and study of waste management, wetlands, water supply and distribution, sewage systems, and water resources. Additional work is performed as part of construction management on projects as well as the legal and real estate professions.

Civil 3D provides for some hydraulic tasks but does use object technology in its pipe networks. Significant control using the pipe style exists for laying out the pipe network and making modifications to it. The seed for formulas can be observed in some of the settings and portends the things to come.

Civil 3D does not provide tools that directly apply to bridge design. Neither does it support tools for some surveying tasks such as data collection and GPS computations.

Of the projects mentioned here, Civil 3D is a *primary solution* for corridors, airports, waste management, subdivision, road, commercial site, and industrial site design. Of the projects mentioned here, Civil 3D is a *strong supporting solution* for a variety of drafting and analyses functions for construction management, environmental engineering, water systems, sewage and storm networks, transportation, wetlands delineation and mitigation, water resources, and the legal and real estate fields.

public sector: The area within civil engineering that provides funding for projects that emanate from tax revenues. This includes federal, state, county, city and town governmental entities, their associated agencies, and PUDs and MUDs.

private sector: The area within civil engineering that provides funding for projects that emanate from private sources. This includes land developers, homeowners, and professionals.

IDENTIFY THE BREAKDOWN AND FLOW OF ENGINEERING TASKS AND HOW CIVIL 3D CONTRIBUTES TO THE WORK EFFORT

By recognizing the tasks performed and the project requirements for each project type identified, it is possible to distinguish which tasks within these civil engineering projects benefit most by applying Civil 3D functionality to them.

Although the Civil 3D software is a revolutionary product and performs many worthwhile and industry leading functions, it would be beneficial to point out where the software offers extraordinary assistance to the user. The first step in accomplishing this task is to break down the types of projects that an engineer might undertake. The purpose here is to identify immediately project areas that are out of the scope of this text, identify project types that are strong candidates for use of Civil 3D as the primary solution, and identify those areas that can use Civil 3D as a supporting tool.

The second step is to identify the functionality that Civil 3D offers in performing computations or drafting assistance of those engineering tasks. The tasks are identified as well as how Civil 3D can provide improved productivity and functionality to those who use it.

The following listing provides a step-by-step description of each project's requirements. **The tasks that benefit most from the use of Civil 3D are denoted in bold type.** <u>Those tasks that can make important use of Civil 3D as a supporting tool are underlined.</u> Those tasks in normal type are outside the current feature set of Civil 3D. The functionality that Civil 3D offers is shown using the following key:

(1) Uses all Civil 3D functionality including alignments, parcels, corridor and grading tools, profiles, and sections

(2) Uses Civil 3D's modification benefits where the changes ripple through the design

(3) Uses alignments capabilities

(4) Uses parcels capabilities

(5) Uses corridor and/or profiles and sections capabilities

(6) Uses terrain modeling, surfaces, and grading capabilities

(7) Uses Civil 3D's drafting and labeling functions

(8) Uses built-in rendering engine

(9) Uses MAP 3D tools

(10) Utility/storm sewer piping

(11) Surveying capabilities for traverse development and data collection

For the Public Sector

The public sector has the following projects and can be DOTs, city, county, state agencies, public utility districts (PUDs), or municipal utility districts (MUDs). They are shown with the workflow milestones they involve.

Corridor Design.   See Figure D-1.

Figure D-1   Corridor design

- **Preliminary planning and alternative layout creation: (1), (2)**
- Communication with decision makers
- **Preliminary engineering: (1), (2)**
- Project funding and approval and notice to proceed

- Surveying activities including property research, zoning issues, ownership, determination of existing site conditions: (7), (11)
- **Terrain modeling: (1), (2), (6)**
- Determination of subsurface and geological conditions: (7)
- Wetlands determinations: (7)
- **R.O.W. determinations: (4)**
- **Curvilinear 2D geometry development, easements, alignments, parcels: (3), (4), (7)**
- **Drafting and labeling: (1)**
- **Corridor profile, section and corridor creation and analysis, roadway design, inter-section ramp and gore development: (5)**
- Paving requirements: (7)
- **Intersection and cul-de-sac design: (5), (6), (7)**
- Utilities crossings, relocations, and conflict resolutions: (7)
- Drainage improvements, storm water piping, and retention: (10)
- Landscape design plans: (7)
- Irrigation design plans: (7)
- **Signage, electrical, and striping plans: (7)**
- **Erosion and siltation control design plans: (7)**
- Submit review plans
- **Make modifications based on review comments: (2)**
- **Construction plan development: (7)**
- Quantity takeoffs and cost estimations: (6), (7)
- **QA/QC and survey stakeout: (6), (7), (11)**
- **Public communication and public hearings with potential for visual renderings: (8)**

Construction Management.   See Figure D-2.

Figure D-2   3D/GPS Machine Control

- Obtain RFP, verifying plans, analyze design documents: (1)
- Quantities, earthworks takeoffs, and cost estimates: (6), (7)
- Proposal preparation: (8)

- Project awarded and notice to proceed
- Surveying activities including establishing project control, verify existing site conditions: (6), (7), (11)
- **Making design changes based on change orders and for constructability: (2)**
- **Curvilinear 2D geometry development: (1)**
- Quantity takeoffs and cost estimations: (6), (7)
- **Terrain modeling for existing and proposed conditions: (6)**
- **Earthworks computations: (6)**
- **Build/rebuild project data for road grading: (2), (5)**
- **Build/rebuild site grading data: (2), (5)**
- Build/rebuild utilities: (6), (7)
- **QA/QC of design plans and construction approaches: (2), (7)**
- **Generate stakeout information and/or GPS Machine Control: (1), (2)**
- **Format for machine control usage: (1), (2)**
- **Construction plan development: (1), (2)**
- Pavement design and analysis as-built surveying and plan generation: (6), (7)
- Project operations and maintenance: (6), (7)

Environmental Engineering

- **Curvilinear 2D geometry development for property lines, Planimetrics, etc.: (1), (2), (7)**
- **Terrain modeling and analysis: (3), (4), (6)**
- Proposed impact studies
- Data collection of above and below ground conditions, chemicals, species, etc.
- Subsurface water analysis, conditions, modeling: (6)
- Air quality conditions, analysis, modeling
- GIS development and mapping: (6), (7), (9)

Water Supply (Which Includes Treatment, Distribution, and Pump Stations)

- **Curvilinear 2D geometry development for waterline trunks, distribution systems: (3), (4)**
- Elevated storage: (6), (7)
- **Planimetrics, etc.: (7)**
- **Terrain development and analysis for waterline depth and conflict resolution: (1), (2), (6)**
- Water pressure analysis, demand loading, etc.
- Location of elevated storage, lift stations, capacities, etc.: (6), (7)
- Water treatment plants and processes (see Industrial Projects): (6), (7), (10)

Sewage Networks (Which Include Collection and Effluent Treatment)

- **Curvilinear 2D geometry development for trunkline, vacuum sewers and collection system, Planimetrics, etc.: (3), (4)**
- Location and design of collection system, lift stations, capacities, etc.: (6), (7)
- **Mapping and GIS tasks: (6), (8), (7)**
- **Drafting and labeling: (7)**
- **Terrain development and analysis of gravity flow systems: (1), (2), (6)**
- System capacity analysis

- Location and design of collection systems from main trunks to treatment facilities: (6), (7)
- Wastewater treatment plants and processes (see Industrial Projects): (6), (7)

Transportation (Which Includes Traffic Flows, Evacuation Planning, Signage, and Signalization).   See Figure D-3.

Figure D-3   Transportation

- **Geometry development: (1), (2)**
- **Planimetrics: (7)**
- Data collection, traffic counts
- Signalization
- HOV development plans and GIS studies: (6), (7)
- Data collection, traffic counts
- **Mapping and GIS tasks: (6), (7), (9)**
- Pavement design and analysis: (6), (7)
- **Drafting and labeling: (7)**

Wetlands

- Delineation, classification, and mitigation: (7)
- **Curvilinear 2D geometry development for wetlands and other boundaries, property lines, treelines, Planimetrics, etc.: (1), (2)**
- **Mapping and GIS tasks: (6), (7), (9)**

- **Drafting and labeling: (7)**
- Data collection and reduction
- **RTK/GPS and traditional surveying: (11)**

Water Resources.   See Figure D-4.

Figure D-4   Water resources

- **Preliminary planning: (1), (2)**
- Project funding and approval and notice to proceed
- Surveying activities including property research, ownership, determination of existing site conditions: (6), (7), (11)
- Determination of subsurface and geological conditions, flows, and magnitudes: (6), (7)
- Surface and groundwater water analysis
- Design/analysis of wells, water transfer systems, irrigation
- Hydrology and water supply
- River conditions and forecasts
- Water quality
- Weather forecasts
- Flood emergency information
- Water use, conservation, and planning
- Design and analysis of dams
- **Geometry development for Planimetrics: (1), (7)**
- Rainfall determinations
- Flood studies
- Wetlands determinations: (6), (7)
- Stormwater analysis and piping
- **Erosion and siltation control design: (6), (7)**
- Landscape analysis: (7)
- Chemical analysis
- **Development of maps: (6), (7), (9)**
- Report generation
- **QA/QC: (2)**
- **Public hearings with potential for visual renderings: (8)**

Airport Engineering.   See Figure D-5.

Figure D-5   Airport engineering

- Obtain FAA and local grants
- **Preliminary planning and alternative layout creation: (1), (2)**
- Communication with decision makers
- **Preliminary engineering: (1), (2)**
- Project funding and approval and notice to proceed
- Surveying activities including property research, zoning issues, ownership, determination of existing site conditions: (11)
- **Terrain modeling: (1), (2), (6)**
- Determination of subsurface and geological conditions: (6), (7)
- **Curvilinear 2D geometry development, runway/taxiways, FAA obstruction/clearance plans, parking lots, service industry access roads: (1), (7)**
- Security considerations: (6), (7)
- **Planimetrics, etc.: (1), (7)**
- FAA and state regulations compliance
- **FAA height contours, clearance analysis, etc.: (1), (7)**
- Pavement design and analysis: (6), (7)
- Runway and taxiway profiles and sections or corridors: (1), (2), (6), (7)
- **Drafting and labeling: (6), (7)**
- **Drainage improvements: (10)**
- Storm water retention: (6)
- Underground retention facilities: (6), (7)
- **Rough grading, finished grade development: (2), (6)**
- **Erosion and siltation control design: (2), (6)**
- **Final design engineering, pad siting for hangars and services: (1), (2), (6)**
- Landscape design: (6), (7)
- Irrigation design: (6), (7), (10)
- **Easement determinations: (4)**
- **Value engineering and review: (2)**
- **Engineering modifications: (2)**
- **Construction plan generation: (1)**
- **Quantities and cost estimates: (6), (7)**

- **QA/QC and survey stakeout: (1), (2), (7)**
- Obtain FAA and local construction grants
- **Public hearings with potential for visual renderings: (8)**

The Legal Field.   See Figure D-6.

Figure D-6   The legal field

- Rezoning issues: (4)
- Study, research, analysis: (1)
- Legal, forensic graphics: (8)
- Expert witness

Bridge Design.   See Figure D-7.

Figure D-7   Bridge design

- **Preliminary planning and alternative layout creation: (1), (2)**
- Communication with decision makers
- **Preliminary engineering: (1), (2)**

- Project funding and approval and notice to proceed
- Surveying activities including property research, zoning issues, ownership, determination of existing site conditions: (6), (7)
- **Terrain modeling: (1), (2), (6)**
- Determination of subsurface, underwater, and geological conditions: (6), (7)
- Wetlands determinations: (6), (7)
- **ROW determinations: (4), (7)**
- **Curvilinear 2D geometry development, easements, alignments, parcels: (3), (4), (7)**
- **Drafting and labeling: (1)**
- **Approach design, corridor profile, section and corridor creation and analysis, roadway design, intersection ramp and gore development: (5)**
- Structural requirements for beams, bents, columns, decks, etc.
- Paving requirements: (6), (7)
- **Intersection and cul-de-sac design: (5), (6), (7)**
- Utilities crossings, relocations, and conflict resolutions: (7)
- Drainage improvements: (10)
- Storm water retention: (6)
- Noise abatement design plans: (7)
- Landscape design plans: (7)
- Irrigation design plans: (7)
- **Signage, electrical, and striping plans: (7)**
- **Erosion and siltation control design plans: (7)**
- Submit review plans
- **Make modifications based on review comments: (2)**
- **Construction plan development: (7)**
- Quantity takeoffs and cost estimations: (6), (7)
- **QA/QC and survey stakeout: (6), (7)**
- **Public communication and public hearings with potential for visual renderings: (8)**

For the Private Sector

Subdivision Design.   See Figure D-8.

- **Preliminary planning and alternative layout creation: (1), (2)**
- Communication with decision makers
- **Preliminary engineering: (1), (2)**
- Project funding and approval and notice to proceed
- Surveying activities including property research, zoning issues, ownership, determination of existing site conditions: (7), (11)
- **Terrain modeling: (1), (2), (6)**
- Determination of subsurface and geological conditions: (7)
- Wetlands determinations: (7)
- **Refined site layout, park, and greenspace requirements**
- **Curvilinear 2D geometry development, easements, alignments, parcels: (3), (4), (7)**
- **Roadway design: (3), (5)**
- Paving requirements: (6), (7)
- **Intersection and cul-de-sac design: (5), (6), (7)**
- **Corridor profile, section, and corridor creation and analysis: (5), (6), (7)**

Figure D-8   Subdivision design

- **Drafting and labeling: (7)**
- **Rough grading, overlot, and finished grade development: (6)**
- **Drainage improvements: (10)**
- Storm water retention: (6)
- Sanitary sewer design plans and profiles: (5), (6), (7), (10)
- Waterline design plans and profiles: (5), (6), (7)
- Landscape design plans: (6), (7)
- Irrigation design plans: (6), (7)
- **Erosion and siltation control design plans: (2), (6)**
- Submit review plans
- **Make modifications based on review comments: (2)**
- **Construction plan development: (7)**
- Quantity takeoffs and cost estimations: (6), (7)
- **QA/QC and survey stakeout: (6), (7)**
- **Public communication and public hearings with potential for visual renderings: (8)**

Environmental Engineering

- **Curvilinear 2D geometry development for property lines, Planimetrics, etc.: (1), (2), (7)**
- **Terrain modeling and analysis: (3), (4), (6)**
- Proposed impact studies
- Data collection of above and below ground conditions, chemicals, species, etc.
- Subsurface water analysis, conditions, modeling: (6)
- Air quality conditions, analysis, modeling
- **GIS development and mapping: (6), (7), (9)**

Water Supply (Which Includes Reticulation Distribution and Pump Stations)

- **Curvilinear 2D geometry development for waterline trunks, distribution systems: (3), (4)**
- Elevated storage: (6), (7)
- **Planimetrics: (7)**
- **Terrain development and analysis for waterline depth and conflict resolution: (1), (2), (6)**
- Water pressure analysis, demand loading, etc.
- Location of elevated storage, lift stations, capacities, etc.: (6), (7)
- Water treatment plants and processes (see Industrial Projects): (6), (7), (10)

Sewage Networks (Which Include Collection, Not Treatment)

- **Curvilinear 2D geometry development for trunkline, vacuum sewers and collection system, Planimetrics, etc.: (3), (4)**
- **Mapping and GIS tasks: (6), (8), (7)**
- **Drafting and labeling: (7)**
- **Terrain development and analysis of gravity flow systems: (1), (2), (6)**
- System capacity analysis
- Location and design of collection systems up to main trunks or lift stations: (6), (7)

Transportation (Which Includes Traffic Flows for Commercial and Large Subdivision Impact)

- **Geometry development: (1), (2)**
- **Planimetrics: (7)**
- Data collection, traffic counts
- **Mapping and GIS tasks: (6), (7), (9)**
- Pavement design and analysis: (6), (7)
- **Drafting and labeling: (7)**

Wetlands Delineation and Mitigation

- Delineation, classification, and mitigation: (7)
- **Curvilinear 2D geometry development for wetlands and other boundaries, property lines, treelines, Planimetrics, etc.: (1), (2)**
- **Mapping and GIS tasks: (6), (7), (9)**
- **Drafting and labeling: (7)**
- **Data collection and reduction: (11)**
- **RTK/GPS and traditional surveying: (11)**

Commercial Design.   See Figure D-9.

- **Preliminary planning and alternative layout creation: (1), (2)**
- Communication with decision makers
- **Preliminary engineering: (1), (2)**
- Project funding and approval and notice to proceed
- Surveying activities including property research, zoning issues, ownership, determination of existing site conditions: (7)
- **Terrain modeling: (1), (2), (6)**
- Determination of subsurface and geological conditions: (7)
- **Access requirements: (4), (7)**
- **Site layout, parking space requirements, curvilinear 2D geometry development, easements, BRLs, parking lots, parcels, Planimetrics: (4), (7)**

Figure D-9   Commercial design

- Paving requirements: (7)
- **Drafting and labeling: (7)**
- **Drainage improvements: (10)**
- **Stormwater retention: (6)**
- Underground retention facilities: (7)
- **Rough grading, finished grade development: (6)**
- **Erosion and siltation control design: (7)**
- **Final design engineering, pad siting: (6)**
- Environmental considerations, oil/water separators, etc.: (7)
- Pavement design and analysis: (7)
- Water and sanitary plans and profiles: (7), (10)
- **Erosion and siltation control plans: (7)**
- Landscape design: (7)
- Irrigation design: (7)
- **Easement determinations: (4)**
- **Value engineering and review: (2)**
- **Engineering modifications: (2)**
- **Construction plan generation: (1)**
- **Quantities and cost estimates: (6), (7)**

- **QA/QC and survey stakeout: (1), (2), (7)**
- **Public hearings with potential for visual renderings: (8)**

Industrial (and Waste Management) Site Layout.   See Figure D-10.

Figure D-10   Industrial (and waste management) site layout

- **Preliminary planning and alternative layout creation: (1), (2)**
- Communication with decision makers
- **Preliminary engineering: (1), (2)**
- Project funding and approval and notice to proceed
- Surveying activities including property research, zoning issues, ownership, determination of existing site conditions: (7), (11)
- **Terrain modeling: (1), (2), (6)**
- Determination of subsurface and geological conditions: (7)
- **Public and staff access requirements: (7)**
- **Site layout, parking space requirements, curvilinear 2d geometry development, easements, BRLs, parking lots, parcels, Planimetrics: (3), (4), (7)**
- **Drafting and labeling: (1)**
- Environmental engineering analyses and considerations
- **Drainage improvements: (10)**
- Storm water retention, underground retention facilities: (6)
- **Rough grading, finished grade development: (2), (6)**
- **Erosion and siltation control design: (2), (6)**
- **Final design engineering, pad siting: (1), (2), (6)**
- Environmental considerations, oil/water separators, etc.: (7)
- Pavement design and analysis: (6), (7)
- Water and sanitary plans and profiles: (1), (2), (6), (7), (10)
- **Erosion and siltation control plans: (6), (7)**
- Landscape design: (7)
- Irrigation design yard piping design for plant activities: (7)
- EPA requirements for spill and containment: (7)

- Disaster and evacuation plans: (7)
- **Easement determinations: (4), (7)**
- **Value engineering and review: (1)**
- **Engineering modifications: (2)**
- **Construction plan generation: (1)**
- Quantity takeoffs and cost estimations: (6), (7)
- **QA/QC and survey stakeout: (6), (7)**
- **Public hearings with potential for visual renderings: (8)**

Hydrology and Water Resources: Surface Water Analysis, Groundwater Analysis, Wells, Water Transfer, Irrigation.   See Figure D-11.

Figure D-11   Surface water analysis

- **Preliminary planning, project funding and approval, and notice to proceed: (1), (2)**
- Surveying activities including property research, ownership, determination of existing site conditions: (7), (11)
- Determination of subsurface and geological conditions, flows, and magnitudes: (7)
- **Geometry development for Planimetrics: (4), (7)**
- Rainfall determinations
- Flood studies
- Wetlands determinations: (7)
- Storm water analysis
- **Erosion and siltation control design: (2), (6)**
- Landscape analysis: (6), (7)
- Chemical analysis
- **Development of maps: (6), (7), (9)**
- Report generation: (1)
- **QA/QC: (1), (2), (7)**
- **Public hearings with potential for Visual Renderings: (8)**

The Legal Field.   See Figure D-12.

- Rezoning issues: (4)
- Study, research, analysis: (1)

Figure D-12   Rezoning issues, shadow studies

- Legal, forensic graphics: (8)
- Expert witness consulting

Civil 3D's Visualization Capabilities

E

Appendix Objectives

- Understand the art of visualizing your designs for display to the public.
- Have an awareness of a variety of examples in which renderings helped projects succeed through public hearings.

INTRODUCTION

This chapter provides you with a brief introduction on the art of visualizing your designs for display to the public. Visualizations can develop stunning and photorealistic computer renderings of projects. The objective here is simple: to introduce visualization to Civil 3D users. This feature should be explored by the user whenever the opportunity presents itself and may actually warrant its own textbook. This chapter commences with some examples of where these renderings might be used in the civil engineering business. Indeed, the examples provided were extracted from some of Harry Ward's actual projects.

In today's very visual society, communicating designs is a paramount necessity for engineers and designers. Civil engineers seem to lag behind other disciplines when it comes to visualizations, and the reason probably goes back to the idea that most engineers do not design in 3D. That is why Civil 3D could cause a paradigm shift in the way engineers work if it assists them in moving into three dimensions.

SAMPLES OF RENDERINGS

Some examples of renderings of projects that Harry Ward has performed include the following.

Figure E-1 shows a 3D model and rendering of a Virginia high school to depict it at night with lighting. It was developed for public hearings for new construction at the school.

The site pictured in Figure E-2 was a 1.5-square-mile model developed for public hearings on the new road and bridge. The graphic is a computer rendering of the site.

The roadway and bridge were cut from this model and overlayed geographically into a photograph of the site to create the photomontage in Figure E-3. The existing conditions can be viewed in the upper right of the photomontage.

Figure E-1   A rendering of a Virginia high school sports field

Figure E-2   A 1.5-square-mile model of a road and bridge for public hearings

Figure E-3   Photorealistic photomontage

The rendering in Figure E-4 was done for a local parks organization for public hearings to show that a quality structure and related grounds were to be built in its neighborhood.

Figure E-4   Golf course maintenance building

The site in Figure E-5 was developed as a 3D model and rendered for use in a litigation case. It had to do with zoning issues and included several scenarios of waivers that might be applicable.

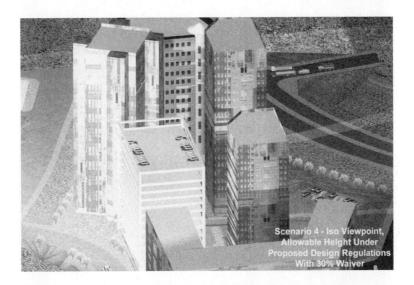

Figure E-5   Zoning issues and shadow studies

The model and photomontage in Figure E-6 were done for a DOT project to show how a lane widening would appear. The lane on the left with its respective shoulder did not exist when this rendering was done.

Figure E-6   Photorealistic photomontage

The rendering and 3D model in Figure E-7 were done for a DOT project and include a new bridge and entrance monument with decorative lighting. The existing conditions are shown in the upper right of the photomontage.

Figure E-7   A new gateway to Annapolis

The 3D model in Figure E-8 was built for an international airport and displayed within the state legislature to show the legislators how the airport would look after construction in the year 2010. New interstate highways, railway spurs, and overhead taxiways were all part of the project. New parking and concession facilities were in the model as well as expanded service areas.

Figure E-8   An international airport

In the model pictured in Figures E-9 and E-10, lighting was a factor, and the office building and parking are depicted with both daytime and nighttime lighting. Everything is done to engineering specifications including parking lot drainage, cross slopes on sidewalks, and so forth.

The example in Figure E-11 is of another airport but shows a 3D model with an orthophoto draped onto it. Some relatively simple structures were placed on the model depicting planned expansion.

Figure E-9   A commercial office building—daylight

Figure E-10   A commercial office building—night lights

Figure E-11   Orthophoto draping

The project shown in Figure E-12 included improvements to both the site as well as the building for this V.A. hospital. It was shown to the directors of the hospital prior to construction so they could visualize what the plans indicated.

Figure E-12   V.A. hospital improvements

The last 3D model and rendering (Figure E-13) was performed for public hearings to allow for a roadway extension to be built. The model was projected into photographs of the site to show a photorealistic view of the project.

Figure E-13   Public hearing presentation for a roadway extension

Exercise E-1: Civil 3D Example

You will now take a short trip into the visualization world by opening a file you have worked on and viewing it in a 3D perspective.

Civil 3D has visualization built in. In order to expedite the lesson, once you open the file, also notice that some closed polylines have been drawn on the **C-Mask** layer. The surface modeling in Civil 3D allows for masks to be placed on the data, which can affect several things, including rendering. The green masks represent grass-covered areas, the blue masks represent sand areas, the red areas indicate gravel drives, and the black mask indicates the paved road. There are five grass areas, three sand areas, two gravel areas, and one paved road.

To access student data files, go to www.pearsondesigncentral.com.

1. Let us begin by opening Appendix-E-a.dwg. You see the surface you have been dealing with in various parts of this text as well as the masks.

2. In the **Toolspace**, under the **Prospector** tab, expand **Surfaces** to see the **Existing ground**.
3. Expand **Existing ground**, and you see an item for **Masks**. Right-click on **Masks** and select **Create Mask....**
4. When prompted, select the **green** colored masks to apply to the grass material.
5. The **Create Mask** dialog box appears, as shown in Figure E-14.

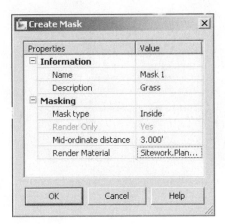

Figure E-14   The Create Mask dialog box

6. Accept the name as the default; enter **Grass** for the description. Click on the **Value** for **Mask type** and select **Inside**. Change the **Mid-ordinate distance** to **3′**, and select **Sitework.Planting.Grass.Thick** for the **Render Material Surface**. Hit **OK**.
7. Right-click on **Masks** and select **Add....**
8. The **Create Mask** dialog box appears.
9. Accept the name as the default; enter **Sand** for the description. Click on the **Value** for **Mask type** and select **Inside**. Change the **Mid-ordinate distance** to **3′**, and select **Sand** for the **Render Material Surface**. Hit **OK**.
10. When prompted, select a **blue** colored mask to apply to the sand material.
11. Repeat steps 7 through 10 for the additional two sand areas.
12. Right-click on **Masks** and select **Add....**
13. The **Create Mask** dialog box appears.
14. Accept the name as the default; enter **Gravel-Mixed** for the description. Click on the **Value** for **Mask type** and select **Inside**. Change the **Mid-ordinate distance** to **3′**, and select **Gravel-Mixed** for the **Render Material Surface**. Hit **OK**.
15. When prompted, select a **red** colored mask to apply to the gravel material.
16. Repeat steps 12 through 15 for the additional gravel area.
17. Right-click on **Masks** and select **Add....**
18. The **Create Mask** dialog box appears.
19. Accept the name as the default; enter **Asphalt** for the description. Click on the **Value** for **Mask type** and select **Inside**. Change the **Mid-ordinate distance** to **3′**, and select **Asphalt** for the **Render Material Surface**. Hit **OK**.
20. When prompted, select a **black** colored mask to apply to the asphalt material. Save the file.

Because the file is developed, you now view it in 3D.

21. Type **V** for **View**, select the view called **Corridor ISO**, hit **Set Current**, and hit **OK**.
22. Turn on all layers and thaw them out.
23. Then select **Visual Styles >> Realistic** from the **View** pull-down menu.
24. Use the **Zoom** command to zoom out and observe the view, and you should see grass, sand, gravel, and asphalt, as shown in Figure E-15.

We are now in a new world and that is 3D modeling and visualizations!

Figure E-15   Materials are applied

SUMMARY

The art of visualizing your designs is an important ability, and this chapter provided a brief introduction to using Civil 3D to do that. With visualizations, you can develop stunning computer renderings of projects. Being able to communicate your designs is paramount for engineers and designers, and this appendix gave examples of renderings.

Glossary

Alignment A series of two-dimensional curvilinear geometry elements, used to represent features such as road centerlines where it is beneficial to understand the relationship that these elements have to each other.

Assemblies Objects that manage collections of subassemblies; used for the basic structure of a corridor object.

Azimuth The North azimuth measures angles from the North axis, in a clockwise direction to 360°.

Bearing/bearing intersect Set points at the intersection of two bearings.

Bearing A point of latitude and longitude that measures a heading and are broken into four 90° quadrants: North, South, East, and West.

Bifurcated highway Where one direction of traffic has an independent PGL from the opposite direction of traffic. The profile may go uphill in one direction and downhill in the opposite direction.

Breaklines 3D polylines representing breaks in the planar slopes of the terrain. A breakline causes the mathematics of the terrain modeling to avoid building triangles that would cross a breakline. The triangle thus has a side adjacent to the breakline but does not cross it.

BRL Building restriction lines indicate the limits for construction of structures inside a property. They ensure that structures aren't built too close to other structures.

Broken back curve An alignment that has a linear segment either coming into or leaving an arc that is not tangent to the arc. This is usually not allowed in most jurisdictions.

CAD Computer aided drafting.

CADD Computer aided design/drafting.

Cartesian A word variation relating to the French mathematician René Descartes.

Civil 3D The short term used in this text for the software package officially called Autodesk Civil 3D.

COGO Software geared toward solving coordinate geometry problems.

Contour A linestring of a constant elevation on the site. It can be open or closed.

Control survey Sets the "monumentation" for the project. All survey shots and references typically come from or tie back to this monumentation.

Corridor A structure that allows passage or conveyance of people or things.

Cross section The cross section for the roadway is defined as an orthogonal view of the terrain model as it crosses the alignment and is draped onto the existing ground terrain model. Users determine the length of the section depending on how far to the left and right they would like information computed and displayed. Sections are usually computed at regular intervals, say, every 20′ along the entire length of the alignment. They can also be computed at irregular or user-defined locations to accommodate pertinent events that might interest the engineer such as driveway locations, cross streets, utility crossings, and the like. There are also occurrences where sections may be computed that are not orthogonal such as stream crossings or utility crossings.

Curvilinear objects These include arcs and spirals. Arcs or circular curves have a constant radius from beginning to end. Spirals have constantly changing radii from start to end.

Daylighting Represents where the slope grading intersects with the existing ground surface.

Description key sets A library of codes that control how points are created, where they are created, and what they represent.

Distance/distance intersect Set points at the intersection of two circles defined by their center points and respective radii distances.

DTM Digital terrain model.

Ellipsoid A mathematical surface that best fits the shape of the geoid.

Existing ground The natural ground conditions of the site before development.

Existing ground profile The vertical alignment for the roadway as defined by the location of the horizontal alignment draped onto the existing ground terrain model.

External data references Additional data files that can augment how point data is stored.

Feature line An object that the grading commands can work with. It represents breaks in the surface features. For example, the edge of pavement, ditches, or daylighting could be feature lines. Their appearance is controlled by feature line styles.

Finished ground The improved conditions for the site.

Geodetic datum A mathematical representation of the Earth.

Geodetic direction and distance Computing a point using a geodetic datum, a geodetic azimuth, and a distance along the mathematical face of the Earth for that part of the country. For instance, 1000′ along the face of the Earth is less than 1000′ horizontally because the Earth is curved.

Geoid Surface that is equal to sea level if it is not impeded or disturbed by any land masses.

GIS Geographic information system.

GPS Geographic positioning system.

Grade A change in elevation over a horizontal distance, usually described in percent (%).

Grading The grading object created in Civil 3D. It is dynamic and interacts with its environment.

Greenspace An area dedicated to the preservation or replacement of vegetation that may be reduced as a result of construction. Planning professionals often ensure that requirements for greenspace are met for a project.

Paradigm shift A fundamental change in how processes are performed.

Parcel A plot of land, usually a subdivision of a larger, quantified area.

PC Point of curvature

PGL The profile grade line is the proposed profile.

Point file formats Preformatted definitions for importing or exporting points.

Point groups A Civil 3D object representing a collection of points grouped by a relationship such as utility points, property points, terrain points.

Point styles A definition of how the point should appear.

PRC Point of reverse curvature

Private sector The area within civil engineering that provides funding for projects that emanate from private sources. This includes land developers, homeowners, and professionals such as doctors and attorneys.

Profile An object containing elevation data that is related to a horizontal alignment. It can apply to existing conditions or proposed conditions. The information within the profile is typically referred to by stations and elevations.

Profile view A Civil 3D term for the location in Civil 3D where profiles are displayed. Each profile view displays new or existing profiles and offsets for one horizontal alignment. Although you can create profiles without displaying them on a profile view, when a profile view is created, the complete list of profiles for the alignment is displayed so that a profile can be selected for display in the profile view.

Proposed profile The vertical alignment for the roadway as defined by the proposed vertical tangents and vertical curves.

PT Point of tangency

Public sector The area within civil engineering that provides funding for projects that emanate from tax revenues. This includes federal, state, county, city, and town governmental entities; their associated agencies; and PUDs and MUDs.

Pull-down menus, toolbars, pop-downs, and **dialog boxes** Interface items.

PVC The point of vertical curvature where the vertical curve begins and departs the tangent. also called *BVC* for begin vertical curve.

PVI The point of vertical intersection of the incoming and outgoing vertical tangents. This is also referred to as the *VPI* or vertical point of intersection.

PVT The point of vertical tangency where the vertical curve ends and returns to the tangent. Also called *EVC* for end vertical curve.

Rate of superelevation These values vary, but numbers on the order of 0.06 ft/ft and 0.04 ft/ft are often observed. AASHTO (American Association of State Highway and Transportation Officials) provides examples of design superelevation rates based on the design speed, the radius of curve, and the superelevation rate. The website for AASHTO is http://www.transportation.org/aashto/home.nsf/FrontPage. Note that these values represent a rate of change, say, 0.04 ft/ft. Thus for a typical template with a 2% cross slope, the edge of pavement will rise 0.04 feet for every linear foot of highway. In this case, it will take 50 linear feet for a 2% cross slope to rise to 0% or flat (example: 2.0/0.04 = 50.0).

Real numbers Expressed by allowing decimals that have an infinite sequence of digits to the right of the decimal point.

Right of way (ROW) The property typically owned by a government agency and usually dedicated for roadway usage. The roads must be built inside the state ROW so that they are not running across private property.

Ripple-through effect A term coined to describe the dynamic modeling characteristics of Civil 3D in performing automatic updates to data.

Roadway assembly fragments Pieces of cross-sectional templates that are applied to locations on alignments where they can be controlled from and then stretched to various targets elsewhere in the corridor.

Rubber sheeting Stretches objects from one set of points to a new set of points, often used to correct scans and to compensate for map distortions.

Secant A line that intersects a circle twice. An external secant is the part of the secant that is outside the circle or arc.

Section view This is a Civil 3D term for the location in Civil 3D where sections are displayed. Each section view must be related to an alignment. The section view displays new or existing sections. You can also create sections by displaying them on a section view, but when you create a section view for an alignment, a complete list of sections is displayed and can be selected for display in the section view. Section views can be created for existing ground, or multiple section views can be developed. The display style of a section view can be altered, and labels and bands can be added as needed.

Slope A change in elevation over a horizontal distance, usually described by a ratio (3:1).

Slope distance The distance measured from point *A* to point *B* along an incline. It will always be longer than the horizontal distance when the slope is not horizontal or vertical.

Station A distance along a horizontal alignment that is usually divided by 100′. Therefore 12 stations is 1200′. In metric, this might represent kilometers such that station 10 is 10 kilometers.

Stationing Distance along a baseline. It is measured in units of 100 feet in Imperial units and, typically, 1000 meters in metric. Therefore, 1 station = 100′ and is illustrated as 1 + 00.

Subassembly The fundamental building blocks used to create assemblies. It defines the geometry of a component used in a corridor section and includes predeveloped components for such things as travel lanes, curbs, side slopes, and ditches. It has intelligent behavior built into it and can automatically adapt to design conditions comprising superelevations and cut or fill requirements.

Superelevation Refers to the cross slope introduced into a cross section of a roadway in order to compensate for the centrifugal forces created by horizontal curves. According to the laws of mechanics, when a vehicle travels on a curve it is forced outward by centrifugal force. On a superelevated roadway, this force is resisted by the vehicle weight component parallel to the superelevated surface and the side friction between the tires and pavement. The pavement is essentially tilted to counter the forces described above.

Table styles A library of styles for constructing tables that report on point information.

Tangent A line that intersects a circle once. A tangent line is perpendicular to the radius drawn to the point of tangency (or point of contact with the arc or circle). If a line is perpendicular to a radius at its outer endpoint, then it is tangent to the circle.

Template A template consists of one or more typical examples of how the roadway will appear for varying conditions, such as a roadway with a curb and gutter at the edge of the pavement or perhaps a shoulder treatment at the edge of the pavement. It is shown in a cross-sectional view and shows the road from left to right looking into the profile grade line (PGL).

3D Three dimensions, characterized by the use of the *X*-, *Y*-, and *Z*-axes in the Cartesian coordinate system resulting in real-world models.

3D-GPS machine control An emerging technology that allows construction equipment to obtain their earthmoving information from on-board computers with 3D data sets of the site. GPS receivers locate the vehicle, compare it to the data set, and automatically adjust the earthmoving blade to the appropriate height and angle to accomplish those goals.

TIN Triangulated irregular network representing the surface.

2D Two dimensions, characterized by the use of the *X*- and *Y*-axes in the Cartesian coordinate system resulting in planar material.

Vertical curves Parabolic curves located around a PVI to smooth the road as it transitions from one tangent grade to another. These curvilinear three-dimensional components of the vertical alignment denoted by a PVI and a length of curve are typically parabolic with an ever-changing radius.

Vertical tangents Linear objects in the profile representing a grade between PVIs. These are linear three-dimensional components of the vertical alignment denoted with a grade usually in percentage (%).

Visualization In the context of CADD, it is used to produce an image of something that does not exist so that the viewer can better understand the project or model being discussed.

Index